ON MY WATCH

JENS STOLTENBERG

with Per Anders Madsen

Translated from the Norwegian by Alison McCullough

ON MY WATCH

LEADING NATO IN A TIME OF WAR

W. W. NORTON & COMPANY

Independent Publishers Since 1923

First published in Norway in 2025 by Gyldendal Norsk Forlag AS
as PÅ MIN VAKT - Å lede Nato i krigstid

Copyright © 2025 by Jens Stoltenberg
Translation copyright © 2025 by Alison McCullough

For information about permission to reproduce selections from this book, write to
Permissions, W. W. Norton & Company, Inc., 500 Fifth Avenue, New York, NY 10110

For information about special discounts for bulk purchases, please contact
W. W. Norton Special Sales at specialsales@wwnorton.com or 800-233-4830

Manufacturing by Lakeside Book Company
Production manager: Anna Oler

ISBN 978-1-324-11117-7
10 9 8 7 6 5 4 3 2 1
W. W. Norton & Company, Inc.
500 Fifth Avenue, New York, NY 10110
www.wwnorton.com

W. W. Norton & Company Ltd.
15 Carlisle Street, London W1D 3BS

Authorized EU representative: EAS, Mustamäe tee 50, 10621 Tallinn, Estonia

For Ingrid

Note

ON MY WATCH IS ABOUT MY TEN YEARS AS SECRETARY GENERAL OF NATO. The events and dialogue described are based on publicly available information and my own notes. A more detailed account of how this book came to be written can be found in a separate chapter at the end.

Contents

PART 6
WAR
August 2021–April 2023

PART 7
PARTNERSHIP
January 2023–March 2024

PART 8
DEPARTURE
March 2024–October 2024

Prologue

WEDNESDAY THE TWENTY-THIRD OF FEBRUARY 2022, JUST BEFORE 18.00.

A light rain was falling from the leaden sky above Brussels. I was sitting in the back of the car, on my way home from NATO headquarters, preparing for a working dinner due to take place later that evening.

My phone rang. David Cattler, the head of NATO's intelligence and security division, wanted a confidential conversation. I couldn't speak to him in the car – we would have to wait until I got home, so that I could use the secure line from there.

I had seen more of Cattler in recent days than almost any of my other colleagues. He was a highly knowledgeable and articulate analyst, adept at communicating complex information in an intelligible way – something I had benefited greatly from over the past few months.

Ordinarily I received a weekly intelligence briefing, but not any more. Now I was receiving updates several times a day. The drama playing out in Russia was changing by the hour.

Most recently, I had learned that a new bridge had been built in a single night, just miles from the border with the north-eastern part of Ukraine. Over 100 battalion tactical groups, around 150,000 Russian soldiers, were positioned close to the borders in the north, east and south. Fighter planes, helicopters, special forces, landing craft, paratroopers, artillery, air defence, field hospitals – they had everything they needed to initiate a massive military offensive. A large-scale military exercise taking place in Belarus extended the front and reduced the advance warning we would receive of any action. I was shown a map and images that supported everything Cattler had said.

On skiing trips back home in Norway, or while cycling along the Belgian country roads, I would often put my phone on silent and stow it in my bag, knowing that if anyone needed to get hold of me, my bodyguards would be notified and come and inform me, no matter the time of day or what I was doing. But now I always kept my phone in ring mode, including at night, and the doors to the hallway and my home office open so that I could hear the telephones with direct lines to NATO headquarters and the White House. If I woke during the night, as I often did in those weeks, I would open my encrypted NATO email and check for updates. If there weren't any, I would scan the online newspapers and read the latest headlines before trying to get back to sleep, feeling ever more uneasy.

Sitting in the car, I thought about what Cattler had told me the previous day. Many of the Russian soldiers were out of their camps. They were living, sleeping and eating in their tanks and other military vehicles, which had now been driven out into the surrounding terrain, ever closer to the border.

Soldiers can only live in their tanks for a few days before they have to return to camp for sleep and rest. Or launch an attack.

Earlier in the day, I had been informed that Russian planes had been loaded with bombs and missiles. Naval vessels were also in position off Ukraine's coast, near Odesa.

Then we learned that the Russian field hospitals had been supplied with large volumes of blood. It isn't customary to bring blood to forces on training exercises. Blood is a perishable product.

Vladimir Putin had long been planning an invasion, there was no doubt about that. For several months, we had been receiving precise intelligence that enabled us to warn against an impending attack. Putin's intention was to invade the neighbouring country of Ukraine, and should the Russian war machine be unleashed, we would see a military conflict the likes of which hadn't been experienced in Europe since the Second World War. It would torpedo the current security order, one that had existed for decades. But a plan can always be changed, or its implementation delayed, if nothing else. I was a little disappointed in the Americans, who suggested a date for when they believed the attack would come. No war starts before an attack is actually underway, before the final order has been given. So until the soldiers began to march and the tanks rolled across the border, there was at least a theoretical possibility that President Putin might change his mind.

It was 18.10 when the car pulled up outside my residence in the Avenue Louise. A security guard opened the car door. I greeted the guards on the pavement, walked quickly inside and went up to the first floor, turning right at the landing where family photographs decorated the walls: images of the children, my wife Ingrid and me; my parents, Karin and Thorvald, when they were young; my older sister Camilla as a child; and my smiling younger sister, Nini, pulled up onto the stage in the middle of a concert and dancing with Bruce Springsteen. I continued into my office, with its wide desk and floor-to-ceiling wall of books. My bag, stuffed full of papers as usual, I slung onto a chair.

I picked up the phone. After a wait of just seconds, David Cattler came on the line.

'Secretary General,' he said. 'I want you to know that the decision has been made. The order to attack has been given.'

PART 1
PREPARATIONS
September 2013–October 2014

1

An unexpected request

THE ROOM WAS DIMLY LIT. THE MAN WHO SAT OPPOSITE ME ON the other side of the table now had a streak of grey in his hair. Barack Obama had just turned fifty-two. He was in good humour and amiable, and as always he pulled the people around him into the conversation. But on this particular evening, the gravity of the moment shadowed us all. Little more than six months into his second term as US president, Obama found himself in the midst of an international crisis.

It was Wednesday the fourth of September 2013, and I was in Sweden. Swedish prime minister Fredrik Reinfeldt had invited his Nordic counterparts to dinner with President Obama, who would soon be travelling on to St Petersburg to meet with Putin. We were gathered in the heart of Stockholm, in Sagerska Huset, the official residence of the prime minister of Sweden, with the Ministry for Foreign Affairs and the Riksdag, the Swedish parliament, close by. In this beautiful, venerable residence, Reinfeldt served Swedish speciali-ties such as Arctic char and venison. We sat close around the table.

Obama was usually surrounded by many people, but on this occa-sion we were few, and those of us from the Nordic countries already knew each other well: Helle Thorning-Schmidt from Denmark, Sauli Niinistö from Finland and Sigmundur Gunnlaugsson from Iceland, in addition to our host Fredrik Reinfeldt and myself.

Before the dinner, Obama mentioned he had seen the stunt from my Norwegian election campaign, in which I had posed as a taxi driver, picking up passengers on the streets of Oslo in order to hear their true opinions from the back seat. The video had gone viral and been seen around the world. He had laughed a lot, Obama said, especially when I hit the brake thinking it was the clutch. Not only was it many years since I had driven a car, but I'd never driven an automatic before. The tone remained friendly and informal for the half-hour before we took our seats at the table.

But then the small talk was over.

The civil war raging in Syria was now into its third year. Two weeks earlier, President Bashar al-Assad had attacked two suburbs of Damascus using chemical weapons. The images rolled across the world's TV screens: people dying agonising deaths, children desperately gasping for air. A total of 1,400 people were killed, 400 of them children. Obama had warned Assad that chemical weapons attacks would have 'enormous consequences'. And he now believed the Syrian regime had crossed the line.

At the dinner, Obama made an impassioned but balanced argument for the need to respond to Assad's attacks militarily. It was far from an easy decision, however. Obama had opposed the invasion of Iraq, which had been undertaken based on what turned out to be erroneous intelligence. But this situation, he believed, was different. The evidence that Assad's regime was behind the attacks was overwhelming.

'I didn't set a red line. The world did,' he said. A clear majority of countries had signed the treaty prohibiting chemical weapons. By neglecting to act, the world would be sending a message to all dictators: breaching international treaties has no consequences.

'If we allow this, then we're also allowing the world to become a more dangerous place. The door to the chamber of horrors the world witnessed during World War I will be opened,' he warned.

But on that evening in Stockholm, Obama invited those of us seated around the table to come with counter-arguments. There is no decision more serious than the one to order a military attack on another country.

Danish prime minister Helle Thorning-Schmidt agreed with Obama, and supported the bombing of Assad's military bases. I advised against it.

Norway condemns the use of chemical weapons just as strongly as the United States, I emphasised, but bombing Assad would solve nothing. Assad would continue to stockpile chemical weapons, and he would become an even more dangerous and less predictable enemy. For Norway, the lack of a UN resolution was also decisive. This was the difference between Libya and Syria – before the bombing of Libya in 2011, the UN Security Council had passed a resolution allowing military action to prevent Muammar al-Gaddafi massacring his own people. Whether the attack on Gaddafi's Libya was justified can be debated, but it was at least legal under international law. It's even possible to claim it would have been wrong *not* to enforce the Libya resolution, since that would have undermined respect for the resolutions adopted by the UN Security Council.

Obama said we couldn't wait for the UN when it came to Syria, because Russia would almost certainly veto any Security Council resolution on the matter, but nevertheless I argued as I had before the Iraq war in 2003: 'We must respect international law. War is prohibited, unless waged in self-defence or mandated by the UN Security Council. Military action without UN backing will set a dangerous precedent and undermine the rules-based international order.'

Everyone listened politely, and nobody was surprised at what I said. As a country, Norway was reluctant to support military action, especially in the absence of a UN resolution. This viewpoint was even stronger in Sweden, and as expected Reinfeldt also argued against bombing Assad's regime.

After a while, Obama took the floor again. He weighed many arguments for and against a military response, and his assessments made a deep impression on me. It wasn't clear that the right thing to do was to simply rely on the prohibition of military action under international law. I thought of the speech Obama had given at Oslo City Hall when he was awarded the Nobel Peace Prize. It had been a homage to peace – but at the same time, he had also convincingly argued that it may sometimes be necessary to use military force to ensure peace. There was strong justification for a military response to Assad's gas attacks. And just as I wasn't entirely sure I had taken the correct stance, I realised that Obama was no stranger to the arguments against bombing.

But there is a time for discussion, and a time for drawing conclusions. And Obama's conclusion was clear – the arguments in favour of using military force weighed most heavily. Assad had to be bombed.

The fundamental ideas and attitudes of two parties can be broadly aligned, and yet in challenging individual cases, those same two parties can end up taking opposite positions.

In retrospect, I thought Obama and his advisers probably regarded me as a security policy dove, my arguments the typical pronouncements of well-meaning, naive Norway. It therefore never occurred to me that what I said in Stockholm that September evening might be an application to become secretary general of NATO. Nor in my wildest dreams would I ever have thought I'd be appointed to the role. I have since been told by Obama's colleagues that it was probably during that dinner at the residence of the Swedish prime minister that I got the job. What Obama apparently saw, was that I am a *politician*. Someone who will always weigh the pros and cons, who understands that a leader has to take overall responsibility for decisions made through a democratic process, and who, ultimately, is a pragmatist. The role of NATO secretary general has been held by experts, diplomats and politicians, but the advantage of the politician is that they are used to taking the initiative and pushing through decisions – even when those decisions provoke opposition. As I would realise over the coming years, not all member states want a politician by trade in this role – someone who has a clear agenda for NATO and how the organisation should be developed. But I'm fairly sure that this was Obama's preference.

I come from a political family. Both my mother and father were committed social democrats and members of the Labour Party. Family conversations around the dinner table covered social issues great and small, and my parents shared their opinions and viewpoints with us children from early on.

When my older sister Camilla, my younger sister Nini and I were in our teens, we used to discuss many things with our parents. The Vietnam War, abortion rights, equality, family policy, arms control and environmental challenges. Our home could be like a seminar, and many of our friends found it exciting to visit. While Nini referred to our parents as Mamma and Pappa, Camilla and I often called them by their first names, Karin and Thorvald. Why we ended up doing this, I'm not entirely sure. One theory is that since we became multilingual while living in Belgrade as children, it was easier to use our parents' first names, which were the same in all languages.

The door to Karin and Thorvald's home was always open, both to family members and to their and our friends. Some guests simply ended up staying, so the true size of the household could vary. Thorvald used to say that on weekend mornings, he would go around the apartment counting the big toes sticking out from under blankets and duvets, divide the number by two, and then he knew how many eggs he needed to boil. He and Karin would serve breakfast to much enthusiastic praise, which Thorvald felt was entirely deserved. My childhood home may not always have been the tidiest; the fridge wasn't always stocked, and dinner plans could be vague. But it was a home full of life – there was always something going on.

Both my parents had political careers. Thorvald served as Norway's minister of defence and minister of foreign affairs, and was the country's ambassador to the UN during the Yugoslav Wars and the dissolution of Yugoslavia in the 1990s. Karin was a state secretary in the Ministry of Trade and the Ministry of Industry, and in the early 1970s served as head of the then Ministry of Consumer Affairs, where she played a key role in shaping a modern family and equality policy for Norway. Yet they had very different personalities. Thorvald was outgoing and social; he loved talking to people, both those he knew and those he didn't. Karin was a more private person who didn't much enjoy public attention. But they shared a strong interest in society and politics, and this bound them together.

Thorvald had told us children about his conservative family and home life, with parents who voted for the conservative right; he had spoken to us about what led him to social democracy and the Labour Party. The 1950s, when Norway was being rebuilt, were key, since it was a time in which maintaining the sense of community of the war years was deemed to be of vital importance. At the local meetings of the Labour Party to which he was taken by friends, my father experienced a sense of solidarity he had never experienced elsewhere.

The couple of years Thorvald spent in the United States around 1960 made a strong impression on him. The class differences were great; the state was weak and capital was strong. Thorvald saw that forces at home in Norway and internationally were pulling in the direction of inequality and unfairness; the principle of the law of the jungle was beginning to gain a foothold, and he believed the trade union movement to be its most important counterweight. Good friends from his student days had connections to the Labour Party, but Karin's influence proved most important. She was more radical than him. By the time Thorvald finally joined the Labour Party in 1963, his slow drift towards membership had become so protracted that everyone around him thought he'd already been a member for years.

Both of my parents spent a lot of time travelling to meetings and conferences when I was a child. They brought many ideas and impressions home with them, and it became natural for us children to form our own opinions on everything from nuclear weapons to European cooperation. As a thirteen-year-old, I travelled around with Thorvald while he campaigned for Norway to join the European Union (or the European Community, as it was called back then); I think I took the 'no' result of the country's 1972 referendum just as hard as he and Karin did. The following year, I joined the Labour Party's Youth Organisation. My local group had sixty members, but nobody wanted to be its leader, so I was handed the role along with my membership card. Only after several months did I realise that the organisation was in the midst of a crisis. In the wake of the EC referendum, the Labour Party and the Youth Organisation were viewed by young people as being out of touch. There was little engagement; hardly anyone came to meetings.

It was off to a tough start, but my love affair with the Labour Party and social democratic values had begun. It is a relationship that has endured throughout my life.

After the general election on the ninth of September 2013, my time as Norway's prime minister came to an end. The Conservative Party's Erna Solberg took over.

On three previous occasions I had moved from the government's departmental offices to the Storting, Norway's parliament, to then return to the departments. But this time, I had the feeling it wouldn't happen again. I had been prime minister for ten years, at the top of Norwegian politics for over twenty and a member of the Labour Party's national committee for over thirty, and I was fairly sure this chapter of my life was now drawing to a close.

I discussed the way forward with Ingrid, and a few other close confidants, and quite quickly concluded that I wouldn't stand for election again in four years' time. But I was also keen to step down as party leader in an orderly and undramatic way. It would have to happen at the party conference in 2015; what I would do after that remained unknown.

Yet I was now evidently one of the former heads of government that Western leaders discussed with an eye to international positions. It was indicated that I might be a candidate to become the next secretary-general of the UN. Ban Ki-moon's successor would be chosen in 2016, and I reportedly had support in many countries – even Russia was apparently willing to accept me. But there was uncertainty about what China would think, because my government had refused to apologise for the Norwegian Nobel Committee's awarding of the Nobel Peace Prize to Chinese human rights activist Liu Xiaobo in 2010.

During a pleasant telephone conversation I had with German chancellor Angela Merkel, she mentioned almost as an aside that the position of secretary general of NATO would soon become vacant, since Anders Fogh Rasmussen was due to leave the post in the autumn of 2014. I expressed neither interest nor disinterest, and Merkel also said it would probably prove difficult to elect two Scandinavians in a row. Nor was it in my favour that Norway wasn't a member of the EU. The role was out of the question, I thought.

In a letter wishing me all the best in my future endeavours, Obama had added by hand at the bottom of the page: 'It has been a great pleasure working with you … I hope we will have the opportunity to collaborate further in future.' A warm gesture, but at the time I didn't think much of it. What I didn't know, was that Obama's closest advisers had spoken to the German chancellor about NATO and me. Angela Merkel and Barack Obama had begun to make a plan.

Around New Year of 2014, the Norwegian minister of defence Ine Eriksen Søreide received a request from Washington. The Americans wanted to nominate me as their pick to lead NATO; Germany and Poland would also support my candidature. Was I interested? This was clearly of much greater significance than a few polite enquiries, and I needed to give the matter some serious thought.

At first, I discussed the request only with those closest to me, and mostly with Ingrid. She was surprised, and sceptical initially. Ingrid felt we had spent more than long enough living in the public eye, and she had been looking forward to life becoming a little more private. Next I spoke to Thorvald, my older sister Camilla and her husband Atle, and my children. Several of the conversations took place in Thorvald's home, in the kitchen of the apartment in Mogens Thorsens gate, where in our youth Camilla, Nini and I had sat discussing politics with our friends until late into the night.

It was here, as a child, that I had heard my parents talk about what it was like to grow up during a war. But it was the stories of my grandfather, Emil Stoltenberg, that were always the most exciting. My grandfather was a fantastic storyteller, and we had become especially close, our intimacy built upon his recollections of the things he had experienced when war came to Norway. He conjured up vivid images of the days in April 1940, when as a forty-year-old captain he had led a company of conscripted nineteen- and twenty-year-olds on a mission to try to stop the Germans' advance through Valdres at

Høljarast bridge. They fought intense battles there, but were eventually forced to fall back. My grandfather could make you feel the atmosphere of chaos and the freezing conditions; the fear and confusion of nothing going according to plan. That was war.

Thorvald was lukewarm about the NATO opportunity. He had become well acquainted with the organisation through his decades spent working as a state secretary and minister in the Norwegian ministries of Defence and Foreign Affairs, and had probably attended more meetings of NATO ministers than any of his compatriots. He thought I would find it too quiet, out there in Belgium. 'What's actually going on within NATO right now?' he asked. Well, a major operation was ongoing in Afghanistan, but the alliance was in the process of pulling out. Other than that, not much. And Thorvald knew his son. He didn't think I would be happy among the generals and diplomats in Brussels.

'You're not made for that kind of work,' Thorvald said. He had seen the other side of NATO: never-ending meetings, drawn-out negotiations, endless back and forth over the wording of statements. Ingrid agreed with him. She knows me better than anyone, and was well aware of my impatient side.

Thorvald thought that instead of pursuing the NATO job, I should keep the door open for making a comeback as Norway's prime minister in 2017. The way he saw it, staying in Norway would also have another major upside, because then I would still be eligible to become secretary-general of the United Nations – a thought he liked very much. Thorvald belonged to a generation with irrepressible faith in the UN. He had been thirteen years old when the Second World War ended in 1945 – old enough for the occupation of Norway and heinous acts of war to have made an indelible impression on him. The UN was the organisation that could bring all the world's countries together in a trusting, collaborative partnership, making another major war unthinkable. In his eyes, the role of UN secretary-general was the most important job in the world.

Personally, I had my doubts about the NATO role. Of course I was flattered, and I felt honoured to have been asked, but to tell the truth

I had never had any strong desire for an international career. Ingrid was a diplomat, and Thorvald had worked on foreign policy his entire life, so this was their field, not mine. I was also unsure about exactly how much power and influence the leaders of various international organisations actually had.

I'm also an economist. I like things that are measurable; anything that can be described using figures, tables and graphs. Concrete issues, clear answers. I like to be involved in building things, everything from oil platforms to sewage treatment plants. As for messaging, deliberation and processes – the kinds of things often handled by the Ministry of Foreign Affairs – I felt myself growing restless just at the thought. There wasn't anything wrong with it, it just wasn't *me*.

And not least: I loved living in Norway. I gave much thought to having to live away from the rest of my family. True, my children were fully grown and living their own lives, but I wanted to be as close to them as possible. If Ingrid and I moved abroad, I would miss our family dinners; my children's company whenever they unexpectedly stopped by to borrow something or have a chat, often with their friends, whom Ingrid and I also knew well. Thorvald was now an old man, almost eighty-three years old. He was fairly fit and self-reliant, still able walk to Frognerveien to do his grocery shopping. And he had Anja. Filmmaker Anja Breien had come into Thorvald's life after my mother Karin died, and she had been a breath of fresh air. Thorvald hopefully still had many good years ahead of him – his father had lived to be ninety-eight.

Then I thought about my little sister, Nini, who had struggled with drug addiction for so many years. Her partner, Karljohn, had died the previous year, and Nini had been severely impacted by his death. She was going through a difficult time, and Thorvald, Camilla and I all felt a responsibility to be there for her. Nini and I would meet up occasionally, but we mostly kept in touch by phone. It therefore didn't really make much difference whether I lived in Brussels or in Oslo. I could come home for weekends and holidays, and besides I would only be in Brussels for four years, maybe five at most. But during those years, I would no longer be in the immediate vicinity, should Nini need me.

I expanded the circle of those I consulted. The attitudes among friends and acquaintances, both within and outside the Labour Party, varied from ambivalent to strongly opposed.

I thought I had plenty of time, that I wouldn't have to make my final decision until the spring. But in early February, I suddenly learned that I needed to tender my reply. The US wanted to avoid the position of NATO secretary general becoming bound up in horse-trading relating to the distribution of leading roles within the EU following the European Parliament elections in the spring. Obama was due to meet with French president François Hollande, and wanted to be able to tell him that I was the candidate of the US. So he needed to know if I was willing to take the job.

I was.

Slowly but surely, I had come to realise that I wanted to be the next secretary general of NATO.

I was used to saying yes whenever my party asked something of me. It had been that way for years; you take the office people want you to have. Now the West's most powerful leaders were asking something of me – and when people like Barack Obama and Angela Merkel ask you to do a job, it isn't exactly easy to refuse. To say no to them because I would rather live in Oslo and go skiing in Nordmarka seemed a little short-sighted.

But nor should one say yes to such an opportunity solely out of a sense of duty. Over the weeks in which I had pondered my decision, a deep, inner motivation to become head of NATO had taken root within me.

I was only fifty-five years old, and the thought of sinking my teeth into a new, large-scale project appealed to me. Of all international work, peace-keeping efforts are the most important. While wars are raging, it is impossible to make headway on combating climate change, fighting poverty, or promoting economic development. Peace is the very foundation of social progress. And NATO stands at the forefront in ensuring peace and security for close to a billion people.

Over sixty years had passed since NATO was established. The organisation was founded to secure a common defence against the communist Soviet Union, and to ensure freedom and democracy within the member states. NATO cooperation was both political and military in nature. The US, Canada and ten Western European countries had been members from the start, but a number of other countries had also joined the alliance since then.

For me, there is a political affinity between the NATO alliance and the social democratic idea that we can achieve more together than we can alone. It is paradoxical that there is often the notion, even among social democrats, that defence and security are issues that primarily belong to the political right. But the truth is that NATO has enjoyed broad support across the political landscape, and social democratic parties have historically been the organisation's driving force. The majority of the European countries who came together and formed the alliance were either led by social democrats, or had significant social democratic participation. The British Labour Party government under Clement Attlee's leadership played a key role, but other social democratic prime ministers such as Willem Drees of the Netherlands, Hans Hedtoft of Denmark and Einar Gerhardsen of Norway also made important contributions when NATO was founded. In the US, democrat Harry Truman was president, and the Liberal Party's Louis St Laurent was prime minister in Canada. Both were left of centre within their domestic political landscapes.

I had mostly worked on issues relating to domestic policy, such as pensions, the administration of Norway's oil fund, and reform of the public sector, and my international engagement had mainly focused on the challenges of climate change and children's health. Still, defence and security policy had always been part of my political life, from the Labour Party Youth Organisation's debates about NATO and nuclear weapons in the 1980s to the major defence investments made during my time as prime minister. I had also worked on Norway's participation in international military operations in Afghanistan, Libya and Kosovo, and beyond.

I believe in strong institutions. In cooperation, through which countries big and small are given a seat at the table; where everyone is heard and common rules are established to constrain the law of the jungle. This, in essence, is what we call civilisation – within local communities, at national level, and, above all, internationally. In order to prevent war and injustice, organisations founded upon international law and democratic principles are needed. It is through organised cooperation that an individual country's interests are best safeguarded, and this is especially true for smaller nations. A binding partnership between the US and Europe is the very foundation of the cooperation we need on defence and security.

On the evening I learned that the Americans needed an answer by the following morning, I sat down with Ingrid. The conversation we had was long. Her scepticism wasn't assuaged entirely, but she believes in international cooperation just as strongly as I do. Together, we made the decision. I agreed to become Barack Obama and Angela Merkel's candidate for the office of secretary general of NATO.

From Washington, I learned that I had broad support from many NATO countries, and that I personally didn't need to do a thing. The greatest campaign manager in the world, Barack Obama, was working for me, I was told. All I had to do was wait.

2

A step change

Thorvald gave me a warm hug. On the twenty-eighth of March, the US and Germany had persuaded all the member states to support my candidature, and I was appointed the thirteenth secretary general of NATO. Just a few days later, we gathered around the kitchen table for yet another dinner in Mogens Thorsens gate.

Once I had made my decision, Thorvald supported me wholeheartedly. For him, the only important thing was that I figure out what was best for me. That I would be working for NATO was all that mattered now. Any suggestion that the alliance was out of date had been silenced.

Moreover, a drama was now playing out, early in the spring of 2014, which had revived old East–West antagonisms, and once again drew increased attention to our collective defence.

The US had not bombed Syria, as Obama had proposed at the dinner hosted by the Swedish prime minister in September 2013. Congress was generally opposed, and Obama decided not to take up the political challenge of going against the elected representatives. Instead, the US and Russia negotiated a deal in which Syria's chemical weapons would be surrendered and destroyed. NATO and Russia also agreed to provide military protection to the ships that would transport the chemical weapons out of Syria.

But then came the crises.

In the early months of 2014, intense clashes broke out in Kyiv after Ukraine's pro-Russian president, Viktor Yanukovych, refused to sign an association agreement with the EU. Several dozen demonstrators were killed by riot police, and the regime's brutality escalated the crisis. At the end of February, Yanukovych was removed by parliament; he fled the country and sought refuge in Russia. A short time later, reports came in that something was brewing in Crimea – Ukrainian military units had been surrounded and threatened by so-called 'little green men', soldiers in unmarked uniforms. But as to where these men had come from, there was no doubt. This was a Russian occupation. On the eighteenth of March, Russia declared Crimea part of the Russian Federation.

A few weeks later, separatists protested in several cities in the Donbas region in the east of Ukraine, taking control of large parts of the area. The separatists were led and financed by Russia, and would have been powerless without this support. In contrast to events in Crimea, in the Donbas intense fighting broke out between the Ukrainian government's soldiers and the separatists.

The security situation in Europe was bumped up the international agenda. Tensions increased. All dialogue with Russia ceased.

But Ukraine was not the only country in which a crisis was unfolding. In Syria and Iraq, the terrorist organisation the Islamic State (IS) was making significant advances, and had taken over large areas. A terrorist state the likes of which the world had never seen had established itself close to NATO's borders.

The world had changed. There were now greater dangers. More uncertainty. Less stability.

We found ourselves in a situation where Western cooperation was suddenly more important than it had been for decades. All this had happened during those brief weeks in which I had been thinking about whether I wished to be put forward for, and was eventually awarded, the role of head of NATO. Of course I felt anxious, but the more difficult the international situation became, the more attracted I was by the thought of the challenges that awaited. I was extremely motivated by everything that happened over the course of that dramatic spring.

To enable me to prepare, I was allocated an office in the Norwegian chief of defence's residence, a beautiful house down at Akershus Fortress in Oslo, where I conferred with my colleagues and other NATO employees who came up from Brussels. Over the summer, I was able to obtain an ever clearer picture of the task I now faced. NATO had become an entirely different organisation from the one it had been during the Cold War. It had gone through several rounds of extensive cuts. The command structure staff had been halved, and year upon year more roles had been cut from among the civil staff, to meet savings requirements.

Most important, however, was the fact that NATO was generally organised and structured to run operations *outside* its own area. In all the years in which NATO had deployed to Bosnia, Kosovo and Afghanistan, European armed forces had been reduced. Military readiness, reaction times, combat capability, high-tech warfare to defend one's own territory – all this had been weakened. Furthermore, NATO had paid too little attention to new challenges, such as China, cyber security and the militarisation of space.

In the chief of defence's residence in Akershus, a major political project gradually began to take shape. The ship had to be turned around. A drastic remedy was required; NATO had to be restructured, armed and modernised. The budget cuts simply couldn't continue – NATO needed increased investment and more staff if it was to once again become capable of achieving its core aim: to secure peace and ensure our common security.

A large part of my preparations involved visiting some important capital cities. One day, towards the end of June, I was led into the German Chancellery on the Tiergarten in the centre of Berlin. Angela Merkel invited me into her office. We drank tea, which she served herself. It was always good to see her – over many years of working together, we had developed a close and trusting partnership. She congratulated me, and I thanked her for her support.

Merkel was deeply concerned about what was happening in Ukraine, and the potential consequences for peace in Europe. She was the Western leader most frequently in contact with Moscow, and she'd had many long conversations with Vladimir Putin following the annexation of Crimea. Her interactions with the Russian president had done little to assuage her unease.

'Putin is living in his own world,' she said.

She spoke about the crucial role NATO played in holding the US and Europe together. Angela Merkel, who before 1989 lived in East Germany, understands NATO's significance perhaps more than most. We went out onto the terrace, where she pointed to the area of the city in which she had lived, and she repeated a phrase I'd heard her use before: 'One has to be patient when waiting for big changes.' It might seem like an eternity, to live behind the Berlin Wall under authoritarian one-party rule and without the freedom to leave. But it took twenty-eight years from when the wall was built until it was torn down. You might think things will never end, but nothing lasts forever.

Merkel was also concerned about the way relations between the US and Europe were developing.

'The Americans are powerful, but I hope you won't do everything they ask,' she said. 'What's important, Jens, is that the United States don't always get their way.'

There is a unique subtleness to Merkel, who is able to make a serious point in a light, almost roguish way. There was both jest and earnestness in her warning. I smiled, and promised her that I didn't intend to give in to the US on absolutely everything.

There was much talk of how the United States was in the process of turning its attention away from Europe and towards China and Asia. The trend had been evident for a long time, but had recently intensified. Yet Merkel wasn't overly concerned about transatlantic cooperation and Europe's standing within the powerful circles in Washington. She got on well with President Obama.

A little later in the summer, I found myself sitting in a deckchair on the beach in Villefranche-sur-Mer, on the French Riviera, just east of Nice. I stared dozily at the blue expanse of the Mediterranean, a cold beer in my hand.

Not long before, I had met French president François Hollande, and like most of his compatriots, Hollande was preoccupied with the French language. When NATO was established in 1949, four of the twelve member states were entirely or partly French-speaking. There are still four French-speaking countries in the alliance, but the number of member states has now risen to thirty-two. This naturally affects the language's position, although French remains NATO's other official language, alongside English.

I had studied German at school, and I would therefore, as far as I knew, be the first secretary general of NATO who couldn't speak a word of French. I wanted to seem obliging towards Hollande, so I told him I would take a French course.

Following my retirement at an extraordinary party conference earlier in the summer, Jonas Gahr Støre was elected as the Labour Party's new leader. 'You're going to try to learn French?' he exclaimed upon hearing my plans (Jonas speaks the language fluently himself). 'It's utterly hopeless,' he said, 'you don't stand a chance.'

But I kept the promise I made to Hollande, and signed up to an intensive three-week course arranged by the renowned Institut Français. The tuition involved eight hours of teaching each day, daily homework, and a prohibition against speaking any language other than French while on the institute's grounds.

Ingrid decided to join me, and we stayed in a small apartment in idyllic Villefranche-sur-Mer. On the first day, we walked up to the language school, which was located in a magnificent villa on a hillside with a view of the town and the sea. Everyone was to be allocated to a group based on their existing knowledge, and we were brought in one by one to be tested. When my turn came, I was shown into a room in which three tutors sat waiting. On the plane from Norway I had practised 'My name is Jens' and 'I am Norwegian' and a few other simple phrases, which I now rattled off. The three tutors stared at me, their faces expressionless.

A short time later, Ingrid disappeared off into one of the groups of advanced students. I was told my level: *Débutant*.

I took the French course seriously, people have to give me that. I went every day, stuck it out for eight hours straight in the summer heat, and always did my homework. But when you're a complete beginner, there's a long way to go before you have even the most basic grasp of the language.

These were delightful days – it's almost impossible not to enjoy life in a place like Villefranche-sur-Mer in the summer. In our free time, Ingrid and I took long walks along the beach; we rented bicycles and sampled excellent food. But as the course approached its end, I took stock. I had indeed learned quite a bit, and I could say some simple, coherent sentences. But I was far from being able to *use* French in any reasonable way. Achieving that kind of proficiency would have required much more effort, and time I simply didn't have.

There in the deckchair on the beach, I drew my conclusion. Jonas had been right.

Later that summer, we were at our summer house in Hvaler, Norway, as usual. I often get a little restless while on holiday, so enjoy doing work around the garden. On Tuesday the twenty-ninth of July I was raking up the leaves when Ingrid rounded the corner of the house and came towards me.

I could see right away that something was wrong. She handed me her phone but said nothing. On the other end of the line was Camilla.

'Jens,' she said, 'Nini is dead.'

Camilla was calling from Nini's apartment. She had found her there.

Ingrid and I looked at each other. She took the rake from my hand, leaned it against the wall of the house and embraced me for a long time. Then she put an arm around me, and together we went inside.

I changed into clean clothes and set off for Nini's apartment; a couple of hours later, I met Camilla and Thorvald there. Nini, wearing a thin silk nightdress, sat in a chair in the kitchen. She looked peaceful. I gently put my palm to her cheek and felt that she was cold. The fear had long gnawed away at me, and now it had happened. My little sister was dead.

That past summer, while I was in France, I had called Nini several times. She didn't pick up the phone. This had worried me, but most of all, it had made me sad. It was fairly normal for her not to answer. Most of the time it meant that she was feeling down and didn't want to speak to anyone. I decided to visit her as soon as I got back to Norway.

When I rang her doorbell a few days later, she didn't reply. 'Nini!' I shouted through the letterbox, but there was only silence. Maybe she was out running errands; maybe she was in but didn't feel up to answering the door. I had brought along some smoothies, because I knew she was struggling to eat properly. I gave them to a neighbour, who had agreed to pass food on to her before.

Now Thorvald, Camilla and I stood in her kitchen. We didn't speak much. Thorvald wept. For years he had done his utmost to help and support his youngest child. I knew how exhausting it had been for him. All the time he had spent on Nini; all the worry. Now she was gone forever. There would be no going out to look for her this time. There was no longer any hope, only grief.

Over the days that followed, people spoke warmly of Nini, and several beautiful obituaries were published in the newspapers. People stopped us in the street; they posted messages on social media and told us what Nini had meant to them. It can be wearing, being a family that is constantly in the public eye, but it was a true gift to experience so much warmth and thoughtfulness from friends and strangers alike.

Uranienborg Church was packed when the church bells rang on the morning of the eighteenth of August. Outside, the rain poured down.

'A big brother is supposed to protect his little sister,' I said in my eulogy. 'I tried to look after you. As did Thorvald, Camilla, and many others. But in the end, death was simply too strong.'

We carried out the coffin. White lilies and roses were spread across its lid. My son walked directly ahead of me. With my eyes fixed firmly on his back, I carried the coffin past all the silent pews and out to the waiting hearse.

In the days following the funeral, Camilla and I gradually began to clear out Nini's apartment. It testified to just how hard Nini's life had been – there was a lot of clutter, and the debris of a life involving drugs. But we also found beautiful things. Small objects, pictures and letters she had kept, and which now brought back fine memories.

I will never fully understand why things turned out the way they did. As children, Nini and I shared a room and set of bunkbeds; I slept in the top bunk, she in the bottom. The same family, the same school, many of the same friends. And yet the trajectories of our lives had been so very different.

Nini's life was unfinished – she had many skills she never got to use, so much potential that was never realised, although we had always hoped she would one day manage to create a better, richer life for herself. But at the same time, I noticed how the *fear* of death released its grasp, now that she was gone. A curious doubleness: grief and loss – but also relief.

Beautiful, poetic Nini, who could come up with the most moving words and sentences; who made the most magnificent greeting cards with her lovely handwriting. As a young person she liked to draw, and made attractive ceramic figurines. I found one of them while we were clearing out her apartment. On it were the words: 'Fly, wild-winged one, fly'.

Ingrid and I spent a lot of time with Thorvald in the period after the funeral. He appreciated our company, but at the same time he was concerned that life must go on, and that I needed to prepare for the tasks that awaited me. Eventually, I would have to make space for a kind of everyday living, a form of normality among everything that seemed so abnormal. I would travel to Wales, to attend a meeting of NATO leaders as a guest, on the fourth and fifth of September.

This would be the first time NATO heads of state and government had gathered since the world had drastically altered over the course of a few short months. The wars in Syria and Ukraine provided a sombre backdrop. In July, a Malaysian passenger plane travelling from Amsterdam to Kuala Lumpur had been shot down over Eastern Ukraine, the rocket fired from an area controlled by Russian separatists; several of the individuals later convicted by the International

Court of Justice in The Hague were Russian agents. A total of 298 people were killed, and the tragedy intensified the sense of insecurity and danger.

At the NATO summit, I met President Barack Obama again, and together we reviewed the most important issues. We were both deeply concerned about the consequences of Russia's illegal annexation of Crimea, and the military encroachment in the Donbas region. It was evident that NATO had to be strengthened, and that Ukraine must be given more support. At that time, Obama and the US were opposed to providing military aid, because it was felt that this might escalate the conflict to a level we were not ready to handle. Obama was keen to emphasise that we shouldn't offer false hope. He also believed Ukraine was more important to Russia than to the West, and that Moscow would therefore be willing to make greater sacrifices.

The message was that we needed to provide extensive political and economic support to Ukraine, not massive military assistance. In return, however, NATO would need to strengthen its defence, in order to deter Moscow from threatening any NATO allies. Obama was especially keen for the European NATO countries and Canada to increase their defence spending – the current situation was simply untenable. The United States' defence budget represented well over 70 per cent of the other NATO members' total defence expenditure. 'This isn't fair, and it won't be possible to justify it to American taxpayers in the longer term,' he said.

It was a subject with deep roots. American dissatisfaction with how the financial burden was shared was almost as old as the alliance itself. 'NATO states are not paying their fair share,' complained President John F. Kennedy to his National Security Council all the way back in 1963.

Now Obama wanted a resolution on a fairer distribution of responsibility from the Wales summit. 'We need a clear resolution, but even more importantly, we need action. And I trust that you'll deliver this, Jens,' Obama said with a gleam in his eye. I smiled and said that yes, of course I would, but I felt extremely unsure as to whether I could live up to his expectations.

At the meeting, Anders Fogh Rasmussen introduced me as NATO's next secretary general. UK prime minister David Cameron also said a few words, keeping the tone light. 'I have great belief in continuity. And now we have another slim and fit Scandinavian former prime minister to follow our previous slim and fit Scandinavian former prime minister,' he said. Fogh Rasmussen was known for donning his running shoes at any opportunity; his first NATO bodyguards had to be replaced because he kept outrunning them. They certainly wouldn't have that problem with me.

In meeting the other heads of state and government, Obama pushed hard on the question of how the alliance's financial burden should be shared. He called countries with low defence budgets 'free riders', who in a crisis simply relied on receiving assistance from the American military. The European member states and Canada wanted the least possible commitment, and no precise figures to be set. But in the end, they gave in to the pressure and agreed that everyone should spend 2 per cent of their gross domestic product on defence.

The closing statement, however, was a compromise: 'Allies aim to move towards the 2% guideline within a decade.' Considered as part of a legal document, such vague wording can open up many loopholes for sidestepping the pledged commitment. But the *political* reality was quite a different one – and this was the crucial point. A promise had been made to significantly increase defence spending, and this was a promise the US expected Europe and Canada to keep.

I realised that increased defence spending and military require-ments were issues that I would be working extensively with in the times ahead. The alliance had made a step change.

PART 2
A NEW START
October 2014–July 2016

3

In Brussels

STARTING IN THE ROLE OF SECRETARY GENERAL OF NATO WAS LIKE jumping onto a speeding train. On the first of October 2014, I arrived at the somewhat run-down NATO headquarters for my first day as head of the alliance. I was shown into my office, immediately dazzled by the wall-to-wall NATO-blue carpeting featuring the alliance's logo. Like many people, I had assumed the logo depicted a star, and commented on how attractive it was. 'Secretary General, that's not a star. It's a compass,' NATO's chief of protocol explained to me, amiably but firmly.

I was then accompanied to the meeting room of the North Atlantic Council, which gathers representatives from all the member states and is the alliance's principal decision-making body. One of the walls featured the Latin quotation *Animus in consulendo liber* – 'a mind unfettered in deliberation' – from the Roman historian Sallust.

I took my place at the table, where the gavel lay, and watched the NATO ambassadors as they entered the room and found their seats one by one. I weighed the dark wood in my hand for a moment, then tightened my grip, rapped the gavel against the table, and for the first time opened a meeting of the North Atlantic Council.

There were no speeches or formal introductions to indicate the organisation now had a new leader, but of course this was obvious to everyone in the room – and not least to me. I wasn't used to leading a body of which I hadn't first been an ordinary member. Every time I wished to give someone the floor, I sought the right person from among all the unfamiliar faces.

At the time of my taking office, NATO had a total of around 13,500 employees. It's a large organisation, responsible for everything from ongoing military operations and exercises to plans to establish NATO standards for member states' weapons and *matériel*.

The secretary general has two main tasks. One is to lead NATO as an organisation – the people who work at the alliance's headquarters in Brussels and in different agencies in the member states, as well as at offices in NATO partner countries. The other is to chair the meetings of the North Atlantic Council. The council meets several times a week, and consists of ambassadors from all the member states, who all have permanent delegations at NATO headquarters. On a few occasions each year, it is the ministers of defence or foreign affairs, or possibly the heads of state and government, who represent their countries at the council. The meetings are then referred to as either ministerial meetings or summits. So the seniority and level of the participants varies, but the meetings are always chaired by the secretary general.

The fact that NATO's secretary general is both an administrative leader – a kind of group CEO – and chair of the organisation's most senior decision-making body, gives the role-holder a unique position compared with the heads of other international organisations, where these responsibilities are often separated. Within the UN, the secretary-general leads the organisation, while other roles chair the meetings of the Security Council and the General Assembly, where decisions are made.

Of course, the secretary general of NATO has limited power, because it is ultimately the member states who make the decisions. Nevertheless, the secretary general has significant influence. Leading a large organisation offers opportunities to take the initiative, set the agenda and establish the conditions for decision-making processes.

I now held the overarching responsibility for the complex activities of this vast organisation, but in practice much was delegated to the group of assistant secretary generals and my other close colleagues. From the very start, I aimed to run the organisation through those closest to me in what is known as the private office. I wanted to spend as much time and energy as possible on the political work.

Some Norwegian former colleagues had also accompanied me to NATO. As director of my private office I chose Vegard Ellefsen, who had served as Norway's ambassador to NATO for the past four years. My head of communications from the Norwegian prime minister's office, Trude Måseide, joined me as my communications adviser. Gjermund Eide, former military assistant to minister of defence Anne-Grete Strøm-Erichsen, accompanied me to Brussels as my military assistant. Randi Ness had been my adviser in parliament after the 2013 Norwegian election, and she also agreed to work for me as an adviser in Brussels. From NATO's defence policy and planning division, I brought in political scientist and diplomat Stian Jenssen, who was already well acquainted with NATO from the inside, and who had assisted me during my preparations.

I felt it vital to have a group of people around me whom I knew well, and who also knew me. I knew that the job would become hectic at times, and my terms as Norway's prime minister had shown me the importance of forging relationships with a small group of people whom I could trust completely. This kind of intimate, close-knit team gave me greater strength in the work of leading the organisation. Every member would need to be able to both act as a political adviser and undertake practical tasks. We collaborated on everything, big and small.

Ingrid and I arrived in Brussels just a few days before I took office, and we moved into the house that Lord Carrington had acquired for NATO when he was secretary general in the 1980s. At first, Ingrid continued to live in Oslo, but as a senior adviser within the Norwegian Ministry of Foreign Affairs, she worked extensively with the EU system and could partly work from Brussels.

Many years had passed since we first moved in together. I got to know Ingrid in 1975, when we were classmates at Oslo Cathedral High School. She was in a relationship with an older boy, who drove her to school in his car. Every morning, I saw the car stop before the school gates; Ingrid would lean towards her boyfriend, thank him for the lift with a kiss, then open the car door and step out. Confident and straight-backed, she crossed the schoolyard like a dancer – which she also was.

Ingrid was sharp, with a great sense of style, and there was something exceptional about her. She didn't much care about the boys in our class. We were young and inexperienced, and we didn't have cars.

But there was one area in which I felt fairly proficient, and that was the political arena. Oslo Cathedral High School was a school with a high level of political engagement, holding intense debates and many elections for various student organisations – elections I stood for, and won. Until the time came to choose the school's representative for the national convention of Norway's student union, in the winter of 1977. Somewhat surprisingly, Ingrid stood as an independent candidate and won by a huge margin. Since I came second, I became her deputy, and we travelled to the convention in Trondheim together. By this point, Ingrid and I had become part of the same circle of friends. I was in love with her, and she had started to take a little more interest in me. We were actually supposed to spend the night camping out in a sports hall with all the other delegates, but neither of us were particularly keen on the idea. We took a room at the Hotel Phoenix instead. We didn't define ourselves as a couple right away, but nevertheless our relationship grew ever more serious. In 1979, we moved in together, into a small apartment we rented in Grünerløkka in Oslo, with no bathroom and a toilet in the hall we shared with our neighbours. It was a happy time, and the start of a long life together.

The house in Brussels we moved into over thirty-five years later was of a rather different standard. The residence, built in the early 1900s, had a floor plan that covered almost thirteen thousand square feet, and was situated in a sheltered part of the several-kilometre-long Avenue Louise. On the ground floor were large reception rooms, well suited to dinners and entertaining. On the first floor I installed my home office, and this was also where we had our private living quarters and bedrooms. Six large rooms on the second floor were excellent for hosting house guests, and in the loft my predecessor had left behind an extensive selection of gym equipment.

At the back of the house, a small set of steps led down from the terrace into a private garden facing the Bois de la Cambre park, where over the coming years I would cover a great many miles, walking both alone and with friends, in sunshine and in sleet, sometimes listening to a podcast, at others speaking on the phone. And occasionally in silence, pondering what on earth I was going to do about all the problems that were stacking up.

A staff of three kept the residence in order at all times. From day one, Berjan Beeuwkes proved himself an excellent cook, and administrated with a steady hand all the activities that took place in our new home. Celine Van Esch and Gizela Oliveira took care of everything else, keeping the place clean and tidy, and welcoming guests and serving refreshments. They made sure I always had freshly laundered clothes, and that my shirts were ironed. I wasn't accustomed to these luxuries back home in Norway, where the prime minister buys and cooks his own food and does his own laundry. I had always believed this was just as it should be, because it's good for political leaders to preserve a sense of connection with ordinary life. But in Brussels, I discovered just how much time is freed up when others take care of the housework for you. It gave me more time to work. The immense benefit of this was something I quickly came to appreciate.

I had been in Brussels many times before, but now that I would be living there, it was as if I *saw* the city in a different way. Brussels is like the little sister of Paris – a slightly run-down but charming capital city. War remains an ever-present backdrop. Many of the wide avenues are named after generals, and there is hardly a park or school without a bust or memorial to this or that war. But what makes the greatest impression are the small plaques scattered across the city, which bear witness to the fates of ordinary people: 'We remember the students who fell for the Fatherland during the war of 1914–1918', followed by the names of all those who lost their lives. The battlefields of Waterloo, Ypres and Ardennes are all located just a short drive from the centre of Brussels, which testifies to the bloody wars that have raged in this part of Europe over the centuries.

Being in close proximity to the places where battles were waged and intense fighting took place gives you a new and deeper understanding of the nature of war – it brings it so much closer than books or speeches can. The history of Brussels has always been tightly interwoven with that of Europe, in times of war and of peace.

4

The challenge of Russia

A GREY-HAIRED, DISTINGUISHED-LOOKING MAN WAS ESCORTED into my office. Russia's ambassador to NATO, Alexander Grushko, had asked to speak with me. The atmosphere in the corridors was a little tense before he arrived – simply speaking with the Russians was contentious, because many feared this might be perceived as acceptance of Russia's aggression in Ukraine.

The encounter, which took place towards the end of November 2014, was the first time I met Grushko. We greeted one another, and I showed him to a chair in the corner of my office. We both knew that the moment we began to speak about Ukraine, the conversation would grow difficult. Grushko looked at me expectantly. He was clearly in no hurry to get to the topic. Nor was I.

'Where in Oslo did you live?' I asked.

'In Sorgenfrigata,' he replied.

Because Alexander Grushko and I had a few old ties. He was the son of Viktor Grushko, who between 1955 and 1972 had worked at the Soviet embassy in Oslo. Alexander Grushko knew my old neighbourhood well; as a boy he had cycled around the park next to Uranienborg School; he knew exactly where the footbridge over to Frognerkilen Bay at Skarpsno was. He was even born in the same building as me, at the Red Cross clinic in Fredrik Stangs gate, just four years earlier.

His father knew Thorvald well, back when my father was a young diplomat in the Ministry of Foreign Affairs, and he had visited our family home in Mogens Thorsens gate several times. During the holidays, Viktor had taken his son Alexander and the rest of the family to Ula in Larvik, and stayed at our holiday home there. He was also well connected among the Labour Party's most senior members. There's a famous photograph of Viktor with former Labour prime minister Einar Gerhardsen and his wife, Werna, taken on a plane's boarding stairs at Oslo Airport Fornebu in 1955, as Gerhardsen is about to embark on a state visit to Moscow. Viktor is handing Werna a large bouquet of red roses, and Werna is patting Viktor on the cheek. The image was much discussed when it later became known that Viktor Grushko was a KGB man.

In the car on my way to NATO headquarters that morning, I had called Thorvald. Oh yes, he remembered Viktor very well, and had known he was a member of the KGB. He had preferred to stay in contact with the KGB's people, he said, quite simply because they were the ones kept most up to date by embassy staff, and who probably wrote the most detailed reports back to Moscow. Thorvald believed this to be unproblematic, just as long as you never forgot that you were speaking to a Soviet intelligence agent.

I met with Grushko alone. Outside my closed office door my staff waited anxiously, wondering how the conversation was unfolding. Little did they know that the alliance's new secretary general and Russian ambassador were reminiscing over their happy childhoods spent in Oslo.

Then it was time to turn to more serious matters.

I conveyed NATO's standpoint. Russia had breached international law in Ukraine. The annexation of Crimea was unacceptable. For us to move forward, we would need to see some fundamental changes. The Russian forces would have to be withdrawn from Crimea and the Donbas.

'Listening to you is pure torture – everything you say is so wrong,' Grushko said, his tone exasperated. 'We had high hopes for you, because you said you support dialogue and cooperation. So we've listened closely to everything you've said, and read the statements you've made since taking office. We've read the declarations from the summit in Wales, and what you've said about them. We disagree with all of it. So I can say nothing other than that we are very disappointed.'

I *had* signalled that I was in favour of dialogue. At the press conference on the day I took office, I was keen to convey that I did not consider Russia an enemy. I saw no incompatibility between a strong NATO and developing a constructive relationship with Russia. Quite the opposite, in fact.

I was basing this approach on previous experience. The partnership we had managed to develop between Norway and Russia over the course of many years had only been possible because Norway had the safety and security that NATO membership provided. Stability and predictability offered the best framework for gradually building trust and cooperation. This was also my message to Grushko.

While Grushko agreed that much had been achieved through the good relations between Norway and Russia, he also believed that NATO's enlargement eastwards and support of Ukraine threatened Russia, and undermined the country's cooperation with NATO. The conversation confirmed that Russia and NATO remained at opposite ends of the spectrum on the question of Ukraine. Still, as the meeting concluded, Grushko said he'd like to keep in touch. He also gave me a copy of the book his father had written about his years in the Soviet intelligence service, *My Life in the KGB*. On the book's title page, he had written a greeting: 'From my father's son to your father's son.'

The challenging meeting with Grushko did not change my basic position. The door to Moscow must not be allowed to close completely. One of the people with whom I discussed this issue most was NATO's principal spokesperson, Oana Lungescu. The two of us met many times that first autumn, when NATO's attitude towards Russia needed to be expressed in draft speeches or statements. When I tried to find the right words to describe our dialogue with Moscow, I noticed that Oana often held back.

Oana was born and grew up in Romania, under one of the harshest regimes in the entire Eastern Bloc. When she was in her twenties, her father was diagnosed with cancer. Oana was sought out by Romania's infamous secret police, the Securitate, who told her they could ensure her father would receive the treatment that could save him – on the condition that she began working for them.

Oana told her father what had happened. 'You must never, ever, have anything to do with those people,' he said. He died shortly afterwards.

Oana managed to flee Romania a few years before the fall of the Berlin Wall, and for many years she worked as a journalist at the BBC, before becoming the NATO spokesperson. For me, her story was a living reminder of the experiences Eastern Europeans carry with them. On more than one occasion, I had referred to 1945 as Europe's great year of liberation. But throughout my time in NATO, I became ever more aware that such descriptions reflected only what happened in *Western* Europe – they obscured and excluded what went on east of the Iron Curtain. In Eastern Europe, 1945, and the subsequent years, marked the transition from one oppressive totalitarian regime to another.

Now Oana was worried that our desire for dialogue would be abused by the Russians, and exploited in their propaganda. A wish for openness could be portrayed as acquiescence.

The Kremlin understood only one language, she said. The language of power.

Post-1989, incredible things had happened. The Berlin Wall had been turned to rubble, and the Warsaw Pact lay in ruins. The pact had been a military alliance controlled from Moscow; the Soviet Union and Eastern Europe's equivalent of NATO. It had consisted of eight countries. Of these, seven became NATO members. The eighth, the Soviet Union, was dissolved, but the Baltic countries, three former Soviet republics, also subsequently joined NATO.

I believed it had been entirely correct to try to use the historic opportunity that arose following the dissolution of the Soviet Union in 1991 to establish a new relationship with Russia. To develop a political collaboration. Expand interpersonal contacts. Increase trade, and find new areas within which we could cooperate.

Others regarded this period during the 1990s with distrust, believing an opening up towards the East to be naive and misguided – that the easing of tensions represented only a brief pause in the rivalry between East and West. Deep antagonisms remained between Russia and the West, and they would come to the fore again. It was just a matter of time.

It was clear from my very first day in NATO that relations between the alliance and Russia were going to pose a major challenge. The fundamental question was: how do we relate to this country?

The NATO-Russia Council had been set up in 2002, with the aim of establishing a permanent structure for cooperation between NATO and Russia. The council had decision-making power, and the ability to implement specific joint projects. Some even hoped the council would be the first step towards Russia joining NATO.

The work to achieve a closer collaboration between Russia and NATO ground to a halt over the course of the 2000s. In the summer of 2008, the flames of the West's scepticism were further fanned by the war in Georgia, where Putin demonstrated his willingness and indeed the ability to re-establish Russia's sphere of influence. When Russia annexed Crimea and Russian forces entered the Donbas in 2014, the thaw was well and truly over. NATO ministers of foreign affairs shut down all practical civil and military cooperation with Russia. The meetings of the NATO-Russia Council were intended to continue, but the political will to make this happen proved lacking. Political dialogue also ceased.

I was keen to get the meetings up and running again, but encountered resistance among the member states and at NATO headquarters in Brussels. The Americans were against it – they wanted any dialogue with Russia to be on a bilateral level, as did the British. The eastern allies were also opposed. They believed engaging in any 'dialogue' would be an expression of weakness, and imply acceptance of Russia's actions. Countries such as Germany, France and Italy disagreed. They supported my view, believing political conversations with Moscow in no way legitimised the Kremlin's aggression towards Russia's neighbours. Dialogue was a necessary channel in seeking to avoid further confusion in relations between NATO and Russia, and, if at all possible, to improve them over time.

It was challenging to reconcile the various internal viewpoints on how the alliance should relate to the Russians. At the very least, we needed to avoid accidents or incidents that might spiral out of control and give rise to truly dangerous situations. In our discussions, I spoke about the old, stable neighbourly relations between Russia and Norway. Even during the coldest period of the Cold War, Norway was able to speak with the Soviet Union about matters relating to military cooperation, energy and fisheries management.

Over the years, I had personally been an active participant in this work. As a young member of the Labour Party's Youth Organisation, I'd had a lot of contact with Russians and other Eastern Europeans. I regularly visited the East German embassy in Oslo; I went to parties at the Polish embassy. We desired contact and dialogue, but were also keen that this should be used politically – to demand that human rights be respected in the Soviet Union and other Warsaw Pact countries. The Youth Organisation supported political prisoners in Poland, and worked with opposition church groups in East Germany. We were open about our contact with Eastern European regimes. Whenever I planned to meet with people whom I knew belonged to the KGB, I would call the Norwegian intelligence service and inform them in advance.

This all seemed completely normal to me at the time. Only later did I understand that it was a little unusual for a young man in his early twenties to have had such close and regular contact with Soviet and Eastern European intelligence agents.

As head of the Youth Organisation, I made my first visit to the Soviet Union in 1986. Among other projects, in 1988 we agreed to work with the young communists in Komsomol to implement an environmental campaign against sulphur emissions in Nikel, and I continued this work in my role as state secretary in the Ministry of Environment. As Norway's minister of industry and energy from 1993 to 1996, I participated in a joint Norwegian–Russian economic commission, through which we facilitated Norwegian investments in Russian oil and gas projects and increased cross-border trade in the north.

The first time I spoke with Vladimir Putin was in August 2000. He had recently become president of Russia, and I had just become prime minister of Norway. Putin called me to express his gratitude for Norway's assistance in the attempts to rescue the crew of the *Kursk* nuclear submarine, which had been wrecked in the Barents Sea. A few weeks later, we had our first meeting at the UN, before I made a larger official visit to Moscow in June 2001.

Putin received me at his office in the Kremlin, the old fortress in the heart of Moscow. The complex is magnificent, with towering palaces, cathedrals, barracks and walls. More than anything else, the facility exudes *power* – you can truly sense how for centuries Russian tsars have sheltered behind those walls and ruled over an empire.

The mood was good, and we were both looking forward to increasing the cooperation between our respective countries. Norwegian companies invested heavily in Russia, in everything from fuel stations and telecommunications companies to newspapers and breweries. Norway financed the scrapping of decommissioned Russian nuclear submarines, and we had expanded joint preparedness plans for search and rescue at sea. But after over twenty years of negotiations, agreement on a maritime border in the Barents Sea – a dividing line between Russia and Norway – still hadn't been reached. Putin also believed Norway was not safeguarding Russian interests on the island of Svalbard satisfactorily, and he was critical of what he believed to be the poor treatment of the Russian mining community in Barentsburg. We agreed to continue to work to strengthen relations between our two countries.

There were many meetings and conversations between us over the years. Putin appeared to be a hard-working, rational and results-oriented man, and for the most part we maintained a civil tone. He obviously read up on and understood the matters we discussed, and despite our disagreements, we were able to take new, important steps in Norwegian–Russian cooperation. And not least, in 2020, we finally reached agreement on the dividing line in the Barents Sea.

The clarification of this boundary made it possible to further expand our energy cooperation, including agreements to develop one of the world's largest offshore gas fields, the Shtokman field, although high costs meant the project was never realised. Strong growth was facilitated by the commercial cooperation between Russia and Norway in the north, and a visa exemption programme was introduced for the population who lived in the border regions on either side. In the Norwegian town of Kirkenes, the Russian-speaking population markedly increased, and many street signs were erected with the names written in the Cyrillic alphabet, in addition to Norwegian.

So I knew from experience that it was possible to work with the Russians, and that they honoured the agreements we entered into.

'It's about expanding the space where agreements are possible, and limiting the space where they are not,' I repeated in my meetings with diplomats and political leaders during this initial period in NATO.

I also told them about the walk I had taken with prime minister Dmitry Medvedev up in Storskog, close to the Norway–Russia border, at the events to mark the twentieth anniversary of the Barents cooperation in 2013. As we made small talk on our way to the Russian border crossing station, I emphasised that the open border and friendship between Russians and Norwegians was a significant step forward. 'There's no reason for you to fear us or NATO,' I said.

'No, I don't fear you,' Medvedev said with a chuckle. 'And nor do I fear President Barack Obama or Chancellor Angela Merkel,' he went on. 'But who will come after you? What history has shown us, is that at least once a century some lunatic from the West comes along who wants to conquer Russia. In the 1700s Charles XII of Sweden attacked, and his great aim was to take Moscow. Napoleon took the city in 1812. In the 1900s, you attacked us twice, in two world wars. In 1941, Hitler stood at Moscow's gates before he was fought off. And don't forget, we've only just entered the current century.'

I honestly don't know how much of an impression my recounting of this conversation made on the various NATO leaders. But it told me a lot. From Moscow, the world looks like a very different place.

It wasn't just the annexation of Crimea and Russian control of the Donbas that worsened relations between NATO and Russia shortly after I took office. Russia also began a comprehensive programme of military rearmament and deployed new weapons – partly in contravention of the disarmament treaties that had been entered into – and launched large-scale military exercises. Of course, any nation is allowed to exercise its forces on its own territory. But what caused unease within NATO was the risk that these exercises might be used as cover for military operations against other countries. To an increasing extent, the exercises also included the use of nuclear weapons, and they were not being carried out in accordance with existing agreements regarding advance notification and transparency, thus making it easier to use an exercise as cover for an actual attack. The entry of Russian troops into Georgia in 2008 and the illegal annexation of Crimea in 2014 both occurred as an extension of large military exercises. In other words, there was reason to criticise what the Russians were doing.

But I was keen to ensure that NATO's criticism should be fair and accurate. Because as it turned out, we were not always precise enough.

Not long after I had taken office, Russian military aircraft activity above the Baltic Sea increased, extremely close to airspace belonging to NATO member states. An incident with a Scandinavian Airlines passenger plane brought the situation to a head. Shortly after departing from Copenhagen airport, the Scandinavian aircraft came dangerously close to colliding with a Russian military jet, and the Russian authorities confirmed that the jet had turned off its transponders – electronic devices that transmit information about the aircraft's nationality, type, speed and course, in order to prevent accidents.

Political leaders in many NATO states condemned the Russian practice of flying military jets with their transponders turned off, and I myself criticised the Russian military aircraft activity above the Baltic Sea. The area has extensive civilian air traffic, and the military activity was significant. In crowded airspace, accidents can easily happen.

But a little while later, I learned that military aircraft from NATO countries also sometimes flew with their transponders turned off. Everyone who had heard me and the other leaders of NATO states criticising the Russians could be in no doubt as to what this criticism implied: *We* flew with our transponders turned *on*.

I had received a range of notes about the dangerous behaviour of the Russians – notes I used when deciding how to express myself when taking the Russians to task. And nobody had told me that we flew with our transponders turned off, too.

I sat down with the heads of several NATO departments. It may well be that we could have criticised much of the Russian activity regardless, I said. Flying a jet without transponders close to Copenhagen airport was clearly on a whole other level than doing it far out in the middle of the Atlantic. But it was unacceptable to give the impression that flying without the use of transponders was reprehensible in itself, when we did exactly the same thing. The grounds for the criticism had to be correct.

Cases like this gave me pause. Sometimes, the desire to criticise one's opponents is so strong that all nuance is lost. The notion had begun to creep in that, when it came to the Russians, it was fine to portray the situation using slightly broad strokes. But an unnuanced view of reality dealt the Russians a good hand in their criticism of NATO. We risked making things easier for the Kremlin's tireless propaganda machine.

The transponder case later led to Russia and NATO agreeing on rules and procedures for military aircraft activity in the Baltic region that would reduce the risk of accidents and misunderstandings. This was an example of a confidence-building measure that was actually implemented, despite the poor relations.

But opposition to resuming the work of the NATO-Russia Council held firm throughout the first six months after I arrived in Brussels. NATO leaders were afraid of sending the message that Crimea and the Donbas had been forgotten, or that these were matters that we did not take very seriously.

On a visit to Vilnius, I met Lithuania's minister of national defence, Juozas Olekas, a friendly and forthcoming man, and both a social democrat and a physician. He accompanied me to the airport as I was leaving, and there in the back seat of the car, the mood turned somewhat confidential. So in an attempt to get him to take a more positive view of maintaining a dialogue with Russia, I decided to tell him about Norway's good neighbourly relations with the Soviet Union and my own experiences of cooperating with the Russians.

Olekas listened to me in silence. Then he turned to me and smiled.

'Jens, you've travelled in and out of Russia in connection with a few environmental projects. I was born in the Gulag.'

In the Second World War, Olekas's grandparents and their families had been exiled from Lithuania to the Siberian tundra, where they were forced to cut timber out in the wilderness. This was where his parents met, and where Olekas was born, not far from the city of Krasnoyarsk, over two thousand miles east of Moscow, in 1955. Krasnoyarsk was the centre of the enormous network of Russian prison camps that became known as the Gulag.

'When we were allowed to return to Lithuania, my grandfather warned me not to get involved in politics,' Olekas said. 'It's understandable advice, even if I haven't followed it.'

He probably thought me a privileged and dewy-eyed politician from the north, who had no idea what the Soviet Union, the Red Army or Russia actually stood for.

Nor did it help when I told him I'd been arrested by Russian police while on a trip to the Kola Peninsula, where we had become a little too interested in taking close-up photographs of factories spewing out vast amounts of sulphur. This, according to Olekas, was naive behaviour.

He considered me with a friendly but firm look.

'Surely you realise we can't trust them?' he said. 'It's easy to talk about dialogue when you come from Norway. In 1944 the Red Army arrived there, but then withdrew again. Where else did that happen?'

'Bornholm, Denmark,' I replied, but immediately understood it was no use. I simply had to accept that I wasn't going to get through to Juozas Olekas with my tales of solar panels on lighthouses and acid rain from Kola.

*   *   *

Between the two major problem areas I faced in this early period in my new role, Islamic State (IS) to the south and Russia to the east, there was an essential difference. Against IS, deterrence was meaningless. The terrorists were prepared to die, and their contempt for life meant that threats and retaliation had no effect. A US-led coalition against IS was established at the NATO summit in 2014, and the coalition and NATO's fight against the terrorist state were closely coordinated. NATO was part of an offensive alliance against IS, which used military force to suppress the terrorist group. Towards Russia, on the other hand, NATO had always been and would always remain a defensive alliance. Here the right approach was not the use of military force, but deterrence. NATO posed no threat towards its neighbour in the east, but Moscow should know that any military attack on any NATO country would cost them so dearly that it wasn't even worth considering. Relations with Moscow were challenging, but had to be managed nevertheless.

I wanted to speak further with the Russians, and it wasn't long before a new opportunity presented itself. The Munich Security Conference is a long-standing event that attracts anyone and everyone who works with security policy. Russia's minister of foreign affairs, Sergey Lavrov, would also be attending the conference in early February 2015. We arranged to meet.

Among my advisers, opinions differed as to how wise this was. 'Lavrov is a difficult man. He quickly becomes angry and aggressive,' they said.

I felt they were wrong, and explained I'd had many civil conversations with Lavrov. As Norway's prime minister, I had met him several times – he had been part of the Russian delegation in the meetings I'd had with Putin and Medvedev. On those occasions he had never been anything but good-humoured and pleasant.

I met with Lavrov at the majestic Hotel Bayerischer Hof, which was packed with experts and politicians. But in a small meeting room, it was just him and me and a few of our advisers.

'It's nice to see you again,' I said. 'We achieved important things when I was prime minister of Norway.'

I mentioned the agreement on the maritime border in the Barents Sea. Lavrov followed my lead. 'I hope you find some oil and gas up there,' he replied.

We eventually steered the conversation towards what we were actually there to speak about. 'I'm intent upon us continuing to talk,' I said. 'We have to meet, maintain a dialogue, try to find a basis for getting out of the difficult situation we're currently in. And as you're aware, the situation in Ukraine is the main problem right now. All parties have to respect international law. The NATO allies will never accept the illegitimate annexation of Crimea and Russia's military operations in eastern Ukraine.'

'But this isn't true, Secretary General Stoltenberg!' Lavrov quickly interrupted. 'There are no Russian soldiers in Ukraine. It's just propaganda. The people in Eastern Ukraine are separatists, just like the Slovenians and the Croats, who broke out of Yugoslavia. Are you against Croatia and Slovenia? They are NATO countries.'

We had precise intelligence showing that the Russians were in Ukraine. But Lavrov continued with his explanations.

'You are the ones who are infiltrating – it was the coup against President Viktor Yanukovych that was illegal. A democratically elected president! You supported the coup leaders at Maidan Square in 2014. And Crimea, why are you going on about Crimea? The people there have decided to join Russia following a referendum, an open and democratic decision. The will of the people. When did you become anti-referendum? Is it wrong to listen to the will of the people? I'm just asking!'

Lavrov is a big man, and with his rugged features and booming voice he can appear even bigger. He gives the impression of being able to withstand any physical challenge anyone might throw at him and exudes a rare hardness. At the same time, he is always well dressed, wears stylish rimless spectacles, and is an eloquent speaker of several languages. Lavrov is a unique combination of an elegant diplomat and a bully.

He leaned across the table, now speaking at a mile a minute.

'This claim that Crimea represents the first border change resulting from the use of military force in Europe since the Second World War – it simply isn't true. What about Kosovo, which after all is a direct result of NATO bombing, Secretary General Stoltenberg? Which many NATO states recognise as an independent country. But not all – not Greece, not Spain. Am I wrong about Kosovo? If I am, then your NATO allies are also wrong. The Spaniards have Catalonia to think about. Perhaps you ought to agree among yourselves before criticising us.'

Lavrov had been in the game a long time. He had become Russia's minister of foreign affairs as far back as 2004; before that, he spent a decade as Russia's ambassador to the UN. He knew all the issues inside out, and had obviously decided he wasn't about to go easy on NATO's new secretary general. He looked me right in the eye.

'What about NATO's bombing of Serbia in 1999, Secretary General Stoltenberg? An unlawful military action, a war crime, and then you accuse *us* of breaking international law? What gives you the right to do that? And since we're speaking of international law – what about Libya in 2011? We trusted you, we supported the resolution of the Security Council. But you used and abused the resolution to kill the country's head of state. How can we ever trust you again? How can you defend such an act? You are the ones who are hypocritical, who have double standards, who invoke international law when it suits you and simply ignore it whenever it doesn't. Just think about the military debacle in Iraq from 2003, and where that has led. You never learn, Secretary General Stoltenberg!'

The meeting lasted forty minutes, twice as long as had been sched-uled. Lavrov talked incessantly, but it was necessary to respond to the incorrect accusations made against NATO. It was entirely unreason-able to compare Eastern Ukraine with Croatia and Slovenia, and Crimea with Kosovo, where the Kosovo Albanians had been perse-cuted. The West had been hesitant to intervene in the war in Bosnia, and consequently we had ended up with the massacre in Srebrenica. We hadn't wanted to risk something similar happening in Kosovo, I told Lavrov. Serbia's leader, Slobodan Milošević, was responsible for ethnic cleansing in Kosovo. Diplomatic solutions had been tried for many years, but the assaults on the Kosovo Albanians had continued. If a leader commits violence against their own population, it undermines that leader's political legitimacy. And Russia itself had guaranteed Ukraine's independence and territorial integrity by signing the Budapest Memorandum in 1994. Ukraine ceded its nuclear weapons, and in return the world powers, including Russia, had guaranteed Ukraine's internationally recognised borders. These were the borders Russia had violated in Crimea and by entering the Donbas.

But I have to admit that I was surprised. In our previous meetings, Lavrov had always been jovial and relaxed. This bullying style of his was new to me. At another meeting a short time later, he began by asking: 'Who was it who said, "If you want peace, prepare for war"?' He allowed his gaze to wander around the room before it settled on me. I suggested Caesar. 'No, there's someone who said it much more recently,' Lavrov said.

I was the one who had said it. I had quoted the old adage in an interview with a Norwegian regional newspaper, and I think I understood why Lavrov was referencing it. As I saw it, this was his way of communicating that, yes, you might be head of an organisation that shouldn't exist, and yes, you might come from a tiny country and give interviews to a few provincial rags, but you should know that we're paying attention. We never sleep. We know about everything you do, every move you make, and every word you say.

Lavrov obviously saw the benefit of adopting a very different approach towards NATO's secretary general than towards the prime minister of Norway. My advisers had had a point when they tried to warn me. But if this was how Lavrov wanted to behave, we would simply have to handle it. NATO's Cold War-era image as the enemy was clearly still alive and well in Russia.

After that first meeting in Munich, I called Thorvald. He was well acquainted with Lavrov.

'Of course he's puffing out his chest,' Thorvald said. He advised me to simply take it in my stride.

'It's nothing to worry about. The more people make a song and dance, the less secure they are. The fact that Lavrov is getting himself all worked up is a sign that, deep down, he's insecure. But it also suggests that Russia is an insecure nation. And that is much more serious.'

5

Ukraine wants to move West

I STOOD ON A MODEST PODIUM OUTSIDE THE UKRAINIAN MILI-
tary academy in Yavoriv, close to Lviv. The blue and white NATO flag
was hoisted into the air, alongside the blue and yellow flag of Ukraine.
An orchestra played the NATO hymn, followed by Ukraine's national
anthem. The sun shone high in the sky.

It was the twenty-first of September 2015, and I was in Ukraine in
my role as head of NATO for the first time. With me on the podium
stood Ukrainian president Petro Poroshenko, and together we opened
a joint civil emergency exercise, in which rescue personnel, police
forces, and ambulance and fire crews from a total of twenty-eight
countries would participate under the auspices of NATO. Afterwards,
Poroshenko and I were accompanied into the mess hall, where we
each collected a tray of food and sat down at a table with Ukrainian
soldiers and some of the American, British and Canadian instructors
who were there to train them.

NATO had been arranging civil emergency exercises like the one
taking place just outside Lviv on that day in September for many
years, to increase the preparedness in countries with which the alliance cooperates. I was there to show sympathy and support for
Ukraine following the annexation of Crimea and the war in the
Donbas, which was now in its second year. President Poroshenko
said that it was of great symbolic importance for Ukraine that I had
come.

After the visit to the base, the president and I flew to Kyiv together. We sat in a small salon aboard his plane, and spent the journey getting better acquainted. Petro Poroshenko had made his career in business following the collapse of the Soviet Union. In the mid-1990s, he had founded a company that produced chocolate and other confectionery, and which had quickly taken a dominating market position all across Eastern Europe. For several years, Poroshenko remained close to the top of Forbes' list of Ukraine's richest people. His long political career began in 1998, with its origins in various parties, and he served as minister of national security and minister of foreign affairs in Viktor Yushchenko's government after the Orange Revolution in 2004–2005. After Russia's annexation of Crimea and war breaking out in Donetsk and Luhansk, the oblasts that make up the Donbas region, in April 2014, a presidential election was held the following May. Poroshenko stood for office, and won by an overwhelming majority.

Poroshenko was open and agreeable. He regarded me with a steady gaze, and was a leader who knew what he wanted. Aboard the presidential plane, the conversation flowed easily over refreshments of beer, rye bread and ham, and Poroshenko spoke at length about Ukraine's history and culture.

A long, shifting and dramatic history forms the backdrop for Ukraine's independence following the collapse of the Soviet Union. Kyivan Rus' was the first East Slavic state, and in the 1000s this kingdom was Europe's largest state by extent. It dissolved during the Mongol invasion of the 1200s, and in the centuries that followed parts of the area we now know as Ukraine belonged to Lithuania, Poland and Russia.

Poroshenko pointed out that President Putin liked to cherry-pick fragments of history to support his view that Ukraine is not a sovereign nation. The country was controlled by the Mongols longer than it was by the Russians, Poroshenko said, but nobody would claim that Ukraine is therefore inextricably linked to Mongolia.

Towards the end of the 1700s, Empress of Russia Catherine the Great expanded the Russian-controlled area southwards towards the Black Sea, and abolished what remained of Ukrainian autonomy.

Areas in the west became part of the multi-ethnic Habsburg Monarchy, the capital of which was Vienna. There were better conditions for the Ukrainian national movement to gain traction in the west than in the east, because the Habsburgs were looking to curb Polish nationalism. In the wake of the Russian Revolution, Russian and Ukrainian Bolsheviks established a Ukrainian Socialist Soviet Republic, which was part of the Soviet Union from 1922 until the country gained independence in 1991.

What Poroshenko wanted to emphasise most was that Ukraine's battle for independence wasn't something that belonged only to the present. 'The fight for independence runs like a red thread through our history,' he said.

Then, between a few bites of sausage and a sip of beer, Poroshenko asked: 'When will we become a member of NATO?'

Poroshenko was keen to ensure that the resolution from the 2008 NATO summit in Bucharest, through which Ukraine had been promised NATO membership, would be upheld. I was Norwegian prime minister at the time of the meeting, and remembered it well. Before the summit, many had expected that Ukraine and Georgia would both be given a so-called Membership Action Plan. This is a reform programme, which aims to ensure democratic control over security institutions, to combat corruption and to prepare countries for NATO membership. US president George W. Bush had been in favour of this, as had the British and the Eastern Europeans. Germany, supported by France among others, was against it. They didn't want to create expectations of membership for Georgia and Ukraine. Norway had agreed with Germany, but I felt it probably wise not to remind Poroshenko of this as we enjoyed our pleasant in-flight conversation above the country he led.

The negotiations in Bucharest had been dramatic, and they had taken place within the meeting room itself. This was unusual, because as a general rule the main points of the resolutions are agreed in advance, and the summit then simply formally adopts them. After a tug of war lasting several hours, a compromise was reached, with the resolution stating that Ukraine and Georgia would become members of NATO in the future, but without specifying when this might happen. Vladimir Putin took part in the summit, and violently protested at the door being kept open for Georgia and Ukraine, but at least we had been sitting at the same table and able to speak with the Russian president. In practice, Ukraine's NATO membership was put on ice. Poroshenko continued to dig into the membership question. 'What would it actually take for Ukraine to be allowed to join?' he asked.

According to the NATO treaty, three conditions had to be met in order for a new country to join the alliance. The country must be European, it must be democratic, and it must be able to contribute to the security of the North Atlantic area. 'This third criteria is the main problem,' I said. What contributes to security in Europe and North America is often contentious, and in the end, it comes down to a political assessment. Some member states believed it would strengthen our common security to allow Ukraine to join NATO as soon as possible, before Russia tried to take more of the country. Others, however, thought granting Ukraine membership would provoke Moscow, leading to an increased risk of crisis and conflict in Europe.

I personally was growing ever more sympathetic towards the Ukrainians' intense desire to gain a foothold in the West through NATO and EU membership. But at the same time, it was important to be honest and not offer false hope. I assured Poroshenko that we would continue to work to bring Ukraine ever closer to becoming a NATO member state – and that it wasn't a case of full membership or nothing. NATO countries like the US, Canada and the United Kingdom were providing Ukraine with economic and military support. We could help Ukraine to strengthen its forces through the provision of equipment and training, as we had observed together in Lviv earlier that day.

'NATO is already helping you to implement reforms, fight corruption and introduce NATO standards and doctrines,' I said.

All this strengthened Ukrainian defence, and that had value in itself. 'And it will also ensure Ukraine is ready for membership as soon as the political conditions are right and we've reached agreement on allowing you in,' I explained, feeling that I had given a fairly convincing answer.

Petro Poroshenko, however, didn't agree. 'So *when* can we join?' he asked again.

'I don't know,' I replied. It was at least an honest answer.

Some Ukrainians felt that giving up Crimea and the Donbas region would be a price worth paying if the rest of Ukraine could then join NATO and the EU. Poroshenko, however, opposed such thinking, because he believed it broke with fundamental principles regarding the country's territorial integrity. Besides, in a 1991 referendum a clear majority in the Donbas and Crimea had voted for severance from the Soviet Union in favour of becoming part of Ukraine.

'This isn't actually about the Donbas region. This is about President Putin wanting control of Ukraine. He'll hold on to the Donbas as a weeping sore, a turbulent corner of the country, where he can turn the heat up and down to prevent us joining NATO and the EU,' Poroshenko said.

A few months earlier, I had met former US secretary of state Henry Kissinger, a highly respected but controversial diplomat and politician. Kissinger's secret diplomacy had paved the way for the historic summit between President Nixon and Chairman Mao in 1972; he also played a major role in the negotiations regarding a ceasefire and peace agreement in Vietnam.

We were both attending a conference in Austria in June 2015, and Kissinger had a message he wished to convey to the new NATO secretary general. He sat slumped in a chair as I entered the room – at ninety-two, Kissinger had trouble walking and was now undeniably an old man, but his self-image and mental condition remained absolutely intact. 'The West must understand that for Russia, Ukraine will never be just another foreign country. Russia's own history begins in Kyiv. Some of the most important battles for Russia's own freedom were fought on Ukrainian soil,' Kissinger said, his voice low but firm. Despite his seventy-seven years in the US, he still spoke with a strong German accent.

Putin was a serious strategist, Kissinger believed, albeit under terms dictated by Russia's own history. But at the same time, he didn't think

Russia would manage to impose its will by military means without isolating itself. If Russia once again forced Ukraine into becoming a state controlled from Moscow, the Russians were doomed to repeat their history of mutual mistrust and suspicion between Europe and the US on the one side, and Russia on the other. A military intervention could lead to a new Cold War.

Kissinger was against Ukrainian NATO membership, and generally sceptical about NATO's enlargement eastwards since the end of the Cold War. He was concerned that the Ukraine crisis was all too often presented as a choice between two mutually exclusive alternatives: whether Ukraine moved towards the East or the West. 'If Ukraine is to survive and grow as a nation, the country cannot become the West's outpost against the East, or the East's outpost against the West. The country must become a bridge between East and West,' he said.

Kissinger paused briefly for effect before concluding. 'The West's demonising of Vladimir Putin is not a policy,' he said. 'It is an alibi for not having a policy. Take care not to isolate Russia. It is a weak country, compared with NATO.'

Foreign policy, according to Kissinger, is 'the art of establishing priorities'. Ukraine was more important to Russia than it was to the West. He therefore urged caution.

It was a thought-provoking conversation. Kissinger was not alone among Western experts in emphasising the unique relationship between Ukraine and Russia; that Ukraine was a divided country that did not unequivocally belong to East or West. But Kissinger believed the annexation of Crimea to be incompatible with what he referred to as the existing world order.

An agreement to bring an end to the war in the Donbas was negotiated in the Belorussian capital Minsk in February, seven months before my trip to Ukraine. It was signed by Russia, Ukraine, the Organization for Security and Co-operation in Europe (OSCE), and representatives for the pro-Russian separatists. The agreement contained provisions regarding a ceasefire, the withdrawal of all heavy weapons, and the exchange of prisoners; a political dialogue would be entered into, and elections would be held. Ukraine's constitution would also be changed to give Luhansk and Donetsk greater political autonomy, although precisely what this would entail was not defined.

But the Minsk agreement was a tottering structure. It was continually breached, with shooting and exploding grenades on both sides of the ceasefire line through the Donbas. The weeks before I visited Ukraine had been the most peaceful since autumn 2014, presumably because Russia had its hands full mustering its troops in Syria and simultaneously wished to ease tensions before the UN General Assembly convened. Yet it was a fragile peace. A political solution was no closer. The Russians had not withdrawn their heavy weapons. A new UN report revealed that many more people had been killed than previous estimates suggested. The war in Eastern Ukraine had become Europe's forgotten war.

Poroshenko and I discussed all this on the flight to Kyiv.

'What's the alternative to the Minsk agreement?' I asked as the presidential aircraft approached Hostomel Airport for landing. 'More war,' Poroshenko replied.

Poroshenko was fighting Russian-backed separatists in the east, corruption within his own country, and an extensive debt crisis. Furthermore, he was under pressure from a nationalist-oriented parliament, which wanted central control and a strong presidential office. Poroshenko had pushed through an amendment to the constitution, which paved the way for decentralisation and increased autonomy for Luhansk and Donetsk, but the changes had not yet been implemented. He faced significant opposition; the amendment was regarded as an expression of weakness and capitulation to the Russians and the separatists.

The Minsk agreement was more of a road map for future peace than a detailed peace agreement, and further progress was dependent upon mutual trust between the parties – a trust that proved non-existent. Among other issues, they disagreed on the order in which events should happen next; the Ukrainians insisted they must regain control of the country's borders before an election could be held, while the Russian-backed separatists wanted an election to be held first.

Both to Poroshenko and in the speech I gave to Ukraine's National Security and Defense Council, I emphasised that it might take time for Ukraine to become a member of NATO.

'It isn't enough to have a majority – all NATO member states have to agree. So let's build our partnership, one step at a time. There's still much we can accomplish, even without Ukrainian membership,' I said. I brought up Sweden and Finland, and pointed out how close our cooperation with these countries had become, both politically and militarily, even though they were not NATO members.

Poroshenko listened, but ceded no ground on what he saw as the core issues.

Ukraine needed more weapons and equipment. They were in desperate need of drones, anti-tank defences and modern air defence. He was grateful that Turkey had supplied advanced Bayraktar drones, but dissatisfied with the fact that the US and other NATO countries were refusing to sell weapons to Ukraine. Poroshenko mentioned Norway, and I explained that the country had a policy of not selling weapons to countries with ongoing conflicts. 'But it's precisely when we are at war that we need weapons,' he protested.

But most important of all was Ukraine being permitted to join the alliance. 'We don't trust Russia,' Poroshenko said. 'Ukraine will not be safe until we are a member of NATO.'

6

Crossfire

ON TUESDAY THE TWENTY-FOURTH OF NOVEMBER 2015, WE HELD
our usual morning meeting in the office. Not long after the meeting's
start there was a knock on the door, and a colleague from our intelligence division asked military assistant Gjermund Eide to step out.

After a few minutes, the pair returned. Gjermund looked
concerned.

'Secretary General, a matter has come up that I think we need to
attend to immediately,' he said.

A tense silence settled over the room as the staff member from the
intelligence division was given the floor. A Turkish fighter jet had shot
down a Russian plane above Syria. Our colleague presented a map of
the relevant area, which showed the aircraft's movements before it
vanished.

A crisis was brewing. A Russian plane had been shot down by a
plane from a NATO member state.

A couple of months earlier, Russia had embarked upon a large-scale
military campaign in Syria, making use of both ground and air forces.
Moscow's official reason for this was to neutralise terrorist organisations in the country, but the main motive was to protect an ally,
President Assad, while strengthening Russia's position in the Middle
East. Russia making itself party to the conflict would force all other
actors to consider Russia's role when shaping their own strategy. This
was Putin's political gain from going in militarily.

After just ten minutes, we ended the staff meeting. Much remained unclear. We needed more information, additional details. And we needed to hear what Turkey had to say.

A little while later we met again, this time with the chair of the NATO military committee, General Petr Pavel, and several of his closest colleagues also present. Now the picture was clearer. It was confirmed that a Turkish F-16 fighter jet had shot down a Russian SU-24 two-seater bomber. For five days, the Russians had been heavily bombing the area where the plane was downed, a part of Syria in which Turkmen militia had taken control. The Turkmen are close to the Turks. Turkish president Recep Tayyip Erdoğan calls them his brothers.

Once again, we looked at the map. In the relevant area the border between the two countries takes a little dip south, so a small spit of Turkish land sticks into Syria. The Russian plane had grazed the airspace above this spit of land, but that was enough for the Turks. They had warned the Russians several times over the past few days, and clearly communicated their intense disapproval of Russian bombing in the area, so close to the Turkish border. Nor was it the first time the Russians had violated Turkish airspace.

Unease spread throughout NATO headquarters. Would there be reprisals?

At 17.00, I chaired a crisis meeting of the North Atlantic Council. I began with a brief statement about why we had convened, before Turkey's ambassador to NATO explained the course of events. The Russian bomber started out above Syria, on course for Turkish airspace. The ambassador played an extremely crackly recording in which a Turkish fighter pilot bellowed that the Russians must change course. At 09.24.05, the Russian bomber crossed the border into Turkish airspace. Five seconds later, at 09.24.10, the Russian pilot was given a final warning. The Turkish F-16 subsequently fired a heat-seeking air-to-air missile, which struck the Russian bomber. Before it crashed, the plane was once again outside Turkish airspace, and it hit the ground in Syria.

The border violation had lasted just seventeen seconds, but it had had dramatic consequences.

The Russians had a different version of events. They categorically rejected that their plane had been in Turkish airspace, and that they had been warned. According to the Russians, the bomber was shot down in Syrian airspace, just over half a mile from the border. The two men on board managed to eject before the plane crashed. One, the pilot, was shot and killed by Turkmen militia on the ground. The other, the weapons officer, survived, and was extracted from the area by a Russian helicopter in a dramatic rescue that cost another Russian soldier his life.

NATO's military authorities confirmed that the plane had been in Turkish airspace, and it was becoming urgent that we go public with a reaction to the incident. We were receiving hundreds of media enquiries, so it was decided that we would hold a brief press conference. Did NATO stand by its ally, Turkey? Was there now a risk of war between Russia and NATO? These were the kinds of questions the journalists were keen to ask. I condemned the border violation. 'NATO stands in solidarity with Turkey and supports the country's territorial integrity,' I said.

My statements expressed a united stance. But the truth is that there was deep disagreement within the alliance. The Eastern European countries supported the Turks in demanding that NATO unreservedly stand behind Turkey's actions, and felt the border violation should be followed up with the deployment of additional air defence, more fighter jets and more batteries of Patriot rockets along the Syrian border.

France and Italy opposed the alliance expressing explicit support for Turkey. Germany, while not against supporting Turkey, wanted a nuanced response. They pointed out that it was one thing to condemn the border violation, but quite another to justify the downing of an aircraft due to a violation that had lasted a total of seventeen seconds.

The atmosphere within NATO was strained. A Russian bomber had entered Turkish airspace for a matter of seconds. Could we really risk war with Russia over this?

The Russians were incensed. The way they saw it, their plane had been shot down entirely unlawfully. They called for condolences from us as a way of expressing their dissatisfaction, and responded by deploying their advanced S-400 missile system in Syria. The flagship of their Black Sea fleet, the guided missile cruiser *Moskva*, was sent to the Syrian coast. A clear rattling of sabres.

That same afternoon, the German minister for foreign affairs Frank-Walter Steinmeier called me. 'What on earth is going on? Is the world completely off its hinges?' he cried. Steinmeier's outburst was a clear reflection of just how fearful many people were, and how tense the situation was. It was obvious the shoot-down could have consequences far beyond Turkey's control.

I had been head of NATO for a little over a year, and I was now discovering just how much of the job is a political balancing act. Major nations disagreed on how the crisis should be handled. I decided to concentrate on the border violation, which nobody defended. It was a way of smoothing over the various disagreements.

I didn't find it hard to agree with those who deemed it an overreaction to shoot down a plane after such a brief airspace violation. But at the same time, the Turks were understandably deeply anxious, because intense fighting was taking place right next to their southern border. It was critical that the war should not be allowed to spill over into Turkish territory.

Nevertheless, my task was to try to build bridges between the various positions, and to formulate a response that was as united as possible. The most important thing was to prevent an escalation – and, *should* an escalation occur, prevent NATO from being dragged into it. I therefore encouraged Ankara and Moscow to maintain close contact, so tensions could be eased.

A few days later, I walked the few minutes from my office to NATO's TV studio. I was to be interviewed by CNN's Hala Gorani.

The interview got off to a good start. Gorani then noted that the Russian bomber had only been in Turkish airspace for a matter of seconds. Wasn't NATO worried that Turkey's shoot-down had been an overreaction?

I repeated the message that all NATO allies supported Turkey's right to defend its airspace. As to whether or not the shoot-down had been an 'overreaction', I deftly neglected to answer.

Then the interview took an unexpected turn.

'Speaking of violating airspace,' Gorani said, 'you may have seen that the Greek prime minister accused Turkey of violating Greek airspace. How does NATO react to that?'

Turkey violating Greek airspace? I was prepared to discuss the relationship between Turkey and Russia and the war in Syria. Relations between Greece and Turkey were complicated, not least because the two countries disagreed on where the border between their airspace ran. The fact that both countries are NATO allies put me in a squeeze. As secretary general, I had to speak on behalf of the entire alliance. I acted as if I had misheard the question.

'I think we have to remember that Turkey is on the front line of a very, very unstable and difficult situation in Syria and Iraq,' I replied, and also pointed to the substantial Russian military build-up in the same area.

But Hala Gorani wasn't going to let me off the hook.

'I was actually referring to the Greek prime minister accusing Turkey of violating Greek airspace,' she said. 'How does NATO react to that?'

When I was Norway's prime minister, being questioned on live television was my favourite way to be interviewed. Everything comes straight out, uncensored and unedited, and viewers can consider the context and background to what is said for themselves. But for such interviews to go well, you have to know what to say.

'But I'm trying to explain that these are *completely* different situations, and that Turkey is—'

'No, I understand that,' Gorani interrupted, 'but there was a violation according to Greece of its airspace by Turkey, so are there two standards here?'

'No,' I replied. 'We underline the importance of respecting the airspace of any nation, but I think we have to understand that Turkey is in a very special situation.'

'So you're saying that Turkey should get a pass because it's in a difficult neighbourhood and a difficult situation right now, for violating Greek airspace, for instance?'

'I'm saying that the airspace of all nations should be respected, and NATO is not in a position where we accept any violations of airspace.'

After what felt like half an eternity, Gorani gave up trying to get an answer out of me. I managed to convey that, after all, there had been no acts of war between Greece and Turkey, and the situation therefore could not be compared to what had happened in Syria, close to the Turkish border. But the interview had been a crossfire of competing considerations. Had I commented on the delicate subject of the conflict between Greece and Turkey any further, I would almost certainly have had one of the parties straight on my case. Instead, I responded evasively and obscurely.

In the wake of the downing of the Russian bomber, the heated situation gradually cooled off and ultimately blew over without dramatic consequences. Nor did I receive any negative reactions from Greece or Turkey following the interview.

'She was tough,' Oana commented as we made our way back to the office. Which was a polite way of saying that my performance had not been all that impressive.

My first months as head of NATO were therefore not without their uphill struggles. One particular meeting of the NATO ministers of foreign affairs in Antalya, Turkey, six months after I took office, is especially difficult to look back on. During the proceedings, the Dutch minister of foreign affairs came up to me and asked: 'Why are we even here?' It was an uncomfortable moment. Several of the other ministers also reacted to the thin agenda, poor preparation and shortage of matters for discussion. As an organisation, NATO was inefficient and not well enough coordinated, a result of our failure to get the top-down management practices into adequate shape.

Furthermore, I hadn't yet found the authority and self-confidence necessary to lead the alliance effectively. This became evident on one of the first occasions I chaired a meeting of the North Atlantic Council. The meetings began at ten, and I arrived just before, took my place, and with a rap of the gavel started proceedings at ten o'clock sharp. One of the ambassadors interrupted me: 'Secretary General, you can't open the meeting yet. Not everyone has arrived.' I hesitated, then acquiesced, and waited until everyone was present.

The consensus principle was another of NATO's processes that took a little getting used to. The idea that no one should disagree with any decision taken was closely guarded by the NATO ambassadors, which sometimes made it difficult to reach decisions and get things done. While chairing the council during a debate, I argued that the alliance had to do more to help Iraq in the fight against IS, and to strengthen the country's defence. I knew a large majority of the allies would support my proposal. 'I find that an increasing number of member states support this thinking,' I said, signalling that I would now move on to the next matter for discussion. One of the most experienced NATO ambassadors then asked for permission to speak, and said: 'What *I* find, Secretary General, is that there is no consensus on this.'

All the years I had spent in Norwegian politics still influenced me. As Norway's prime minister, I was able to make various decisions, and a majority vote was enough for a resolution to pass. This was not the case in NATO. And so a still rather green secretary general was put in his place by an ambassador who didn't care what the majority thought, knowing that as long as one country said no, the decision would not be made.

And there were more challenges to come.

The war in Eastern Ukraine continued apace, and within the alliance there was constant disagreement on how we should respond to Russia. NATO was also split in terms of how great a role we ought to play in the work to fight terrorism and stabilise our neighbouring countries to the south. The terrorist attack on Brussels in March 2016, for which IS claimed responsibility, reminded us that this was also about the security of Europe's cities. And I had to campaign constantly for the member states to increase their defence spending, as they had promised at the summit in Wales.

During the refugee crisis of the spring of 2016, the prevailing attitude among ambassadors was that NATO should keep out of it. I disagreed. The alliance had resources that might prove beneficial.

Luckily, German chancellor Angela Merkel and her minister of defence, Ursula von der Leyen, agreed with me. They suggested that NATO ships be employed to implement the agreement made by the EU and Turkey to limit the flow of refugees across the Aegean Sea. A meeting of NATO ministers of foreign affairs adopted the overall framework for the deployment in line with the German government's proposal, but it was left to NATO ambassadors to decide how it should be put into practice. NATO ambassadors are highly experienced and skilled individuals, but diplomats to the core, and therefore concerned with every detail and nuance of each decision that is made. Often, there would be just a single person or handful of individuals holding things up. At the meeting of the council at which the implementation and operation plan were to be adopted, several ambassadors attempted a renegotiation, looking to stop the deployment from becoming a reality. The meeting dragged on and on.

This was when my patience finally ran out. Once a political decision has been made, diplomats shouldn't attempt to hinder its implementation. I interrupted the discussion.

'You can call your respective capitals to confirm what's been decided. We're going to sit here until we come to an agreement,' I said. An oppressive silence settled over the room.

During the break, I sent texts to the ministers of defence in the countries that were dragging their feet, asking them to ensure their ambassadors were instructed to stick to what had been agreed. Nobody would be permitted to leave the room until we were done.

Only at one o'clock in the morning were the last of the kinks finally ironed out, and we adopted the resolution we needed for the NATO operation in the Aegean to begin.

I have realised in retrospect that it was precisely *this* meeting that changed many people's perceptions of how I would fill my new role as head of NATO – including my own. In our discussions about whether I should take the job, Ingrid and Thorvald had said that they felt my restlessness would make me unhappy. But ironically enough, it was this impatience that ultimately enabled me to command people's respect. I had achieved the self-confidence I needed to cut through when necessary, and concluded that the best thing I could do was be myself. Perhaps my impatience would prove a useful counterweight to the NATO system's tedious processes.

I also subsequently began every meeting I chaired on time, regardless of whether or not some seats remained empty.

7

Teaming up with the EU

BOIS DE LA CAMBRE IS A VAST, LUSH PARK THAT EXTENDS INTO the centre of Brussels from the south. It is around the same size as London's Hyde Park, and is named after the La Cambre Abbey, which once owned the land on which the park sits. Huge oak trees tower against the sky; footpaths and promenades wind their way around a small lake. It is an area that resounds with history. British officers played cricket here before the Battle of Waterloo in June 1815, when Napoleon suffered his final defeat.

At weekends in particular, the park teems with life. People ride their bicycles or take a stroll; families with young children play ball games on the grass slopes beside the lake and eat lunch sitting on large picnic blankets. I enjoyed cycling or taking a walk through the park whenever I had the time, and my bodyguards were good at keeping a discreet distance. As I passed people I could hear all the different languages being spoken, including English, German, Spanish and many Slavic languages, in addition to French and Dutch – even in Bois de la Cambre one notices what an international city Brussels is. On these walks my thoughts could wander freely, and that did me a lot of good.

One of the things I spent a lot of time reflecting on over those first months in Brussels was the relationship between NATO and the European Union. The organisations have much in common. They are built upon the same values of freedom and democracy. They work for peace. They face many of the same challenges and have the same neighbours – Russia to the east and the Middle East and Africa to the south. And the vast majority of EU countries are also members of NATO.

Both organisations were headquartered in Brussels, but still there was little contact between them. As I saw it, this was a situation that needed to change.

One beautiful June day in 2016, I was standing on the steps outside my NATO residence when Jean-Claude Juncker's car pulled up before the entrance. 'When I see this house, I know I've made a huge mistake in life,' Juncker said as he stepped out and we completed the customary greetings. 'That mistake was becoming president of the European Commission, and not secretary general of NATO.'

Not long before this, I had met with the European Council, which includes the heads of state and government of all the EU nations. 'No one at this meeting has fought harder for the EU than me,' I said. Some of the other delegates looked a little confused.

'Norway is the only country in the world that has managed to negotiate a membership agreement with the EU, only to vote it down – not just once, but twice,' I continued. 'On both occasions, I participated with great enthusiasm on the losing side. So you mustn't listen to me if I start offering advice on how to win referendums.'

It wasn't a given that NATO's secretary general would be permitted to speak on defence and security policy at a meeting of EU leaders – that's how limited NATO's contact with the EU was. No attempts had been made to identify areas that might facilitate cooperation, and there were no regular meetings at the highest level. Within the European capitals, there was also poor coordination between the senior officials who worked with the EU and those who worked with NATO, with the result that the same country could have two different standpoints on one and the same issue: one within the EU, and another within NATO.

The EU's two top officials – the president of the European Commission Jean-Claude Juncker, and the president of the European Council Donald Tusk – and I agreed to strengthen our cooperation, deciding that we would regularly participate at each other's top meetings and hold informal working dinners. And it was to such a dinner that I welcomed them on this sunny day in June.

Juncker had been prime minister of Luxembourg for eighteen years, and Tusk had previously spent many years as prime minister of Poland. We knew each other well. We had met at meetings of NATO and the European Economic Area, and made bilateral visits to each other's countries. Many years of service at the highest levels of politics had given both Juncker and Tusk self-confidence and authority, but neither had lost the ability to grant themselves a few moments respite from the seriousness of their professions. It was always a pleasure to spend time with them.

As a young man in the 1970s, Donald Tusk had demonstrated against the deployment of Russian nuclear missiles in Eastern Europe, and had been arrested by the Polish police. Not long afterwards, I had marched in protest against American missiles in Western Europe, albeit without being arrested. 'Well, you radicals certainly had plenty of opinions when you were young, but you've come around to good sense in the end,' Juncker said.

Out on the terrace, the light conversation continued. My two guests were so in sync that one could start a sentence and the other finish it. Since this was a working dinner I had invited them to, Juncker wanted to be sure that the usual division of labour could be expected – Tusk would do the work, while he would do the eating and drinking. He was also fond of poking fun at his own country. 'I've told President Putin there's only one reason Luxembourg never attacked the Soviet Union,' he said. 'And that's that we wouldn't have had space for all the Soviet prisoners our soldiers would have taken.'

Humour isn't necessarily indicative of an inability to make difficult decisions – quite the opposite, in fact. An informal and light tone can encourage trust and openness, which can in turn help drive progress on important issues.

On that summer's evening, we discussed a comprehensive framework agreement for cooperation between the EU and NATO, which we would sign together at NATO's upcoming summit in Warsaw in

July. We identified specific areas for cooperation, such as cyber security, where we would exchange real-time information on hacking and other data attacks – there were no existing agreements regarding the sharing of such information. The agreement would also facilitate cooperation in the Mediterranean, where the EU had an ongoing naval operation, Operation Sophia, whose aim was to stop human trafficking to Europe and which NATO supported with ships, supplies and fuel. We began a collaboration in Iraq, through which the EU worked to enhance the country's civil capacity, and NATO the country's military capacity. Our patrols in the Aegean Sea supported the migration agreement between the EU and Turkey. We partnered on some exercises, through which we tested various scenarios. Nowadays crises can be highly complex, with military threats, cyber-attacks against civilian and military infrastructure, large movements of refugees, and massive disinformation directed at the population. All this demands that the EU and NATO work closely together.

The situation in Kosovo offers an example of effective cooperation between NATO and the EU. Serbia doesn't recognise Kosovo as a state, while at the same time a large Serbian minority lives in the northern part of Kosovo. The wounds of the war that took place in the 1990s have still not healed, and mistrust and suspicion are prevalent among the various ethnic groups – seemingly innocent episodes can be enough to spark a crisis. To prevent this, the EU leads a political normalisation process between Belgrade and Pristina, which NATO supports. The EU provides law enforcement support, while NATO's Kosovo Force (KFOR) of around four thousand soldiers provides the crucial security guarantee. In Kosovo, the EU and NATO are working together to stabilise an area of unrest not far from their own borders. This is precisely how such cooperative partnerships should be arranged.

The framework agreement that was negotiated that summer took the relationship between the EU and NATO to a new level. The agreement was reached only after much hard work – not because Tusk and Juncker had trouble agreeing with me, but because certain countries have a deep mistrust of one another. Turkey blocked any joint military exercises, since that would involve exchanging classified information it didn't wish to share with EU member Cyprus. We eventually resolved this by arranging what we called 'parallel and coordinated exercises'. The EU and NATO would each hold their own exercises, with their own programme, but these would just happen to be held simultaneously, using the same scenario and with mutual invitations. This was one of many examples of a pragmatic solution that made cooperation easier without anyone having to compromise on their principles. In achieving this solution, I had to drag an acceptance out of Turkey, while Tusk and Juncker had to expend significant energy convincing Cyprus.

Tusk and Juncker never allowed themselves to be overwhelmed by complex challenges, and they were serious, solution-oriented leaders who, rather refreshingly, didn't take themselves all that seriously. But at the same time, they were fearless. With their extensive experience, they refused to surrender to the bureaucratic machine when they wanted to cut through and get specific projects off the ground. It's good to have strong people at the top, who can achieve breakthroughs for the things they want to accomplish. The framework agreement enabled us to clear old obstacles from the path towards our shared objectives.

Tusk had a deep affinity for Norway following a period spent as a construction worker in Tromsø early in the 1990s, although this had clearly been a somewhat mixed experience. Just as we were finally about to sit down to dinner in my dining room, Juncker said that he hadn't much cared for the Danish specialities he had been able to sample when my predecessor Anders Fogh Rasmussen had invited him to dinner. Norwegian specialities, on the other hand, he was very much looking forward to trying.

'I wouldn't get too excited,' Tusk said.

8

An important supporter

'NATO'S NEXT DEPUTY SECRETARY GENERAL HAS TO BE A German!'

Angela Merkel said the words with emphasis, eyeing me with a level gaze. We were in the elegant new Chancellery in Berlin on a fine day in June, 2016. As usual, we had a few minutes for private conversation out on the large terrace before the working lunch began. At times like this, we were able to raise topics that were better discussed one-on-one, rather than with everyone else around the table. On this occasion, she took the opportunity to remind me of an appointment she had brought up several times over the past year.

The term of office for NATO's then deputy secretary general, Alexander Vershbow, was about to come to an end, and we were in the process of appointing his successor. Merkel's pick was Martin Erdmann, an experienced diplomat who, after having worked at NATO, knew the organisation inside out. He had also been Germany's ambassador to the alliance.

For a long time, it had seemed that the job would be his, partly because the US had failed to put forward a candidate. But now they had. President Barack Obama was pushing hard for diplomat Rose Gottemoeller, and brought up her candidature in the meetings I had with him at this time. Gottemoeller was not a NATO insider, but she was an arms control expert, could speak Russian, and had worked extensively with the Intermediate-Range Nuclear Forces (INF) Treaty,

Strategic Arms Reduction Treaty (START), and other similar agreements.

'I'll certainly consider Erdmann,' I told Merkel. And then there was no further mention of the deputy secretary general role. But I knew it would not be as easy to fulfil her wish as I had first thought.

Angela Merkel was the NATO head of government with whom I most saw eye to eye. We had many good conversations founded on our shared fundamental attitudes towards the major challenges. She was pragmatic, and took a rational approach to most matters. I regarded her as an extremely important supporter.

We first met back in the mid-1990s, when I was minister of energy and she minister of environment, nature conservation and nuclear safety. But we had got to know each other well from 2005, when we both became head of our respective governments. We had met many times since, but really hit it off during the dramatic Copenhagen climate summit in 2009, at which a group of the world's leaders led by Obama, Medvedev and Merkel sat down to compose a draft agreement text in a cramped meeting room with cold coffee and slightly stale sandwiches. I had also received Merkel's wholehearted support in my work within global children's health and vaccination programmes.

When I took office as head of NATO, I was determined to nurture the organisation's relationship with Berlin. Of course, this wasn't just about my personal working relationship with Angela Merkel. She was Europe's most powerful politician, and head of the country that represented by far the EU's biggest economy. This in itself made Germany important. But Merkel was also leader of one of the countries besides Norway in which I felt most at home. I had grown very fond of Germany.

I have immense respect for what Germany has done since the Second World War. I know of no other country that has caused others so much suffering, but which has managed to confront its own past as Germany has done. Because instead of pushing this painful history away, Germany confronts itself with it.

I was reminded of this on my visit to the Federal Foreign Office in Berlin. The ministry is located in the old central bank building on Werderscher Markt in the historic city centre. When the Nazis were in power, the central bank was responsible for financing the German war machine and for retrieving occupied countries' gold reserves; after the war, the bank's director was sentenced to life in prison. At the time of the German Democratic Republic, the building was on the east side of the wall, and for many years housed the Communist Party's central committee. Every time I walked into the building, I noticed the small exhibition in the ground-floor vestibule, which relates its bleak history in text and images. Extremely few people would have reacted if this exhibition *hadn't* been there. Perhaps even fewer would have actively campaigned for it to be created. But the Germans choose to highlight even this small piece of the larger story of Nazi Germany and put it on display, for themselves and for others. To me, this is a small but important example of how Germany is keen to learn from history.

The Norwegian Labour Party maintained close contact with its German sister party, the Social Democratic Party of Germany (SPD), and as a young politician and head of the Youth Organisation I had many interactions with the SPD's youth arm. Leaders like Willy Brandt and Helmut Schmidt were important role models for me. Thorvald felt a special affinity for the country after serving in the Independent Norwegian Brigade Group in Germany after the war. When he was minister of defence, and to an even greater extent when he was minister of foreign affairs, he found Berlin willing to listen and take the interests of a small country like Norway into consideration.

For years, my family had even believed that we came from noble German stock in Schleswig-Holstein. That our lineage was German was something Thorvald had heard from his grandfather. Whenever I've attended events in Germany, it has always proved a success to open my speeches by saying that I'm actually German.

But then, in 2013, Thorvald took part in the Norwegian version of *Who Do You Think You Are?*, the TV series that digs through the records of national archives and other sources to uncover the family backgrounds of famous people. It didn't take long to find out that the first person to use the Stoltenberg name was Thorvald's great-great-great-great-great-grandfather, Vincent Henriksen from Larvik, who had lived during the 1700s. He had studied in Germany for a time, close to the small town of Stoltenberg, and took this name after he returned to Norway. He probably thought it more refined, to have a foreign place name as his surname.

Thanks to one of my snobby ancestors, my name is therefore Jens Stoltenberg, and not Jens Henriksen. But my family was one illusion poorer.

In the first eight months after I took office as head of NATO, I travelled to Germany five times on visits of varying duration. The trip in June 2016 took place just a few weeks before I was due to chair my first NATO summit. It was important to have Germany's support on the major issues, but that wasn't all. I also believed the country could, and should, play a more prominent role within NATO.

Angela Merkel was under no illusions when it came to Vladimir Putin. She believed he had never actually accepted the outcome of the Cold War, and that he wanted to return Russia to its former status as a strategic superpower – which was why he was trying to take control of Eastern European countries that were not NATO allies. The way Merkel saw it, Putin wasn't interested in maintaining good relations with the West. On the contrary – he could become more important and achieve greater influence by having a difficult and adversarial relationship with us. Merkel emphasised how crucial it was that NATO stand united in its support of Ukraine, precisely to deter Putin from choosing such an aggressive and confrontational course of action again in the future.

But at the same time, Merkel was adamant that we mustn't cease all dialogue with Moscow. Like me, she didn't believe deterrence and dialogue to be mutually exclusive, but rather that we had to make use of both. She often pointed out that we share the Eurasian continent with Russia, and therefore must maintain relations with the Russians, regardless of who holds the power in the Kremlin.

Before the summit, NATO had prepared concrete plans for building up our military presence within the Baltic countries and Poland. Germany was sceptical at first, believing it would kindle Russia's fear of having NATO come too close, and thereby increase tensions across Europe. But of course the Germans also understood that Russia's aggression in Ukraine had triggered deep unease, especially among our Eastern allies. Merkel therefore agreed that Germany would lead one of the four battalions that I proposed should be approved for deployment at the summit. If this went ahead, it would be the first time NATO had deployed forces in the east of the alliance, and the first time German soldiers had been stationed there since the Second World War.

Germany's relationship with NATO was not problem-free. The Germans had a deep-rooted reluctance to engage militarily, but were now providing valuable assistance to NATO's operations in Afghanistan and Kosovo. Our efforts to stabilise Iraq, however, were more difficult for them. They believed NATO ought to stay out of the region, because the alliance had a bad reputation there.

I struggled to understand the German scepticism about participating in certain NATO-led operations when they had already agreed to engage militarily elsewhere. But on the question of NATO's engagement in the south, the Germans felt much as the French did. Both countries were opposed.

Defence spending was always a topic that came up in conversations between Merkel and myself. At that time, very few member states were meeting the target of spending at least 2 per cent of their gross domestic product on defence. Germany was lagging far behind, at just over 1 per cent of GDP. This mattered for the alliance's total defence expenditure because Germany's economy was so large – the largest in Europe.

Germany was extremely hesitant to act as a leading military force in Europe, and this reticence was understandable in light of the country's history. But I encouraged the Germans to increase their defence spending to a level that at least approached the target everyone had agreed on at the Wales summit two years earlier. Personally, Merkel didn't really disagree with me – not in her view on her country's defence spending or on NATO's involvement in Iraq. But she was head of a coalition government that contained substantially differing viewpoints, and she had many considerations to balance.

An intense debate was ongoing regarding natural gas and the construction of the Nord Stream 2 pipeline, which would run from Ust-Luga a little west of St Petersburg in Russia, and through the Baltic Sea to Greifswald in Germany. The Nord Stream 1 pipeline had already begun operation a few years earlier. The project had become much talked about within NATO, not least because the Americans were so critical of it. The US believed Europe was making itself strategically vulnerable by becoming so dependent on Russian gas – Nord Stream 2 was a security policy issue. Merkel and several other European leaders, however, argued that the pipeline was a commercial project that had to be considered on commercial terms. This split within the alliance on such an important question made my job more difficult.

Ever since my time in the research department at Statistics Norway, and later as a politician, I'd had significant involvement with the European gas market. As Norway's prime minister, I was able to get the development of the Snøhvit field voted through – a large facility for liquid natural gas and the first development in the Barents Sea.

Norwegian gas fulfils around 30 per cent of Europe's gas consumption. So in a certain sense, Russian gas competes with Norwegian gas, but getting more Russian gas to Europe involves the construction of more pipelines and infrastructure, so the total gas market becomes larger. Viewed from a broader perspective, the European import of Russian gas has therefore also been advantageous for Norway, and Norway's position has been not to advise European countries against buying Russian natural gas.

Like Germany, Norway also believed that increased trade across the East–West divide in Europe would help to bind countries together and reduce the risk of war and conflict. Even during the Cold War, the Soviet Union had proved to be a reliable supplier of energy to NATO countries. Many Norwegian politicians, myself among them, had often pointed out that there was little to suggest Moscow would suddenly begin using natural gas as a means of political coercion.

After I started in my role at NATO, however, my views on this issue gradually changed. I had less faith in Russia as a reliable energy supplier, and grew more concerned about the security of Europe's supply.

Despite the unsolved problems, Merkel was a constant source of support for me. She was constructive, always seeking solutions that all the NATO allies could rally behind. Now she wanted Martin Erdmann to become NATO's next deputy secretary general. After the meeting in Berlin, the Germans reiterated their desire for Erdmann's appointment to the role through several channels, while the Americans kept pushing for Gottemoeller. I interviewed both candidates thoroughly. There was no doubt that both were highly qualified, but Gottemoeller held a central role within the US State Department, was an expert on Russia, and had extensive knowledge of arms control. I believed we would need her in the work to strengthen our dialogue with the Russians going forward.

Towards the end of June, I had decided on Gottemoeller, and she was officially appointed deputy secretary general on the twenty-seventh of June 2016. We immediately received an email from Angela Merkel's security policy adviser. The Germans were deeply disappointed. They had supported me all the way, and this was the thanks I had given them.

Straight afterwards, on the twenty-eighth and twenty-ninth of June, an EU summit was held in Brussels. I had been invited to speak on the partnership between the EU and NATO on the summit's first day.

As I walked into the area outside the conference room I noticed Merkel, and nodded to her. She didn't nod back. Perhaps she hadn't seen me. I spoke briefly with Italy's prime minister, Matteo Renzi. When I tried another nod in Merkel's direction, I managed to make eye contact with her. She only stared at me, straight-faced.

Just as I was about to give my speech, Merkel strode straight past me. As I spoke, she flicked through some papers. I had made similar speeches at previous EU summits, and on those occasions Merkel had always paid close attention, taken the floor in the subsequent discussion, and commented on my points in a supportive way. This time she only continued to shuffle through her sheaf of pages without looking up.

On the way out, she finally turned to face me. I prepared to exchange a few pleasantries. Merkel did not.

'I'm so disappointed in you, Jens,' she said. 'You've considered only the Americans' interests. The US cannot be permitted to decide everything within NATO.'

This, of course, was what Merkel had been keen to impress upon me when I visited her in Berlin a few months before I took office. 'What's important, Jens, is that the United States don't always get their way,' she had said, and now, in her view, I had facilitated the exact opposite. For Merkel, it wasn't just about appointing a German to the position of deputy secretary general. It was also a symbolic matter, a test to see whether I would always do what the Americans wanted. And in Merkel's eyes, it was a test I had failed.

'I couldn't reject Gottemoeller just because she's American,' I replied in an attempt to explain. But I was unable to say anything further, because Merkel turned on her heel and left. I stood there watching as she determinedly strode away.

It often happens that top executives receive input from the people around them regarding the appointment of this or that candidate to a leading position. I had hoped this was the case here, too – that Merkel had supported Erdmann because it was her job to do so, but that she would also be fine with an American in the role. Obviously not.

I had no doubt that Gottemoeller was the strongest candidate, and that she represented something NATO needed. But I didn't like the thought that I had disappointed someone who had supported me for so many years. In the worst-case scenario, I had weakened my good relationship with Merkel, and I was afraid this could have political consequences.

But the decision was made and the appointment announced, and the responsibility for it was mine. In just a week and a half, I would see Angela Merkel again in Warsaw. And for the first time, it was a meeting I was not looking forward to.

9

'Ready to fight tonight'

NARODOWY IS THE LARGEST AND MOST MODERN FOOTBALL stadium in Poland. It was built for the European Championships in 2012, and is situated just outside Warsaw city centre, on the same plot where another stadium previously stood. One in which the communist regime of the 1950s and 1960s drummed up some of its biggest propaganda performances.

The Polish national football team always play their home games at Narodowy, the stands packed with almost sixty thousand excited Polish fans. The arena is also used for concerts, and the Rolling Stones, Ed Sheeran and Madonna are among the stars who have played here. Narodowy represents the modern, outgoing Poland, receptive to ideas from beyond the country's borders. At night, the arena is bathed in red and white light, the colours of the Polish flag.

On the eighth and ninth of July 2016, the stadium had been transformed into a congress centre, ready to receive NATO heads of state and government. In the months leading up to the summit, the office had shifted into high gear. Torgeir Larsen had taken over from Vegard Ellefsen as director of my private office the previous autumn, bringing with him wide experience from his career as a journalist, diplomat and politician. He soon fitted right in to the NATO environment.

Issues had been raised, discussed and thrown out again; others had been brought forward. But throughout the process, one question had overshadowed all others: the alliance must build up militarily. To adapt to a new reality, we had to deploy NATO forces in the east.

An important part of these preparations involved following up the resolution from the summit two years earlier, which stated that each ally was to spend 2 per cent of GDP on defence. Increasing the member states' defence budgets was something I worked on continuously. Not only was it important for our own security, but I knew the Americans were keen to ensure the decision didn't become a promise made solely on paper. My job was to push the allied countries to achieve the targets they had set themselves.

The message was simple. After the Cold War, we had all reduced our defence budgets. This was only right – but we had to now be willing to boost them again as tensions were rising.

'You have to deliver on what you promised. If you believe two per cent of GDP not to be necessary, then at least be honest enough to say so. The worst thing you can do is say that you agree to the two per cent target,' and then not follow up with action,' I repeated at the many meetings I had with prime and cabinet ministers in the lead-up to the summit.

Reluctant coalition partners within government, major pension expenses or EU budgetary discipline requirements were often used as explanations for why it wasn't possible to achieve the 2 per cent target. Some countries were struggling with their economies, and asserted they simply didn't have the resources to spend so much on defence. For others, it was the exact opposite. They were too rich. Two per cent of a large gross domestic product is a staggering sum, and far too much money to spend on defence. Many of my former political colleagues in Norway were among those who spoke this way. And in a sense, they had a point. Two per cent of a large cake is more than 2 per cent of a small cake.

'But ninety-eight per cent of a large cake is in fact much, *much* more. You have ninety-eight per cent of a large GDP to spend on other worthy causes. It's not a disadvantage to be rich,' I said.

Another frequently used argument was that GDP fluctuated, and was therefore unsuitable as a defence spending target. This, too, was a relevant point, but the problem was that the defence budgets of most of the NATO member states fluctuated around levels *far below* 2 per cent of GDP. So it all boiled down to a lack of willingness to allocate adequate resources to defence.

In Norway, I encountered the argument that I myself had not achieved the 2 per cent target, even though the NATO resolution had been adopted after I had completed my final term as prime minister. But while I rolled my eyes, I also had to admit that it was much easier to be secretary general of NATO, travelling around and demanding increased investment in defence, than it was to be a prime minister and actually allocate the required sums. For every extra billion spent on defence, there is one billion less for other worthy causes like healthcare, education or public transport. I had felt how painful this was when we increased Norway's defence budget during my time as prime minister. And now the need was even greater.

In some European capitals at this time, I gained the nickname 'Mister Two Percent'. But luckily, reports with positive figures began to roll in. Yet another country, Poland, was set to achieve the 2 per cent target that year. Others were also increasing their budgets.

My ambition to maintain a dialogue with Russia had been met with intense resistance, but before the summit in Warsaw this had eased somewhat. A conversation with UK prime minister David Cameron in London was a particular turning point. There was no need to nag the British about defence spending or to remind them of the promises made in Wales, since the United Kingdom was already meeting the 2 per cent target. But when it came to their view of the NATO-Russia Council, which I was trying to resurrect, they were still sceptical. At the meeting, Cameron had three of his advisers with him, and I had three of mine. When the topic of dialogue with Russia came up, Cameron turned to his people: 'What's our position on the NATO-Russia Council?'

The UK secretary of state for defence Michael Fallon leaned forward. 'We are reticent. We want to wait.' I subsequently took the floor and made an almost missionary plea for my standpoint. 'Dialogue is not weakness,' I said. 'Dialogue is strength. If you daren't even speak with the Russians, *that* is an expression of weakness. As long as we are firm and predictable and have a strong defence, we can always meet them.'

Cameron and I had previously been united on many issues, and I felt that might be the case here, too. And it was, perhaps even more so than I had realised, because when I finished speaking Cameron looked at his colleagues and said: 'Agreed. We must support resuming the dialogue with Russia.'

Cameron's advisers glanced about the room. The British ambassador to NATO was sitting there, and he had quite rightly defended the official British stance, expressing his nation's reticence, rejecting the idea of dialogue and setting new conditions. It is the job of the civil service to implement the political decisions that are made in accordance with the guidance that is given, and this understandably makes diplomats cautious about announcing new positions. While a confident prime minister can abruptly take a new stance. Just as David Cameron did.

And so the UK was on board. At around the same time, the United States adopted the same view. Slowly but surely, the Eastern Europeans also resigned themselves to the fact that we needed to increase our dialogue with Russia.

I felt we were on the right path, but I was somewhat apprehensive before the Warsaw summit. Unforeseen problems could always arise, no matter how thoroughly we had prepared; new factors might crop up and overturn the resolutions that lay ready to be adopted. I had been NATO secretary general for a year and nine months. The summit would be a kind of political test piece, and there was no guarantee we wouldn't stumble at the finish line. Nor was it in my favour that I had recently managed to annoy someone as important as Germany's chancellor over the relatively small matter of appointing the next deputy secretary general.

On the first day, we gathered outside Narodowy Stadium so the photographers could take the traditional family photographs. I have never been especially fond of the organised mingling before meetings and dinners – I find it easier to meet around a table, with an agenda detailing the matters to be discussed – but I've grown better at it over the years, and as head of NATO I found the socialising easier than when I had attended the summits as Norway's prime minister. I now had a clearer role. I had something important to discuss with almost everyone in the room, and found that it was both enjoyable and useful to have an opportunity to meet with so many people at once. Here, I could not only bring up major issues like insufficient defence spending, but also make specific enquiries about additional soldiers for NATO battlegroups in the Baltics, or contributions in Afghanistan or Kosovo. For these kinds of small but focused conversations we might agree so-called 'pull asides' in advance – meetings of just a few minutes in which I stood with one of the heads of government one-on-one, often in a corner of the room.

Inside the stadium, Angela Merkel's bright green jacket stood out among the dark suits of the other leaders. After a while, I managed to make eye contact with her, and understood that she was ready to talk. We drew away from the crowd, and she got straight to the point.

'When I disagree, I disagree,' she said. 'And I disagree with the deputy secretary general appointment. But you should know, Jens, that I don't bear grudges. I'm done with the matter. Finito!'

Angela Merkel hardly knew the impact it had had on me, to know she was so dissatisfied with a decision I had made. Just days had passed since she had so obviously been irritated with me at the EU summit in Brussels, and it was a great relief that we were now back to being friends and confidants.

The rest of the summit also continued favourably. Poland had long desired a stronger NATO military presence in the easternmost regions of the alliance. They were feeling extremely vulnerable and exposed following Russia's aggression in Georgia and Ukraine.

'Think about the Cold War,' they said. 'Back then, West Germany was NATO's eastern flank, and there were several hundred thousand American soldiers there.' Now Poland was NATO's eastern flank. The country had been a member of the alliance since 1999, but hardly a single NATO soldier had been deployed there. 'NATO has given us a few hundred middle-aged officers who sit behind desks,' they said. 'That scares no one.' They were exaggerating slightly, but they were right in that we had no combat-ready forces in Poland or the other countries which had joined the alliance after the end of the Cold War.

Now the summit adopted a resolution to establish four multi-national battlegroups in Estonia, Latvia, Lithuania and Poland. Obama supported the build-up in order to clearly mark for Moscow where NATO's eastern border ran. At no point must President Putin think he could treat the former Soviet republics of Estonia, Latvia and Lithuania, for example, in the same way he was now treating Ukraine – also a former Soviet republic. The British supported the Eastern Europeans. The Germans, as usual, had been reticent, but agreed to lead one of the battlegroups as long as the path to resuming a dialogue was also followed up. The United States, the United Kingdom and Canada would each lead their own battlegroup.

For the Eastern Europeans, increased military presence in their own countries was crucial before they could agree to maintaining a dialogue with Russia. As long as the battlegroups were deployed, we could hold meetings with the Russians without anyone thinking that the aggression in Ukraine had been forgotten.

The summit also adopted a resolution to increase the alliance's military presence in Romania. It was decided that NATO's forces in the area would be increased threefold, and that a dedicated rapid deployment force would be established. Greater preparedness. More exercises. Faster decision-making processes.

Ready to fight tonight. Which meant we were also ready to speak to the Russians. As President Theodore Roosevelt once said: speak softly and carry a big stick.

NATO was founded to secure the defence of Europe's democracies. The resolutions adopted in Warsaw removed any doubt that this was, and remains, NATO's most important task.

In the evening, we gathered for a working dinner in the column hall of the Presidential Palace, where the Warsaw Pact had been signed by the Soviet Union and other Eastern European countries on the fourteenth of May 1955. Sixty-one years later, NATO was holding a celebratory dinner in the very room where the Moscow-led military alliance had been founded. It would be hard to find a stronger symbol of the Soviet system's failure. I couldn't help but think about it, and I'm sure I wasn't the only one. But nobody commented on it, a clear indication of a certain sensitivity, and the fact that nobody wished to gloat over the fate of their neighbours in the east.

We had adopted important resolutions that led to the most significant build-up of NATO forces since the end of the Cold War, and which erased any distinction between the eastern member states and the rest of NATO. For me, these achievements elicited mixed feelings – it gives me far greater immediate pleasure to help cut greenhouse gas emissions, invest in education, or ensure vaccines are available for all the world's children. But emotions cannot determine political priorities. Defence and security are of fundamental importance. Before the war in Eastern Ukraine and the annexation of Crimea, such a military build-up had been unthinkable. Now, unfortunately, it was right and it was necessary.

The battlegroups in the east were the most important, but the resolutions on training and capacity building in Iraq and supporting the fight against IS with AWACS surveillance planes were also of great significance. When our neighbours are more stable, we are more secure.

The working dinner wasn't exactly a relaxing affair – especially not for me, since I was the one responsible for chairing it. It was as much a meeting as it was a dinner, with microphones and papers among the dinner service, flower arrangements and several kinds of wineglasses, all accompanied by a list of speakers I had to manage. We went around the table. Some of the speeches were reflective and analytical, others more directly political and bordering on the polemical.

Eventually I saw people around me beginning to glance at the clock. It had been a long day. I was just preparing to conclude the evening when a note was handed to me. Barack Obama wished to say something. He had already made his speech, but he was now asking to take the floor one more time. This wasn't usual. I thought he maybe just wanted to offer his thanks, because this would be his last NATO summit. But Obama had more on his mind.

There were two things he would like to say, he began. First, he wanted to thank Prime Minister David Cameron for his cooperation (Cameron had lost the Brexit vote a couple of weeks earlier, and was stepping down). Then Obama moved on to his second point. Earlier in the evening, Greek prime minister Alexis Tsipras had pointed out that Vladimir Putin would probably be happy to hear that NATO's leaders had spent the entire dinner speaking about Russia and the threat the country represented. It would strengthen Putin's self-image.

'I'm sure Alexis is absolutely right. But as I listened to our conversation this evening, it occurred to me that we're not talking about Putin or Russia,' Obama said. 'What we're *actually* talking about is ourselves, who we are, what's important to us, the values we're willing to fight for.' Several of the other leaders had mentioned that a fair number of voters were quite keen on some of Putin's policies; that the currents the Russian president represented were not unknown in the West. 'This is true,' Obama said. 'There exists an antiliberal sentiment in all our countries, and that is understandable.'

All eyes were turned on Obama. There was no longer any glancing at the clock.

'Many people feel they have lost the fixed anchor points in their lives. Globalisation has created uncertainty and resignation. A primitive form of nationalism and xenophobia has returned. Yes, there *is* fertile ground for whipping up hatred towards immigrants, Muslims and the LGBTQ+ community,' Obama said. But just how willing, he asked, were we to confront such attitudes? 'It's so easy to exploit these currents,' he said. Those who chose to flirt with them would get their desired response.

'But the truth is,' Obama said, 'that Europe has walked this road before. And if you start down that road again, if you start to dislike Muslims, or immigrants, or members of the LGBTQ+ community, then pretty soon' – here he leaned forward and pointed across the table – 'pretty soon you'll start to dislike Poles, Germans and Turks, too. And then you'll be back in the twentieth, nineteenth and eighteenth centuries. Times in which things didn't go so well for Europe. So I think it's important to understand what we're actually fighting for.'

A deep silence had settled over the table. There sat Angela Merkel and François Hollande, representatives of Germany and France, Europe's historic arch enemies. There sat Andrzej Duda from Poland's nationalistic Law and Justice Party. There sat Recep Tayyip Erdoğan, who back home in Turkey faced accusations of undermining democracy and gathering all the power in his own hands. There sat Hungary's Viktor Orbán, the creator of what Orbán himself referred to as 'illiberal democracy'. Now they were forced to listen to a burning appeal for freedom and tolerance from the president of the United States.

'If we don't hold on to the values upon which our society is built, things will not go well for us,' Obama said. 'We won the Cold War not because we had the most missiles, but because of our values.' He asked the gathering to look closely at Russia and Russian society. Life expectancy was plummeting, to the level of that of a developing country. The Russians were able to sell gas, weapons and vodka, but little else. And they didn't really know what they wanted with Ukraine.

Obama concluded:

'All Putin represents is an attempt to deny that Russia is a country in decline. We should be constructive, we should take Russian interests into consideration when they are reasonable, but ultimately, we're going to do just fine. We will win, as long as we know who we are. But if we *don't*, then Putin, or people like him, will sweep away everything Europe has built since World War II. It will be a tragedy for the world, and a tragedy for all Europeans. Even if you don't realise it yourselves.'

The Warsaw summit marked the end of the beginning of my long term as head of NATO. The organisation was more united than it had been before, and the atmosphere among the allies was good. I felt that I had managed to take control of the moving train onto which I had jumped two years earlier, but as secretary general, my role was to a significant extent a function of the member states' fundamental attitudes – what *they* wanted from the alliance.

No other country is more important to the alliance than the United States. And in the United States, Barack Obama was on his way out. A presidential election was just around the corner.

PART 3
BURDENS

July 2016–July 2018

10

A president like no other

THE MEETINGS OF THE NORTH ATLANTIC COUNCIL GATHER ALL NATO member states. All countries – one voice. But the United States holds a unique position among these countries due to its political, economic and military weight. No other nation means more for what NATO is, what NATO can do, and what NATO can become. Which is why the forces that dominate American politics – and who is in the White House – are such decisive factors.

The presidential election in November 2016 was therefore not only important to the United States, but also to all of NATO.

Observing all the attention around the election over the course of the year had caused me to reflect a little more closely on my relationship with America, a country I had been highly critical of in the 1970s, when my political consciousness was being shaped. The US's foreign and security policies were the overriding reason that the Labour Party's Youth Organisation had been against NATO membership. *Sing 'Norway, Norway out of NATO' when the red revolution comes!* – this refrain was sung to the melody of 'Glory, Glory Hallelujah', and I sang it many times myself at the summer camps on Utøya, the island owned by the Youth Organisation, near Oslo. We held discussions, presentations and concerts there every year, and the camps were important political workshops.

On the way to Utøya sometime in the 1970s, members of one of the Youth Organisation's local groups had driven over to NATO's northern command, which at the time was located at Kolsås, and taken down a huge black-and-white NATO sign from outside the fence. When they arrived at the camp on Utøya, they erected it as a road sign pointing towards the island's largest outdoor toilet. The facility was known ever after as 'the NATO WC'.

So as to the Youth Organisation's prevailing opposition to NATO, there was little doubt. This opposition was part of our identity, and when I became the YO's head in 1985, I said what everyone was used to hearing. 'The Labour Party's Youth Organisation believes that in the long-term, Norway should withdraw from NATO' was the message I conveyed in my first interviews. And the reason for this was primarily everything the United States had been and remained involved in: the Vietnam War, the bloody coup in Chile, the covert support of counter-revolutionary rebels in Nicaragua. We didn't want to belong to an alliance in which the most powerful country pursued policies that ran counter to a rules-based international order.

But in 1985, I was in fact already moving towards a different viewpoint. It wasn't credible to argue that Norway should withdraw from NATO, because we didn't really mean it – or at least, we didn't believe we should withdraw *right now*. Being covered by NATO's security guarantee outweighed the negative aspects of the United States. Our anti-NATO stance was mostly just for show.

I began preparing the ground for a turnaround, working on the programme committee for at least a year to garner support there. When trying to get people to change their minds, you have to make it as least painful as possible for them – you have to come up with a new narrative that ensures much of the old stance can be carried over into the new. One could be in favour of Norway's membership of NATO, for instance, but against Ronald Reagan and much of what he stood for. We spoke about 'fighting from within NATO' – it was a plank we set out so that everyone could make it safely across, from one stance to the other. We would remain a member of the alliance and fight from the inside for our views on issues such as US policies in Latin America, nuclear-free zones and disarmament.

In my address to the Labour Party Youth Organisation's national conference in 1987, I vehemently argued that we should also take a clear stand *for* transatlantic cooperation on security and defence. The Youth Organisation supported Norway's membership of NATO with a solid majority.

I remain proud of that turnaround to this day, and I thought about it a lot over the weeks in which I considered whether I wished to be put forward for the role of head of NATO. The first major fight I took up as a young politician had been about international security and NATO. And despite my former scepticism towards the US, there was also another America, one to which I had always been attracted, and for which I had always felt an affinity. My maternal grandparents emigrated to the United States in the 1920s, before returning to Norway towards the end of their lives. Karin was born in the United States; she and my aunt Marianne spoke English together. Transatlantic ties are woven into my family's history.

The United States is home to people with backgrounds from all across the world, and represents an unparalleled creative force within technology, economics and culture. US history shows us a country plagued by slavery and discrimination, but also one that gave rise to the civil rights movement and Martin Luther King. The US waged a bloody and misjudged war in Vietnam, but it was also on US soil that opposition to the Vietnam War grew strongest and finally won out. The US invaded Iraq, but later elected a president who was against the war. We should be grateful that the most powerful country in the world is a democracy that permits criticism, freedom of the press and open debate – that it is a country able to change course when something isn't right. America's ability and willingness to self-correct is something I have always admired.

For the first six months of 2016, Hillary Clinton was ahead in every poll. She maintained her lead throughout the autumn, and the predictions of election experts also pointed to a Clinton victory. I, too, had a strong gut feeling that this would be the election's outcome. I think this had something to do with most of us – or I myself, at any rate –

being so used to political continuity being the norm. It's hard to conceive of changes that abruptly break with long-term trends. And Donald Trump making it to the White House would represent such a break.

Within NATO, emphasis was placed on the importance of political neutrality, but nevertheless, many American staff were happy to hint at the result they were hoping for. 'We're looking forward to welcoming the next president of the United States to the summit in May 2017, and it will be a great honour to meet *her*,' they said.

In the spring, Mike Scaparrotti had taken over as NATO's SACEUR, or supreme allied commander Europe – the most senior commander for NATO's forces, and a role with proud traditions. Dwight D. Eisenhower, the general who led the Allied invasion of Normandy on the sixth of June 1944, and the subsequent liberation of Western Europe, had been appointed NATO's first SACEUR in 1951. A few years later, he became president of the United States.

In September 2016, I invited Scaparrotti to my home on the Avenue Louise for our first working dinner.

I had never worked with Scaparrotti before. He arrived from being head of the US forces in South Korea, and had previously served in Iraq and Bosnia. He had closely cropped dark hair and a level, penetrating gaze, and, like many military personnel, he spoke in short, precise sentences. His authority and gravitas were no surprise – there are few four-star generals, and they report directly to the president. We went through the topics from the summit in Warsaw a couple of months earlier: Ukraine, relations with Russia and the fight against IS, and how these challenges ought to be handled going forward.

Before the dinner was over, we also had a chance to speak more informally. Scaparrotti had just been home to the US on vacation, where of course there had been much talk of the upcoming presidential election.

'I think Donald Trump is going to win. I know lots of people who usually vote Democrat, but they've turned their backs on Hillary Clinton,' he said. Clinton represented power, she was the elite. Donald Trump, despite being a billionaire, was regarded as a man of the people.

I secretly thought that NATO's SACEUR, while undoubtedly a respected general who knew a lot about leading military forces, probably didn't know all that much about politics.

On election night, Ingrid and I arranged an election party with friends and colleagues at the residence in Brussels. We rigged up a large television in the living room, and hamburgers were served. A long day awaited me the next morning, so I turned in before midnight. Sitting on the edge of my bed, I checked my phone and saw that the projections had evened out. Still, feeling fairly sure my gut feeling was right, I went to sleep.

I woke at five in the morning, as I often do, and still half asleep checked my phone. Trump had taken Pennsylvania and Ohio. It still wasn't 100 per cent certain, but CNN had reported that he was going to win. When I came down to our agreed election breakfast at six o'clock, the others were clearly just as surprised as me.

I had underestimated Trump's chances of winning, and I hadn't managed to undertake a cool-headed analysis of the figures.

I've studied and worked with statistics – I should know what probability is. Before the election, I had visited websites that predicted the two candidates' chances of winning. The American statistician Nate Silver had been pretty much spot on with his probability calculations when Obama won, and had also made his predictions in 2016. Just before the election, he released an analysis that indicated there was a 71.4 per cent chance that Clinton would beat Trump.

After the election, many people said that Silver and other analysts had been wrong, but that wasn't necessarily the case. They relayed what was most *probable*. Which is not the same as excluding another outcome. And since there was a 28.6 per cent chance that Trump would win the election, then it was actually also rather probable. That I didn't fully take in the possibility of a Trump victory illustrated my own unwillingness to accept reality. For many months, the figures had shown that Trump *could* win. I sent my congratulations to the newly elected president.

I was anxious about what would happen next, because I had noticed how critical of NATO Trump had been during his election campaign. In a television interview towards the end of March, he had said that 'NATO is obsolete'. It was a view that undermined the American foreign policy of the past seventy years. Trump received pushback from a number of Republican heavyweights, but it simply seemed to glance off him. At around the same time, he was asked who he would consult when he needed foreign policy advice. 'I'm speaking with myself, number one, because I have a very good brain,' he replied.

The American people had elected Donald Trump as their president, and we had to respect the result. I wanted NATO to establish a good working relationship with him as quickly as possible, in order to get Trump and his administration to take a more positive view of the alliance. Within the organisation, self-discipline would also be necessary – I made it clear that exasperated groaning at internal meetings was unacceptable. There would be no eye-rolling at Trump's tweets or public appearances; no mocking laughter over videos; no jokes about golfing or his mannerisms. Zero tolerance for such behaviour was absolutely necessary. Just a small group of individuals poking fun at some statement or behaviour can spread throughout the ranks of an organisation and trickle out. And should that happen, it would take little for it to reach Washington that staff in NATO headquarters were sitting around laughing at Donald Trump. It would be ruinous.

We were going to work with President Trump. It was our duty to try to ensure that his view of NATO evolved, and that the US relationship with the European allies stayed strong.

I called General Michael Flynn, Trump's pick for national security advisor. Flynn believed Trump to be a NATO supporter, and that we would work well together. Reading between the lines of what Flynn told me, Trump hadn't meant what he had said during his election campaign.

I wanted to speak with Trump myself as quickly as possible, but none of the Americans in NATO had the right contacts. Usually, so-called transition teams are rolled out within the departments, but the Trump team was behind schedule, and didn't have people in place. From his contacts in Washington, the head of my private office Torgeir

Larsen heard that I was one of twenty-five people on a call list. But the person who had made the list had been fired, and nobody knew who was currently managing it. In the end, we set up a phone call with Trump through Flynn's chief of staff, Marshall Billingslea. We did so just in time. When Torgeir called Billingslea again a little later, he was astonished at how much time he seemed to have on his hands. Billingslea was watching his daughter play soccer, he said, and he chatted away about all kinds of things. As it turned out, he had been fired, too. But the call wasn't cancelled, and on Friday the eighteenth of November, I got Trump on the line for the first time.

'I'm a big, big, big fan of NATO! Great to speak with you, Secretary General, looking forward to working with you,' he said. During our conversation, I was a little shocked that we mostly seemed to agree on the crucial matters. Trump believed the European member states needed to spend more on defence. 'On that I completely agree with you,' I said. Fairer burden sharing and increasing defence spending were of course what I had spent most of my time working on since taking office. NATO needed to be better prepared in the fight against terror, Trump said. 'On that I completely agree with you,' I replied again.

Trump also wanted to hear my thoughts on the individuals he was considering for key positions. I was somewhat surprised that he would consult *me* on such appointments, but I didn't contradict him. Rex Tillerson for secretary of state? I knew him a little from the oil industry, and I had met him at energy conferences at Sanderstølen in the 1990s. He had often been mentioned in media speculation about who would become secretary of state. 'A good choice,' I said.

Jim Mattis for secretary of defense? At this I was surprised – his name hadn't come up, and I didn't know what to say. The truth was that the little I did know about Jim Mattis came from the HBO series *Generation Kill* about the Iraq war, which I had watched with my son. In the series, Mattis is portrayed as a mythic figure, a general both feared and admired who goes by the call sign 'Chaos' when he communicates over radio. I had enjoyed the series very much, but I couldn't exactly recommend Mattis for secretary of defense on the basis of a TV series. There was a slightly embarrassing pause before Torgeir, who was listening in on the conversation, handed me a note. It said: *Jim Mattis is great. He knows NATO.*

'Jim Mattis is great. He knows NATO,' I told Trump.

I'm sure my recommendation made no difference, but a few weeks later Jim Mattis was appointed defense secretary.

Trump invited me to Trump Tower, so we could meet and get to know each other a bit better before he took office, and I was ready to accept – I wanted to forge relationships with him and with the people around him as quickly as possible. I also thought it would be quite exciting to see the fabled skyscraper from the inside, but we quickly came to understand that this wasn't a good idea. Japan's prime minister, Shinzo Abe, had visited Trump, and we learned that the outgoing administration hadn't exactly appreciated it. At any given time there is only one president, and Barack Obama was still in the White House. We didn't follow up on the invitation.

After that first conversation with Trump, I felt things looked brighter. We needed to distinguish between form and content, I thought. His style was crude and tough, but I didn't see that as an insurmountable problem. Like many others, I disagreed with Trump's views on climate change, abortion rights and trade policy, but the substance of what he had said about NATO in our conversation was absolutely something I could work with.

Shortly after the election, Obama invited the incoming president to the White House. It was a conciliatory affair. Trump praised Obama and said some kind words about him. He thanked him for his efforts, while Obama said everything an outgoing president should say.

This appearance, too, I found encouraging. Things are going to calm down, I thought.

You campaign in poetry, you govern in prose, as they say. I believed that now the election was over, Trump would be shaped by his new role and its accompanying responsibilities. That he would become more predictable, closer to the norm. With competent people around him, Trump would become more like his predecessors in the White House.

That was the second incorrect assessment I made of Donald Trump.

On Friday the twentieth of January 2017, I sat down in the living room on the first floor of our house in Brussels to watch the president's inaugural address. I was excited. This was Trump's big opportunity to step up and lead the American people. He had run a hard-hitting election campaign, but now he could tone down the brutal rhetoric.

Trump started agreeably. He thanked Michelle and Barack Obama for their help and support during the transition phase, and said that they had been fantastic. But that was the end of the kind words.

Trump launched straight into saying that former presidents had abused their power at the people's expense. They had caused 'American carnage', he said. The elite had celebrated in Washington, while ordinary families struggled. 'Mothers and children trapped in poverty in our inner cities; rusted-out factories scattered like tombstones across the landscape of our nation,' Trump boomed. Nobody learned anything at school. Gangs, crime and drugs made life unsafe. The United States was used and abused by other countries. But now this was all over, now it was America first!

I had expected reconciliation. But the tone of the address was exactly the same as that of Trump's election campaign.

It slowly began to sink in. Trump wasn't going to change now that he was president.

But one assessment I had made still stood: it was vital that we develop a good working relationship. I had to convince Trump that NATO wasn't just important for Europe, but also essential to the United States. The inaugural address changed none of this.

We worked to make contacts within the new administration, and the signals we received from several key individuals were encouraging. The Trump administration would stand by its obligations towards NATO, we were told. And the reassurances increased in strength the closer the sources were to Trump. We had started making plans for a summit in Brussels in May, with burden sharing and the fight against terrorism at the top of the agenda, along with an opening ceremony for NATO's new headquarters, which we were in the process of moving into. Our partners in Washington supported the plans, and everyone pointed out that it was important that I meet with Trump in person fairly soon. He liked speaking to people and was available.

On Saturday the fourth of February I had my second telephone conversation with Trump, the first after he had taken office, and as I so often did I struggled a little with the introductory small talk. My advisers, who were listening in on the conversation from a neighbouring office, later teased me for my propensity to talk about the weather in such situations. According to them, I almost always began important telephone conversations by saying that the sun was shining in Brussels, no matter what the weather was actually like.

Trump asked whether I had a lot on my plate, and I replied by saying I was sure he had more. He laughed, clearly in a good mood. So we talked through the most pressing issues: terrorism, Russia and defence spending. He was especially concerned with the latter.

'I was pretty surprised when I learned that Germany owes us billions of dollars, money they haven't paid, but they will,' he said. He lingered on this point for a long time, speaking about these sums of money as if they were dues Germany had neglected to pay. I tried to explain that that wasn't the case, but he only repeated what he'd said. It was clear that he was critical of Angela Merkel. I tried to defend her, while also making sure to praise Mattis, Tillerson and Flynn, people it was important Trump put his trust in.

At the end of March I travelled to Washington, not to meet Trump, but to establish working relationships with other key individuals. Secretary of defense Jim Mattis was a strong supporter of NATO, and would be important for us. I wanted to invest as much time and effort as possible in maintaining good contact with him. Mattis was highly respected – to many Republicans working on foreign and security policy, he was important in enabling them to support the new administration, and they hoped he would ensure the president took a responsible line on defence policy. I repeatedly heard that getting rid of Mattis would cost Trump dearly – that to do so would drive a wedge between Republican heavyweights and the president, and send shockwaves through the American military, which holds a unique position within American society. But at the same time, many saw the source of a potential conflict there – a popular and respected Mattis, who was praised by the same establishment that lacked respect for Trump and his team.

I had a conversation with Mattis in the Pentagon that lasted for over two hours. He had previously been head of US Central Command, responsible for the Middle East, East Africa and Central Asia, and head of Allied Command Transformation, one of NATO's two strategic military commands.

He began the meeting by providing a quick summary of the military operation at Åndalsnes in Norway in 1940; the landings of the British soldiers and the problems they faced during their advance. He talked about Crown Princess Märtha's escape to Sweden, and about how she and Crown Prince Olav had stayed with President Roosevelt. I had to admit that in several areas, he had a better overview of Norwegian military history than I did myself.

We didn't talk solely about military history, however, despite it being a subject that interested us both. Mattis was worried that Trump's criticism of Europe would weaken NATO.

'Americans can't be more worried about the future security of Europe's children than you are yourselves,' he said. 'If Europeans want to prevent the United States reducing its involvement, they need to show that they actually support our common defence.'

Mattis wondered whether there might be ways to reward the NATO states who spent 2 per cent of their GDP on defence, such as by holding more exercises with countries who fulfilled the requirement. This kind of arrangement would be extremely politically sensitive, but I had to say that we would look into it.

Secretary of State Rex Tillerson was as difficult to get hold of as Mattis was open; he ultimately cancelled a meeting that had finally been scheduled after much back and forth. My staff tried in vain to contact his people, but they never called back. After the press got wind of the cancellation, however, a fifteen-minute meeting with Tillerson was hastily arranged. Just before our conversation, I was sent a brief memo from a colleague acquainted with Tillerson from his time at

ExxonMobil. It was almost a warning. Tillerson never agreed to attend meetings unless deals could be signed or other concrete results achieved. When he believed he had done his part, he would simply get up and leave, even if the meeting wasn't over. He refused to spend time on meetings which, in his opinion, were purely ceremonial. According to the memo, Tillerson was 'extremely introverted' and loathed the press.

Predictably enough, the quarter of an hour we spent together didn't result in much; he probably thought the meeting pointless and vacuous. But worse was the fact that Tillerson wasn't planning on attending the meeting of NATO ministers of foreign affairs in early April. He claimed the timing clashed with another meeting, but I got the impression he didn't intend to prioritise the NATO session regardless. 'It's important that you attend, so we'll move the date,' I said.

Tillerson attended, and we eventually managed to get our cooperation up and running smoothly. But the initial refusal lingered somewhat. If Tillerson regarded a meeting of the NATO ministers of foreign affairs as 'ceremonial', then his attitude was deeply worrying.

11

Donald Trump in
the White House

IN MID-APRIL, I WAS BACK IN WASHINGTON. READY TO MEET Donald Trump for the first time.

There is a uniqueness to the meetings that take place in the Oval Office. Coming face to face with the world's most powerful head of state demands clear messaging – you have to get to the most important points and ensure the time is used well. Before the meeting, I sat in my hotel room preparing, just as I had on the occasions Barack Obama received me in the White House. The delegation accompanying me on these visits to Washington usually left the hotel an hour before me, to make it through all the security measures and be in situ before I arrived. I would therefore be left alone in my hotel room, with only my own security guards and the Secret Service just outside the door.

That hour alone always felt a little strange. I was constantly surrounded by people on such trips – I was always being ushered on, into another meeting or to hold a press conference. But all at once, my room would be empty and quiet. It was good to have this downtime to think through my main points and check my notes. Meetings with the president of the United States have no written agenda, but they are prepared for by the people around us over the course of several weeks. Telephone calls are made and emails sent back and forth; memos are drafted. So there is an agenda in the sense that we agree the subjects to be discussed in advance. And to a certain extent, there is also agreement on what the outcome of the meeting will be.

My meetings with Obama followed a fixed routine. When the president was almost ready in the White House, there would be a knock at my hotel door a few blocks away. I would be notified that it was time to leave, and we would make our way down to the car. In the vehicles used on these occasions – even the huge SUVs – security is prioritised above all else. They have additional armouring in the floor and roof, but this means the car's interior isn't quite big enough for me, so I have to sit with my bottom almost hanging off the seat to have enough headroom. The cars are undoubtedly extremely expensive, but they don't offer passengers the most comfortable experience. Luckily, the drive was a short one.

Upon arriving at the White House, I would be shown into the room where my delegation was waiting. Shortly afterwards, we would be accompanied to the Oval Office. The door would open, and President Obama would be standing there. 'Jens, so good to see you! How are things? Is Ingrid well?' This was how the meetings proceeded, seamlessly and cordially, every time. Obama impressed me with his detailed knowledge of personal matters. He was always up to date, and might ask whether I'd had a chance to go skiing lately, or wonder about something to do with Ingrid's job. I, on the other hand, usually hadn't remembered to prepare something thoughtful to say about Michelle or the children – Afghanistan and defence spending were the topics I had read up on. I always managed to say that I hoped Michelle was keeping well, but I never managed to make it seem as natural as his genuine care and concern for me and my family.

After the welcome, we would each sit in our respective chairs beside the fireplace for the 'warm words', as this is referred to in the schedule – a brief meeting in the presence of the press. Obama was on home ground here, too. 'I always look forward to meeting this guy,' he might say. There's something incredibly sincere, but also a little strange, about the way Americans always make it sound as if you're practically childhood friends.

Once the press had asked us a few unsuccessful questions about American domestic policy and then left the room, things would turn serious. Obama would take us through the points that had been agreed in advance, one issue at a time. Iraq. Afghanistan. Russia. Arms control. Terrorism. Defence spending. And when an hour had passed – pretty much exactly to the minute – he would conclude the meeting.

As I prepared to meet Trump, the process was very similar, with many of the same issues on the agenda. Upon arriving at the White House, I would first meet with Secretary of Defense Jim Mattis and National Security Advisor H.R. McMaster. McMaster had taken over as security advisor when Michael Flynn was forced to resign despite being in post for just a few weeks, after it emerged he had misled the administration over conversations he'd had with Russia's ambassador to Washington.

The motorcade stopped at a side entrance, and I was led up the side steps to McMaster's office for the meeting. Mattis was sitting there, along with a couple of younger colleagues. McMaster was nowhere to be seen. The Americans were somewhat taken aback – where was McMaster, if he wasn't with me? He was still waiting for NATO's new secretary general at the main entrance. Someone ran out to fetch him, and McMaster soon came hurrying into his office, where the rest of us sat waiting. We laughed a little at the misunderstanding, before we spent an hour going through the plans for the summit in May.

Afterwards, we went into the Roosevelt Room, named for former US presidents Theodore Roosevelt and Franklin D. Roosevelt. It's a beautiful, relatively small room, with a long table in the middle and the banners of each branch of the United States military adorning the walls. We relaxed there for a few minutes, and were served fruit and the legendary White House cookies; we signed the guestbook that had been set out. Then came the message that the meeting could begin. I had prepared a few pleasantries about the election victory and Melania, Trump's wife and the first lady. The door opened, but no president stood there waiting. Trump lounged casually in a chair.

'Come on in, guys,' he said, smiling and looking up. It was a pleasant welcome, albeit a different one.

When Trump had greeted Japanese prime minister Shinzo Abe a few weeks earlier, the handshake lasted fifteen seconds, and Trump had squeezed so hard that Abe winced in pain. Canadian prime minister Justin Trudeau was subjected to similar treatment. A little later, French president Emmanuel Macron chose to grip so hard that his knuckles turned white. All this had been much reported on in the media, with some commentators believing Trump was trying to assert his superiority through his handshake; others pointed out that he was concerned with his masculine image, which he tended to display somewhat carelessly. Not long before my visit, he had met German chancellor Angela Merkel, and refused to shake her hand in front of the photographers. Much was written about that, too.

In our preparations, my team and I had therefore discussed Trump's handshake. We tried to imagine how the encounter might play out, but a handshake wasn't all that easy to plan for. When Trump got up from the sofa and I had to take his outstretched hand, I was slightly apprehensive.

But then Trump's handshake turned out to be so normal I felt almost disappointed. His grip was neither hard nor loose.

When the conversation began, however, it quickly became apparent that this was going to be *extremely* loose. We jumped from one topic to the next. At one point, we were talking about Russia when Trump suddenly exclaimed: 'But why can't you guys in NATO join us in Korea? They're developing nuclear weapons, and that's something we can't accept.'

A couple of months earlier, North Korea's leader Kim Jong Un had declared that preparations for the testing of an intercontinental nuclear missile were now in their final stage; this announcement was then followed by the firing of medium-range missiles, which landed in the Japan Sea. On Twitter, Trump's response to North Korea acquiring long-range nuclear missiles was: 'It won't happen.' He also made it clear he would like China to help stop North Korea's nuclear weapons programme, but 'If not, we will solve the problem without them!'

So Trump bringing up North Korea in his conversation with me wasn't completely out of the blue. But I was unsure as to exactly what he meant. Did he want NATO to intervene in North Korea?

'Mr President, all the allies are concerned about the nuclear weapons, but I don't think there will be any support for bombing North Korea,' I said.

'But you're in Afghanistan. Why can't you be in North Korea?' Trump replied, before the conversation swiftly moved on. We touched on terrorism and IS, of course, with Trump declaring: 'We have to kill them, we have to bomb them, they're really evil people.'

Soon our conversation returned to the topic of Russia, and I tried to seize the opportunity to offer my thoughts on maintaining a dialogue with Moscow. I repeated the points I had been keen to make since taking office in NATO.

'We must be strong and predictable, but at the same time we need to be open to maintaining a dialogue with Russia. Russia is here to stay. It's a neighbouring country, not a terrorist organisation that needs to be eradicated, like IS,' I said.

Then, as I had done in many other conversations, I referenced Norway's experiences.

'You know, Mr President, as former prime minister of Norway, I know that it's possible to speak with the Russians.'

Trump cast a questioning look in my direction.

'Are you Norwegian?'

I understood why he was asking – over the years I've received many secretary generals and heads of various organisations myself, and it isn't always easy to remember where each of them comes from. They are there as representatives for an *organisation*. And at this meeting in the White House, I was *NATO*. If Trump was unsure of my home country, that was understandable. I smiled.

'Yes, I'm Norwegian.'

'Do you know Celina Midelfart?'

'Yes, I've met her several times. She's a well-known person in Norway,' I replied.

'Nice girl. What they wrote about us in the Norwegian papers – was it good or bad?'

I remembered seeing some newspaper images of Trump and Norwegian cosmetics heiress and investor Celina Midelfart at some sporting event or other, but more than that I couldn't recall. I had no idea what the papers had said.

'Oh yes, the reporting was positive. She's married to a rich Norwegian now,' I said.

'He's not rich.'

So the president of the United States clearly knew who investor Tor Olav Trøim was. But were you rich if you had a few billion kroner to your name? Possibly not, in Donald Trump's eyes.

After about twenty minutes, our private conversation was over. Mattis and McMaster entered the room, and several members of my delegation also joined us. I noticed my colleagues looking on anxiously as Trump and I shook hands once more for the photographers. But everyone was cheated out of a potentially amusing anecdote.

For Trump, the most important issue was NATO members' defence spending. I wanted him to take a more positive view of the alliance, and had therefore brought along a graph which illustrated that the trend in Europe had turned, and that defence spending was increasing. Trump was most concerned with the fact that only five member states had achieved the goal of spending 2 per cent of GDP on defence. I pointed out that several countries were close, and six or seven were set to reach the target in the near future. And then there was Iceland. The country has no armed forces, so would consequently never spend 2 per cent of its GDP on defence. It was therefore actually five out of *twenty-seven* countries who had achieved the goal, rather than five out of twenty-eight, I said, immediately thinking that I was probably coming across as rather nerdy with all these figures.

But this caught Trump's interest, if not entirely in the way I had intended.

'Then what do we want with Iceland?' he asked.

Before I could say anything further, Jim Mattis came to my aid. He concisely explained how important NATO's bases on Iceland were for the alliance's submarines, ships and planes. 'Mr President, they're good to have if you want to track down Russian subs,' he said.

Trump thought for a moment.

'Well, then we'll let Iceland stay a member,' he said.

I noticed that it wasn't just on the question of Iceland that Mattis contradicted Trump. He did it several times. Trump spoke at length about how other countries were 'not paying what they owe'. He had worked out that Germany owed NATO $374 billion, having arrived at this sum by taking the difference between what the Germans had spent on defence and what they would have spent had they met the 2 per cent target, then totalling this over a ten-year period. At his meeting with Merkel shortly before I visited the White House, he had apparently written the number on a kind of invoice, which he wanted her to pay. He had even calculated and applied interest retroactively.

Trump spoke as if these sums were a fee all the countries needed to pay in order to be a member of the alliance. Mattis asked to speak.

'Mr President, this isn't about debt or fees to NATO. It's about the total each country is spending on its own defence,' he said.

I don't know whether Trump neglected to listen because he thought his own point too good to let go, or whether he simply disagreed. But Mattis stood his ground.

Maybe I allowed myself to get a little carried away by the informal and direct tone, because when I presented the graph illustrating how European defence spending was on the rise, I called it 'the Trump effect'. Trump liked the expression so much that he encouraged me to use it at the subsequent press conference, but I couldn't – it would be going too far. The increase in spending had begun before Trump became president. I instead said that Trump had 'helped' to boost defence budgets, while in the period following our meeting Trump himself occasionally referred to 'the Trump effect' and how he had made the money come pouring into NATO.

The press conference that followed the meeting went well. I gave Trump the praise I thought he deserved with regard to increasing the allies' defence spending, but without exaggerating. True, Trump continued to talk about money that needed to be repaid, but most important was his conclusion: 'I used to say NATO is obsolete. But NATO is no longer obsolete.'

From the day Trump was elected, I had continually been asked about how I, as NATO secretary general, could trust an American president who believed the alliance had lost its relevance. Now Trump had finally gone back on that statement. NATO was once again important in Trump's eyes because he had managed to get Europe to jack up its defence spending, and because we had listened to his demands to ramp up the war on terror. The full story was more nuanced than that, of course, but all in all it was a good day. Trump expressed strong support for the alliance and for me, and this was good for NATO. The American media, with the national TV stations at the helm, gave the meeting broad coverage, with commentaries and analyses in addition to wide reporting. All the attention was also good for NATO's cooperation with the United States.

I repeated it time and time again in the interviews and speeches I gave in the US following this first meeting with Trump: NATO is important for Europe. But NATO is also important for the United States, because the alliance makes the United States stronger.

This had been my message in meeting with the president. But after an election campaign in which Trump had constantly questioned America's ties with NATO, it was also important to get through to the American public. Article 5 of the North Atlantic Treaty states that an attack on one country shall be considered an attack against all. The only time the article has ever been invoked was in the wake of the terrorist attacks against the United States that took place on September 11, 2001. Tens of thousands of European and Canadian soldiers had fought alongside the Americans in Afghanistan. And over a thousand of them had given their lives in doing so.

It is in the United States' interest to be part of a strong and effective NATO. After that first meeting with President Trump, I started to think that maybe he believed this, too.

12

Teeing up the shot

IN NATO, WE NEVER ROLL OUT THE *RED* CARPET – WE ROLL OUT A blue one. And we do this during summits and on other prominent occasions.

On Thursday the twenty-fifth of May 2017, we rolled out an extra-long and extra-wide bright blue carpet, all the way from the main entrance and through a small avenue of trees to the road leading to NATO headquarters. The blue was reflected in the colour of the NATO flag, which in turn symbolises the Atlantic Ocean, around which the alliance is gathered. The NATO emblem adorned the walls, and everything was ready for a grand ceremony with all NATO heads of state and government in attendance.

On this day, President Trump would make his first appearance at a NATO summit. Emmanuel Macron had also recently been elected, and few of us had yet had the chance to meet France's new, energetic president. This would be a special summit, because we would also be inaugurating the alliance's new headquarters. After fifty years in premises that were only ever intended to be temporary, NATO finally had a brand-new building.

While I was looking forward to leading the proceedings, I also felt somewhat apprehensive. Despite this being a celebration of NATO's new premises and continued solidarity, I felt nervous about how the summit would go. Following our meeting in the White House some weeks earlier, uncertainty as to how Trump really viewed NATO had arisen again. He had sown doubt about whether the United States would in fact come to the aid of any NATO nation subjected to a military attack.

Article 5 of the North Atlantic Treaty is NATO's collective defence clause, and represents the very core of the alliance: one for all and all for one. Trump had refused to offer a clear 'yes' to the question of whether the US continued to stand behind this assurance, despite persistent questioning by the press. And not least, doubt had arisen around whether the US would defend the NATO countries deemed to be spending too little on their defence. 'Why should we protect countries that aren't willing to pay for their own security?' Trump said. This made many of the allies uneasy. The way they saw it, Trump was reducing NATO to little more than a protection racket.

Security guarantees must be incontestable and absolute, not partial and with reservations. Each and every possible aggressor has to know that should they even think about touching Finnmarksvidda in Norway, or try to take so much as a square mile of the wetlands in eastern Estonia, then NATO, including the Americans, would be there in an instant.

If the United States' attitude in a crisis can be perceived as something along the lines of, 'well, we might come help you, but you'll have to pay up first' – if there is even the *tiniest* seed of doubt – then of course the risk of someone taking a chance and launching an attack increases. Article 5 loses its value.

Feeling hopeful, I received the delegates in a room set up for small talk and mingling. Here was Emmanuel Macron; there was British prime minister Theresa May at the centre of a small group. Others sat on a sofa, speaking with Italy's prime minister Paolo Gentiloni. I stood at the top of a flight of stairs, welcoming people as they arrived before they moved on into the building. Such occasions provide opportunities to speak to many people about all kinds of things, in a way that isn't possible around a table.

Last to arrive was President Trump. The Secret Service wouldn't allow him to use the same entrance as everyone else, due to a fear of snipers. I therefore met 'The Beast', the presidential armoured car, on a more sheltered side of the building. Many hundreds of Americans accompany the president on a presidential visit, and on this occasion they had occupied every last room of the Hotel Brussels, one of the city's largest hotels. They had brought along their own security, with motorcycles and cars, and now I saw Trump in the back seat of the largest of them as they pulled up outside the building. It truly *is* a beast of a vehicle. I noticed him quickly scribble something on the manuscript he was holding, before he stepped out.

After shaking hands and exchanging a few pleasantries, we began our walk through the building and across the long atrium that connects the various wings. The plan was to take Trump to a place where the text of Article 5 is carved into the wall, so photographs of the two of us could be taken in front of it.

I had intended to offer Trump a few facts about the new building and NATO, but his constant questions kept cutting me off. 'Do you really need such a big headquarters?' he asked. 'What do you need all these people for?'

I replied that while the organisation itself isn't all that large, the member states' delegations also use the building. Less than half the people who work at NATO headquarters are on the organisation's payroll, but it's good to have everyone gathered under the same roof – it makes it easy to meet with security measures in place, and everyone uses the same cafeteria. But that means the building is double the size of the one the organisation alone would need. The United States has the biggest delegation, consisting of several hundred people.

I continued by telling Trump who had designed the headquarters: renowned architects Skidmore, Owings & Merrill, who also designed the Trump International Hotel and Tower in Chicago.

'I know those people. They're extremely expensive,' Trump exclaimed. 'I don't understand why you chose those expensive architects. Extremely expensive!'

I had promised Trump's colleagues that I would walk us slowly through the building and keep Trump talking, to ensure the press photographers following the American president would have time to make it around to the other side of the building and immortalise

Trump's first meeting with all the other leaders. I did my best to drag things out, but the president strode off ahead. I prattled on, pointing this way and that as I described various aspects of the new building, but he seemed only mildly interested. Nothing came of the plan to take him over to the Article 5 text, because Trump simply marched on, staring straight ahead. I felt like a tour guide whose group of tourists clearly doesn't think him worth listening to.

All the heads of state and government were clustered together when we reached them. I introduced Trump to them one by one, somewhat randomly, depending on who was standing closest. During the seconds in which Norway's prime minister Erna Solberg spoke with him, she managed to say that she had beaten me in Norway's general election a few years earlier. I replied: 'Well, Mr President, my party clearly received the most votes. Many more than hers!'

Trump just gaped, seemingly confused. He was completely indifferent to this bickering between two party leaders from a country with fewer inhabitants than his home city of New York.

But there were more important matters on the agenda. In front of the main entrance a small avenue of newly planted trees had been constructed, with lawns on either side. On one of these lawns stood a twisted steel girder from the Twin Towers in New York; on the other a couple of segments of the Berlin Wall. Two monuments and testaments to some of the most momentous events in NATO's history. I introduced Angela Merkel as a speaker by reminding everyone that she had been living in Berlin not only when the wall was erected in 1961 but also when it was torn down in 1989 and Europe changed forever.

'Each day, all those who will enter this building will pass this memorial. They will understand that freedom will never be defeated. And that NATO will always defend the values on which our alliance is founded,' I said. Merkel expressed her gratitude for NATO's presence during the Cold War. She emphasised how the fall of the Berlin Wall symbolised that democracy wins out, even after many years of struggle. It was a solemn, but also forward-looking and optimistic speech, which I admired very much.

Then it was Trump's turn, standing before a piece of the mangled remains of the Twin Towers. The memorial's full name is the 9/11 and Article 5 Memorial, to emphasise how it symbolises the solidarity within NATO. I introduced Trump by stressing this unity. 'NATO's greatest strength is the enduring bond between North America and Europe. We saw the strength of that bond after the 9/11 attacks against the United States,' I said.

'And President Trump,' I continued, 'those attacks struck at the heart of your own home town, New York. And for the first time, NATO invoked our collective defence clause, Article 5. One for all, and all for one.'

I had teed up the shot for him. All Trump needed to do was highlight NATO's efforts when the United States was attacked, and reassure everyone present that the same would apply to them should they ever find themselves in need of help. Here, in front of the monument named after Article 5, I presumed Trump would acknowledge the obligations of the clause.

Trump began by speaking at length about the threat of terrorism. This wasn't so strange – just three days earlier, on the twenty-second of May, a suicide bomber had attacked the city of Manchester in the United Kingdom. Trump condemned the attack, which had killed 22 people and injured 119. After this, he touched on the threat represented by Russia.

But then came the accounting accusations.

'Twenty-three of the twenty-eight NATO nations are still not paying what they should be paying, what they are supposed to be paying, for their defence,' Trump said to the heads of state and government standing behind him on the lawn. 'This is not fair to the people and taxpayers of the United States. And many of these nations owe massive amounts of money from past years.'

There stood Merkel, Macron and all the other world leaders, and Trump was speaking about them as if they were tenants who were late paying their rent.

This was not the speech I had been expecting. On the previous day, we had privately been handed a copy of the speech the president would give. It was excellent, with all the important points covered, including the Article 5 obligations. But somewhere along the way, Trump must have chosen to give a different speech than the one that had been prepared.

As I stood beside Trump, I was able to glance down at the script from which he was reading. A few words had been added in thick, black marker: 'MUST PAY' and 'NOT FAIR'. And a little further down: '2% is the absolute minimum!' He had clearly crossed out certain things and added others, to amplify the message. I presumed these were the changes I had seen him make at the last minute, just before he stepped out of the car. Here he was, dedicating the 9/11 and Article 5 Memorial, and yet he hadn't said a word about Article 5.

The delegates walked back to the other side of the building, where the formal inauguration of the new headquarters would take place. I stood beside the prime minister of Montenegro, the alliance's newest member state. Suddenly Trump ploughed his way through the group, pushing the Montenegrin aside to attain a prominent position towards the front. The episode was captured by the TV cameras and attracted significant attention.

The flags were raised as the NATO hymn played.

When the ceremony was over, there was a brief break in the programme ahead of the working dinner. As the break was coming to an end, I went to collect Trump to accompany him to the dining hall. I entered Trump's room and saw him sitting at the end of a table, a Diet Coke in front of him. With him were Secretary of Defense Jim Mattis, National Security Advisor H.R. McMaster and Stephen Miller, one of the president's advisers and speechwriters. It was the first time I had met Miller. I had been told he was the man behind the speech Trump had given at his inauguration.

The four of them continued their discussion, hardly noticing my arrival. They were concerned with the address Trump was about to give during the dinner. I gathered from the conversation that there were two alternatives: a speech by Miller, and another favoured by Mattis and McMaster. The first was sharp in tone towards the Europeans, the other more conciliatory.

Trump weighed the pros and cons of each. Should he take the soft approach, or the hard one? Miller was in no doubt. 'You should take a hard line, Mr President. The Europeans need to be sent a clear message.'

McMaster tried to coax a different decision from Trump. 'They're both good,' he said, while also making it clear that he preferred the second, less confrontational speech. The discussion between the president and his advisers continued, and it was clearly a tug of war as to who had the greatest influence, who Trump listened to: the more moderate NATO-supporting Mattis and McMaster, or Miller, who was more of a NATO-sceptic.

Trump had been informed of the media's ongoing coverage of the summit. Commentators were already issuing some harsh criticism, pointing out that the president had neglected to express support for Article 5, and this irritated him.

He turned to me. 'Don't you agree, Secretary General, that it's unfair for them to criticise me for this? There's no reason to doubt the United States' support.'

Instead of responding to the question directly, I tried to recover the message and tone of our meeting in the White House. I reminded Trump that he had described himself as a strong supporter of NATO. 'The best way to express this is to emphasise your endorsement of Article 5 by referring to what the United States is actually doing. The US is increasing its military presence in Europe, which clearly illustrates that the US stands behind the security guarantee – not just in words, but also in action,' I said.

We left the room together. On the way out, I reminded Trump of the working dinner's programme. 'Do you think I should read from my speech, or is it better if I speak without a script?' he asked.

My impression was that he had decided to go for the more confrontational address. 'I don't think you need to give a pre-prepared speech,' I said. 'It's better … how can I put this … more *inspiring*, to listen to someone speaking more casually. This is an informal dinner, after all.'

Maybe he'll soften a little once he's in the room and sees everyone, I thought.

We walked in, and I showed him to his place next to mine. After starting with a brief introduction, I gave Trump the floor. 'It's great to be here,' he said, and followed up with a few friendly words about some of the individuals present. But his tone quickly changed. It was time to be even clearer than he had been earlier in the day, he said.

'I didn't want to say this so strongly out there, but I can do it in here. I have to tell you that the United States is not being treated fairly. Or – we've been pretty stupid for many years, with the Iran agreement and other things. But with NATO, there's no doubt. We're not being treated fairly.'

Mattis stole a glance at me, but his expression remained unchanged.

'I have to tell you,' Trump went on, 'that the United States isn't getting as much out of NATO as the rest of you around this table, no matter what everybody keeps telling me, including my own generals. And we pay much more.'

The complaint had become a hobby-horse for Trump. But this was the first time he had expressed it so directly to all the NATO leaders.

Then came what sounded ominously like a threat.

'It's important that you remember the United States is here. We're willing to show up, but we can't pay two, three and four times as much as everybody else. We're getting to the point of saying: We can't do this anymore, we don't want to do this. That moment is coming. Maybe we're almost there already. So people have to cough up the money. You have to pay.'

'I have a lot of respect for everybody in this room,' Trump said in closing, 'and I have a lot of respect for the secretary general. We're with you. But I hope you'll remember what I've said, because you'll never have a better partner than us. You can't use the United States. You just can't do it. Thank you.'

As Trump spoke, I glanced at the script he had in front of him but wasn't following. Even in the hard-line speech, the Article 5 obligations had been mentioned. It would have been better if he'd read the pre-prepared speech, instead of speaking off-the-cuff.

Other American presidents had also been critical of the fact that the majority of NATO countries were spending too little on defence.

But Trump's complaint was much more strongly worded. And what was truly new, was that he went so far as to say that if Europe and Canada didn't spend more, the United States would no longer guarantee their security.

The summit was drawing to a close. And among the gathered prime ministers and presidents, the seriousness of what had just taken place began to sink in.

13

A promise in Afghanistan

I CAST A GLANCE AT THE MAN I WAS FLYING WITH, US SECRETARY of defense Jim Mattis, as always smartly dressed in a suit and tie. The plane rattled and shook, but then again the C-17 Globemaster isn't exactly built for comfort. It's a huge American military transport aircraft, capable of carrying tanks and other heavy *matériel*. The soldiers sit in the cargo hold wearing earplugs and surrounded by all the equipment, which is tethered in place using straps. In the centre is a kind of campervan – the 'Silver Bullet'. This is the transport aircraft's answer to first class, and contains deep armchairs, sofas and desks. And it was there, in this box with no windows, that Mattis and I sat. It was the early hours of the twenty-seventh of September 2017, and we were on our way to Afghanistan.

We landed in Kabul in the splendid autumnal morning light. At the airport, we transferred to Chinook helicopters and were flown towards the city centre, to a meeting with President Ashraf Ghani.

A couple of years earlier, NATO's large-scale military operation in Afghanistan, the International Security Assistance Force (ISAF), had been replaced by a smaller training operation known as the Resolute Support Mission, which deployed around thirteen thousand soldiers. The United States was also running a counter-terrorism operation in the region, with special forces, drones and planes. The plan was for Resolute Support to last two years, and that after this, NATO would no longer need to have any military forces in Afghanistan. But things hadn't worked out that way. President Obama had not been able to end the war in Afghanistan, as he had promised in his 2012 election campaign. The price of sticking to the schedule that had been set for a full withdrawal was simply too high.

The aim was to enable the Afghan security forces to defend themselves in the war against both the Taliban and smaller terrorist groups. But the CIA briefings I received were discouraging, and presented a far bleaker picture than the reports NATO's military leaders were giving me. Desertion was an ever-increasing challenge for the government army, and many divisions suffered from poor leadership. Corruption was also a major problem. And the Afghans were vulnerable. The Afghan security forces had lost more soldiers in just twelve months than the ISAF force had in fifteen years, and they remained more dependent on US and NATO military forces than we had hoped. I doubted whether NATO's new strategies and our plans to withdraw could hold.

But someone who was in no doubt as to what he wanted in Afghanistan was Donald Trump. He was certain the American forces ought to be brought home. 'Why are we even there? We have to put an end to this war,' he had said at my first meeting with him in the White House. He would rather 'rebuild the United States' than Afghanistan, he said.

I argued for staying in Afghanistan. 'If we withdraw, it won't just be a tragedy for the Afghan people, but the country may once again become a hotbed of international terrorism,' I said.

Afghanistan's government had many weaknesses, but there was at least a governing team with which we were able to communicate. If we abandoned the Afghans, that would no longer be there should we be forced to return to the country in a few years' time. And then we would have to start the immense task of stabilising the region all over again.

This, after all, was what had happened in Iraq. The US withdrew its forces in 2011; just a few years later, Islamic State terrorists moved in and took control of large parts of the country, which had resulted in the United States and NATO allies being forced to return to Iraq, in order to neutralise IS.

Both Obama and Trump had been informed by their military leaders in no uncertain terms – any withdrawal from Afghanistan could not slavishly follow a pre-determined plan working to a deadline. To do this would allow the enemy to simply sit and wait, and then proclaim their victory the moment the withdrawal was completed. 'You have the watches, but we have the time,' as the Taliban liked to say. Commanding officers on the ground insisted that any withdrawal must be 'condition-based', and only undertaken once certain requirements had been fulfilled and concrete objectives achieved.

That military leaders viewed the situation this way wasn't unexpected. But more surprising was the input I received from German chancellor Angela Merkel. She was firm in her belief that NATO forces should remain in Afghanistan.

'We Germans might be a little slow off the mark,' she said, 'but once we've made a decision, we stand by it.' Merkel made no attempt to hide the fact that this was a matter of conscience for her. German forces were stationed in the Kunduz Province in northern Afghanistan, and in the years that they had been there, over fifty German soldiers had lost their lives. Merkel couldn't stand the thought of withdrawing from Kunduz only to see the Taliban move in. We had to ensure our soldiers hadn't died in vain. We owed that much to their families, Merkel said.

At the time, I too thought this way.

Staying in Afghanistan was the lesser of two evils. After all, our presence there in 2017 was much more limited than it had been previously. The political objective was to force peace negotiations – to make the Taliban realise they couldn't win on the battlefield, and that a solution would have to be carved out at the negotiating table.

During the spring and summer of 2017, over fifteen NATO member states declared they were prepared to stay in the country. But from the United States, there was only silence. We were promised clarification on the way forward as early as the upcoming summit in Brussels in

May, but it never came. Again, the same promise was made at the meeting of NATO ministers of defence in June; the clarification didn't arrive then, either. We'll have the decision for you in July, we were told. But July came and went.

The Afghans were anxious, and the press were growing impatient. I reassured everyone that we remained in close contact with the Americans, but this wasn't entirely true. We were in close contact with Secretary of Defense Mattis, but he wasn't in a position to deliver what he wanted due to the ongoing tug of war within the American administration, between those who wanted to stay and those who wanted out.

At the end of August, Trump finally laid out the United States' new strategy. The principle of a condition-based approach had been approved; instead of withdrawing, the US deployed a further three thousand soldiers to the region. Fighter jets were moved from Iraq and Syria to Afghanistan. The Taliban's havens in Pakistan would be dealt with. The threshold for the use of fighter jets and other offensive weapons was lowered, to make it easier to launch attacks on the terrorists.

The discussions within the American administration had been tough. McMaster and Mattis expended significant time and energy on getting Trump to change his mind, and I supported them. On the opposite side of the table was Trump's adviser and chief strategist, Steve Bannon. He was keen to see US troops withdrawn as soon as possible.

When Jim Mattis and I arrived in Afghanistan on that day in September, the situation in the country was challenging but not without its bright spots. At our meeting with President Ghani, we were informed that for the first time in a very long while, the Taliban no longer controlled a larger territory than it had the year before. The strategy of providing training, advice and assistance to the Afghan government's security forces seemed to be working more effectively. But for the time being, our military presence was important to keep the Taliban in check.

Ghani himself was forthcoming, and spoke in a slightly academic manner. He had studied and taught at American universities, and had worked at the World Bank. His government had been strengthened by Trump's decision to send more troops to the region, but it nevertheless remained a rickety structure. Ethnic tensions smouldered just below the surface, and Ghani was accused of favouring the Pashtun, the community to which he himself belonged. Leading cabinet members were in reality opposed to a national unity government in delicate ethnic balance.

IS didn't seem to be succeeding in its attempts to gain a solid foothold, and this was one of the meeting's main discussion points.

'We need extremely good reasons to send our boys and girls here to risk their lives, but the war on terror is such a reason,' Mattis said. The message that Mattis and I both wished to convey was that Afghanistan could never again serve as a safe haven for international terrorists. This was what we risked by withdrawing too early. And the more stable Afghanistan was, the safer we would be.

As we sat with Ghani, an attack was attempted on the airport at which we had landed just a few hours earlier. Grenades fired from mortars struck the area directly beside the terminal building. The intended target was US secretary of defense Jim Mattis and his huge military aircraft, but by the time the grenades began to rain down on the airport the plane had already been moved to the Bagram base north of Kabul. Afghan security forces, supported by Norwegian special forces, located those responsible in a building in a residential area around half a mile away; four Taliban fighters were killed when the special forces struck. American helicopters also fired two Hellfire missiles as part of the counter-attack. One of them missed the target, and a civilian was killed.

After the meeting with Ghani we were transported back to the airport to travel to the Gamberi base, more than ninety miles east of Kabul. Due to the attack on the airport our journey was delayed by an hour, and we circled above Kabul for a long time before being cleared to continue on to Gamberi. The helicopter was hot and clammy. I sat there wearing my suit and tie, but also a helmet; I had terrible jet lag and was so tired that I kept nodding off, waking myself with a jolt every time my head, weighted by the helmet, dropped forward. Machine gunners manned the doorways on either side, and the soldiers occasionally fired off flares to counter heat-seeking missiles, so the missiles would target the flares instead of striking the helicopter. A stark reminder that Afghanistan was far from the peaceful country we wished it to be.

We landed in a field fortified by sandbags and were led into the camp at Gamberi. During the day, the soldiers went out and patrolled the wild desert landscape bordering the Himalayas and Hindu Kush. In the distance, jagged, snow-covered peaks towered against the sky; below them, hillcrests undulated towards the horizon. It was an immensely beautiful but dangerous area. Taliban fighters might be hiding in the valleys. Mines might lie hidden along the footpaths. Suicide bombers might have infiltrated civilian areas. And when the soldiers returned to the camp, it was unsafe there, too.

Relations between the Afghan soldiers and NATO forces were generally good. They helped each other, supporting one another on their day-long patrols, and as often as not, they saved each other's lives. They were comrades-in-arms.

But not always. The phenomenon that had become known as 'green on blue' posed a mortal threat. Afghan soldiers recruited by the Taliban would suddenly draw their weapons inside the camp and open fire on the NATO soldiers who were there to train and help them. It wasn't always easy to know who was friend and who was foe.

To reduce the risk of such inside attacks, the Gamberi camp was divided into two strictly separated areas. You first entered the largest part of the camp, which was home to the Afghan forces, around two thousand men. To enter the NATO area, you had to pass through massive barricades and other security measures. So this is what's become necessary, I thought, as I moved through the checkpoint inside the camp. I couldn't shake the thought that the security measures were a sign that there was something deeply wrong in the relationship between those of us in NATO and the people we were in Afghanistan to help. Only once we were deep into the NATO area did we see a memorial wall with the images and names of our soldiers who had lost their lives. *Fallen but not forgotten.* It was a reminder of just how great a risk people took in choosing to come here.

Before our visit, the soldiers had tidied, cleaned and decorated the camp as best they could, but there was no hiding the fact that it was a somewhat run-down and spartan place. Bombproof concrete walls, barbed wire, surveillance cameras and makeshift containers out on a windswept, sandy plain – this was Gamberi. All the security measures made me feel safe, but the claustrophobic sense of being confined was a constant feature of my time there.

We were given a briefing in a map room, along with an explanation of the tactical assessments made before various types of mission. This was where Jim Mattis showed how things ought to be done – he combined academic knowledge with pragmatism and humility, and in the mess hall afterwards he was even more in his element. Here, surrounded by the young soldiers, Mattis stood and spoke as he gestured around him; he had served in the area himself, and was well acquainted with it.

'Surely you've been to the little stream just over the crest of that hill?' he might say. Or: 'Don't let the officers bully you over polishing your boots and making your beds' – to howling cheers and whistles from his audience.

'You are Black and white, Christians and Muslims, you come from different ethnic backgrounds. Every day, here in this camp, you show how the world's most diverse society can stand united,' Mattis said to several hundred NATO soldiers gathered in the mess hall, most of them Americans.

This was right after a heated debate had broken out about whether trans people should be allowed in the US military, and just over a month after the terrorist attack in Charlottesville, in which a right-wing extremist had driven his car into a group of protesters, killing one of them. Mattis's speech was a response to the divisions within American society. Here, far from home in Afghanistan, there should be no doubt as to which ideals were important. 'We can do this. No matter our race or our sexual orientation,' he said.

'We have a common goal,' Mattis went on. 'It's why you get up every day. To fight for freedom. Together. Our enemies think we're fat and lazy. That our democracies aren't strong enough to send soldiers to fight for what we believe in. You're proving them wrong.'

The atmosphere was electric. The message hit home.

Mattis concluded with a story from the war in Iraq. One night, when Mattis was in his tent, some of his soldiers came by with a man they had taken prisoner. They had caught him trying to plant a home-made bomb nearby. The bomb had been intended for Mattis.

'Why did you try to kill me?' Mattis had asked the prisoner, who sat before him with zip ties around his wrists. The man managed to stammer that the Americans were imperialists who wanted to take Iraq's oil. Mattis cut the zip ties and offered the man a cigarette – to the soldiers in Gamberi, Mattis explained that he 'figured it wasn't the time to tell the guy just how bad for you smoking is'. Instead, he told the prisoner he might be sent to the Abu Ghraib prison. After another cigarette, and then another, the prisoner asked Mattis if he thought it would be possible for him to emigrate and seek political asylum in the United States.

The man who wanted to murder the American imperialists also wanted to become an American. *That* was the point of the story. The power of intimidation and the power of inspiration. The threat of Abu Ghraib, but also the alluring freedom of the United States of America.

'We won't always win, we won't always succeed. We're not perfect, but we'll always be the good guys,' Mattis said.

He spoke in an open and direct way. In one of the corridors I saw him pass a soldier who stood ready in his helmet, sunglasses and bulletproof vest; earpiece in place, machine-gun in hand, a knife in his belt. Mattis looked at him and said: 'You are ready to kill.' Norwegian officers don't speak this way. Still, it was a fairly accurate description of the soldier's task. 'Kill' was a word I heard Mattis use quite often. But at the same time, when speaking with the soldiers, he would also say things like: 'You must do everything within your power to avoid civilian losses. Try to get on the same wavelength as the ordinary

Afghans. Show them openness. Take off those sunglasses when you meet people.'

Mattis wanted to take a hard, offensive approach in Afghanistan, because he was convinced that was the fastest way to end the war. The mission was actually simple, as he formulated it in his meetings with the soldiers: 'We're here, and we're not going to surrender. We want a political solution, but those who refuse and want to fight, we'll go up against. Some will flee, some will negotiate, and some will join us.' He left a brief pause.

'The rest we're going to kill.'

After a few hours at Gamberi, we flew back to Kabul. That evening, the head of the bodyguard force, a Danish officer, sought me out. He said I could go to bed, but asked me to make sure I had some clothes on – if the alarm sounded I would have ten seconds to get out of the room and under the stairs. We were quartered in a property inside NATO's base, with high walls and extensive security on the ground. But the roof was vulnerable. It wouldn't withstand a missile strike.

So I went to bed fully clothed that night.

I struggled to sleep, so took out a book I had brought with me: *Return of a King* by the Scottish historian William Dalrymple. The British invaded Afghanistan for the first time in 1839, but three years later great swathes of the population rose up in protest against the king the British had appointed. The British Army was forced to withdraw, and almost twenty thousand men lost their lives during the freezing-cold campaign. It felt strangely close to home to read about the Khyber Pass, Jalalabad, Kandahar, Mazar-i-Sharif. The same mountain passes, valleys and cities often referred to in current war reporting.

Alexander the Great entered the area with his mighty army as early as the 300s BC, and described the intense opposition he encountered. He was unsuccessful in his attempt to conquer this part of Asia, and died while returning home from the campaign. In our time, the Soviet Union had tried to take control of Afghanistan, first by offering support to a communist-led coup, and then through military intervention and war. The Soviets didn't manage to win, however, and the humiliating defeat in their neighbouring country to the south helped trigger the Soviet Union's fall.

It is not for nothing that Afghanistan is referred to as the graveyard of empires.

And now NATO was there. With a large-scale military operation, offering extensive economic and political support to a government in Kabul that was fighting a rebel movement that showed no signs of giving up. After sixteen years, there was still no peace.

Earlier that day, I had met one of Afghanistan's most famous music artists, Aryana Sayeed. The Taliban had threatened to kill her – they were going to liquidate her, they said, if she didn't stop holding concerts. But Sayeed refused to bend, and continued with her career. She had recently played a concert in front of thousands in Kabul.

I also met two students in their twenties from Kabul University, a woman and man. As our conversation was drawing to a close, the woman gently took hold of my arm and said: 'You have to stay. You can't go now.' Her fellow student followed up with: 'Everything will be lost if you abandon us.'

There existed a young, forward-looking Afghanistan, one people like Sayeed and these two students stood for. They represented a possible future. Young, progressive individuals, who wanted women to be able to get an education and be involved in building the country. Who believed in modernisation, knowledge, equality and freedom of the press. Who believed it was possible to fight corruption. They would never forgive us if we left.

The cost of withdrawing versus the cost of staying. This was what it came down to in Afghanistan. NATO countries paid a high price for being in the region, both in blood and treasure. But the costs involved in leaving the country would also be significant. An increased risk of terrorist attacks, and a tragedy for all Afghans who dreamed of freedom and democracy. The country's women in particular would face dark times.

NATO and the United States had just decided that we would remain in Afghanistan until the government's security forces were able to defeat the Taliban themselves. I promised the students we were going to stay. And back then, in 2017, I was sure it was a promise we would keep.

14

European illusions

ALL AT ONCE THE SKY ABOVE ME WAS FILLED WITH PARACHUTES. Below them hung tiny human dots, which grew larger and larger as they approached the ground. Soon they landed all around me. First to touch down was a man of around fifty. He unhooked from his parachute, pulled off his suit, took his weapon in a firm grip and strode towards me. A moment later he stood before me in full uniform, saluted and said: 'The lead element of the 82nd Airborne Division at your service, sir!'

I was on the sun-scorched plains that surround Zaragoza in Spain. Beside me stood the head of NATO's land command, General John Nicholson Jr., who a few months earlier had become head of the United States' and NATO's forces in Afghanistan. NATO's biggest military exercise in several decades, Trident Juncture 2015, was well underway. It was happening simultaneously in a number of countries, and all branches of the army were participating. The land-based part of the exercise was taking place in Spain, and we had just observed how modern infantry enter urban settlements.

The paratroopers completed their airdrop. They had come directly from Fort Bragg in North Carolina, one of the world's largest military bases, in huge transport aircraft. The scenario for the exercise was that an acute crisis requiring American military assistance had arisen in Spain. The moment the order was given, the soldiers loaded up their equipment and boarded the planes. A few hours later, they were hanging from their parachutes above Zaragoza, on the other side of the Atlantic.

The 82nd Airborne Division is one of the most legendary units of the American army. The division was brought in during the invasion of Normandy in June 1944, and in the bloody Battle of the Bulge at the end of the same year. It played a key role in the liberation of Kuwait in 1991, and has served in Kosovo as well as in several other NATO operations.

The division consists of around fifteen thousand highly trained soldiers, divided into four brigades. One of these brigades is always combat ready at Fort Bragg, 24 hours a day, 365 days a year. Within eighteen hours, the soldiers can be deployed into combat anywhere on the globe.

I had attended many meetings at which NATO's Article 5 and the United States' security guarantee had been discussed. I knew it was invaluable, and I was well aware that it was the very core of the alliance. But on this sunny autumn day outside Zaragoza, I saw what it truly meant. Just how critical the United States is to Europe's security. The planes that crossed the Atlantic, coming directly from North Carolina. The parachutes that rained down from the sky in rapid succession. The brigadier who came up to me and reported his soldiers ready for battle. The security guarantee was being demonstrated before my very eyes.

Throughout my first couple of years in NATO, General Philip Breedlove held the position of SACEUR, the supreme commander of NATO's forces in Europe. Breedlove was a knowledgeable man and former fighter pilot. He liked to wander around in his battledress, and it suited his slightly rough and ready style. Ukraine was a topic we discussed often; Breedlove was constantly pushing for more support, and felt frustrated at the allies who were hesitant to provide it.

Once, when I visited him in Mons, around an hour's drive from Brussels, he told me why NATO's military headquarters had ended up precisely there. 'In 1966, President Charles de Gaulle decided to throw NATO and the United States out of France. Our headquarters had been in Paris, so we went north, over the border into Belgium, and in Mons we found this castle. It was so beautiful we just had to stay here. The Belgians pay for it, so we're very happy.'

The relocation operation described by Breedlove, albeit in his rather unceremonious way, came about as a result of internal tensions that had existed ever since the alliance was founded – that is, France's relationship with NATO. It was a matter of national self-image, political priorities and prominent figures. When President de Gaulle threw NATO out of Paris, he also withdrew France from NATO's military command. This meant the country was still party to the political cooperation, but would no longer participate in the alliance's defence cooperation. No French officers would serve in NATO's command structure, and all overseas soldiers had to leave the country.

US president Lyndon B. Johnson was furious. His secretary of state, Dean Rusk, was scheduled to meet with the French president not long after, and Johnson instructed Rusk to ask de Gaulle if the order to leave French soil also applied to the sixty thousand American soldiers killed in France during the Second World War, and who now lay buried in French war cemeteries. Rusk was hesitant, believing that such a question would offend the French president. But Johnson insisted: 'Ask him about the cemeteries, Dean!' The request was made a presidential order, so when Rusk met with de Gaulle, he had no choice but to ask. De Gaulle is said to have got up and left the room without responding.

De Gaulle nursed a deep-rooted mistrust of the United States' dominance within NATO. After the Soviet Union had developed intercontinental ballistic missiles capable of reaching the American continent, he had little faith that the Americans would actually defend Europe. Would they really risk New York to protect Paris?

In de Gaulle's eyes, France was a superpower with its own nuclear weapons and means of deterrence. He wanted his country to play an independent role in international politics, autonomous from the United States and the Cold War's East–West conflict.

In 2009, France chose to rejoin NATO's military cooperation, but the attitudes and viewpoints from de Gaulle's time endured. Shortly after

Emmanuel Macron was elected president in 2017, he gave a speech at the Sorbonne, in which he spoke at length about his vision for a strong and independent Europe, including when it came to the region's security policy. He subsequently reiterated this message a number of times by supporting the idea that Europe should distance itself from both the United States and China. Basically, this was about Europe having what Macron referred to as 'strategic autonomy'. And to achieve this, an independent European defence would be necessary.

Various European politicians take differing views of the term 'strategic autonomy' and of the desire for increased cooperation on defence within the EU. If it involves increasing defence budgets, making the European defence industry more competitive and focusing on the development of military technologies, then this is nothing but advantageous for all NATO countries. But if it means the EU is to build up its own military structures and plans to take over more of Europe's defence, then it will rapidly weaken NATO, and consequently our common security.

There are many significant challenges relating to the economy, the environment and technology that the EU should solve independently, but when it comes to defence and security, I am convinced that Europe and North America have to stand united – through NATO. The EU cannot defend Europe. This is partly about resources; around 80 per cent of defence expenditure in NATO is provided by countries that are not members of the EU. It's also partly about geographical facts, which become obvious the moment you take a glance at a map. There is Turkey in the south-east, Norway in the north, and the United Kingdom, the United States and Canada in the west. None of these nations belong to the EU.

Furthermore, the vision of 'strategic autonomy' is a concept on which Europe is divided. The countries in the east have been traditionally opposed to weakening Europe's ties to the United States; they know the US alone has sufficient military strength to guarantee their security.

NATO has no army of its own, but it does have a standing command structure manned by military officers. In the event of a crisis, each

NATO country can plug its army and other armed forces into this framework. If the EU wishes to become independent – 'autonomous' – from a military point of view, EU countries will also have to establish this kind of command structure. But since almost all the EU nations are also members of NATO, that would take away resources from the alliance, and duplicate critical functions. Two half-filled command structures are far less effective than one that is fully staffed.

The EU also has a solidarity clause, which states that the member nations must assist one another if an EU country is subjected to a terrorist or military attack or major natural disaster. While the EU clause isn't worded like NATO's Article 5, in the event of an attack on a country that is a member of both organisations it is still technically possible to question which of these clauses ought to be invoked. Any shred of doubt around this illustrates the problem of having two solidarity clauses – if there is something we *don't* have time for in the event a nation is attacked, it's a debate between Washington, London, Paris and Berlin over whether NATO or the EU should come to that nation's aid.

I have brought up Europe's military dependence on the United States many times, including in a presentation I gave to the German government in the magnificent Schloss Meseberg palace north of Berlin in the spring of 2018. The palace was once owned by a Prussian prince, and in the interwar period Nazi leader Hermann Goering managed to get his hands on it. Towering at the end of a long, paved avenue and surrounded by lush deciduous trees, the whitewashed palace is currently in use as a venue for conferences held by the German government.

I emphasised that I strongly supported a close cooperation between the EU and NATO, and said I was happy that I, together with EU leaders Donald Tusk and Jean-Claude Juncker, had succeeded in strengthening this partnership. I also made it clear that I support European nations both spending more on, and taking greater responsibility for, their own defence. But the EU's defence efforts must take place from *within* NATO – not in competition with the transatlantic alliance.

This was my main message at Schloss Meseberg. In Germany and within EU circles there were many who supported the idea of European 'strategic autonomy'. But I believed the EU's ambition to develop its own defence and an independent security policy, separate from the United States, to be dangerously naive. To illustrate this point, I spoke about what had happened in Libya in 2011.

The bombing of Libya was a European initiative, with then French president Nicolas Sarkozy in the driving seat; as Norway's prime minister, I had been present at the Palais de l'Élysée in Paris when the decision to go forward with the military intervention was made. US secretary of state Hillary Clinton was also there, and made it clear that while the United States supported the operation, they would not take on any central role. NATO's secretary general at the time, Anders Fogh Rasmussen, wasn't invited to attend the meeting in Paris. NATO wasn't involved – not in the operation's planning, preparations or implementation. This was France and the United Kingdom's intervention, but they would receive assistance from several smaller European countries, Norway among them. It soon became apparent, however, that the Europeans needed help.

'Before the French and the British could begin bombing, the Libyan air defences had to be knocked out. That required advanced missiles and aircraft with electronic weapons. The Europeans don't have much of that kind of equipment, but the United States does,' I told the German ministers.

The Europeans asked the United States if they could help out by eliminating Gaddafi's air defences before they started bombing. And that's exactly what happened.

The next obstacle was identifying suitable targets. This was about finding the right building and making 100 per cent certain that it was a military target – nobody wanted to strike the neighbouring mosque or school. To enable such precise attacks, detailed intelligence from advanced drones and satellites was required, often accompanied by people on the ground who could positively identify the target and lead the bombers towards it.

'The Europeans didn't have enough of any of this. But the United

States had the resources necessary to run intelligence, surveillance and reconnaissance, ISR. And so the Americans also assisted with finding appropriate targets to bomb,' I said.

The Europeans quickly ran out of ammunition, and didn't have access to enough fuel. Precision bombers were brought out of their hangars in the United States, and the Americans provided special aircraft for refuelling in the air. Most critical was the lack of qualified personnel to lead the operation around the clock, day after day. The whole thing soon ended up becoming a NATO operation, in which the alliance's permanent command structure was activated.

'We must have no illusions about what Europe can accomplish alone,' I concluded.

The Libya operation was contentious, and questions were raised about whether it went beyond the UN Security Council mandate, which had been intended to force a ceasefire and prevent attacks on civilians. But what I said at Schloss Meseberg was not delivered as part of that debate – my point was to illustrate how the Europeans had been forced to rely on US military resources.

At the time of the Libya operation, Barack Obama had been president of the United States. Now Donald Trump was in the White House. After that challenging first summit with him in 2017, most European NATO nations believed the entire transatlantic cooperation ought to be deprioritised until the US had elected another president. In their view, Trump was too erratic, too difficult to work with. Many quite simply wanted to put NATO on ice.

My colleagues and I did our utmost to challenge this view. If NATO was going to survive, there was no alternative but to work with the US president. We had to get President Trump to stand behind the alliance.

The question of whether it was possible to trust a United States led by Donald Trump was constantly being asked in Europe, and with increasing urgency. The president's attacks on European politicians and his unpredictability were used as arguments in favour of 'strategic autonomy'. Trump was therefore fuelling the forces within the EU who believed Europe should stand alone. And in much the same way, the Americans could use those same forces within Europe to promote Trump's message in the United States. The more President Macron and others spoke about an autonomous EU defence, the more tempting it would be for Trump to take them at their word: The Europeans want to defend themselves? What could be better! We'll save billions of dollars!

Trump was firmly rooted in a long isolationist tradition – there has always been strong support in the US for keeping the country out of any conflict in Europe, and understandably so. There have to be good reasons for sacrificing American lives on European soil. The United States stayed neutral when the First World War broke out in 1914, and only joined the conflict in April 1917, after the Germans had resumed their unrestricted submarine warfare in the Atlantic, which hit the US hard. Only in the spring of 1918 were there enough American soldiers on the battlefields of France for their presence to have a decisive impact on the war's outcome.

As late as during his election campaign in the autumn of 1940, when the war in Europe had been raging for over a year, Franklin D. Roosevelt made a promise to all American parents: 'I have said this before, but I shall say it again and again and again: Your boys are not going to be sent into any foreign wars.' Nevertheless, he became the American president who decided to send American forces to Europe to defeat Hitler.

For over seventy years, NATO had managed to withstand external pressure and internal tensions. The Soviet Union had dissolved, the Cold War was won. But what now, with Donald Trump in the White House?

I had become head of NATO to help fortify the bridge across the Atlantic. The importance of remaining united was my main message in all my conversations with political leaders, in the meetings of the North Atlantic Council within NATO, and in the interviews I gave. But over the course of the spring of 2018, in advance of NATO's July summit, the distance between the two continents seemed to be growing ever greater. The political currents were driving Europe and the

United States in different directions, and they amplified each other in a negative spiral. It was not a given that the transatlantic partnership would hold.

In the weeks before the summit I often thought of the American paratroopers floating down above the plains outside Zaragoza. We knew how much they meant, what they represented. A world in which the United States neglected to come to Europe's aid in a crisis would be a more dangerous world. We must not end up there, under any circumstances.

15

An atmosphere of crisis in Brussels

'HERE COMES MY BIG MONEY COLLECTOR!'

These were the words with which Donald Trump welcomed me as I entered the Oval Office in mid-May 2018. Meeting the president of the United States was always an important part of preparations for any NATO summit. Now just two months remained until the next one, and like the previous year's summit, it would be held in Brussels.

As usual, Trump jumped from one topic to the next, constantly going off on a tangent. But he was in a good mood and said many positive things about NATO, although he once again complained that many countries were still spending far below 2 per cent of GDP on defence. He lashed out at Germany in particular, but also mentioned Denmark, the Netherlands and Norway. Rich countries who had a moral obligation to do more.

'Can we kick them out?' Trump asked. 'Can't Norway just go with the Swedish model, if they don't want to pay?' This was Trump's business mentality talking – if Norway wasn't willing to pay for 'full NATO', maybe they should go for the 'half NATO' option instead, a looser connection to the organisation, like the one the Swedes had. If you want full coverage, then you have to pay the full insurance premium. This was Trump's logic. I told him that Norway did not want to loosen its ties to NATO.

Back in Brussels, I knew that the summit might prove difficult. A G7 summit in Canada in June had ended in a somewhat dramatic fashion. After intense negotiations, the heads of state and government from the world's economic superpowers had managed to agree on a joint statement. But the fragile consensus was short-lived. Aboard Air Force One directly after the meeting, Donald Trump learned of Canadian prime minister Justin Trudeau's concluding press conference, at which Trudeau criticised the tariffs the US president had introduced on imports of steel and aluminium.

A furious Trump tweeted that he was retracting his support for the joint statement. Trudeau had 'acted so meek and mild' at the summit, only to criticise him at the press conference. 'Very dishonest & weak,' Trump tweeted.

We had to avoid the NATO summit ending in a similar breakdown. I knew how preoccupied the president was with fairer burden sharing, and that this would be one of the main topics of discussion. Nevertheless, I felt fairly sure the summit would go according to plan, because we had a positive story to tell: European countries had now made greater increases to their defence budgets than they had for many years, and Trump had helped to bring this about. He could take ownership of something that was a real success. It was therefore my hope that this would prove to be a unifying summit.

One Friday, a couple of weeks before the summit, I was due to speak with Trump by telephone. It was a call he had requested, and since we had recently met in Washington, it wasn't immediately clear why he had asked to speak to me again.

I sat in my office at NATO headquarters in Brussels and waited. It always took the operators at the White House a little time to establish the connection to the Oval Office, and on this occasion, it seemed to take even longer than usual. But I finally heard Donald Trump's unmistakable voice on the other end of the line.

'Hello, how are you?'

'Thank you, very good, Mr President! It's very sunny here in Brussels.'

I was about to say more about how lovely the weather was in Brussels that day, which for once it actually was, but Trump interrupted me.

'Well, Brussels is always sunny for me. But it used to be a lot more sunny, if you know what I mean.'

I didn't, but I had no time to reflect any further on Trump's meaning, because he launched into telling me how great things were going in the United States. The economy was running in high gear, despite the fact that he'd been handed a country in ruins. But he hadn't called me to brag about how he had managed to get the United States back on an even keel. Defence spending, and the sharing of the financial burden between NATO's member states, was what he really wanted to talk about.

'Germany is paying one per cent! It's shocking.' According to Trump, Angela Merkel was in trouble.

I told Trump that Merkel was working to increase Germany's defence budget, but that she was leader of a coalition government, and it wasn't always easy to reach a consensus. Trump cut me off.

'Migration is the big problem. It was a terrible decision.' He was referring to all the refugees that had fled to Germany during Europe's refugee crisis.

Then he returned to the subject of the defence budgets. Spain was spending less than 1 per cent of GDP on defence. King of Spain Felipe VI had just made a state visit to Washington, and Trump had received him at the White House.

'They were here and they said: "Thank you for the military protection." But Spain's economy is good. This is very unfair.'

Trump had recently met with Merkel, too, and told her things simply couldn't carry on the way they were, with Germany spending only 1 per cent of GDP on defence.

'I said, "Angela, you have to cough up. You need to spend two per cent." She said, "Maybe in 2030" – and she laughed as she said it. She's a criminal. She *laughed*!'

Trump said the United States was spending 4 per cent of GDP on defence, and that they covered 80 to 90 per cent of NATO's expenses.

'And we're not doing it anymore. We're gonna pay what Germany pays.'

'I agree that currently, the burden isn't equally shared,' I said. 'But the good news is the trend has turned. The Europeans are paying more. I've often said that the pressure you applied, Mr President, has given results, and—'

'Tell the media that!' Trump interrupted me again. 'You feel like an idiot when you're paying eighty to ninety per cent. Listen – I'm a businessman. And I've decided to pay the same as Germany.'

We had spoken about how the financial burden was shared among NATO nations many times before. Trump usually liked to be reminded of how the trend in Europe had changed – this was the source of his many statements along the lines of 'the money is flowing in thanks to me'. At a rally in Florida a few months earlier, Trump had said: 'I will tell you the Secretary General Stoltenberg is [my] biggest fan.' I had said several times that Trump's message had worked, and this recognition was something he obviously appreciated.

Of course, it was hard to measure Trump's impact as compared to what had been achieved under Obama. Had the Europeans increased their defence spending because Obama pushed them to promise to do so at the summit in Wales in 2014? Or was it due to Russia's aggression? Or because they were fearful of Trump's threats? We'll never know for sure, but it was entirely reasonable to say that Donald Trump's messaging had indeed contributed to the increases in defence spending.

Yet on this occasion, my praise had no effect. Trump's anger, especially towards Germany, dominated the conversation. Trump continued to speak about it with a focused energy, while I tried to paint a more positive picture.

'Clear promises on sharing the burden more fairly, and a successful summit, will be a great victory for you,' I said.

'Do it before the summit,' Trump said. 'It's a terrible deal. This country was run by idiots.'

I tried to remind Trump that NATO was also a source of support for the United States – that the Americans didn't go to war alone. In Afghanistan, we stood shoulder to shoulder.

But the president didn't want to hear about this, either, claiming he'd prefer it if the Europeans kept their soldiers at home.

'It's just another way of trying to pacify me. They send a few people. Germany has two hundred in Afghanistan. And Angela *laughs*. My grandfather came from Germany, but from a much tougher region than she comes from.'

In an attempt to change the subject, I brought up Russia again, which we had touched on briefly at the start of our conversation. Trump was due to meet President Putin directly after the NATO summit.

'It's good that you're in dialogue with Russia,' I said. 'I've always maintained that's important. I've negotiated with Putin myself several times, and we agreed on some important questions.'

But Trump refused to be derailed. He said he would rather spend his money on the United States. Germany was now under Russian control because they imported Russian gas, he said.

'They are feeding the beast. You should have prevented this. Get things cleared up before the summit – I'm not going to explain it to them. I have to go now. You explain it to them.'

The call was over. Stian Jenssen was sitting opposite me, and he had been listening in on the conversation. A couple of years earlier, when Torgeir Larsen left his position as head of my private office, I had been in no doubt as to who I wanted to replace him in this key role. Ever since he had joined my team before my taking office, Stian had proved to be an outstanding colleague with a deep understanding of how NATO functioned.

Now I looked at him. And Stian looked at me. It was a while before either of us spoke.

There was no mistaking Trump's warning: 'Look, if we leave, we leave. You need NATO, desperately. We don't need NATO.'

The president of the United States was angry. He would no longer accept Europe and Canada paying too little. He simply refused to allow it.

If the United States withdrew, the alliance would be dead. Trump had made me responsible for NATO's possible dissolution. He wanted me to set things straight before the summit. And the summit was twelve days away.

Luckily, I wasn't starting from scratch. Defence spending was increasing, but it simply wasn't happening fast enough. To help pick up the pace, I had spoken with many heads of state and government that spring to emphasise the urgency of the situation. On the ninth of April, it had been Angela Merkel's turn. She listened, but reminded me that in a parliamentary democracy you can't simply click your fingers and conjure up huge sums for defence. 'I'm doing my best, Jens, but it's your social democratic friends in the Bundestag who are holding things up.'

As I hung up the phone, I considered the historic irony. On the ninth of April, the day Germany had invaded Norway in 1940, I had called the German chancellor and begged her to spend more money on the country's military. If I got my way, Germany would once more become the largest military force in Europe. Today, when Polish leaders are asked if they fear a militarised Germany, they say that what they fear is a *weak* Germany. That's how much the world has changed.

Trump had replaced his security advisor, H.R. McMaster, earlier that spring, and appointed former UN ambassador John Bolton to the role. Bolton had been listening in on my conversation with the president, and called me straight afterwards. There was no one else listening in on his end, he said, and he asked me to send out anyone present on mine. This would be a conversation between just him and me.

'This is no joke. The president is serious when he says the United States is going to pay the same as Germany,' Bolton warned. 'You have to find a solution.'

Bolton referred to the press reports that claimed there were a handful of 'adults in the room' – people in Trump's circle who made sure to clean up after the president whenever he went too far.

'The president reads those articles, and he doesn't like them. Don't underestimate him now. This issue isn't going to be solved by any "adults",' Bolton said.

I already understood that we mustn't underestimate Trump's ability to make good on his threats. But what had he actually meant when he said he wouldn't pay more than Germany? Bolton didn't know, either.

As the sun shone over Brussels, the weekend became one long shift at the office. Our telephone conversation had been a warning that Trump intended to confront NATO head-on. Preparations for the summit had been comprehensive, and we wanted to show that the alliance was still able to function well, even in challenging times. Trump had recently shaken the Europeans by withdrawing the United States from the Iran agreement, which detailed how sanctions against Iran would gradually be lifted if the Iranians refrained from developing nuclear weapons and permitted inspection of their nuclear facilities. On Twitter, he was critical of Europe and of the region's refugee, trade and energy policies. But I still hoped that Trump would see that NATO was delivering. We were doing more in the war on terror and we had increased our defence spending, but clearly this wasn't enough. We had to come up with something else.

The critical question was how we were going to accommodate Trump's repeated demand that the United States and Germany should 'pay the same'. At that time, Germany's defence budget comprised around €40 billion, while the American budget was as much as fifteen times larger. Even when calculated as a percentage of GDP, the difference between the two countries' defence budgets was vast. So any notion that each country's total defence expenditure should be 'the same' was entirely unrealistic.

Luckily, we found another way forward – one that enabled us to show that the United States was not paying more than Germany – and that was by looking at NATO's own budget. This budget covers expenses relating to the operation of the organisation's civilian head-quarters, some of the costs associated with the military command structure, and a number of investments in military facilities and capacities such as AWACS surveillance planes and drones, while the major costs of maintaining standing armies and deploying them on various NATO missions are covered by the member states themselves.

The United States was paying much of the NATO common budget at €2.5 billion. By adjusting this figure, it was possible that we could enable the United States and Germany to pay the same without the involved sums becoming excessive. The question was whether this would be enough for Trump. It all came down to whether it was the symbolic or the actual amounts that were most important to him. We simply didn't know.

By Sunday evening, our first draft of the document was complete. We calculated that in the previous year, the allies had spent $33 billion more on defence – a figure we could present to illustrate that things were moving in the right direction. This was the most important point in the draft. Another was to get the allies to agree to more concrete increases in their defence budgets. A third was that the Europeans would pay a large portion of the costs incurred by the US in having American forces stationed in Europe. At first, we shared the draft with just a few close colleagues, because several of the proposals would be contentious.

The United States incurred significant costs associated with its forces stationed in Europe. European countries contributed to a certain extent, by providing bases and facilities, but most of the expenses were covered by the Americans themselves. The allies had previously paid for American military assistance in the past – in 1991, for example, when a US-led coalition liberated Kuwait from Saddam Hussein's occupation, Germany paid almost $6 billion in compensation for not sending their own troops. So the Germans could also pay for American soldiers to be stationed in Europe, we reasoned. Especially since the number of American soldiers had increased since 2014.

This was clearly a controversial proposal. And we hadn't yet got everyone on board with the idea of adjusting the contributions to NATO's common budget so that the United States and Germany paid the same. Both proposals were intended as emergency measures, should the summit reach breaking point.

We also calculated the effects of the member states' plans to further increase defence spending, which showed that the sums would rise significantly in the years ahead. And these increases represented a win for Trump.

Over the days that followed, I spoke with Bolton and Mike Pompeo, who had taken over from Rex Tillerson as US secretary of state some months earlier. In Washington, everyone now had a single focus – the work to get conservative judge Brett Kavanaugh nominated to the Supreme Court. The nomination would take place just before the NATO summit.

The nomination of judges to the United States' highest court is of major political significance. The Republicans had a slim majority in the Senate, and it would be a huge victory for Trump to get Kavanaugh appointed. Bolton and Pompeo wanted to use this to their advantage to the greatest extent possible. They therefore tried to convince the president not to threaten that the United States would leave NATO – conflict at the NATO summit would attract significant attention, and overshadow the Kavanaugh victory.

Trump didn't disagree with this. But Bolton told me he still continued to ask why they couldn't just pull the United States out of the alliance.

The proposals we had managed to prepare were a way of testing the waters, and I showed them to Bolton. He seemed interested, but was more concerned with the manner in which we should proceed. To avoid a breakdown, it was vital that we agreed on everything in advance. 'Did you see the images from the G7 summit, where the president alone was seated, while all the other leaders stood over him? He didn't like that. We can't have anything that reminds him of that, a situation in which everyone is pressuring the president,' Bolton said. 'We need to avoid any negotiations at the meeting itself.'

I took his point, but such a plan broke with the way in which the summits were usually arranged. While it was customary to have most issues agreed upon in advance, a certain pressure on the heads of state at the meeting itself was often necessary to get the final resolutions over the line. But there was no mistaking Bolton's message.

'If it ends up like that, Secretary General, I'm afraid we won't get any resolutions through at all. And then I fear the president will make good on his threats.'

Bolton insisted that everything had to be ready within the next few days. The United States was approaching a long weekend with the Fourth of July celebrations, and straight afterwards Kavanaugh would be nominated. And then it would be the NATO summit.

Over two days, I spoke with eleven heads of government and ministers of foreign affairs and defence.

In preparing for such conversations, I always ask to be informed of developments in each country's domestic policy and the latest opinion polls – this makes it easier to understand the political reality in which the person I'm speaking with is operating. It's also nice to send occasional texts to the other political leaders, and to exchange congratulations and family photographs. This informal contact helps to build a sense of community, and to create a better basis for conversations when difficult matters have to be discussed.

Like now, as I made my round of calls. I was glad I was already well acquainted with many of the leaders. No negotiations at the table. After Trump's retraction of his endorsement of the G7 joint statement, everyone knew what was at stake.

In Brussels, NATO diplomats worked under intense pressure to pull together the final statement. Before the summits, many issues are worked on that never make it into the newspaper headlines. These might be about new tasks within the command structure, or the wording of agreements NATO has with its many partner nations.

Out of fear that the summit would break down, the member states reached a consensus before the meeting. This had hardly ever happened in NATO's long history. Talk about a 'Trump effect'.

We agreed to launch a training operation in Iraq. Offensive cyber-security measures. Efforts in the Balkans. When it came to defence spending, the declaration stated that the aim was still to spend at least 2 per cent of GDP on defence by 2024. The member states thereby reiterated their commitment to follow up the decision from the 2014 summit, no more, no less.

The final declaration was complete. And while we still didn't know how the summit would go, certain stumbling blocks had at least been cleared away by completing the negotiations in advance.

Just before the summit, I wrote a piece for the *Wall Street Journal* under the headline: 'America's NATO Allies Are Stepping Up'. My message was that Europeans were now spending more on defence than they had just a few years earlier, and that it was in our common interest that the United States, Canada and Europe stand together.

Senator John McCain tweeted his wholehearted support of the article, and I sent him some warm words in return. At the same time, I thought back to my political awakening in the early 1970s. The first protest I took part in had been against the United States' bombing of North Vietnam. Alongside my sister Camilla and many other anti-war protesters, I marched to the US embassy and shouted: 'Stop the bombing!' While I was protesting, McCain was a naval aviator with the US Navy; he had been captured by the North Vietnamese and became a prisoner of war. Almost fifty years later, I was secretary general of NATO and regarded McCain as an important ally.

The final days ticked past and the summit neared. Trump gave a speech before an excited crowd at a rally in Montana. Again he lashed out at the Germans, criticising Angela Merkel for spending just 1 per cent of GDP on defence.

'We're paying for anywhere from seventy to ninety per cent to protect Europe,' Trump said, 'and that's fine. Of course they kill us on trade. They kill us on other things … And, on top of that, they kill us with NATO.'

'I'm going to tell NATO,' Trump said, 'you got to start paying your bills.'

16

On the precipice

JOHN BOLTON AND I HAD AGREED THAT ON WEDNESDAY THE eleventh of July 2018, the first day of the summit, President Trump and I would eat breakfast together. The idea being that we would exchange a few pleasantries and start the day on an optimistic note.

Our preparations had been exceedingly thorough. We had done our utmost to steer the summit safely into port.

Bolton had brought up the unpredictability of the situation in one of the last conversations I had with him, before Trump and the rest of the American delegation arrived in Brussels. 'The president still might tip the table over,' he said.

Of course I was apprehensive. But I also knew that we could not have done more, so I was feeling relatively calm.

At the breakfast meeting, held at the US embassy in Brussels, a long table had been set in a small room. Trump and I sat directly opposite each other. I had some close colleagues with me on my side of the table; Trump had several of his most important advisers with him.

The plan was clear. As host at the embassy, Trump would wish everyone welcome. Then there would be a couple of minutes from him, followed by a couple of minutes from me, before the doors were closed to the press. *Warm words.* The usual procedure.

But this time, things didn't quite work out that way.

I began by saying that defence spending would be one of the topics discussed at the summit, and that everyone had agreed that we needed to spend more.

'The good news is that the allies have started to invest more in defence,' I said. 'After years of cutting their defence budgets they have started to add billions … and last year was the biggest increase in defence spending across Europe and Canada in a generation.'

'Why was that last year?' Trump interrupted me as the cameras continued to roll. A clear invitation. Fair enough, I thought, and went on.

'It's also because of your leadership,' I said to Trump. 'Your clear message …'

'They won't write that, but that's okay,' Trump said, pointing at the journalists.

I briefly explained how important NATO was to both Europe and the United States, and concluded by remarking that I was looking forward to hearing Trump's thoughts on his upcoming meeting with Vladimir Putin, whom he would meet in Helsinki in a few days' time.

Things could have ended there, but Trump kept going.

'I think it's very sad when Germany makes a massive oil and gas deal with Russia,' Trump said. '… So we're supposed to protect you against Russia, but they're paying billions of dollars to Russia, and I think that's very inappropriate.'

Trump felt the agreement regarding the new pipeline in the Baltic Sea, Nord Stream 2, was a mistake.

'It should have never been allowed to have happened,' he said. 'But Germany is totally controlled by Russia. Because they will be getting sixty to seventy per cent of their energy from Russia and a new pipeline. And you tell me if that's appropriate, because I think it's not, and I think it's a very bad thing for NATO.'

Trump then moved straight on to the German defence budget. So much for my idea of starting the day on a positive note.

'On top of that, Germany is just paying a little bit over one per cent, whereas the United States in actual numbers is paying 4.2 per cent of a much larger GDP. So I think that's inappropriate also. We're protecting Germany, we're protecting France, we're protecting everybody ... This has been going on for decades, this has been brought up by other presidents, but other presidents never did anything about it ... but I have to bring it up, because I think it's very unfair to our country, it's very unfair to our taxpayer[s].'

Trump looked straight at me as he spoke.

'Germany is a rich country. They talk about how they can increase [their budget] a tiny bit by 2030, well, they could increase it immediately – tomorrow – and have no problem ... We're not going to put up with it, we can't put up with it, it's inappropriate,' he said.

Trump sat calmly; he didn't raise his voice, and he wasn't angry. But he spoke with an intense, persistent energy. Trump was a man who did not easily give up.

It slowly dawned on me that this breakfast had become something entirely different from what I had intended. All at once, I had been cast in a leading role in a theatre production for which I had not seen the script or stage directions. The journalists were permitted to stay in the room far longer than was usual during such meetings.

I began to respond.

'You know, NATO is an alliance of twenty-nine nations, and there are sometimes differences and different views ... and disagreements. A gas pipeline from Russia to Germany is one issue where allies disagree. But the strength of NATO is that despite these differences we have always been able to unite around our core task, to protect and defend each other, because we understand that we are stronger together than apart.'

The president looked me in the eye.

'But how can you be together when a country is getting its energy from the person you want protection against?'

'Even during the Cold War,' I said, 'NATO allies were trading with Russia—'

'I think trade is wonderful,' Trump interjected. 'I think energy is a much different story than normal trade. And you have a country like Poland that won't accept the gas ... they don't want to be captive to Russia. But Germany, as far as I'm concerned, is captive to Russia ...

So we're supposed to protect Germany, but they're getting their energy from Russia. Explain that. And it can't be explained, you know that.'

What could have been said behind closed doors had been said with the world's press in the room. Trump continued to criticise the NATO nations in general, and Germany in particular. Every time I tried to protest or to refute something he had said, Trump shut me down. Had I continued to speak, we would have ended up with the president of the United States and the secretary general of NATO bickering on live mics, with the result broadcast on live television all across the world. So Trump was able to continue his tirade about the sorry state of affairs within NATO.

After what felt like an eternity, the press were sent out. But Trump was just getting started.

The next topic he wanted to discuss was the new NATO building. 'Why do you need it? It's made of glass! One shot from a tank and it's gone. And why is it so big? You don't need all those people working there. You should have had a little bunker, that's much cheaper. And the United States has paid for ninety per cent of it. Three billion euros!'

Obviously, the price tag for NATO's new headquarters was not the most important matter at hand, but I was still keen to respond.

'The building was completed within budget,' I said. 'It cost one billion euros, not three, and the United States didn't cover ninety per cent of the cost, but twenty-two per cent.'

Trump refused to be derailed.

'I'm so disappointed. We're paying ninety per cent,' he said.

After the breakfast, I met with John Bolton. After all our telephone conversations before the summit, this was the first time I spoke with him face to face.

'We just have to try to calm this down,' he said. 'And let me give you a piece of advice. Don't get into any discussions with the president, especially not about numbers. It won't help.'

I also met with Jim Mattis immediately afterwards, and he was more direct.

'We're so ashamed,' he said. Mattis was sorry for both the form and content of Trump's outburst. The idea had been that it would be best for all concerned if we managed to agree on the message: recognise the progress that had been made, while acknowledging that we could do more.

Mattis was quiet for a moment. Then he said: 'I don't know how long I'm going to be in this job.' He had received no hints that he had fallen out of favour, but we had also previously established that with Trump, it was impossible to know for sure. Still, in this conversation, Mattis was most concerned about me. 'What's important now, Secretary General, is that we make sure you stay where you are. You are the only stable point here now, so you quite simply have to stay.'

It was a rather dramatic conversation.

'If I realise I'm on my way out, I won't tell you. I don't want you getting caught in the undertow,' he said.

According to the American media, Mattis was the last remaining 'adult in the room' among Trump's circle, following the departures of Rex Tillerson and H.R. McMaster. I actually doubted the claims that the president had no good advisers around him, but all the same, Jim Mattis was my most important contact within the Trump administration. Now it seemed he was getting ready to lose his job. He almost seemed to be acting a little recklessly in those days in Brussels – it was sink or swim for him. Or at least, he spoke with unusual candour, including when he took the time to talk with some of my closest colleagues straight after the breakfast. 'It must feel like you're hosting a birthday party, and then in comes this dog that runs around, jumps onto the sofa and knocks all the glasses off the table,' he said. He turned to Oana, who had also been at the breakfast meeting. 'I'm impressed you managed to keep a straight face. That must have been pretty hard to do,' Mattis said.

'We should be grateful,' Mattis went on, 'that the founding fathers had George III in mind when writing the constitution two hundred years ago.'

King George III was the last British king to also rule over what until the American War of Independence were British colonies in America.

The founding fathers were concerned that the United States Constitution must be built upon the separation of powers principle, so there would be a limit to how much damage the head of state could do.

Mattis knew he held an important role, and he felt he had support from many quarters. But he was also aware that he was operating within a thorny landscape. 'You know, Jens, I have a strange job,' he said to me. 'I get up in the morning. I read the newspaper. And if it doesn't say that I've been fired, I go into the office.'

The first part of the summit itself didn't go too badly. I did as we had planned. The normal procedure would be for me to ask everyone to take a look at the documents before them and approve the summit declaration towards the end of the meeting. But not wanting to risk being derailed later, I focused on ensuring the documents were approved at the very start of the meeting. 'I would like to wish everyone welcome, and thank you all for your endorsement of the documents we have negotiated,' I said. There was nothing that formally prevented me from proceeding this way, although I did notice a few puzzled faces. But no one protested. The documents were approved. It happened so quickly that some delegates almost missed it, I later heard.

Bolton and Pompeo had been worried that Trump might try to use the declaration as a means of punishing the other member states – that he might refuse to approve it, should he be provoked by something others said during the debate. With the declaration in place at the start of the summit, much was already achieved in terms of the meeting's content. Still, I felt constant uncertainty about how the rest of the summit would pan out.

Trump gave a critical address, but it was no more critical than expected. The other leaders promised, in various ways, to invest more in defence; I summarised the meeting's main points, and felt that, for the most part, the summit was over. Things were under control.

In the car on the way from NATO headquarters to the evening dinner that would follow the first day's meetings, I called Thorvald. In all the brief pauses, in each and every fleeting moment of calm throughout this hectic period, he was in my thoughts. My father had suffered from various health complaints for many years now, but he was an irrepressible optimist and never complained. In recent weeks, however, his condition had changed, and he had been forced to admit he wasn't doing so well. When I took a trip home to Norway in June, his skin had taken on a yellowish hue.

'You have to come home, Jens,' he said now. He spoke slowly, and his voice was weak.

Camilla had said the same when I had spoken to her in the preceding days. Thorvald had almost stopped eating. A few days earlier, he had been admitted to Diakonhjemmet Hospital to receive intravenous fluids, before being sent home again. It was gradually dawning on me that the situation was more serious than I had realised. Thorvald knew that his bowel cancer had spread to his liver and that his treatment options were few, and for a long time, he had lived without this affecting him too much. Then, on the first of May this year, he had given a speech in Eidsvoll – the cradle of Norwegian democracy. He had returned home, happy and enthusiastic as usual, but a few days later he grew weak, his skin turning sallow. Over the weeks that followed, he was forced to cancel various speeches and appearances. This was something he hated having to do, but he had remained hopeful that his health might improve.

I had already decided to travel to Oslo on the weekend directly after the summit. A few days earlier, feeling uneasy, I had managed to book a flight on the Saturday, and planned to stay in Norway until Friday the thirteenth of July. After speaking with Thorvald on the telephone, I didn't actually know anything new. No recent developments in his physical condition indicated that I ought to change my travel plans. But my gut told me otherwise. What I really wanted to do was drop everything right there and then and jump on the first flight to Oslo. This wasn't possible, of course, but I wanted to get home as fast as I could. I managed to book a ticket on the seven o'clock flight on the Thursday evening, just hours after the summit was due to end.

'I'm coming,' I told Thorvald.

17

'I am not happy'

THE SUMMIT DINNER WAS HELD AT THE ART & HISTORY MUSEUM in the magnificent Parc du Cinquantenaire, with its French gardens and countless monuments and sculptures. The museum building looks like a towering temple, with rows of columns on various levels, and from the top of the small hill with its huge triumphal arch flanked by arcades there is a magnificent view across Brussels. The premises date from the 1880s, and were built in connection with the fiftieth anniversary of Belgium's independence. The venue certainly wasn't lacking in pomp and ceremony.

I met Slovenian-born Melania Trump in the reception tent that had been erected on the lawn in front of the museum. We had a pleasant conversation, which touched on subjects that included the years I spent in Yugoslavia during my childhood. I was glad Ingrid was with me. She had taken on a kind of hostess role, and as always was adept at ensuring everyone felt included.

The music played, the dance performance was stunning, and it was a lovely July evening. This is going to go well, I thought.

After the opening performance, the heads of state and government took their seats around the table for a working dinner in one of the museum's halls. Only one adviser was permitted to accompany each leader. We were seated close together, and the atmosphere was expectant.

Trump was the evening's first speaker. He was served his own menu and a Diet Coke, all brought to the table by his own waiter. We had asked him to say a little about North Korea, because he had met Kim Jong Un in Singapore a few weeks earlier – the hope was that this would set a good tone, because we knew Trump had been enthusiastic about the meeting with North Korea's leader. Trump told a story about a golfer who had called him from a plane when he was on his way to Singapore, although since I know hardly anything about golf, I didn't understand much of it. He then spoke about former basketball player Dennis Rodman, who is a friend of Kim Jong Un, before he returned to describing his visit. 'There wasn't a thousand photographers taking pictures of us, there were lots more. Three thousand!' Trump said excitedly. 'More than at the Oscars! Click-click-click! The widest red carpet I've ever seen!'

I remember thinking there was something wonderful about the enthusiasm Trump exuded. He was due to speak with Vladimir Putin in Helsinki in just a few days' time, and we had also asked him to say something about his thoughts on the upcoming meeting. But I think he became so caught up in his own stories that he simply forgot about Putin. This did no harm, of course.

As I went to bed that night, I was feeling fairly relaxed about the summit. Just before I fell asleep, I told Ingrid that despite a challenging start at the breakfast with Trump, I was sure we'd manage to bring the gathering safely into harbour. Ingrid, who is a realist and much more level-headed than me, said she hoped I was right. 'But don't be too sure,' she added.

The next day started early. At the summits, it was customary to hold a separate session with the organisation's partner countries, and this time I wished Ukrainian president Petro Poroshenko and his colleague from Georgia, President Giorgi Margvelashvili, welcome to NATO. I reassured them of the alliance's solidarity, but both were rather disappointed that we hadn't arranged separate meetings with each of their countries. They were even more disappointed when it became apparent that President Trump wouldn't be present when we began the meeting. He arrived sometime later, after several leaders had already made their speeches and offered their assurances that NATO would never accept Russian aggression against independent states. They expressed their full support for Georgia and Ukraine. When Trump was given the floor, he cast a glance at Poroshenko and Margvelashvili and offered them a few supportive words, before quickly moving on to something else entirely.

'I have to make an official complaint,' Trump said. 'Because I'm not happy. Yesterday we had a nice dinner, and I saw that all of you were happy. But I just have to say: I am not happy.'

I hadn't sensed any tension in the air the previous evening. But Stian, who had been sitting right behind me, had noticed Trump's body language when some of the other leaders spoke about how sharing the burden wasn't just about money, pointing out everything their countries contributed to the NATO cooperation through other means.

Trump's statements were not new to me. But most of the other leaders at the meeting hadn't heard him express his grievances with the directness and intensity he did now.

'The United States is paying ninety per cent of NATO's expenses. I know there are some people who say seventy per cent, others say seventy-three per cent. There are all kinds of ways of working it out, but the way I see it, we're paying ninety per cent. NATO is important, but it's way more important for Europe than the United States,' Trump said. 'American presidents have come here and said this for many years. Then they've gone home, and nothing has happened. It's only gotten worse. We're paying more. The others aren't paying very much. I have great respect for Angela. My father was born in Germany. My mother was born in Scotland. So in a way, I'm part of the EU. But this has to stop.'

Some of the things he said were clear warnings.

'The US doesn't need NATO. Why should I continue to pay for this organisation when I don't need it?'

There was complete silence around the table. Trump continued to talk at length about the trade imbalance with the EU, another hobby-horse.

'I don't like linking these two things together, but we have to do it. The EU has enormous tariff walls that make things very difficult for our automotive plants, almost impossible for our farmers. The EU sends its BMWs and Mercedes into the United States, almost tariff-free. It can't go on like this. It won't go on like this.'

Then came more criticism of Europe.

'I think the borders you have here in Europe are terrible. Angela has said that many of the people streaming in over the borders are young men. That doesn't sound good. They might be enemies,' Trump said. 'I have great respect for Europe. I have great respect for the secretary general, who has managed to bring in more money. But it's very little compared to what we need. And as I've said: we can be an even better partner than we have been – even though I don't think we can be much better. We need a new agreement. You have to pay your share. Angela could pay two per cent today, if she wanted to! Instead she says 1.5 per cent by 2025!'

Trump then moved on to expressing his frustration at the other allies.

'I don't want people leaving this meeting saying everyone was happy. I am not happy. I'm not happy. You could have made me very happy. When a rich country doesn't pay, it's because they're trying to trick us, the way they tricked every single president since Reagan. You have to pay. Two per cent is so little. It's a joke! You need to aim for four per cent if you want proper protection. Either you pay two per cent immediately, within a few months, or by January first. Otherwise, we're going to … do our own thing. We have no choice. And as you already know, I really disagree with this building. Three billion dollars for a building like this! It's ridiculous! The United States is paying! It's a beautiful building, but a single shot from a tank and this building will collapse.'

The delegations from Ukraine and Georgia looked somewhat confused, and more than a little exasperated – this meeting was supposed to be about them, not internal problems within NATO. The moment Trump finished speaking, Angela Merkel stood up, came around to my side of the large meeting table, and leaned over me.

'We have to respond to this,' she whispered. 'We can't just let it pass.' It was clear she feared the meeting might end up spiralling out of control. I nodded in agreement.

There were still many people left to speak, but after a while I decided the meeting with Ukraine and Georgia had to be concluded. I cleared the room of everyone but the people I needed to be there, and set another meeting date. The only nation to remain sitting there with a large delegation was the United States. Rumours of a crisis began to leak out to the TV crews.

We took a break of a few minutes. I conferred with Angela Merkel, Emmanuel Macron and Dutch prime minister Mark Rutte in a corner of the room, while Trump sat close by, his arms crossed, speaking with Bolton and Pompeo. We agreed it was out of the question to change the 2014 decision that had set the 2 per cent of GDP goal of investment in defence, but discussed how we could best handle the situation that had arisen and pacify the president. My staff were also in contact with their colleagues in many delegations, and we tried to establish a shared basis for the way forward.

When the meeting resumed, I attempted to define this basis in three brief points: that we couldn't end the meeting without renewing our endorsement of NATO's security guarantees, that everyone had to acknowledge the importance of increasing their defence spending, and that at the next summit we needed to be able to provide evidence of actual defence budget increases.

In doing this, I wanted to try to get Trump to commit to NATO's security guarantee, while the other allies committed to spending more on defence.

Trump got up and walked towards me as I was speaking, then practically cut me off. 'Next year?! What does next year mean? That's way too late. This is what always happens. We can't have it! We need an increase now. Two per cent by the end of the year. And Angela, you can pay two per cent now! I've seen your budget, you have an excess. I'm borrowing money to pay for defence, including Germany's defence, while you're saving money because you expect me to defend you.' Again, he spoke with that same insistent energy.

Trump looked me right in the eye.

'We can't say: "We'll talk about it, see you next year." Because that's what you said! We can't defend anyone who doesn't pay their bills. Simple as that.'

He had previously been satisfied with the job I'd done in getting the allies to spend more on defence, but now there was an accusation in his voice. He held me responsible for not delivering what he had asked for.

Trump spoke about the gas pipeline again, and reiterated his demand for immediate promises of increased spending.

'We have to talk about this now. Otherwise – you know, otherwise, we're not going to be friends,' he said.

Then, finally, it came, the moment I had feared since our telephone conversation twelve days earlier, when Trump had said the United States would only continue to be a member of NATO if Germany and the United States paid the same.

'I'm leaving this meeting. There's no reason for me to be here anymore,' Trump said.

Now everything's going to fall apart, I thought. I looked around the room. All the leaders wore grave and focused expressions, some pressing their earpiece to their ear to hear better. Others, who sat closer to Trump, took their earpiece out to listen to him directly. Everyone understood things were on the brink of collapse – the entire summit, all the declarations of agreement. And all at once, NATO was in serious danger.

There in the meeting that day, I feared that NATO was about to stop functioning. Not necessarily that the alliance would be formally dissolved, but that it would no longer have any meaning. NATO stands or falls by the security guarantee. If an American president says he no longer wishes to defend the other allies and leaves a NATO summit in protest, then the NATO treaty and its security guarantee aren't worth very much. The world is full of worthless treaties – and now the NATO treaty might be about to become one of them.

This might be the meeting at which NATO is ruined, I thought. And it's happening on my watch. The alliance had managed to operate successfully for seventy years – but not after the twelfth of July 2018.

Trump wanted 2 per cent by the first of January 2019, with further subsequent increases. Now his delegation had packed their bags. They were ready to leave. Trump had already explored the possibility of the United States withdrawing from NATO. He had formerly spoken at length about bilateral agreements as an alternative to the multinational alliance, and this was his preferred solution. With bilateral agreements, he could provide military protection only to the countries who paid their way. A much better arrangement, in his view.

When I took the floor again, I knew what was at stake.

'Yes, President Trump is right,' I said. 'We have to talk about this now. It's the very reason we are holding this extraordinary meeting. The allies must fulfil their obligations. And the two per cent target is what we have agreed on.'

I reiterated that this would be a significant increase for many nations.

'No matter one's feelings on whether or not this is enough, this is what we must now aim for. I mentioned next year because that is when our next summit will take place. And by then, we must be able to see real progress,' I said. I then opened the floor to the other leaders.

Angela Merkel expressed what many were thinking.

'We have to take this back to our parliaments and national assemblies,' she said. 'This is the system within which most of us must operate – we aren't able to make the decisions here. I will fight hard to meet the two per cent target in 2024. But I simply don't have the majority for anything more than that right now.'

Then Trump did something that hardly ever happened at such meetings. He interrupted another head of government.

'That's too long,' he said. 'Way too long.'

But Merkel kept speaking.

'Thirty-seven to thirty-eight per cent of German gas comes from Russia. It's been that way for several decades – we are not importing more than previously.'

Then she used an expression we often heard from Trump.

'I have to say,' Merkel said, 'that *I* don't feel I'm being treated fairly here. You speak frankly, Donald, so I will do the same. Germany is the second largest contributor of forces to NATO. 9/11 and Afghanistan are the only time Article 5 has ever been invoked. This has contributed to protecting the United States, despite intense opposition in my country, where many asked what Afghanistan has to do with us. Germany can do more, and we can probably do things better. But now we must stick to the commitments we have made.'

Macron supported Merkel.

'We cannot, sitting around this table right now, say that by January we will be spending two per cent,' he said. 'We cannot pretend that this is possible, it is not a serious way to move forward.'

Everyone agreed that the member states would increase their defence budgets to 2 per cent of gross domestic product. But the problem was that Trump insisted on it happening *this year*. The other nations set the goal of achieving the target in 2024, something which had also been adopted in the summit declaration the previous day.

Trump took the floor again. He began to rattle off how much each member state spent on defence as a percentage of GDP, as if he were announcing the results of the Eurovision Song Contest.

'Belgium: 0.9. That's less than one per cent. Croatia – oh, I'm so disappointed in you, I can't believe it: 1.26 per cent. You must feel rotten,' he said, searching for the relevant leader with his eyes. 'Estonia: 2 per cent. Thank you! France: 1.79. Not bad, Emmanuel. Not bad for you. You haven't been president long enough, it'll probably go down. Germany: 1.2. Come on, Angela! Come on!'

He sought out Xavier Bettel, the prime minister of Luxembourg. 'Luxembourg, you're such a nice guy, where are you? 0.46. I'm not going to talk to you anymore. But I'm sure it'll be fine. My wife thinks you're a nice guy.'

Trump continued to speak.

'Poland: 1.99. So I'll call that two. You've been super. Thank you, Poland, wherever the hell you are. Slovenia: less than 1 per cent. I'm not surprised. I know my wife, I know what she spends money on.'

Up next was Turkey.

'The nice thing about Turkey,' Trump said, 'is that he, Erdoğan, can say anything, there's nobody controlling him. When he got sixty-one per cent of the vote in the election, I said: why don't you just say it was eighty per cent? That sounds much better.'

And finally:

'United Kingdom: 2.1. Thank you. That's very good. United States: 4.2 per cent, of the biggest gross domestic product of all. So you may as well call us idiots. But I haven't been at this party very long. How stupid is this? That's all.'

He leaned over towards Theresa May and said something. Then he turned to Erdoğan, who was sitting on his other side, and high-fived him.

Several other leaders spoke. Some sympathised with Trump's demand for immediate increases in spending, while others were as reserved as Merkel and Macron.

Then I gave the floor to Mark Rutte. This was no accident. During the deliberations in the break some minutes earlier, we had discussed who should convey the message we had agreed on, giving Trump credit for the fact that several countries were now paying more, while at the same time promising to increase our budgets. It wouldn't be appropriate for Merkel to do this, since Trump was so furious at Germany for importing Russian gas. Nor did Macron wish to take on this role, but he understood it was important that someone did. It had to be Rutte. He and I had met for lunch in The Hague a week before the summit, where we had discussed how we could get Trump to support NATO, including by pointing to the fact that defence spending had increased by $33 billion.

'Mr President, you have urged us to spend more, and I agree with you,' Rutte said. 'And that is exactly what we are doing. Just last year, we spent thirty-three billion dollars more on defence because of your leadership. So this is good news for you.'

Trump liked this. *Thirty-three billion.* He nodded.

I had highlighted Trump's leadership many times before, and now Rutte did so too, at a critical juncture. He foregrounded the new figure and gave Trump credit. It worked.

After a while, Trump took out the thick black marker he always used, jotted something down on a sheet of paper, then leaned over and handed me the note. His handwriting was neat and rather attractive. The note said:

'Secretary General, if you can say that the NATO allies have significantly increased their defence spending thanks to me, then I think we can agree.'

I finally glimpsed an opportunity to bring the meeting home. I took the floor myself.

'At the press conference after the meeting, I will state that the NATO allies have significantly increased their defence spending thanks to President Trump's leadership and clear messaging,' I said, practically reading straight from Trump's note. Then I added: 'And at the same time, that all member nations remain committed to NATO and to Article 5 of the treaty.'

I hoped against hope that this would be enough to bring the meeting to a close in a way that was acceptable to everyone. Trump would be given political recognition and a strengthened promise on increased defence spending, while the rest of us would receive a renewed commitment to NATO and our collective defence clause.

The problem was that there were still twelve leaders remaining on the list of speakers. If I allowed the debate to start up again, it seemed extremely likely that at least one of them would say something that irritated Trump, causing the fragile consensus to be broken. I therefore looked pleadingly around the table, at Merkel, Macron, May, Trudeau, Erdoğan and all the others, and suggested something highly unusual – that we move to stop the discussion now, with everyone in support of my proposed conclusion. 'Can we agree?' I asked.

There were nods around the table, and for a moment I thought that both the day and NATO were saved. But no. Lars Løkke Rasmussen raised his hand, pushed the button on his microphone, and made it known that he was not going to withdraw his name from the list of speakers. That everyone else was fine with ending the debate there and then seemed to make no difference. Denmark's prime minister wanted to take the floor.

Lars Løkke Rasmussen and I were old colleagues. I liked the cheerful and down-to-earth Dane very much, but now I felt only exasperation and extreme irritation towards him. If I gave him the floor, I risked others wanting to jump on the bandwagon, and then the entire debate would be reopened. There couldn't possibly be anything it was so vital to say on Denmark's behalf that Løkke Rasmussen couldn't simply hold his tongue, as all the other heads of state and government were willing to do.

Reluctantly, I gave him the floor. Løkke Rasmussen began cautiously, saying something about the importance of us standing united in difficult times, and that of course he agreed it was important to share the financial burden fairly. Then he fixed his gaze on Trump and paused.

'But sharing the burden isn't just about money, Mr President. It's about blood and sacrifice,' Løkke Rasmussen continued. 'Denmark is a country of only five million people, and we have lost forty-five soldiers in Afghanistan, in an operation that is a response to an attack on the United States.'

Denmark's prime minister was hitting back. After a morning in which the US president had accused the European allies of not doing their share, of paying too little and leeching off the United States, Lars Løkke Rasmussen had clearly had enough. His voice shook, and he was practically on the verge of tears as he said: 'By population, Denmark has lost more soldiers in Afghanistan than the United States.' He refused to look the fallen service members' families in the eye and say that their loved ones' lives mattered less because Denmark hadn't met the 2 per cent target.

The episode reminded me of a scene in the movie *Love Actually*, where Hugh Grant, playing the British prime minister, stands up to the American president. But this was no movie – it was reality. I realised that it was right and of great import that Lars Løkke Rasmussen had been permitted to speak.

Still, I held my breath when he was done. I cast a quick glance around the table and saw he had made a deep impression on many. Trump stayed quiet. Everyone understood they were at a historic meeting, and several leaders now wished to become part of the story by taking the floor; they pushed the buttons on their mics and raised their hands, but I wasn't going to allow them to speak. The meeting was over. It was time to bring things to a close.

'Now let us agree on my aforementioned points. Can we do that?'

I looked around the room. There were no further protests. 'Thank you,' I said. 'We have concluded. The meeting is closed.' I raised the gavel and rapped it against the table.

I felt indescribable relief. I knew that our problems were far from solved – the meeting had revealed a deep rift between the United States and major European nations. But we had clawed our way back from the precipice edge. The meeting was saved without us having to present the emergency proposal that the European countries pay more for having US forces stationed in Europe. We had managed to buy ourselves some time.

Trump held his press conference immediately after the meeting.

'The United States' commitment to NATO is very strong, remains very strong, but primarily because everyone – the spirit they have, the amount of money they're willing to spend, the additional money that they will be putting up has been really, really amazing to see it. To see the level of spirit in that room is incredible,' he said.

He also brought up the $33 billion.

'The allies will spend at least thirty-three billion dollars more, in addition to what we had previously agreed. We are more united than ever. No problem.'

We had scheduled the press conference straight after the meeting to be able to balance Trump's statements should we need to, but this proved unnecessary. I had a brief conversation with Mike Pompeo, and he was on cloud nine. 'This really was great, congratulations!' he said.

A little later, I was interviewed on live television by CNN's Christiane Amanpour. Which was challenging, to say the least, because the media had already been given two completely different versions of what had happened at the summit: President Trump said we had a new resolution on increased defence spending, while Merkel and Macron said no such new resolution had been adopted. It was my job to relay that we were all actually saying the same thing.

'So, first and foremost,' Amanpour said, 'has President Trump secured a pledge from NATO allies, as he said today, to immediately start spending more?'

'All allies agree that we have to make good on the commitments we have made,' I said.

'So, let me be specific again. I want a clear answer from you, please. President Macron denies that the allies agreed to up their spending beyond the two per cent. Can you confirm to us what are the facts?'

I couldn't, of course. There was no new agreement, no new pledges beyond the 2014 resolution. But I couldn't simply come out and say that, because then I would be contradicting Trump, and risk him withdrawing his support for the fragile consensus we had just reached.

'The fact is that we have a clear commitment to increase defence spending. And we all agreed that we have to deliver on that,' I said. And so we went on, for several confusing rounds. Amanpour asked clear and precise questions, and received vague and unclear answers.

But even though there was no new resolution, a new political reality had been established – a new understanding of what was at stake – and that was just as important. It wouldn't be possible for everyone to convene again in a year's time without having delivered something that truly made a difference. We had to take Trump at his word. Fundamentally, he was right, and what he said was in essence the same as what American presidents had been saying for years.

To this day, I remain surprised at how Trump accepted the summit's conclusion. Something had clearly happened during the proceedings. Had he made good on his threat to leave the summit in protest, we would have been left to pick up the pieces of a shattered NATO. I think he realised he was banging his head against a wall with his demands of immediate budget increases, but at the same time, he departed Brussels convinced he would have more money by the new year. And in January, Trump would balance the books to find out whether the allies had fulfilled the promises he believed they had made.

But for now, the $33 billion was the formula for success Trump had needed. When I met him at the UN headquarters in New York a few weeks later, he smiled, satisfied.

'Is the money still coming in, Secretary General?' he asked.

'Mr President, the money is flowing in,' I replied.

PART 4
FRIENDSHIP
July 2018–April 2019

18

Sunset from all sides

A LARGE BED STOOD IN THE MIDDLE OF THE LIVING ROOM. Thorvald smiled weakly when he saw me.

'There you are,' he said. 'I'm so glad you came. I've been waiting for you.'

The summit had ended on the afternoon of Thursday the twelfth of July. All my appointments scheduled for later that afternoon and the following day had been cancelled, and I had made it onto the 7 p.m. flight to Oslo. I sank into my seat feeling drained and uneasy, having pushed all thoughts of Thorvald to the back of my mind during the summit. As I leaned back and stared at the clouds below, my concern for him crept to the fore.

From Oslo Airport Gardermoen, police officers drove me straight to Mogens Thorsens gate. It was 9.30 p.m. when I finally walked through the front door of my childhood home.

Camilla and her husband Atle were there, along with Thorvald's partner, Anja, and the grandchildren. The others withdrew a little when I arrived, and I sat down beside him. The balcony door was open, and the curtains shifted gently in the breeze. An intense heat had settled over Oslo that summer, it seemed to radiate from the apartment's brick walls. Thorvald was clearly bothered by it.

'So here you are in your castle, gazing out across your kingdom,' I said.

'Yes, in my castle,' he replied. Thorvald loved this apartment with its view of the Oslo Fjord, so open and full of light. In the evenings the sun was reflected in the glass panes of the old Norsk Hydro building close by. 'The only place in the world where you can see the sunset from all sides,' as Thorvald would say.

We talked about the life he had lived; how satisfied he was with it. It had been a rich and exciting life, he said. Our time in Yugoslavia, when I was a little boy and Thorvald worked at the embassy in Belgrade. Years that bound us so tightly together as a family, and which taught me the immense value of friendship, between countries and between people. Throughout his life, Thorvald had stayed in close contact with many of his old friends from his time in Yugoslavia.

It was good to sit there, in the peace and quiet. Thorvald was utterly clear-minded, but exhausted and weak.

Nobody could tell stories like him. At our cabin in Ula, he used to conjure up images of the 'Urde troll' who had urinated the long icicles that hung from the surrounding rocks and cliffs. Then he might suddenly incorporate stories from the Six-Day War, speaking at length about Moshe Dayan, Israel's minister of defence, who wore a black patch over one eye. Norwegian resistance fighter Max Manus was a figure to whom he returned constantly. And the immense explosion that took place at Filipstad, Oslo, in 1943, when eight hundred tonnes of ammunition went up in smoke. His grandmother had been making a red fruit compote that day, Thorvald said. The force of the blast sucked the compote out through the kitchen window and back in through the window of the apartment below, where it stuck to the ceiling with a slap. We children had sat and listened, rapt and wide-eyed. The story broke more than a few laws of physics, but to this day I can still see that red fruit compote hanging from the ceiling.

Thorvald's roots were firmly planted in a mythical narrative tradi-tion, in which fact and fiction, true and false, were transformed into a higher entity. His stories bound the world together, imbuing it with meaning and excitement. He made things seem so real that I had the sense I'd lived in Norway through the 1940s and 1950s myself. Later,

Thorvald was open about how he sometimes gave reality an added dash of colour. 'I might not always tell it exactly as it was. But you have to exaggerate a little, so those listening can understand how things actually felt,' he said.

Sitting there beside the hospital bed I saw how bone-tired he was, this man who had always been so strong. His words emerged slowly and with great effort, punctuated by long pauses that gave me time to think back on our lives and everything he had given me; all the warmth, care and love. Adversity and disappointments had always spurred him on to work harder, and I think this was down to his irrepressible optimism. He *chose* never to give up hope, no matter the challenges he faced, great or small. This attitude to life was a gift to everyone close to him, and it was his mantra as a politician.

When I got into politics myself, I followed in Thorvald's footsteps in my belief in social democratic values. But at the same time, I chose a different path; one that went the way of economics and domestic policy. Only when I took office within NATO did I truly immerse myself in the matters *he* had been concerned with all his life. War and peace. Defence and security. Transatlantic cooperation.

In my first years at the highest level of Norwegian politics, people often said that I was conflict-averse. That I wasn't much of a politician, steering clear of any uncomfortable confrontations and never daring to have it out with people. This was when Thorvald had come up with his theory that the world actually had far too few conflict-averse leaders. Because many leaders actively sought out conflict. If there was anything the world needed more of, he said, it was politicians who wanted to avoid fighting and disputes. This would raise the threshold for hostility and conflict, he emphasised in his speeches and interviews. These interpretations of and musings on avoiding conflict appeared to represent Thorvald's life philosophy. But in reality, he was simply defending his son.

Thorvald was a real father hen. He would constantly ask me to check the smoke detectors at home. I tried to tell him I had people around me who looked after that sort of thing, but no, that wasn't good enough – I had to check the smoke detectors myself. And never set out on my bicycle without wearing my helmet. When I was Norway's prime minister, I often claimed I spoke with Thorvald on the phone every day. This was a slight exaggeration, but after I moved to Brussels, I actually did. Often in the car, on my way to or from work, for anything from two to twenty minutes. Thorvald always got straight to the point.

'How are you?' he would ask.

'Fine,' I would reply, no matter how I was feeling.

But there was no fooling him. He could hear it in my voice, how I was really doing. Which enabled us to have many honest conversations.

As I sat there at his bedside, the July evening slowly darkened. I peered down at his head, which lay unmoving on the pillow, and waited patiently for him to complete his next sentence. His hand rested in mine. We talked a little about the summit I had just attended; I reported back on the most important conversations I'd had, and the work within NATO.

'It's great that you're speaking with the Russians,' Thorvald said. He had told me many times that most of us simply didn't understand just how humiliated Russia felt by the United States and the West. We didn't understand that the Russians felt inferior. Contact and dialogue were the only passable path to understanding each other better.

'You have to speak with the Russians,' he repeated.

This was one of the very last things he said. Thorvald wasn't naive, and he supported a strong military defence. But he retained his belief in dialogue to the last.

After a while, the nurses from the Fransiskushjelpen charity came in. They helped to turn Thorvald in the bed and gave him a small dose of morphine. He accepted the offer of a glass of water, and drank a little. Not long afterwards, he fell asleep.

Later that evening, I went home to Nordberg. Compared with all the other events of my long political career, the NATO summit I had concluded earlier that day was certainly up there when it came to drama and nail-biting moments. The adrenaline still coursed through my body.

The next day, Friday the thirteenth of July, I woke feeling considerably better rested. I had seen how frail Thorvald was, but I was looking forward to spending the day with him, sitting at his bedside, recalling memories, talking about this and that and listening to his slow words as I had the evening before.

When I went over to the apartment that morning, I stopped to consider Thorvald from the living room doorway. He lay there in the bed, his hands atop the sheet. The silhouette of his head, angled slightly towards the window. So still. So peaceful and calm.

As I took the final steps towards him, I realised that Thorvald was dead. He had died in his sleep, just moments before I arrived.

Only then did I understand the true meaning of his words the previous evening, when he said he had been waiting for me.

Thorvald had clung to life so the two of us could meet one last time.

It was the last gift my father gave me.

The funeral was held on Thursday the second of August in Oslo Cathedral. Thorvald had planned the event in detail – he had asked Camilla to write it all down, point by point. Uranienborg Church had been mentioned as a venue, but then Thorvald had intervened. 'Uranienborg? No, my funeral isn't going to be a quiet affair. It has to be Oslo Cathedral,' he had said.

And he had made it clear that the Labour Party should be given a prominent role in the service.

I had to return to Brussels for a few days – there was always much to do after a NATO summit, resolving issues, getting in touch with the various ambassadors. But I noticed I felt somewhat distant, disconnected from it all. I was most present when being interviewed by Norwegian journalists, who were more interested in Thorvald and my relationship with him than they were in the way forward for NATO. So I was able to speak about the thing that dominated my thoughts. It felt good to return to Oslo and take part in the final funeral preparations.

And no, it certainly wasn't a quiet affair. The cathedral was packed, crowds thronged outside, and the media covered the service. The King

and Queen of Norway sat in the front pew. Priest Sturla Stålsett offici-
ated, and three of Thorvald's oldest and closest friends gave eulogies.
As did Gro Harlem Brundtland, who had led the last two Labour
governments of which Thorvald had been a member, and Jonas Gahr
Støre, the Labour Party's current leader. One person we missed was
Thorvald's good friend Kofi Annan, who had been deeply moved
when I called to tell him what had happened. He had been determined to come to Oslo, but then fell seriously ill himself. A little later
in August, he died, too.

Then it was time for Camilla and me to speak, and we went up to
the casket together. It was just the two of us now. Karin, Nini and now
Thorvald were gone. They had been my closest confidants throughout
my childhood, and later in life they had always supported me and
surrounded me with so much life and warmth. Now only my big sister
remained of what for so many years had been our close-knit family. It
was so painful and strange.

In my eulogy, I emphasised Thorvald's incomprehensible ability to
reconcile apparently irreconcilable differences. I spoke about the time
the family had been on a beach holiday on the coast of Croatia. We
children had found it boring, staying close to the shore, and wanted to
swim out towards the open sea. Thorvald had been against this – he
thought it wasn't safe. 'Let's swim *out towards land* instead,' he said. It
was a solution the whole family happily embraced.

Long-standing former minister of culture and musical artist Åse
Kleveland was master of ceremonies at the reception in
Arbeidersamfunnets Plass directly afterwards, where there were more
speeches and more singing. The earnest address given by Arild
Knutsen, who for many years was head of Norway's Association for
Humane Drug Policy, made a profound impression. He thanked
Thorvald for the ways in which he had spearheaded the fight for a new
illegal drugs policy in Norway. His speech was actually a burning
appeal from an old comrade-in-arms, utterly in Thorvald's spirit.

Because Thorvald wasn't just a constructive reconciler and
mild-mannered consensus-builder. He could fight like a lion for what
he believed in, and he never gave up. And Arild Knutsen reminded us

of this perseverance. When he finished speaking, the entire room gave him a standing ovation.

We ended the church service by singing Violeta Parra's magnificent 'Gracias a la vida' in Swedish: 'Jag vil tacka livet'. At the reception, we ended by singing 'To the Youth' by Nordahl Grieg. I couldn't imagine a finer framing of the day on which we said our last goodbyes to our dear Thorvald.

What defined Thorvald above all else was his unfailing zest for life and infectious hopefulness. On those busy workdays in Brussels, I had imagined that I made those countless phone calls to Thorvald back home in Norway for his sake. But now that he was gone, I knew that wasn't true.

They had been for mine.

19

The return of nuclear weapons

'NUCLEAR ALARM!'

The cry resounded through the barracks at Evjemoen on a bitter spring day in 1979. We quickly pulled on our hoods and mittens, tightening them as best we could, then threw ourselves to the ground, every soldier covering himself with the tent canvas we carried in our packs. In our hands, we each held our own 'nuclear brush', which we would use when the attack was over, to brush the radioactive fallout from our clothes.

I pulled the canvas to one side and peered up at the sergeant leading the exercise.

'What do we do now, Sergeant?'

'Wait for further orders,' he replied.

There was really nothing more to say. A nuclear bomb had exploded; Norwegian foot soldiers had little option but to seek shelter under their tent canvases and wonder what would happen next.

That conscripted soldiers like us were participating in such exercises at the end of the 1970s says something about how the nuclear threat was perceived.

But the idea of nuclear war was associated more with total destruction than it was with smart survival tricks and curious lint brushes. At that time, nuclear weapons and the arms race overshadowed all other security policy concerns. The Soviet Union had deployed new intermediate-range ballistic missiles, the SS20s, which could carry both conventional and nuclear warheads – and they were pointed at Western Europe. In December 1979, Soviet forces marched into Afghanistan, heightening the sense of tension and fear.

That same month, in response to the Soviet military build-up, NATO decided to deploy 579 intermediate-range ballistic missiles in Europe. These, too, were capable of carrying nuclear warheads. But NATO would only deploy them should negotiations with Moscow prove futile. The NATO decision was therefore both carrot and stick – an invitation to negotiate *and* a decision to deploy new weapons. This so-called Double-Track Decision became one of the most contentious in NATO's history.

The thinking behind the Soviet SS20s was clear. They could only strike targets in Europe, and they therefore ushered in a new phase of the great nuclear arms race. The mutually assured destruction, or MAD doctrine, expressed a brutal logic: nuclear war was unthinkable, because both the United States and the Soviet Union could be certain they themselves would be destroyed the moment they fired off their long-range nuclear weapons. But the Soviet intermediate-range missiles drove a wedge into this logic. Ultimately, they might enable Moscow to strike without triggering a US counter-attack involving strategic nuclear weapons. The SS20 blew a hole in NATO's deterrence strategy – *limited* nuclear war was now a possible scenario. And the threshold for nuclear war actually breaking out was consequently also lowered.

The Double-Track Decision was intended to be a response to this new threat. The Russians should know that any attack using intermediate-range missiles might elicit a response using equivalent American weapons in Western Europe. The deterrent therefore remained credible, and the United States would not simply be a bystander to any conflict in Europe.

The Double-Track Decision was of immense significance for those on the left in Norway and Europe. For me and the Labour Party's Youth Organisation, it was a source of the utmost concern. We believed NATO's decision to respond to the Soviet Union represented yet another turn of the armament screw, and that it posed a threat to world peace. I went on anti-nuclear protest marches; I gave presentations and passionate speeches. As vice president of the International Union of Socialist Youth, I cooperated with Olaf Scholz and Sigmar Gabriel from Germany, Anna Lindh from Sweden, Manuel Valls from France and Alfred Gusenbauer from Austria, all of whom would later become cabinet ministers or heads of government in their respective countries. The fight against nuclear weapons shaped an entire generation of European politicians, and the disputes surrounding these intermediate-range missiles defined my own understanding of security policy.

The apartment in Mogens Thorsens gate was also full of life in this period. Despite having moved out ourselves, Camilla, Nini and I brought friends home to our parents' place – young people with links to the Red Youth, Socialist Youth and the Labour Party's Youth Organisation. My sisters and I probably held some of the most moderate views at these gatherings. On New Year's Eve, as we sat there drinking beer and wine, the minister of defence himself walked in; Thorvald sat down at the kitchen table and joined the discussion. He was firm in his conviction: the Double-Track Decision was right and necessary. Not because nuclear weapons were a good thing, but because NATO had to combine dialogue with force.

'We need to play tough to prevent these weapons from ever being used. We have to look the Russians in the eye and say: don't go thinking you can start a limited nuclear war. You'll face all of NATO regardless,' Thorvald said.

We were firm in our convictions, too. Throughout 1980 and 1981, we protested against the Double-Track Decision and NATO's missile plans. But I was somewhat conflicted in my view even then, and influenced by the discussions at home. I realised there was a crucial difference between *unilateral* and *reciprocal* disarmament. There was also an imbalance, or an asymmetry, to the peace movement's protests. It had been pretty quiet when Moscow deployed the SS20 missiles. Only when NATO responded did we take to the streets.

The Labour Party emphasised the 'negotiation' aspect of the Double-Track Decision, but the negotiations were deadlocked. Hardly anyone believed it possible that *all* medium-range weapons could be banned. The first step had to be to stop the nuclear build-up, and this was therefore the peace movement's main demand. This was most clearly expressed through the Nuclear Freeze movement, which advocated for a bilateral halt to all further deployment of nuclear weapons by the United States and the Soviet Union. But sometimes, reality can surpass even the greatest optimism.

In 1985, the reformist politician Mikhail Gorbachev came to power in the Soviet Union. He was a strong supporter of disarmament, for reasons that included being able to focus more on the production of the consumer goods his country so sorely lacked. In 1987, what everyone had thought impossible actually happened. Soviet general secretary Gorbachev and US president Ronald Reagan signed the Intermediate-Range Nuclear Forces, or INF, Treaty. It covered all weapons with a range of between 310 and 3,420 miles, and was not limited to a halt on new deployments. All land-based intermediate-range missiles would be prohibited *and* current deployments would be removed, and the treaty contained detailed provisions regarding how the disarmament would be managed and verified. Reagan and Gorbachev declared that the ultimate goal was a world free of nuclear weapons. The INF Treaty was a milestone, and an important source of inspiration for other disarmament agreements. In the years that followed the fall of the Berlin Wall in 1989, the fear of nuclear war between the superpowers largely disappeared.

When I took office in NATO in 2014, my fear of nuclear weapons was primarily linked to countries such as North Korea and Iran, or the possibility that terrorists might obtain access to nuclear weapons. There was far less reason to worry about a nuclear arms race between the United States/NATO and Russia. After all, we had several agreements that set strict limitations on the number and type of nuclear weapons that were permitted. But this would soon change.

I received the first warning during one of the briefings the CIA gave me at least once a week. By this point, I had been head of NATO for about a year. We sat around my meeting table, but didn't speak until we had ensured all telephones and other electronic equipment had been removed from the room. When everything was ready, the CIA staffer said: 'Secretary General, today we would like to inform you of something serious. We regard it as extremely probable that the Russians are breaching the INF Treaty on land-based intermediate-range missiles.'

I was shown a map. The staffer pointed to Kapustin Yar, east of Volgograd, a rocket launch complex where the Russians had tested various weapons systems throughout the entire post-war period. Now they were in the process of developing, producing and deploying a new intermediate-range missile, the SSC-8, capable of carrying nuclear warheads.

Other maps showed rings undulating across Europe from Russian bases, illustrating where the various missiles might strike. First they would take Berlin, then Rome, then Paris. 1,200, 1,800, 2,400 miles. At around 3,100 miles, Lisbon would also be hit. Oslo would go up in smoke early, around the same time as Berlin. The Russians had three battalions, and were in the process of deploying a fourth. Each battalion had four launchers, located on trucks, and each of these launchers carried four SSC-8 missiles. Four times four times four – that gave a total of sixty-four missiles. Of a type the Russians had pledged not to possess.

Ever since Barack Obama was president, the Americans had suspected the Russians might be breaching the INF Treaty, and they were growing ever surer that this was in fact the case. An extensive new – and banned – weapons programme was in development.

I later received more briefings and additional details, but on the whole the conclusion was the same. The Russians had deployed nuclear intermediate-range missiles, which they could transport around the endless Russian forests, while the INF Treaty stipulated that the development, testing and deployment of such weapons was prohibited. The threat of nuclear war became more real. The unthinkable became more thinkable.

The INF Treaty was the cornerstone of a comprehensive system of agreements that had also enabled a dramatic reduction in other types of weapons. Throughout the 1990s, NATO had reduced the number of nuclear warheads in Europe by 90 per cent. Now the Russians' treaty breach sent a deep crack through this impressive political construction. A world without the INF Treaty would be a more dangerous world.

Why were the Russians doing this? NATO's experts pointed to many different explanations, and it likely came down to a combination of all of these.

Russia had nuclear weapons on ships, submarines and aircraft, but these were easier to eliminate than the ground-based systems covered by the INF Treaty. The more exposed the Russians felt, the more important it would be for them to have access to ground-based intermediate-range missiles. Such missiles were cheaper, less vulnerable, and easier to use and maintain than weapons on ships and aircraft.

China was not party to the INF Treaty; only the United States and the Soviet Union were. While the Americans and the Russians had been bound by the treaty's prohibition, the Chinese had been developing their own intermediate-range missiles. Russia has a long border with China, and was easily within range of these missiles. Pakistan, Iran, North Korea and India had also developed intermediate-range missiles of the type prohibited under the INF Treaty. Even though these were nations with which Russia had close relationships, it made Moscow uneasy that these countries were increasingly acquiring weapons systems that Russia was not permitted to have.

The INF Treaty stemmed from a time in which the United States and the Soviet Union were the dominating nuclear powers. Paradoxically enough, it was other countries' military build-ups that had direct and destructive consequences for the relationship between the United States and Russia.

There were therefore rational reasons behind the Russians' breach of the treaty. But that didn't improve matters. Quite the opposite, in fact.

For the Americans, the picture was different. They didn't share a continent with other countries who were in possession of land-based weapons capable of reaching the United States. In terms of their own defence, it was the long-range nuclear missiles that were most important. But the Americans were also keeping an anxious eye on China's nuclear arms build-up, and they felt the INF Treaty was out of date.

The Americans had discussed the INF breach with the Russians a number of times throughout 2016 and 2017, but without the conversations leading anywhere. Moscow acknowledged they had the missile we referred to as SSC-8 in their arsenal, but claimed its range was less than 310 miles, and that it was therefore not in violation of the INF Treaty. But American intelligence reports left increasingly little doubt that the missile's range was in fact much greater.

Eventually, the Americans began to publicise some of what they knew about Russia's breach of the treaty, and the first thing that struck me when details started to trickle out into the public sphere was just how little attention it received. The parallel with the 1970s was striking – the Russians could deploy nuclear weapons without people seeming to care all that much. These weapons also undermined the most important disarmament agreement we had, but nor did that seem to make any significant impression.

This caused me to reflect on how society reacts to crises, and how we are perhaps unable to take in more than one crisis at a time. The climate crisis is an existential crisis. We know that it is coming, and that it will trigger natural catastrophes, unrest and conflict, and waves of migration. Nevertheless, it makes sense for us to discuss how this crisis can be limited, and how we can adapt. It will hit the world's poorest hardest, while the richest countries will be able to implement mitigating measures. A nuclear war, however, would affect everyone. In this respect, the nuclear threat is democratic, and it makes little sense to talk about adaptation. Risk is probability multiplied by impact. Even though the probability of nuclear war is small, the resulting destruction would be so vast that the risk has to be taken extremely seriously.

I struggled to get people to pay attention to Russia's nuclear arms build-up, but received help from President Putin when he held his state of the nation address in March 2018. As much as the content of Putin's speech, it was the way in which the new weapons were presented that attracted attention. On huge screens, large-scale animations showed new cruise missiles, ballistic missiles and underwater drones. Putin also spoke about a new hypersonic cruise missile. The video simulations depicted it zigzagging its way past anti-aircraft missiles above the Atlantic, rounding South America, and heading straight for the coast of California. Then the screen turned black.

'As you no doubt understand, no other country has developed anything like this. There will be something similar one day but by that time our guys will have come up with something even better,' Putin said.

He neglected to mention the weapons systems most discussed within NATO – that is, the intermediate-range missiles. They were illegal, so he showed no video simulations of them.

Russia's new weapons systems rendered NATO's anti-missile defence systems useless, Putin claimed. He said that Russia had long attempted to get the United States to refrain from developing anti-missile defence systems that disrupted the balance between the US and Russia. 'Nobody wanted to listen to us. So listen now,' Putin said.

We had been listening, of course. But above all else, we now noticed how Putin stood there bragging about his new weapons systems, illustrating his speech with animations of deadly attacks to resounding applause from his audience. Our experts reviewed the address in detail. Some of what Putin said was pure fantasy. But some of it was reality.

The Nuclear Posture Review is a document in which the United States formulates its political doctrine in the area of nuclear weapons. In the report that was issued in the winter of 2018, the US reiterated its assessments of how Russia was breaching the INF Treaty, and showed how the threat could be countered with submarine-launched nuclear missiles that were not prohibited. The Americans wanted to develop so-called 'low-yield' nuclear weapons – extremely precise nuclear weapons with less explosive force. Washington clearly signalled that they would implement these countermeasures.

In NATO, nuclear weapons are regarded as political weapons – their function is to deter an opponent. In all doctrines, plans and exercises, a clear distinction is therefore made between nuclear weapons and conventional ones. The purpose of this is to prevent any conventional war gradually developing into a war in which nuclear weapons are used.

Moscow, however, does not make an equally clear distinction. The Russians operate using more of a sliding scale, from cyber-attacks, limited military operations and comprehensive conventional warfare to the use of smaller tactical nuclear weapons and finally full-scale nuclear war. Nuclear weapons have become a more central part of their doctrine, and the Russians' threshold for using nuclear weapons is lower.

Russia's strategy is to have the ability to strike, either with superior conventional forces locally or using smaller, precise nuclear weapons, in order to take control of a limited area. This then forces their opponent to have to choose – to either go to war, or to surrender.

Jim Mattis, in the conversations I had with him at that time, was keen to ensure we didn't end up in a situation where we would become vulnerable to such pressure. 'They have to know that whatever they attack us with, we'll be able to counter them at the right level, with just the right amount of force. That they shouldn't even *think* about using their nukes, because we'd checkmate them immediately. But for that, we need capacity in low-yield nuclear weapons,' he said. Mattis was concerned that while the Americans must abide by the INF treaty, the deterrent also needed to remain credible.

It's easy to think that smaller nuclear weapons are less dangerous than larger ones, but actually almost the reverse is true. Low-yield nuclear weapons have a lower threshold for use. Mattis emphasised that the US's decision to undertake research into new intermediate-range missiles, and the plans to develop low-yield nuclear weapons, were intended as a means of exerting pressure, and a bargaining chip that could be used with the Russians. It strengthened my hope that it might be possible to bring the Russians back to the INF Treaty.

'Try to convince the Russians that everyone is served by the treaty holding. Offer them a new agreement,' I told Mattis. He assured me that this was exactly what the Americans were doing.

But as time went on, my hopes began to fade. By the summer of 2018, I could tell that the Americans were losing patience, and I was afraid they might decide to act alone. As I began to accept that the Russians were not going to return to the INF Treaty, I adjusted my goal: now, it was simply to keep NATO united.

This was no simple task. Several European countries were hesitant to come out and say that Russia was breaching the treaty, because such an acknowledgement might initiate a process that ended with NATO deploying equivalent missiles, thereby opening the door for a new arms race. The inflamed relationship between the United States and Europe also made everything more difficult. In Germany in particular, many believed the US could no longer be regarded as a reliable partner. The Germans felt that President Trump was more interested in offending than defending them. Internal conflict around the INF Treaty would increase the risk of the US and Europe drifting even further apart.

I met with John Bolton and Mike Pompeo in Washington in September. Bolton's opinion in particular was clear: 'We are two countries who signed the INF Treaty. If one country breaches it, then the treaty is of limited value to the other.'

Both Bolton and Pompeo were professional and knowledgeable, and both were loyal to the US president. While they were part of the Trump administration, which I generally felt far from in terms of my political views, they were also enthusiastic supporters of NATO, and we worked well together.

During a dinner at home in the residence in October 2018, one of my bodyguards came over to me at the table. He had received a phone call from NATO headquarters. 'Secretary General,' he whispered into my ear, 'National Security Advisor Bolton wishes to speak to you in an hour.' I had regular phone conversations with Bolton, but we usually agreed the time for these a day or two in advance. Clearly something was brewing.

I took the call in my office.

'We're no longer in any doubt,' Bolton said. 'Russia is not complying with the INF Treaty. The seriousness of this breach demands a response.'

Bolton told me that the Russians claimed the United States was breaching the treaty, which he deemed utterly ridiculous.

'The final decision hasn't been made. But everything is moving in the direction of declaring that Russia is in breach of the treaty, and that we're therefore withdrawing from it,' he said.

As I slowly put down the receiver on that day in October and leaned back in my chair, I remember with absolute clarity what I was thinking. The INF Treaty was dead. A cornerstone of Europe's security was about to crumble.

Bolton expressed his concerns regarding China. The Americans also felt the pressure of the Chinese intermediate-range missiles, which could threaten American aircraft carriers and the American territory of Guam in the Western Pacific. China had long been acting with carte blanche in the South China Sea, building military bases on small islands they claimed were Chinese territory.

I understood that Bolton ideally wanted the United States to withdraw from the treaty as quickly as possible. But at the same time, he knew how sensitive the matter was for the Europeans, and that we might be in for a battle over the perception of what was going on. He accepted that a deliberate withdrawal process would be necessary.

The best thing undoubtedly would have been for the INF Treaty to be maintained – presuming it was adhered to, that is. No serious attempt was made to bring China into the agreement, because the Chinese would have rejected the proposal outright, but both the Russians and the Americans could have done more to involve China. As late as the summer of 2018, such an approach might have been possible, but after my conversation with Bolton in October, I realised it was game over. It was no longer in NATO's interest for the Americans to comply with the treaty while the Russians were breaching it. We might require a military response to the Russian missiles, and moreover, it was about the treaty's credibility. The Russians had to see that breaching agreements had consequences. Were they to draw the conclusion that the West would naively fulfil its obligations, while they recklessly did as they pleased, the very purpose of arms control measures would be undermined.

One weekend towards the end of October, I was back home in Oslo when I learned that John Bolton wished to speak to me again. Early on the Sunday morning I went down to the Ministry of Defence, to use the secure line there. Bolton got straight to the point. 'The President has just said we're withdrawing from the INF Treaty.'

Trump had been interviewed following a campaign rally in Nevada, and he had been asked about the nuclear treaty's current state. The president referred to Russia's breach and China's military build-up. 'If Russia's doing it and if China's doing it and we're adhering to the agreement, that's unacceptable,' he said.

'It came as a surprise to us,' Bolton said. He had immediately called Mike Pompeo, who hadn't received advance notice of the announcement, either. The two of them scrambled and managed to inform a number of key players. 'I wanted you to know that Trump has said we're pulling out. I can no longer keep a straight face and tell the Russians the US has yet to make a definitive decision,' Bolton said.

'So is this a final decision in practice?' I asked.

'If you ask me, it looks that way,' he said.

Bolton's plan to discuss the matter with the other allies before anything was announced fell by the wayside. As did the idea of trying to achieve a coordinated phasing out of the treaty, in cooperation with the Russians. These plans went up in smoke because Trump, who had never publicly mentioned the INF Treaty before this point, made short work of them. It happened in passing, as he was making his way up the steps to Air Force One.

An ever increasing number of NATO allies were realising that the current situation, in which Russia violated the treaty while the United States respected it, could not continue. But the way in which the INF Treaty was terminated was of the utmost importance. If the Europeans felt the decision had already been made, then it would be more difficult to close ranks. Those desiring a more independent security policy role for Europe would receive grist to their mill. The rift between the United States and Europe might grow both deeper and wider.

Over the weeks that followed, we tried to get the process back on track. I met with all the key players in Paris in mid-November, in connection with the centenary of the end of the First World War. The European leaders were disheartened by the turn of events. Just before a dinner at the Musée d'Orsay, I met with Angela Merkel, and I was completely open with her. 'I need your support to keep the alliance together,' I said.

Merkel was clear about what Germany needed.

'You have to convince the Americans to give Russia one last chance to come back to the treaty. We have to do this in the right order, give them sixty days before we do anything else. A last chance for a diplomatic solution,' she said.

The national security advisers of France, Germany, the United Kingdom and the United States had just discussed precisely this in Paris. But according to Bolton, enough was enough. He wanted the US to show its strength and withdraw from the treaty immediately.

'Exactly *when* the United States withdraws surely isn't crucial,' I said to Bolton when I met with him. 'What's crucial is that you first give Russia a final deadline.'

Either Russia would do a one-eighty at the last minute, and the INF Treaty would be saved, or the United States would at least obtain much broader political support among the NATO allies for terminating the treaty.

I presented the Americans' arguments in my conversations with the Germans, and used the Germans' arguments when I met with the Americans. Both parties were fairly stubborn.

'This is important to us,' Merkel said. 'But we'll find a solution, Jens.'

This gave me cause for optimism, in spite of everything. An internal split along the lines of the one we experienced during the Iraq war in 2003 would be deeply serious. In a speech I gave in November, I said that NATO had no intention of responding to Russia's breach of the INF Treaty by deploying new nuclear missiles in Europe, which gave rise to internal friction within NATO. A number of the Eastern European nations were of the opinion that we should retaliate in kind. The entire question of missiles in Europe could be taken off NATO's table; nations such as Poland and the Baltic states might negotiate directly with the US regarding the deployment of missiles on their territories. Germany and France might then withdraw their troops from Eastern Europe, deeming the American missiles so provocative as to put their own forces in danger. It would mean a major splitting and weakening of NATO.

Such was the seriousness of the possible consequences of a split around the INF Treaty.

Vladimir Putin was also present at the commemorative ceremonies in Paris. At this time, I still perceived Putin as a leader it was possible to have rational interactions with. I also thought he could exhibit brief flashes of a sense of humour, although I realised I was probably the only person in NATO who thought this. As head of NATO, I would normally have had more frequent contact with Russia's president, but the prevailing poor relations meant we hardly met. The last time I had seen Putin was at a lunch at the United Nations General Assembly three years earlier. Then, I had mentioned all we had achieved together, back when I was Norway's prime minister. Putin had replied with a crooked smile. 'Yes, you should go back to Norwegian politics,' he said. 'That would be best for both Norway and NATO.'

'Sure. I'll go back to Oslo the day you go back to St Petersburg and get back into local politics there,' I said.

And now, in Paris, I essayed another soft lead-in to a serious matter. I told Putin I was glad to see him, and again reminded him of our successful cooperation during my time as Norway's prime minister. For Putin and the other Russian leaders, NATO stands for something far worse than each of the organisation's member nations separately, so I thought a reminder that the two of us had previously managed to work well together might have a certain positive effect.

'Mr President, many allies are concerned that you are breaching the INF Treaty. We want to try to save it, but you have to help us,' I said, after we had shaken hands.

'Secretary General, Russia is abiding by the treaty,' Putin replied. 'The United States is the problem. President Trump has said straight out that they are withdrawing from the treaty.'

'But you have to pacify the Americans, submit evidence that there is no breach.'

'I'll discuss the INF Treaty when I meet with Trump at the upcoming G20 summit in Buenos Aires,' Putin said, before reiterating that the problem was the United States.

'Then I would ask that you make an honest attempt to come to an agreement with him,' I said. Just then, Angela Merkel came walking towards us. Putin waved and greeted her in German, gesturing for her to come over and join us. From a distance, Merkel waved and shouted: 'No, no, Vladimir. You have to talk to Jens about missiles. That's what's important right now.'

The United States postponed their withdrawal, and Russia was given a deadline of sixty days within which to begin removal of the missiles that were in contravention of the treaty. This proved unsuccessful, however, and no agreement with the Russians was reached. On the fourth of December 2018, the meeting of NATO ministers of foreign affairs concluded that Russia had developed and deployed a new land-based missile system that constituted a breach of the INF.

And so it was done. The meeting of NATO ministers of foreign affairs was a worthy funeral for a jewel in the crown of international arms control. We did our utmost to save the agreement, but Putin would rather have his new nuclear missiles.

The INF Treaty's burial was tedious but predictable. On the second of February 2019, the United States declared that the sixty-day deadline had expired, and then a six-month notice period began. A month later, the Russians suspended the treaty. On the second of August that same year, the entire process was concluded. Early in the morning, the Americans announced their withdrawal from the treaty. At the same time, I made an official statement which made it clear that all NATO members supported the United States' decision. It's almost painful to realise just how relieved you can feel when something you've worked so hard to save is terminated in an orderly fashion.

The world had passed a milestone on a march in the wrong direction. But NATO managed to preserve its solidarity. All the allies agreed that Russia had breached the treaty, and we had managed to get the Americans to agree to give the Russians an opportunity to turn things around. They were given the deadline Angela Merkel, with my support, had so forcefully desired. I was happy for the political signal this gave. The United States listened to its allies.

Nevertheless, we had now experienced our first major setback in the work of international disarmament. A huge block had tumbled out of the construction. And more bricks could fall.

20

The closeness of war

IN THE FLAT, GREEN LANDSCAPE OF FLANDERS STAND THE REGI-
mented lines of white gravestones in Tyne Cot, just outside the small
city of Ypres. It's possible to wander between the cemetery's rows of
headstones for hours, reading names, stopping to reflect on yet
another fate, yet another young life lost. It's in such war cemeteries
that we can feel the true weight of it: that the catastrophes we call
world wars are the sum of an infinite number of human lives suddenly
cut short. Hopes lost, dreams never realised. There are few places in
which all this pain is as present as it is in Ypres, the scene of some of
the bloodiest battles fought during the First World War.

I have been there several times, but made my first visit just six
months after we had moved to Brussels. Ingrid and I had invited some
close friends along for a kind of combined celebration of my birthday
and a history seminar. One of the things I found difficult about
moving to Belgium was that I missed my good friends, so the trip was
also about spending time with some of the people who mean the most
to me. We have since visited Verdun, Sedan and Ardennes in France,
and Arnhem in the Netherlands – important places in the history of
the First and Second World War.

Accompanying us as our guide in Ypres was the chair of NATO's
military committee, Danish general Knud Bartels, who had previously
been head of the Danish forces in Afghanistan. He knew his history
inside out, and showed us where the Germans and the British had

held their positions opposite one another, pointing and explaining as we went.

'It's always about taking higher ground. Those who manage that have the upper hand,' Bartels said as we trudged along the green hill-crests surrounding Ypres. He thought this had to be one of the places on earth that has seen the most suffering, because so much death and pain were concentrated in such a small area over such a long period of time.

The reconstructed Menin Gate has now been made into a war memorial. In the first months of the war, the soldiers marched through this gate on their way out to the trenches. The names of the fallen were engraved here, but soon there were so many names that there was no space for more, and the inscriptions were moved to one of the church-yards outside the city. Every evening at eight o'clock, a bugle call, the Last Post, is sounded here in honour of the dead. The call has sounded every single day since the early 1920s, with the exception of a few years during the Second World War, when the area was occupied by the Germans. The bugle call was then sounded at a churchyard in London.

At one of the area's war cemeteries, Bartels stopped and asked us to gather round. He then recited one of history's most famous war poems, 'In Flanders Fields', written by Canadian physician Lieutenant-Colonel John McCrae after he attended the funeral of a friend who was killed at Ypres in May 1915. The first verse reads as follows:

In Flanders fields the poppies blow
Between the crosses, row on row,
That mark our place; and in the sky
The larks, still bravely singing, fly
Scarce heard amid the guns below.

Bartels's voice trembled slightly. 'I can never read this poem without thinking of the children of the soldiers I was responsible for in Afghanistan who didn't return home to Denmark,' he said. Nor did McCrae survive the war, but through his poem the red poppies that grew on the graves have become an immortal symbol of the fallen.

In the small hollow in the landscape within which Ypres is situated, the suffering began in October 1914 and did not end until the autumn of 1918. The Germans wanted to avoid the strongly fortified border with France; their plan of attack was therefore to go through Belgium, around the French fortifications, and straight to Paris. They managed to take Ypres in the autumn of 1914, but withdrew from the city after a few days due to supply and logistics problems. The Germans dug themselves in among the dense hills around the city, where they remained, while in the meantime the British took control of the city centre. The static battle had begun.

It was interrupted by bloody offensives, from each side in turn. Trench warfare was a miserable, meaningless nightmare of despair and death. The soldiers leaped from their trenches and stormed towards the enemy's positions, only to be mown down. Ypres was razed to the ground. Across the landscape, which was shattered by exploding shells, all the vegetation vanished. And when the autumn rains came, the soldiers found themselves drowning in mud. To this day, the earth here regurgitates skeletons, helmets, belts and unexploded grenades. When I visited the German war cemetery in 2019, eighty-seven German soldiers had been recently buried there after their remains were discovered during excavation works.

A total of 610,000 soldiers were killed at Ypres: Germans, British, and soldiers from the British Commonwealth. Millions were severely wounded. They managed to move the front line just a couple of miles in four years.

The gravestones of the British soldiers who fell at Ypres are inscribed with the words 'Victim of the Great War' – this is the name by which the war was referred to in many European countries until 1940. The First World War was the first truly industrial war; the advent of tanks, machine guns, submarines and gas changed warfare forever. Technological advances have always had their impact, but in the past, events unfolded infinitely more slowly. The Roman legions with their spears and lances might have managed to stand their ground in the Napoleonic wars two thousand years later. After another hundred years, on the other hand, Caesar's soldiers would have fallen wretchedly short.

The tragic thing was that the Great War's infantryman fell short, too. Although they should have known better, the military planners of the day failed to fully grasp the new weapons' annihilating power. Just before the war broke out, there was a great debate in the French parliament about the army's attire. Those who argued that the uniform ought to provide camouflage lost the debate. In 1914, French soldiers therefore ran straight towards the enemy's machine guns wearing red trousers, and hats – they would only be supplied with helmets later on. In the second battle at Ypres, in the spring of 1915, the Germans used gas for the first time. Gas masks existed, but hardly any of the soldiers had them. The consequences of new military technology had simply not been reckoned with.

Fundamental misjudgements were made back then, but it is far from certain that we handle the challenges associated with the threats and weapons systems of our age any better. Missiles that find their targets themselves. Drones equipped with facial recognition technology to kill specific individuals. Autonomous weapons systems that have been developed using artificial intelligence. Technological advances are happening so rapidly that we are struggling to keep up. We are unable to take in the true breadth of these technological developments, and the consequences they may have for how wars are fought.

Another lesson learned from our recent war history concerns deterrence. In 1914, there existed a treaty through which the European powers guaranteed Belgium's neutrality. The security guarantee involved the British coming to the country's aid in the event of an attack. Historians have pointed out that Germany didn't think Britain would stand by the treaty – the Germans simply couldn't believe that the British would risk a major war over defending tiny Belgium. This turned out to be a fatal error in judgement. The British declared war on Germany, and sent significant forces to defend Belgium. The deterrent had failed.

NATO is about present-day deterrence. Everything rests on any potential adversary knowing that an attack on one NATO country is an attack against all. As long as this remains credible, no military attack will be attempted. Which is why the deterrent has to be a reality in the mind of any potential enemy. There can be no doubt that NATO nations stand by their commitment to each other.

In several NATO capitals, many felt that Trump was sowing doubt about the credibility of the alliance's deterrent, because he failed to express clear and unconditional support for the Article 5 security guarantee.

This doubt was further intensified by a statement the US president gave on Fox News in the summer of 2018. Host Tucker Carlson asked about Article 5 of the NATO treaty. 'Why should my son go to Montenegro to defend it from attack?' he said.

'I understand what you're saying,' Trump replied. 'I've asked the same question. Montenegro is a tiny country with very strong people … They're very aggressive people. They may get aggressive, and congratulations, you're in World War III.'

Senator John McCain was among those who tweeted that the statement was a gift to Vladimir Putin, who was extremely unhappy that Montenegro had recently joined NATO. Only two years had passed since an unsuccessful pro-Russian coup in Montenegro, which also involved agents from Russia's military intelligence agency, the GRU.

I called Montenegrin prime minister Duško Marković, and assured him that NATO stood by its obligations, although in all honesty, I'm not sure how much it helped. If the president of the United States says he doesn't intend to defend your country, the secretary general of NATO saying the opposite will offer little in the way of reassurance.

Strength, steadfastness and predictability can prevent war. Uncertainty and ambiguities, on the other hand, can provide space for misunderstanding and misjudgements that can lead to it.

Rivalry between major powers caused them to stumble into a world war in 1914. Europe's leaders misjudged the consequences of their decisions.

Only very few had imagined that a major war might be possible. Following the end of the Napoleonic wars in 1815, the 1800s had by and large been an era of peace in Europe's history. Over the next hundred years, trade significantly increased. National economies became more interlinked. New methods of transportation and communication, such as steamships, railways and the telegraph, bound countries and people together. Productivity within agriculture and industry saw a major upturn. Between 1900 and 1914, overseas investments almost doubled. Globalisation reached heights the world had never seen.

A notion of lasting peace took hold – the idea that where merchants cross borders, no soldiers will follow. The illusion that a full-scale war was unthinkable, that it simply couldn't happen, turned out to be exactly that – an illusion.

On the eleventh of November 2018, a number of leaders came together in Paris to mark the centenary of the end of the First World War.

I had been looking forward to the event. The heads of the nations that sent their soldiers out onto the battlefields, coming together and remembering all those who died. The centenary also highlighted how old adversaries can put their differences behind them. The close cooperation within today's European Union is perhaps the best example of how former enemies can become trusting friends.

The conditions for the ceremony were not the best on that day in November. The rain fell heavily over the French capital as the various heads of state and government and EU and NATO leaders walked together down the Champs-Élysées. A podium had been set up by the Arc de Triomphe. Only once we were there, and a good while after everyone else, did President Donald Trump turn up. Vladimir Putin arrived even later. He seemed a little sullen, possibly due to the conflict surrounding the INF Treaty, which had dominated the previous evening's conversations and dinner.

As host of the event, it was French president Emmanuel Macron who gave a speech, in his winter coat and with a thick wool scarf around his neck. He highlighted the influences that had led to the catastrophe in 1914, and warned that these 'old demons' were resurfacing again. 'Patriotism is the exact opposite of nationalism,' he said. 'Nationalism is a betrayal of patriotism. In saying "our interests first, whatever happens to the others", you erase the most precious thing a nation can have, that which makes it live, that which causes it to be great and that which is most important: its moral values.'

I stood on the podium beside the Arc de Triomphe along with the heads of state and government. French flags waved around us, their colours visible everywhere. Many of the bloodiest battles fought in the First World War took place in France. The country suffered incomprehensible losses.

Trump stood in the front row, stony-faced. During a speech he made in Houston not long before, he had lashed out at all the corrupt, power-hungry globalists and called himself a nationalist. He was now forced to listen to Macron confronting nationalism, which the French president believed to be the driving ideological force behind the bloodbath that ended in 1918.

Just after the ceremony, Trump posted a hailstorm of tweets: 'MAKE FRANCE GREAT AGAIN!' He mocked France's capitulation in 1940: 'They were starting to learn German in Paris before the U.S. came along!'

The centenary of the Armistice of 11 November 1918 was an opportunity to highlight the importance of cooperation, reconciliation and friendship, but it wasn't used as it should have been. The world order as we know it today was created by the leaders of the countries that had gathered there. It was an order that had given peace to our part of the world for over seventy years. Now we're drifting apart, I thought. Things were already bad, and they might get worse.

That same autumn, I returned to Ypres with some students from the two Norwegian schools in Belgium. Just as the head of NATO's military committee, General Bartels, had done for me on my first visit, I read the poem 'In Flanders Fields' to the Norwegian teenagers. The second verse reads as follows:

We are the Dead. Short days ago
We lived, felt dawn, saw sunset glow,
Loved and were loved, and now we lie,
In Flanders fields.

The youngest of the British soldiers buried at Ypres was just seventeen years old. As one of the students thoughtfully pointed out: 'They weren't that much older than us.'

If we are to truly understand that peace is something precious and fragile, our experiences of war have to be kept alive. We must grasp the vast suffering of war, in order to be able to fight for peace. We must understand what is at stake.

This is why I have made multiple journeys to Ypres. And it is why I will go there again.

21

A rescue operation on Fox News

IT WAS PRESIDENT DONALD TRUMP'S BELIEF THAT AT THE SUMMIT in the summer of 2018, the Europeans had committed to fulfilling the requirement to spend 2 per cent of gross domestic product on defence immediately. As 2018 moved into 2019, he looked over the accounts – and found that most countries were still spending far below the target.

We received clear signals that the president had decided to make good on his threats to break with NATO, and make a move that, to all intents and purposes, would render the alliance's security guarantee worthless. We had avoided sustained damage at the last summit, but the risk of a breakdown was ramping up again.

On the fifteenth of January, Tucker Carlson mocked NATO in his Fox News show *Tucker Carlson Tonight*. 'On multiple occasions the president has privately floated the idea of pulling the United States out of NATO. Let that sink in: *leaving NATO*. This is a huge story – or it would have been a huge story in 1983, when the Soviet Union still existed and it was still clear what the point of NATO was … Vladimir Putin runs Russia now, he does not plan to invade Western Europe, *he can't*. So why do we still have NATO?'

Carlson entertained his viewers with quick-witted anti-NATO rhetoric, and we knew that the Trump administration and Fox News were closely connected.

In February 2019, Trump would give the annual State of the Union address. We were told by people in the White House that two drafts existed as to how NATO would be mentioned: one in which Trump announced he wanted to pull the United States out of NATO, and one in which he made it clear that he would only protect the countries who spent 2 per cent of GDP on defence. An article in the *New York Times* confirmed this – according to the newspaper, Trump had expressed his wish to leave the organisation in several contexts.

By now, Jim Mattis had resigned as secretary of defense. Without warning, Trump had announced that he was withdrawing US troops from Syria, and it had been the final straw for Mattis. I had understood during the summit in Brussels that Mattis was unsure how long he would remain in office. The Syria announcement triggered his resignation, but the reasons for it were more complex.

Mattis had called me between Christmas and New Year, to thank me for our cooperation. He felt that Trump was no longer listening to him, and that it was therefore impossible to effectively fulfil his role as secretary of defense.

Trump claimed he had fired Mattis, called him the world's most overrated general, and talked down his achievements. Mattis himself seemed mostly relieved. 'I just had to quit,' he said to me.

We agreed to meet. 'I'll buy you a Norwegian beer, and we can talk about everything that's happened and all we've seen and done,' he said.

There was no point dwelling on Mattis's exit. That's just how it is in politics. People come and go.

Facing the renewed possibility that Trump might be about to pull the United States out of NATO, we couldn't just sit around in Brussels. I had to travel to Washington and speak with key individuals. Get a feel for the atmosphere, understand more of what was going on and see if anything could be done. As ever, it would be about showing that the recent developments within NATO were a victory for Trump, so a public appearance would help to get the message out. The president of the United States had to be engaged, not isolated.

I agreed to be interviewed on Fox News. On Sunday the twenty-seventh of January, I made my way to the studio in Washington for the channel's morning broadcast. I was asked about how things really were within the alliance, and what I thought of President Trump. I didn't want to become part of the debate around US domestic policy, and nor could I defend everything Trump had said and done. What I could do, however, was stick to my well-worn message that Trump's clear demands had had an effect, and that he had been heard.

'By the end of next year,' I said, 'NATO allies will add a hundred – one hundred billion extra US dollars toward defence.' This was a new, collated figure we had calculated for how much more Europe and Canada had spent on defence since Trump became president. Now we were diligently trying to sell this number to the American public, so that Trump himself could use it in his State of the Union address and other speeches. I also emphasised that Europe and the United States continued to stand together.

I don't know how large an audience was watching the Fox News broadcast that Sunday. I was actually only speaking to one faithful Fox viewer. And sure enough, after just a few minutes, he tweeted:

'Jens Stoltenberg, NATO Secretary General, just stated that because of me NATO has been able to raise far more money than ever before from its members after many years of decline. It's called burden sharing. Also, more united. Dems & Fake News like to portray the opposite!'

In this interview with Fox News, I did perhaps give Trump a bit of a helping hand in the domestic debate, where the Democrats were criticising him for weakening NATO. But it was a price I was willing to pay to achieve the most important thing – keeping NATO united. I would much rather he used me as a witness to prove he had helped make the Europeans pay up. And besides, it was true.

During my visit to Washington, I attended a formal dinner at which former White House chief of staff John Kelly confirmed that Trump had indeed been ready to leave the summit six months earlier. His bags had been packed.

I also met with Mike Pompeo, and asked if he thought the new figure I was using, $100 billion, would be enough to convince Trump to stay in NATO. Pompeo said he thought so. I was also buoyed by my first meeting with the new secretary of defense, Patrick Shanahan, who expressed a genuine interest in working with us.

All in all, I felt reassured. The staff around Trump gave no sign that anything dramatic was about to be announced, as I had feared before we arrived. Whatever came next, it would stem directly from Trump himself, not from the people around him. When it came to Trump, nothing was certain. We knew this. But Bolton believed we had nothing to fear when it came to the State of the Union address.

He was right. Trump gave his speech on the evening of the sixth of February, European time. He said nothing that threatened NATO. On the contrary. The president referred to NATO as one of his foreign policy victories.

Everything indicated that Trump had been ready to withdraw from the alliance but ultimately decided not to. The efforts of several individuals in Washington and those of us in NATO had likely contributed to this.

At my meeting with Mike Pompeo, he brought up a confidential request. 'I haven't discussed this with anyone,' he said. 'But would you be prepared to stay on in NATO?'

My immediate reaction was that I would. It might be a slightly lonely job, and I missed my family and friends back in Oslo, but being head of NATO was so important and meaningful. Every day, I felt privileged to work with some of our time's truly great questions.

NATO was a heavy ship to turn, but we were in the process of developing an organisation with improved management at all levels. I wanted to continue this work. The turnaround demanded new political efforts every day. President Trump wasn't always easy to work with, but I was motivated by the challenge of interacting with him, and of keeping NATO united.

Now the US secretary of state was asking if I would like to extend my term in office. I was unprepared, and needed to take some time to think about it. And to discuss it with Ingrid. She and I had made many plans for all we would do when I came home. Ideas and dreams we could finally realise when I was no longer so tied down.

It was not a conversation I was looking forward to. Especially since this wasn't the first time my post had been extended.

My term as head of NATO had been originally set to run from 2014 to 2018. But late in the autumn of 2017, my term had been extended by two years, until 2020. The norm was one, but during the work on the extension we realised fairly quickly that many countries would support an additional year. They clearly wanted calm and stability around the person who would lead NATO, at a time when Brexit and Trump were causing more than enough unpredictability and uncertainty. Many wished to extend my term to avoid the NATO role becoming a bargaining chip in complicated negotiations over leading international positions.

Ingrid had been far from enthusiastic. On the morning I had to confirm whether I was willing to stay on for two more years, she sent me a text: 'If you have to give your answer today, then make sure you have an exit strategy.' This was her way of saying yes.

For over thirty years, my career had been a source of tension in my relationship with Ingrid. In reality, this began in 1989, when I became a researcher at Statistics Norway, and Ingrid had travelled to Hungary with our son, who was just a few months old. She would be working at the Norwegian embassy in Budapest, and the plan was that I would move out there later in the autumn. But before I managed to do so, I received a call from the minister of environment Thorbjørn Berntsen, who asked me to become his state secretary. And with that, my research career was over before it had ever really started, and I never moved to Budapest, but commuted back and forth instead.

Later, I was nominated to parliament, then leading positions within the Labour Party's Oslo branch, deputy positions and cabinet posts, until I became the party's parliamentary leader. Every single time, I convinced Ingrid that these were short-term offices and roles: just *one* term in parliament, just *a few years* in the party leadership, cabinet minister just *once*.

Of course, things never turned out that way – quite the opposite, in fact. They snowballed, and in 2000, I ended up becoming Norway's prime minister. There's a big difference between being a cabinet minister and being prime minister in terms of the responsibility and workload – and not least, the public attention. The 2001 Norwegian parliamentary election was a catastrophe, and I was out of the prime minister's seat after just two years.

The next time, I was prime minister for eight years, and I remained head of the Labour Party until 2014. I had also presented the NATO job as a short-term affair – four years would pass quickly, I had said.

Ingrid herself had never sought a life in the public eye. This was something that had been forced upon her, as a result of my choices and desires. We had always agreed that she would pursue her own career, but of course my decisions had consequences for her life, too, both professionally and privately. Ingrid is a diplomat, but for all those years between the period in Budapest until she became an ambassador in Brussels in 2015, she was never stationed overseas. My career had come first.

Ingrid didn't say no to this life of ours. But nor did she offer a resounding yes, either. She more or less begrudgingly agreed to it. Of course she wanted to take overseas posts as a Norwegian diplomat, and I've always known that Ingrid desires a quieter, more withdrawn family life. She placed great emphasis on protecting the family's privacy. We never allowed reporting involving our children, wanting them to decide for themselves whether they wished to become publicly known.

Nevertheless, Ingrid chose a husband with a job that constantly interrupted our shared free time, and which could torpedo our holiday plans at short notice. Over the years, I had developed a few special techniques to ensure my work would intrude as little as possible when we were together at weekends or on holidays. I would take work calls while I was out for a walk, for example, or when I was out shopping or tidying up the cellar.

I could probably have made married life much easier for both of us by being less conflict-averse. But instead, I have repeatedly stuck my head in the sand and delayed discussions about important decisions, or waited until the very last minute to deliver bad news about appointments I wouldn't be able to keep.

It's often the case that expectations haven't been fully clarified, so when I have to have these kinds of conversations about a new job or office, I never look forward to it. I therefore delayed the conversation about the NATO extension for as long as possible. Just as I always did.

Nobody within the American administration had discussed the extension with the European leaders. But once Pompeo had taken the matter up with me, the ball got rolling pretty quickly. I needed to sit down with Ingrid. The conversation went better than I had feared. Yet again, she understood the arguments in favour of me continuing in the role. This was an expression of her fundamental support for the work I was doing. When, after some back-and-forth, we had made equivalent decisions together at similar crossroads in the past, she always supported me. She offered comfort and encouragement, and made the practical side of things work for the family.

So the Americans could proceed. When my term was extended the first time, it took a while before the confirmation came. This time it happened more quickly, and that was because the United States had initiated the request. NATO ambassador Kay Bailey Hutchison did much of the work by speaking with her colleagues and persuading key individuals within the member states' governments. As to why the Americans wanted me to continue in office, I can only speculate. Perhaps Pompeo and his colleagues saw that their president and I actually worked quite well together. If that was the case, then I helped to make their jobs a little easier.

At the end of March it was decided. France, as the last country to do so, had green-lit extending my term.

Now my time in post was due to end on the first of October 2022. Another two years was a vote of confidence that gave me greater authority, and having more experience made the role less demanding. When I now looked around the table during meetings with the heads of government, there were very few others who had been there as long as I had.

Trump's many objections to NATO helped to mobilise strong support *for* the alliance within the United States. The fact that both parties in Congress were concerned about Trump wanting to withdraw the United States from NATO led to a measure to prevent the president from unilaterally withdrawing the US from the organisation without Senate or congressional approval. Of course, I was glad to see the immense support for NATO, but it also posed some challenges. Once, when I joined a meeting of the Senate Foreign Relations Committee, the chair of the committee, Democrat Bob Menendez of New Jersey, leaned towards me and said: 'I would like to know whether it helps you in your work when President Trump says he isn't certain we'll defend Montenegro should a conflict arise. I hope to hear a clear response from you, Secretary General.'

Menendez knew very well what he was doing – he wanted me to criticise Trump. I was aware that if I criticised the president for undermining NATO's security guarantee before the Senate Foreign Relations Committee, it would make it harder for me to work with him. But at the same time, I couldn't defend what Trump had said about Montenegro in the much-discussed Fox News interview. I sidestepped: 'It isn't my role to participate in domestic policy debates within the United States,' I said, sticking to the line I had so often repeated in the American media. The United States' increased presence in Europe was what really mattered. Actions speak louder than words. This was true, but it wasn't the whole truth. President Trump's statements were a problem.

In February 2019, I met the majority leader of the House of Representatives, Nancy Pelosi, who was visiting Europe with a large delegation. We had known each other for a long time, and she was a major source of support in the work to defend NATO within the United States. She never said so directly, but I had the sense that she felt I went too far in defending Trump, pointing out that European defence budgets had begun to increase under President Obama. Indeed, Obama had also been responsible for stepping up the US military presence in Europe, she said. She was absolutely right, of course. But at the same time, I tried to explain how important it was to say that Trump's clear message had contributed to further increasing the European defence budgets.

It was probably my conversations with Pelosi and the other representatives that gave them the idea I might do even more to garner support for NATO within the United States. Because not long afterwards, I was invited to address Congress.

My assignment was crystal clear, as formulated in the letter from Nancy Pelosi and Republican Senate leader Mitch McConnell: 'In a critical time for the United States, NATO, and the EU, the American Congress and the American people look forward to hearing your message of friendship and partnership.'

The bar had been set. There was nothing to do but get writing.

22

It's good to have friends

I VISITED THE UNITED STATES IN THE SUMMER OF 1980. I WAS twenty-one years old, had just completed my military service, and a long holiday awaited me. I was met at the airport in New York by embassy counsellor Arne Treholt of the Norwegian UN delegation, and would be staying with him. He was a popular figure at the centre of a large social circle in New York. Little did we know that the FBI, at the request of the Norwegian Security Service, were in the process of implementing a major surveillance operation against Treholt. His apartment in Manhattan was watched around the clock.

Thorvald came over, together with the rest of the family. Treholt, elegant and well dressed as ever, accompanied me to the airport to meet them. After saying our hellos, and while we were still in the arrivals hall, Treholt cast a sceptical glance at Thorvald's slightly worn and not especially well cut suit, and said: 'You can't go around looking like that, Thorvald. You look like some mediocre KGB agent.'

Just a few years later, Arne Treholt was sentenced to twenty years in prison for spying for the Soviet Union and Iraq.

Thorvald had come to the US on business, in his role as minister of defence, but he also managed to insert a few days' holiday into the trip, so it became a combination of work and leisure. The US Army offered the Stoltenberg family the use of a dedicated, comfortable plane, and flew us to Thorvald's various meetings all across the country. A somewhat exotic experience, and an informative trip.

One thing we heard several times during our travels was how the United States was increasingly orienting itself westwards, towards the Pacific region. The generation that had lived through the war against Hitler's Germany was now disappearing. Silicon Valley was becoming the engine behind a mighty economic upturn, which affected California and other states in the west far more than those in the east. Demographic trends were also moving in the same direction; political, economic and demographic weights were all tilting the scale westwards. As the United States placed more emphasis on the Pacific region, the parts of the country with the strongest connections to Europe were weakened. The transatlantic ties and security policy cooperation with Europe were at risk of disintegrating.

This was back in 1980, so concerns about the United States turning towards the Pacific are not new. But these developments have continued and intensified. Immigration from parts of the world other than Europe is changing the US's demographic make-up. The significance of the groups within American society with the strongest European connections is decreasing. And in addition, there is China's growth. In 1980, China's gross domestic product was just 10 per cent of that of the United States. Today, China's economy is around the same size as that of the US, taking into account the cost differences between the two countries. The Soviet Union was never any real technological challenger, while China competes with the United States to a much greater extent.

China's military build-up has led to US military authorities viewing the world in a different way than they did previously. Even the Pentagon, with its formidable military budget, does not have unlimited resources. China's growth is pulling the Pacific region up everyone's priority list. That things have gone well for NATO over the forty years that have passed since I first heard about the US turning towards Asia in 1980, doesn't necessarily mean that things will go well for forty more.

These major trends were in the back of my mind when I began working on my congressional address. One of my aims was to say something about China, but we struggled to find the right words. At the time, in April 2019, relations between NATO and China were unsettled and contentious. Many NATO countries were concerned about their trade links with the country, and wanted to avoid the alliance giving signals that might be perceived as NATO making China a new enemy. Within NATO, we had analyses and intelligence assessments of China, but we had no agreed policy. There was no single NATO declaration, not one document, that I could build upon. So I ended up not mentioning China at all.

The day before I was due to make my way to Capitol Hill, I was invited to the White House and a meeting with Donald Trump. During our conversation, he hopped from one question to the next as usual, but he spoke well of NATO. 'Would there have been any NATO without me?' he asked, before answering his own question: 'I don't think NATO would have existed without me. Or at least it would be a very different NATO.' He believed the alliance had been on the brink of bankruptcy, since the organisation's income had been plummeting before he stepped in.

'Why are we in Afghanistan?' he suddenly asked. He had asked the same question many times before. My reply was the same, too.

'To combat international terrorism,' I said.

'So are we going to have soldiers in every country where there are terrorists?'

He had a point. Trump might ask simple, direct questions, but there was a logic behind them that couldn't easily be dismissed. No NATO country believed it should have its own forces stationed in every country harbouring terrorist organisations. Sometimes, Trump reminded me of the boy in the fairy-tale about the emperor's new clothes, who comes straight out with what no one else dare say. He broke with political correctness, and at times this could be quite liberating.

Trump continued to complain about the NATO nations who were paying too little, and he remained just as critical of the Nord Stream 2 gas pipeline. 'The Germans are getting eighty to ninety per cent of their energy from Russia. I hear forty per cent. But it's eighty per cent,' he said. Nonetheless, his tone was lighter and less confrontational. He had noted the message Congress wished to send by inviting me to speak – that is, that NATO held a prominent position within the United States. I think Trump realised that he ought to try to pocket a victory around NATO, rather than keep hacking away at the organisation. I heard it said that Trump was on truly good terms with only two foreign leaders: Israeli prime minister Benjamin Netanyahu, and me. It's on such occasions that I can start to wonder what on earth has become of my life.

When the meeting was over, vice president Mike Pence and I stood together beside the door. 'The President would appreciate it if you could say in your address that he's made NATO stronger,' he said.

This was something I couldn't promise to do.

'It's in the speech that Trump's clear message on defence spending and a fairer sharing of the burden has had a real impact,' I replied. Perhaps Trump and Pence had been hoping for more. But as ever, I couldn't stand by any statement that went further than this.

Nancy Pelosi was my host at Congress the following morning. At the time she was seventy-nine years old, and combined a good-natured humour with sharp repartee. She showed me her office, with its magnificent view of the National Mall, the vast park with its famous sights like the Lincoln Memorial and the Washington Monument. Slightly off to one side, I glimpsed the White House.

I was collected by a select group of representatives, consisting of both Republicans and Democrats. It was similar to when a delegation of Norwegian MPs escort the King into parliament at the annual formal opening of the Storting – only this was the United States Congress, and I didn't exactly feel like a king.

I was anxious. I was about to speak to the world's most important national assembly, and millions would see me on their TV screens. My address was about what the entire NATO alliance rests upon: the organisation's relationship with the United States. Would the representatives be inspired? Would my speech galvanise support for NATO in the way I hoped?

The procession marched in, and I was announced to a packed chamber. I walked up to the lectern, and before I had said a single word, I was met with a standing ovation, and yes, even cheers. We were off to a good start. My audience was obviously going to be attentive and kindly disposed.

It was almost seventy years to the day since the North Atlantic Treaty had been signed in Washington. The recurring theme of my speech was how throughout those years, NATO has served us well in the fight to preserve our peace and our freedom.

'Yes, allies have been involved in conflicts in different parts of the world. And allies have suffered the pain of terrorist attacks. But no NATO ally has been attacked by another country,' I said.

I pointed out that America has been the backbone of the alliance. That Europe would not be the Europe we know today without the support of the United States.

'NATO has been good for Europe. And NATO has been good for the United States. The strength of a nation is not only measured by the size of its economy. Or the number of its soldiers. But also by the number of its friends. And through NATO, the United States has more friends and allies than any other power,' I said.

The chamber was with me, my audience appreciative. They clapped, both my incisive and not-so-incisive statements. Pence and Pelosi sat directly behind me, and were just as enthusiastic as the rest of the room.

I spoke about how I had looked out of the window, down at the mighty Atlantic Ocean, on my flight to Washington.

'For adventurers like Leif Eriksen, the Atlantic Ocean was never a barrier. Rather, it was a great blue bridge to new lands and new possibilities. For millions of Europeans, it has been a bridge to freedom, sanctuary, and hope. My grandparents were among them. My mother was born in Patterson, New Jersey.'

At this, a representative seated in the middle of the chamber jumped up, threw his arms wide and looked about him, smiling. It was the representative from Patterson, New Jersey. Everyone laughed and clapped.

The Atlantic Ocean does not divide America and Europe – it unites us. Our solidarity strengthens our will to defend our values. I spoke openly about how an alliance consisting of so many member nations cannot possibly agree on everything. Trade, climate change, energy and the Iran nuclear deal were matters upon which the allies held differing views, but I also reminded the chamber that the alliance had experienced deep disagreements before.

'The strength of NATO is that despite our differences, we have always been able to unite around our core task. To defend each other. Protect each other. And to keep our people safe. We have overcome our disagreements in the past. And we must overcome our differences now. Because we will need our alliance even more in the future.' I listed the challenges we faced – Russia, the war on terror, cyber security, and a shifting global balance of power. No one nation could face these unprecedented challenges alone.

I emphasised the importance of fair burden sharing. 'NATO allies must spend more on defence. This has been the clear message from President Trump. And this message is having a real impact,' I said.

Behind me, Vice President Pence jumped up and clapped enthusiastically. The chamber followed him in doing so. Beside him, Nancy Pelosi stood, too, although considerably more slowly. When she had got to her feet, she picked up the glass of water in front of her and took a sip. In doing so, she didn't have to applaud.

'In just the last two years, European allies and Canada have spent an additional forty-one billion dollars on defence. By the end of next year, that figure will rise to one hundred billion.'

Pence stood again. This time, Pelosi remained seated. The other Democrats in the chamber followed her example.

Towards the end of my speech, I spoke about the formidable strength NATO has when we simply stand together. 'Our alliance has not lasted for seventy years out of a sense of nostalgia. Or of sentiment. NATO lasts because it is in the national interest of each and every one of our nations. Together, we represent almost one billion people. We are half of the world's economic might. And half of the world's military might. When we stand together, we are stronger than any potential challenger – economically, politically and militarily.'

I was speaking to a joint session of Congress that day, at which both the Senate and the House of Representatives were gathered. The atmosphere was relaxed and ceremonious at the same time. Many members of Congress were worried about what President Trump might do. They were looking to strengthen their belief in the transatlantic cooperation, and to find some new arguments for why NATO is so important. And the two members upon whose initiative I had been invited, Nancy Pelosi and Mitch McConnell, were exceedingly pleased. They had achieved exactly what they had wanted – to demonstrate Congress's strong cross-party support of NATO.

This support flooded me as I stood there at the lectern. I was relieved and happy. We had succeeded with one of the most important speeches of my life.

I rounded off with the only possible conclusion: 'Madam Speaker, Mr Vice President, it is good to have friends.'

PART 5
DEMOCRACY

March 2019–August 2021

23

Utøya

I WAS FIFTEEN YEARS OLD WHEN I ATTENDED A CAMP ON UTØYA for the first time, in 1974. The island, which is situated in the Tyrifjord just under an hour's drive west of Oslo, has a long and complex history. In the mid-1800s, it was purchased by local merchants who built a large holiday home there; the house was later used as the summer residence of Jens Bratlie, Norway's Conservative prime minister for a brief period in the early 1900s. The Labour movement acquired Utøya in 1932, and the island was used as a holiday camp for working-class children. Later in the 1930s, Russian revolutionary Leon Trotsky stayed there. Trotsky had sought asylum in Norway, and lived close by for a time. He was working on his great polemics against Stalin, and it isn't improbable that he wrote parts of his book *The Revolution Betrayed* while on Utøya.

In 1950, the Labour Party's Youth Organisation received the island as an anniversary gift from the Labour movement, and over the years that followed Utøya became a place that would exert a huge influence on Norwegian politics. Generations of Youth Organisation members have been schooled there. Political leaders have visited; visions for the future are developed there, and many initiatives have been launched from the island's podium.

True to tradition, in 1974 the camp gathered young people from all over Norway. And it opened up a whole new world to me.

I became friends with people who worked at the ironworks in Mo i Rana, who came from small farms in Vestlandet, or from one of the new housing developments in Romerike. I was used to taking the tram or getting around by bicycle; they had cars with fox tails attached to their aerials and Little Trees dangling from their rear-view mirrors. I enjoyed listening to the music of Bob Dylan and Ole Paus; now I met people who listened to Dolly Parton and the New Jordal Swingers. I tasted home-brewed beer and heard dialects from across the country. I loved all of it. In no time at all, I became a devoted member of the diverse community of the Youth Organisation.

Utøya bonded us. We slept in tents, swam in the fjord, flirted on the forest trails and played football in the fields – and, of course, we discussed politics. Higher education for all. The fight for abortion rights. The coup against Salvador Allende in Chile in 1973. In the evenings, there were parties with endless sing-alongs. Utøya captured my heart, and I have returned to the island every year since.

After 2011, making that regular journey has become even more important to me. On Friday the twenty-second of July at 15.25, a two-thousand-pound bomb planted by an extreme right-wing terrorist exploded in front of the prime minister's office in the government quarter of Oslo. Eight people were killed and many others injured.

I wasn't at the office when the bomb went off, but in the prime minister's residence not far away, where I was working on the speech I would give at Utøya the following day. After leaving the van filled with explosives in the government quarter, the terrorist transferred to another vehicle and drove out to Utøya. For over an hour he stalked the island, shooting defenceless young people who had gathered to attend the Youth Organisation's summer camp. Sixty-nine people were killed, the youngest two of whom were just fourteen years old.

That Friday is the darkest day of my life. One of my colleagues at the prime minister's office was killed. On Utøya, I knew many of the young people who were shot, and I was friends with several of the parents who lost their children. The party I led, the Labour Party, and its Youth Organisation, were the target. The country in which I was prime minister was subjected to the bloodiest attack ever experienced during peacetime. The government quarter lay in ruins. Utøya, the paradise of my youth, was transformed into hell on earth.

The following morning, I met with survivors of the attack and their relatives at Sundvollen, close to Utøya. I visited Ullevål Hospital, where the injured had been taken, and met the medical staff who were treating them. US president Barack Obama called me. As did German chancellor Angela Merkel, Israeli prime minister Benjamin Netanyahu and Palestinian president Mahmoud Abbas. From Russia, two people called. Both Vladimir Putin, who was prime minister at the time, and Dmitry Medvedev, who was president. They expressed their sympathies and offered assistance. Compassion streamed towards us from across the globe. We were in shock, we were grieving, we were devastated, but we also felt more intensely than ever before that we were part of a greater community.

On Sunday the twenty-fourth of July, a mourning service was held in Oslo Cathedral. It was hot in the packed church. I had hardly slept in two days, but it was important that I speak to all those who had been affected, and to the Norwegian people. I ended with the words: 'We are a small country, but we are a proud people. We are still shaken by what happened, but we will never abandon our values.'

The act of terror shocked, but also galvanised, the Norwegian population. On the twenty-fifth of July, all across the country, from north to south in cities and tiny villages, hundreds of thousands of people walked in torchlight processions and carrying roses, to condemn the terrorist attack and show we would not yield to fear and hate. Flowers were laid everywhere – in front of churches, at fountains and in parks. The centre of Oslo was so densely packed with people that the procession was unable to move through the streets. Outside Oslo City Hall, 150,000 people gathered in a massive, dignified demonstration. The 'rose parades' of that day became a powerful expression of the sense of community and solidarity felt so intensely by the Norwegian people in the days that followed the attack.

The Norwegian people stood together in their grief, across all political, religious and ethnic divides. That which united us was stronger than that which divided us, and it was vital to show that our open society could withstand this test. The answer to violence was more democracy, more openness and more humanity, but never naivety.

A middle-aged couple stood as I entered a VIP room in the run-down airport terminal in Tbilisi, one day in March 2019. I was in the process of concluding an official visit to Georgia. The conversations I'd had with the country's political leaders had gone well, but the most important meeting on my schedule still remained. I felt anxious as I prepared to meet with Avtandil Liparteliani and Leila Asatiani.

The couple had had a daughter, Tamta. She was a member of the Youth Organisation's sister group in Georgia, and had been invited to Norway to take part in the summer camp on Utøya in July 2011 – an opportunity she and her friend Natia had jumped at. Tamta's parents had managed to get in touch with her just after the bomb exploded in Oslo's government quarter on the afternoon of the twenty-second of July. Then, there was only silence.

Tamta tried to hide down at the shoreline. But after seventy minutes the terrorist found her, shooting her twice in the back. She died there, one of the very last people to do so. She was twenty-three years old.

Tamta had travelled from turbulent Georgia to peaceful Norway, but she never made it home again.

I knew before meeting with them that Tamta's parents couldn't comprehend how the perpetrator had been allowed to continue his murderous rampage for so long before the police finally managed to stop him. They were critical of the Norwegian authorities, and of me, since I, as prime minister, held the overall responsibility on the day of the attack. I understood completely, and was prepared to respond to some difficult questions and painful accusations. But they never came.

Leila Asatiani and Avtandil Liparteliani met me with nothing but warmth and openness. We had a lovely, bittersweet conversation about Tamta. This couple, who had lost their only child, told me about the person she was and the dreams she'd had. I told them that every year a memorial is held for those who were killed, at which Tamta's name is read aloud. 'She is remembered by many,' I said.

If Tamta's parents felt any bitterness towards Norway, they didn't show it. I had wanted to see them to offer my deepest sympathies, but they were the ones who said they were so grateful I had taken the time to meet with them. I felt almost ashamed.

Terrorists hide behind various religions and political ideologies to defend their acts of violence. At Utøya, it was a white man from an affluent neighbourhood of Oslo who abused Christianity and its religious symbols to justify murdering people he regarded as too welcoming towards Muslims and too positive about immigration. Other times, it is Islamic extremists who are guilty of abusing Islam. But no matter what they might claim, terrorists have more in common with each other than they do with any of the rest of us. They believe they can kill and put themselves above democracy to achieve their political aims.

NATO has been deeply involved in the war on terror. NATO allies went into Afghanistan to fight Al-Qaeda, who were behind the 9/11 terrorist attacks on the United States. At the operation's peak, we had as many as 150,000 soldiers in the country. NATO allies also played a vital role in the fight against IS in Syria and Iraq; extensive bombing and the provision of support to local forces made it possible to neutralise the terrorist state that IS was in the process of establishing. In March 2016, thirty-two people were killed and over three hundred injured in terrorist attacks on Brussels. The airport just outside the city, not far from NATO headquarters, was among the locations where the terrorists detonated their bombs.

For me personally, it is nevertheless Utøya that remains the strongest expression of the horrors of terrorism, and I have carried its story with me. It reminds me that when we are faced with acts of terror, the differences and disagreements between us become vanishingly small. When we are forced to fight for the values that truly matter, we manage to stand united.

Today, the Labour Party's Youth Organisation has reclaimed Utøya. Once again, young people gather at the island's summer camps, but other organisations also use the island as a venue for their events. People from all over the world come to Utøya to learn, discuss and make connections in the fight for democracy and human rights, and for peace and reconciliation. The island has become a meeting place and political arena that gives me hope.

When I met with Tamta's parents in Tbilisi, I told them a little about what Utøya is like today, and the plans for the island's future. The inside of the old café building, where thirteen young people died, has been preserved. The bullet holes in the walls bear witness to the island's terrible history. But a new building has also been erected around it, with sixty-nine columns reaching towards the sky and supporting the roof – one column for each of the dead. Outside stand another 495 columns, representing those who escaped the island alive. They preserve the memory of Tamta, and all the others who were killed.

24

Servant of the people

AS WE MADE OUR WAY DOWN TO THE HARBOUR, THE ROADS WERE closed to all other traffic. Our cars were decorated with NATO flags; people on the pavements stopped to wave and clap as we passed.

I had known it before I arrived, but now, driving through Odesa in October 2019, I saw it with my own eyes – NATO's presence was strongly appreciated in Ukraine.

My visit to the country began in this beautiful and strategically important city of a million inhabitants beside the Black Sea, not far from the border with Moldova. It wasn't so far from Crimea, nor from the Donbas, where, despite the ceasefire agreement, fighting still continually broke out between the Russian-backed forces and Ukrainian soldiers. At the entrance to the port area we passed the Potemkin Stairs, named for General Grigory Potemkin. At the end of the 1700s, Russia, led by Catherine the Great, conquered the Crimean Peninsula and the areas within it, and Potemkin was the man responsible for this achievement. He was also Catherine the Great's lover, and brought her to Odesa to show her his conquests.

Odesa grew into a large port city, and throughout the 1800s became an important centre of Jewish culture. In the wake of the 1917 revolution, and during the Second World War, intense battles were fought here.

The drive down to the harbour ended at a quay where a mine-sweeper was moored, one of four NATO vessels bearing the NATO flag, from Italy, Spain, Bulgaria and Romania respectively. The visit demonstrated how the cooperation and partnership between NATO and Ukraine were developing.

After our tour aboard the minesweeper, I was driven to the naval academy, where I was escorted into a room full of young men in uniform and some older officers, who all sat waiting for the NATO delegation.

'No matter how difficult the challenge, no matter how grave the threat, I am confident that by standing together – friends and partners – we can overcome any challenge,' I said, thinking this was a moment in my speech where there might be applause.

Instead, there was complete silence. I saw the disappointment in the faces before me. The cadets had wanted and hoped for more.

The Q&A session afterwards ended up being almost exclusively about Ukraine joining NATO. One of the young men challenged me directly.

'We're fighting for the same things as you. Why can't we join NATO?'

I understood the mix of anger and desperation behind his question. I represented NATO, and the basic security we were apparently unwilling to provide.

I replied by pointing out that there were several areas in which Ukraine did not yet meet NATO's standards, including the principle of the rule of law, fighting corruption, and ensuring democratic control over the country's security institutions.

'I was born in Luhansk, a city in the east that is occupied for now,' said one of the others. 'I would like to ask: what's the exit from this situation?'

I had no good answers. In meeting these cadets in Odesa, I felt some of the same sense of inadequacy as I had when meeting the two students in Kabul two years earlier. We were trying to do the right thing, we wanted to support those pushing for freedom and democracy, but at the same time we were reluctant to take full responsibility for Ukraine's security out of fear of being dragged into a direct conflict with Russia. Whether we were doing enough for the Ukrainians was a question I constantly asked myself.

My response to the cadet was somewhat long-winded and vague.

'If we can't join NATO, then at least give us weapons and equipment,' came another voice from the packed room.

I replied that we were doing what we could, and that the United States, United Kingdom and Canada in particular were providing support and training Ukrainian soldiers, but that some of the other allies were hesitant to do so. 'I understand that you feel this is taking too much time. If it's any comfort, all I can tell you is that sometimes, when it seems very dark, when it looks like there is almost zero progress, suddenly there can be new momentum and things can really start to change,' I said.

Sudden and dramatic changes that no one had predicted, such as the fall of the Berlin Wall, had happened before and could happen again. With any real signs of a solution and an end to the war in Eastern Ukraine lacking, the possibility that history might take a surprising and promising turn was as much an appeal to myself not to give up hope as it was to the naval cadets in Odesa.

But I don't know if it was any comfort to the cadet from Luhansk and his comrades.

Over five years had passed since Russia annexed Crimea. The war in the Donbas region had become Europe's forgotten war. Over thirteen thousand Ukrainians had lost their lives since the war's start in the spring of 2014, and over a million people had fled their homes. Ukraine was high on NATO's agenda and on my own personal agenda. The war in the Donbas was a weeping wound that undermined peace and stability across Europe, and which cast long shadows over the alliance's relations with Russia.

The main purpose of my visit to Ukraine was to meet the country's new president, Volodymyr Zelenskyy. Six months earlier, President Petro Poroshenko had lost the election to outsider Zelenskyy, an actor and artist who had shot to fame for his role in the popular Ukrainian comedy series *Servant of the People*, in which he played a history teacher who becomes president of Ukraine.

A smiling Zelenskyy received me at the presidential palace in Kyiv; the forty-one-year-old radiated energy and enthusiasm. He impressed me during our thirty-minute private conversation and the subsequent meeting of the NATO-Ukraine Commission, the body responsible for NATO's political and day-to-day contact with Ukraine. Zelenskyy was full of vitality, despite all the problems he faced. 'Had I known during the election campaign how hard it is to fight corruption, I might have given up. Now I think the most important thing I can do is fight even harder. There is corruption everywhere,' he said.

Over the months in which he had been president, Zelenskyy had managed to submit five hundred draft bills. He fearlessly grabbed Ukrainian society with both hands to bring about reform and plot a course towards a better future for his country.

Zelenskyy was in favour of holding elections in Eastern Ukraine and giving the region separate status; he had not insisted that the Ukrainians must first have control of the entire Donbas region before such elections could be held. The opposition in Kyiv, however, mercilessly struck this down, because they believed it an expression of weakness. Zelenskyy therefore increased his demands for a Russian withdrawal from the Donbas. I believed it unlikely that the Russians would bend, despite the promised elections. It was the conflict and unrest itself that gave Russia power in Ukraine.

The intensity of the fighting in the Donbas region varied. For periods it would be extreme, and then it would peter out, before ramping up again. Heavy Russian military equipment was sent to the Russian-controlled rebel forces in Eastern Ukraine: tanks, armoured vehicles, artillery and air defence.

Ukraine sank into an economic quagmire, with a drop in gross domestic product and increasing inflation and unemployment. The country was unable to pay its debts. They were forced to borrow more and more – not least to pay for their defence. Corruption was ingrained, and made it difficult to implement the reforms within taxation, healthcare and pensions. Just a few families controlled large parts of key industries and the banks, and these families had their loyal supporters among the country's politicians.

The authorities in Kyiv kept a close eye on how much attention the war was attracting in the West. When hostilities flared up at New Year 2017, it was two days before Washington made a statement. And when it finally came, the Americans neglected to make it clear that it was the Russian-backed separatists who had broken the ceasefire first. Nor did the statement mention Russia. President Poroshenko had called me, deeply concerned about what he interpreted as a lack of support from the United States.

On the other hand, US support did arrive in 2018. The Americans decided to sell Ukraine precision rifles, along with the Javelin advanced anti-tank guided missile system, which the Ukrainians had been especially keen to acquire. The Javelin is a missile that first aims straight for its target, before shooting upwards in order to attack the tank from above, where its armour is thinnest. When Obama was president, he had been reluctant to supply Ukraine with Javelin missiles out of fear of provoking Russia. For years, Kyiv had been on at me to get Washington to change its stance. Now Donald Trump had given the green light, to the Ukrainians' great satisfaction.

My conversations with President Zelenskyy gave me the sense that Ukraine had elected a leader we could trust and cooperate with. But on my visit it also became clearer than ever that the Ukrainians wanted more from us than we were able to give.

I did not leave Odesa and Kyiv unmoved. The war in the east of the country raged on. Arms support and NATO membership were what the Ukrainians wanted. Everyone I met – parliamentarians, the press, Zelenskyy and other political leaders – they all begged for Ukraine to be allowed to join the alliance. And I felt this most strongly in Odesa when meeting with the young cadets, who would soon go out to fight for Ukraine's independence. At my meeting with them, it was the new Ukraine that spoke to me.

The Ukrainians wanted to move West. They were fighting for freedom, to break free of Moscow's grasp. A large majority in parliament and among the Ukrainian people wanted Ukraine to join NATO, but I knew that many of the allies were still not ready to let them in.

For the foreseeable future, the door was closed. On my flight back to Brussels, it felt harder than ever to accept that this was simply how the world was.

25

On Erdoğan's home turf

IN THE AUTUMN OF 2019, I WAS BUSY PREPARING FOR THE NATO
summit that would be held in London that December. I had extensive
contact with the various heads of state and government; it was important to check in on people's attitudes and positions, and to clarify any
matters that needed to be addressed.

While I was working on these preparations, something dramatic
happened on NATO's southern flank. On the ninth of October,
Turkish tanks rolled across the border into Syria. I had previously
been notified that Turkish forces were preparing to move into northern Syria to combat the Kurdish People's Defence Units, better known
as the YPG; President Recep Erdoğan had also issued public warnings. But there was much uncertainty, and the Turkish plans met with
intense protests. Until the moment the tanks crossed the border, I did
not know if the Turks would actually strike.

We put out a statement as soon as the military operation was
underway, in which I expressed my 'deep concern' and stated that the
move might undermine the progress we had made in the fight against
IS. If the Kurdish militia were defeated, IS terrorists might retake areas
they had lost.

I didn't want to criticise Turkey any more strongly than I planned
to during the visit to Istanbul that was already on my schedule. If
there's one thing I dislike, it's people throwing criticism around until
they're standing beside the person they've been finding fault with.

A couple of days after the entry of Turkish troops into northern Syria, I sat down with President Erdoğan in an old sultan's palace in Istanbul. The city has long been a crossroads for meetings between East and West, religious and secular powers, Christianity and Islam; a place for the peaceful exchange of cultural impulses and trade, but also for fighting and war. Together, we admired the view towards the Asian side of the Bosporus Strait, where a few years earlier a large mosque had been built. It had become a landmark, and an expression of just how important Islam was to Erdoğan.

Erdoğan and I were old acquaintances, and we had met fairly regularly during the years in which I was Norway's prime minister. In January 2012, I had made an official visit to Ankara, and Ingrid and I had been invited to visit Erdoğan and his wife Emine at their home. It had been a pleasant afternoon, with tea and Turkish sweets.

Erdoğan is an engaged and knowledgeable leader, who always has a good overview of the details in whatever is to be discussed, and he is easy to get in touch with. He would frequently bring an iPad to our meetings, using it to show figures, tables and video clips to support his viewpoints.

Turkey has always been an important country for NATO, and the nation played a key role in the fight against IS. Turkey's border with Syria is 511 miles long – four times as long as Norway's border with Russia. The Turks were criticised for allowing the border to remain open; IS fighters were able to cross back and forth, transporting weapons and supplies. Many believed Ankara wasn't doing enough to combat the terrorist state.

But instead of just criticising, it was important I also show support. Which was why Turkey was the second country I visited, just days after I had taken office as NATO secretary general. The country had to be kept within the alliance – among other things so that we could succeed in the fight against IS. I went to a military base outside the city of Gaziantep close to the border with Syria, where NATO had deployed advanced Patriot air defence missiles. I was taken up to a ridge near the military base. As I looked across the border, I was reminded that Syria and Iraq are NATO's neighbours; Aleppo in Syria is closer to NATO's borders than the Donbas region of Ukraine. Directly to the south-east lay the border city of Kobani, which IS had begun to besiege just a few weeks earlier. At the time, the terrorists controlled a territory the size of the United Kingdom, and over the course of just a few months, IS had gone from being a small terrorist group hardly anyone had heard of to an organisation with many thousands of soldiers and an extraordinary ability to gain ground. They took Raqqa. They took Mosul in Iraq. The Iraqi army collapsed, and it was feared IS would take Baghdad.

The heat quivered above the golden landscape outside Gaziantep that day. I gave a brief speech to the soldiers from Turkey, the United States and several other NATO countries that manned the Patriot batteries. But what I said was first and foremost intended for the Turkish authorities and the Turkish people: 'Turkey's border is also NATO's border.' There should be no doubt that we stood with Turkey.

In the summer of 2016, military forces tried to overthrow Erdoğan and his government. On a visit to Ankara not long afterwards, I was able to see just how dramatic the attempted coup had been. Chunks of concrete and rubble lay scattered across the assembly hall of Turkey's parliament building. Above me was a gaping hole, where a bomb had blasted through the roof. Many elected representatives had been in the next room at the time, said the parliamentarian who showed me around. They had gathered there over the course of the evening of the coup to protect the parliament building. Had the bomb struck just a few feet closer, many would have been killed. It was the equivalent of one of the Norwegian Storting's largest rooms being blown to smithereens.

On the day the coup was attempted, the fifteenth of July, the chief of the general staff of the Turkish armed forces Hulusi Akar had been working in his office into the evening. At around 20.30, two officers came in and ordered him to go with them, he told me. He didn't know what they were talking about. 'A takeover is happening. You have to come with us,' they said.

Akar refused. 'So they drew their weapons, pointed them straight at my head and forced me down onto the ground,' he said. The officers tried to sedate Akar using ether. Then they dragged him out to the courtyard and into a helicopter, in which he was transported to an airbase controlled by the coup's leaders.

'Again they threatened to shoot me, wanting me to read a statement on TV in support of the coup,' Akar went on. But he refused to read out any such statement.

Around dawn on the sixteenth of July, the attempted coup was fought off by military units loyal to the government, and Akar was released. The fighting had cost 300 people their lives, and over 2,100 were wounded. But Erdoğan and the other members of the government were safe. Had the coup leaders managed to extract the chief of general staff's support, it would have been much more difficult to galvanise resistance among the military's ranks. A short time later, Akar was appointed Turkey's minister of defence.

On the night of the coup, I came out in support of Turkey's legally elected government. The Turks were deeply disappointed at other reactions in the West, which they believed to be too timid and too late. 'Only Theresa May, Carl Bildt and you stood behind us,' Erdoğan said to me. He was exaggerating, but it was good that he had noticed NATO's support.

The Turks felt that they were treated differently from the other allies. There was a clear pattern, Erdoğan believed – Turkey was not *seen* the way other NATO countries would have been seen, had they just been through a similar drama. Erdoğan and his people considered the attempted coup an act of terrorism, and sought support from the wider world. 'What demonstrations of solidarity are organised each time *we* are the victims of terrorism?' Erdoğan asked me.

Viewed from Paris, London or Oslo, Turkey can seem remote. The unrest and violence linked to the country's complex political and ethnic conflicts are something with which most Europeans have a distant relationship. As prime minister of Norway, my relationship with Turkey and the country's problems was no different from that of most of the other heads of government in Western Europe. But in my job as NATO secretary general, this changed. Turkey became the centre of my attention due to the country's strategic significance in the fight against IS – and eventually also in the work of admitting new countries into NATO.

Following the attempted coup, I pointed out how important it was that *all* parties respected the democratic ground rules. In this was a plea to avoid overreactions – the way in which Erdoğan responded had to be proportionate.

But just a few days later, it became clear the countermeasures were going to be immense. Military and police officers, judges, governors, university employees, journalists and teachers were imprisoned. Erdoğan accused Sunni Muslim preacher Fethullah Gülen, who was living in exile in the United States, of having pulled the strings. Anyone who could be associated with the Gülen movement ended up under lock and key.

Erdoğan became a challenge both for NATO and for me. Turkey was already low on the Democracy Index published by the Economist Group each year, and fell further after the attempted coup. During my visit to Ankara, it had struck me how much the new presidential palace exuded power. You drove in through high gates and entered a large park, which contained a mosque and several other buildings in addition to the palace itself. My delegation and I were escorted through enormous halls and up stairs, through more rooms and into yet another hall, where we waited for a short time. Then came word that the president was ready, and we were accompanied into yet another colossal room. We greeted each other, and Erdoğan said 'Welcome' and 'How are you?' He took a seat in his chair, which sat slightly higher than all the other chairs in the room.

I had always got on well with Erdoğan. But at the same time, I had to think of my own political integrity, and was forced to reflect on how best to handle a leader like him. In our meetings, I gave him recognition when I thought it right to do so. Which meant that I, apparently much more strongly than many others, sympathised with Turkey's deep problems relating to terrorism and the refugee crisis.

But the negative political developments could not be allowed to pass without comment. The principle of the rule of law and the European Convention on Human Rights apply to everyone.

'NATO allies are following the recent developments with concern,' I said.

Turkey is not like Russia. Erdoğan has to engage with a genuine political opposition. His party has lost important local elections, defeats he has accepted. Nevertheless, recent developments in the country brought with them dilemmas I had to balance as best I could.

NATO doesn't just defend the member nations and their territories – the alliance is also about values. Fundamental values such as individual liberty, democracy and the rule of law are enshrined in the organisation's founding document, the Washington Treaty of 1949. But NATO looks outwards, not inwards. The alliance was not established to deal with internal political affairs in the member states. It has neither the means nor the institutions to intervene in cases where individual countries are rightly or wrongly accused of violating NATO's founding principles. This is reinforced by the fact that decisions within NATO have to be made by consensus. This means, for example, that if sanctions were to be imposed against a member state, the country in question would itself also have to vote for it.

The challenge of ensuring that NATO adheres to its democratic principles is not new. When the alliance was established in 1949, many countries, including Belgium, the United Kingdom and France, still had colonies. Over the years that followed, national liberation movements were opposed with violence and war. In the United States, not all Black Americans had true voting rights until the 1960s. Despite being a dictatorship, Portugal was invited into the alliance upon its creation because the country was strategically important; two world wars had shown how critical it was to defeat enemy submarines and dominate the Atlantic to protect the supply lines between North America and Europe. In this context, the Azores and Madeira were deemed more important than a lack of democratic institutions in Lisbon.

Every time I encountered the demand that sanctions be imposed on Turkey, or on Hungary, for that matter, I pointed out that this was not one of the means at the alliance's disposal. But I also added that it was therefore even more important that we all used NATO as a political platform for expressing our concerns and formulating policy. In the past, Portugal had been criticised at meetings of NATO ministers for waging war on its African colonies. In much the same way, NATO is also used to put political pressure on allies that do not abide by the organisation's values today.

A glance at a map shows why Turkey has been so important for NATO since the country became a member of the alliance in 1952. The country borders Georgia and Armenia, which were part of the Soviet Union. It also borders Russia across the Black Sea, Iran in the east and Iraq and Syria in the south. The Bosporus and Dardanelles straits that connect the Black Sea and the Aegean Sea continue to be of great strategic importance. A NATO without Turkey would weaken European security.

As secretary general, my job was to keep the alliance together. NATO forms a framework through which the allies meet with the Turks daily. We sit around the same table, we can discuss the various problems, and everyone can bring up their concerns. A Turkey outside NATO would not promote human rights in the country. Quite the opposite.

On that day in October 2019, when I was once again visiting President Erdoğan, he welcomed me as usual by saying a couple of words in English before switching to Turkish. We were given earpieces, enabling the simultaneous interpretation to be streamed straight into our ears. Erdoğan continued with some small talk about how glad he was to be in his hometown of Istanbul, where his family live and where his grandchildren could visit him. He was obviously proud and happy to be a grandfather.

When we got down to business, I repeated what I had said when the Turkish military operation in Syria began. In diplomatic language, saying I was 'deeply concerned about the ongoing operations' constituted clear criticism. It was important that I say this to Erdoğan directly. I also repeated my concern that the Turkish operations might undermine the fight against IS.

As I spoke, I noticed that Erdoğan was growing impatient. He didn't become angry, but he had an urgent need to explain. 'We are not against the Kurds,' he said. 'Millions of Kurds live in Turkey. We have many hundreds of thousands of Kurds among the Syrian refugees, and nor are we against them. What we *are* against is this militia group, the YPG. They are terrorists. They are carrying out deadly raids on our own population, here in Turkey.'

Erdoğan did not make a distinction between the Syrian Kurdish militia group, the YPG, and the separatist organisation the Kurdistan Workers' Party, or PKK, who were behind the attacks within Turkey.

It had become known that the United States was going to train a so-called 'border force' in Syria, in association with the Syrian Democratic Forces. The force of around thirty thousand soldiers would be led by the Kurds in the YPG. And it was this that had caused Erdoğan to react so forcefully.

'When the United States equips and trains the Syrian Kurds, that is an attack on Turkey. It's completely unacceptable. You must tell the Americans we will not stand for it,' he said.

The United States had promised to help Turkey in the fight against the PKK, so in Erdoğan's eyes what the Americans were doing was beyond belief. They were training one wing of a terrorist movement while at the same time fighting the other.

In all the conversations I'd had with Erdoğan, both face to face and on the telephone, he had been concerned with just one thing: establishing a safety zone within Syria. This would provide a buffer against the various military groups in Syria and make Turkey safer. He wanted NATO to help with this, and for the United States also to assist. This would have involved NATO forces taking control of part of the territory of one of Turkey's neighbours. Time and again, I had to explain that there would never be consensus within the alliance for violating Syria's territorial integrity in this way. Erdoğan was disappointed that help wasn't forthcoming, because he feared the YPG would take control of areas in the north of Syria. He believed this to be an existential threat to Turkey. And he was convinced that if another NATO country had been in the same situation, such a safety zone would have been established long ago.

And so Erdoğan decided to go it alone.

This was what had happened over the preceding few days. Erdoğan and Trump had spoken on the phone, and Erdoğan had made it clear he was going to launch a large military operation in northern Syria. Immediately afterwards, the White House had announced that American troops would be pulled out of the area.

Trump had announced such a withdrawal previously, too; it was the reason Jim Mattis had resigned ten months earlier. But on that occasion, John Bolton and the Pentagon had managed to get the president to change his mind. A small number of American soldiers remained, undertaking a kind of joint patrol alongside Turkish forces. But the situation was complicated. For the Americans, the YPG were allies in the fight against IS, but they were the Turks' arch enemy. Two NATO allies were on a collision course, with reasons for being in northern Syria that were completely at odds.

Trump's attitude was that the Americans had been in northern Syria more than long enough; the Europeans and neighbouring countries would have to clean up the mess by themselves. The Kurds had been excellent in the fight against IS, but then again they had also received weapons, equipment and large sums of money from the United States. All this would have to stop sometime. Erdoğan's invasion gave Trump the excuse he needed to pull the Americans out.

Erdoğan was crystal clear as we sat there in his palace on that day in October. The Turkish military operation was absolutely necessary, he said.

'The YPG are terrorists. You've said as much yourself before. So why do you no longer think this? Ah, you need them to fight IS, of course. But that makes them no less terroristic.'

Erdoğan has a habit of using 'you' to mean the West in general – the region that, in his eyes, never learns from its own fatal missteps. 'Surely you don't believe it's possible to use one terrorist organisation to fight another. You saw what happened in Afghanistan in the fight against the Soviet occupation in the 1980s. You supported the

Mujahideen and ended up with the Taliban and Al-Qaeda. Don't make the same mistake again.'

Erdoğan rattled off the names of Turkish towns and cities, with the dates on which terrorist attacks had been committed there and the number of people killed. There were fifteen victims here, five school students there; a youth camp attacked here, a village there. He kept it up for quite a while. I couldn't vouch for the accuracy of his figures, but it was a fact that no other NATO member had been subjected to more acts of terrorism than Turkey. I had said as much myself many times, most recently at the press conference just a few hours earlier.

The president leaned forward in his chair.

'Don't even try to tell me that the YPG is different from the PKK. And the PKK are on your own list of terrorist organisations,' he said.

NATO doesn't have formal lists of terrorist organisations. But the EU does, and the PKK is certainly listed there. Erdoğan knew this, of course.

I mostly sat and listened, not without good reason. The United States and many other NATO countries had previously considered the PKK and the YPG as two parts of the same organisation. But it had now become more important that the YPG were effective in fighting IS than it was that they were in league with the PKK. None of the other groups in Syria that the Americans had tried to collaborate with had managed to combat IS. For the United States and other NATO nations, it was impossible to maintain that the YPG were terrorists after they had begun to equip them to overcome the IS terrorist state.

'Secretary General, do you like sweetcorn?' Erdoğan suddenly asked. We were sitting in deep armchairs around a small table, and had been offered coffee and tea. As usual, I had chosen tea, which was served in small glass cups. I must have looked confused, because Erdoğan repeated the question: 'Do you like sweetcorn? We are in the middle of sweetcorn season.'

'I like sweetcorn,' I confirmed.

'Then we'll eat sweetcorn,' Erdoğan said, gesturing to a member of his staff over by the door.

A moment later a huge platter of golden corncobs was brought in. There were perhaps eight or ten people in the room, and everyone munched away, eating corncobs with their bare hands. Delicious roasted chestnuts were also served.

'The protocol department hates this,' Erdoğan said, reaching for another corncob.

'You know the difference between the Taliban and the protocol department?' he asked, peering at me expectantly as sweetcorn and salt sprinkled onto the floor.

I shook my head. Erdoğan smiled.

'It's possible to negotiate with the Taliban.'

The mood lifted, and the Turks began to squabble among themselves about which area of Turkey produced the best sweetcorn. We also talked about how Americans ate a lot of sweetcorn, and it was agreed that Trump probably chomped his way through mountains of corn on the cob. I tried to refrain from engaging too readily with the casual, unrestrained talk. We had received reports of fatalities and huge waves of refugees as a result of the Turkish military operations. I had conveyed protests on behalf of several NATO allies. The situation didn't exactly warrant amiable chit-chat and jokes.

But Erdoğan clearly wasn't intending on letting me off lightly anyway.

'You know, Secretary General, I've been asking for this safety zone for a long time. And you haven't given it to me. Now NATO allies are telling me that we are breaching international law by going into Syria. But then, what are you doing, when you're bombing the region and have specialist troops there?'

It wasn't actually a question. Erdoğan went on.

'Why do the Americans have reason to be there under international law, but not us? We've lost thousands in terrorist attacks, you've lost maybe a few hundred. So if I'm breaching international law by going into Syria and killing terrorists, what right do the United States, the United Kingdom and other NATO nations have to send their soldiers and bombers to kill members of IS?'

I didn't have an easy time of it in Istanbul. Yet again, I was reminded that one person's terrorist is another's freedom fighter. But I had encountered Erdoğan like this several times before, and I was prepared. I listened to his defence of Turkey's military operations, but all the while urged caution.

'You have to be careful. Turkey's military response must be proportionate, and you mustn't strike civilians,' I said.

'We're killing terrorists. You're the ones hitting civilians while bombing IS in Raqqa and Mosul. Nobody is protesting against that,' Erdoğan replied.

Again, Erdoğan had a point. Through the US-led coalition to which NATO was also a party, we were running a comprehensive military operation on the ground and in the air to annihilate IS. We were doing this without a clear resolution from the UN Security Council. And we were acting in what we believed to be self-defence. Just like Turkey.

I tried to emphasise how important it was that everything didn't unravel in the fight against IS. 'Both Turkey and the United States are NATO countries. You both have soldiers in northern Syria to fight terrorists. True, not exactly the same terrorists, but you have to be able to cooperate, to remain within the bounds of international law and spare civilians wherever possible,' I said.

Some referred to the invasion of northern Syria as the biggest crisis for NATO's unity since I became secretary general. Erdoğan had marched into Syria without any form of coordination with the other NATO nations. The French believed Turkey's conduct to be completely unacceptable. They had also come down hard on the United States for Trump pulling out most of the American soldiers without consulting any of the other allies. So while Turkey had been reprimanded for going into Syria, the United States had been reprimanded for withdrawing. And again, it wasn't exactly easy to make all this cohere within NATO.

The Americans had long been asking European nations to do much more in northern Syria. Secretary of Defense Jim Mattis practically begged them to help provide support to the Kurds. European NATO countries had some forces in the region, but these were relatively small contributions. Some special forces soldiers and intelligence agents who were totally dependent upon the Americans when undertaking missions.

The Americans were doing all the work. As per usual.

And now the Europeans, and especially the French, were angry because the United States was reducing its presence. The reactions across Europe caused irritation on the other side of the Atlantic. Or as one American colleague put it: 'Europe will defend the Kurds to the last American.'

The Turkish invasion of northern Syria gave Trump a good excuse to withdraw American troops. But at the same time, he cautioned Erdoğan. 'Let's work out a good deal! You don't want to be responsible for slaughtering thousands of people, and I don't want to be responsible for destroying the Turkish economy ... Don't be a tough guy. Don't be a fool!' Trump wrote in a letter to Erdoğan on the ninth of October. The letter's tone shocked the Turks. When Erdoğan visited Trump at the White House a month later, he quite simply handed it back.

The Turkish military operations met with more intense resistance than expected. The Kurds quickly aligned themselves with President Assad's government forces. The resistance on the ground was probably the reason Erdoğan agreed to a ceasefire deal, which US vice president Mike Pence negotiated relatively quickly, and in which the Russians also played an active role. The Turks finally had their safety zone, but it was smaller than they had hoped for.

I was mostly concerned with preventing the alliance's internal rifts becoming so wide as to be unbridgeable. Erdoğan talked with contempt about 'you in NATO' and how 'NATO has failed us'. If he wasn't met with greater understanding for Turkey's problems and demands, he was going to 'flood Europe with migrants'. The splits on the western side allowed for greater Russian influence in the region, and we had to avoid the Turks being pushed into the arms of Russia as a result of the condemnation served up by NATO countries. Without cooperation from Turkey, the refugee crisis would also become entirely unmanageable.

That autumn, deep cracks appeared in the alliance's unity along several lines at once. Between the United States and Turkey in their views of the Kurds. Between Turkey and European NATO nations, due to the Turkish military intervention. And between the Europeans and the United States, as a result of Trump's decision to withdraw American troops.

Things could not go on this way. Arguing in the public spotlight hands the forces that wish to sow discord free rein. Allies cannot hurl mud at one another in full public view.

26

Stubborn presidents

WHEN NATO WAS FOUNDED IN 1949, THE UNITED KINGDOM WAS IN the driving seat. The British wanted close security policy cooperation between democratic countries in the West in response to the threat posed by the Soviet Union. In Eastern Europe, country after country had been subjected to Soviet domination. The coup in Czechoslovakia in February 1948 made an especially strong impression.

To many people's surprise, Labour leader Clement Attlee had won the parliamentary election that took place after the end of the Second World War, unseating Winston Churchill. Churchill was the war's great hero, but he also symbolised attitudes and values from a class system that, after the war, seemed outdated, and to which the exhausted and run-down British did not wish to return. After the trials of war, the British were looking to the future, and gave their support to a programme of mixed economy, welfare state and reducing social differences.

Attlee's foreign secretary, the former trade union giant Ernest Bevin, was a driving force behind the work to establish NATO. Bevin came from difficult circumstances. Who his father was is unknown, and his mother died when he was just eight years old. Bevin was forced to quit school at eleven, and eventually became a day labourer at the docks in Bristol. He was involved in creating the British Transport and General Workers' Union, which he led for many years.

Bevin's heart beat strongly for what would become NATO's solidarity principle. For him the promise that an attack against one country would be regarded as an attack against all was a direct extension of the unity and community he had fought for within the British trade union movement.

The relationship between the United States and the United Kingdom is often referred to as a special one. It rests on a shared history and language, as well as parallel economic and political interests. This closeness is also reflected in the intimate relationships between the two nations' leaders, such as Ronald Reagan and Margaret Thatcher in the 1980s; Bill Clinton and Tony Blair developed a similar relationship some years later.

Both as prime minister of Norway and head of NATO, I saw how the 'special relationship' between London and Washington played out in the military arena. The two countries closely cooperated on intelligence, and shared their assessments of classified information. The British had been quick to respond with strong support for the United States' intervention in Afghanistan following the terrorist attacks on New York and Washington on September the eleventh, 2001; they also joined the contentious invasion of Iraq in 2003. And after 2014, the United States and the United Kingdom, along with Canada, were quick to offer training to Ukrainian soldiers.

Ever since the days of Attlee and Bevin, the British had been strong supporters of NATO. Every year, the UK spent over 2 per cent of its gross domestic product on defence. The British supported the vast majority of my initiatives, whether these related to new battlegroups in the eastern part of the alliance, or the war on terror. The UK was a country I could always count on, even during times of changing governments with various prime ministers.

Through a referendum in 2016, the United Kingdom chose to leave the EU. I had hoped they would stay, because an EU without the UK would represent a weakening of a peacekeeping institution of which I was a strong supporter. Brexit broke with the long-standing trends in Europe, which had been moving in the direction of greater cooperation and integration.

The consequences of Brexit for defence and security policy across Europe were ambiguous. The United Kingdom had always fought for NATO's defence of Europe, and acted as a guarantor for NATO's primary role. When the British left the EU, however, this guarantee vanished. But on the other hand, it would now be even more challenging for the EU to defend Europe alone. While the vision of an EU defence met with less resistance on a political and rhetorical level, it became harder to realise, because when the UK left the EU, so did one of the union's strongest military powers. In that respect, Brexit meant that NATO became even more important, including for the British.

So it was a strong and loyal NATO nation that hosted the heads of state and government when they gathered for the summit in London in December 2019. Upon the organisation's creation after the Second World War, NATO headquarters had been situated in London. It wasn't much of a headquarters; more a small secretariat for member nations. The position of secretary general didn't exist – it was only established some years later, along with the position of NATO's supreme commander. In many ways, London was the perfect place to hold a summit and also celebrate the alliance's seventieth anniversary.

The run-up to the summit could have been easier, however. A few weeks before we gathered in London, President Macron gave a major interview to the *Economist*, in which he followed up on French dissatisfaction at events in northern Syria. Macron went further than he had done previously, stating that NATO was brain-dead. The organisation's most important member state by far, the United States, was making decisions of major political and strategic importance without consulting the other allies; according to Macron, NATO could therefore be described in no other way. Of course, the subtext was Macron's message of the need for greater European autonomy when it came to the region's security policy. NATO was ostensibly losing its political value.

When Macron's 'brain-dead' statement went public, I was in Berlin, which proved helpful. Angela Merkel and I could literally stand shoulder to shoulder and reject Macron's claims. 'I don't think that such sweeping judgements are necessary, even if we have problems and need to pull together,' Merkel said.

I had long since concluded that the most effective defence of NATO was to concede that our cooperation did not always run smoothly. Denying something that was obvious to everyone would only undermine my credibility, and therefore that of the alliance. But whenever I acknowledged that there were problems, I also pointed out that what united us was stronger than what divided us.

My assessment was that Macron had gone public with a long-held belief. In Macron's eyes, the United States under Donald Trump was no longer a reliable partner. In part, he was pointing out a problem that was undeniably real. Trump's isolationist instincts and his regular public criticism of Europeans generated discord. But Macron also had another agenda – one that Trump was indirectly helping him with. The French president wanted to strengthen the EU's position within the region's defence policy, and thereby France's role in security policy cooperation within Europe. After Brexit, France was the EU's only nuclear power. My impression was that Macron wanted to appear strong and independent, in order to obstruct the right and Marine Le Pen – a motive with which I sympathised.

It might have been tempting for European politicians to jump in behind Macron, because Trump was so unpopular in Europe. Anything of the sort would have intensified the splits within the alliance and made our job of keeping NATO united more difficult, but Macron gained no support from other European capitals.

We realised that his actions had sparked immense criticism in the German press. German MPs and other political leaders supported Merkel and her response throughout November. They said yes to strengthening European defence efforts within NATO, no to Macron's European strategic autonomy. There was a fundamental difference between the two approaches.

Three presidents therefore dominated the run-up to the summit that autumn: Recep Erdoğan, Emmanuel Macron and Donald Trump. In different ways, all three of them posed challenges for NATO and for me. Holding the summit seemed like a risky project. Erdoğan might block important decisions due to the allies' criticism of the Turkish invasion of Syria. Macron had already written off the alliance's ability to think independently, and there was a chance of a full-blown confrontation between him and Trump.

Early in the autumn, Trump made a statement that attracted significant attention. He wanted to buy Greenland, the world's largest island, his interest in the region fuelled by both Greenland's strategic location and a desire to secure the US access to the area's minerals.

But the idea of American ownership of Greenland was rejected outright by Danish prime minister Mette Frederiksen and Greenlandic prime minister Kim Kielsen. The island was not for sale. I supported Denmark's position. In my conversations with Mette Frederiksen, I also agreed it should be possible to find solutions for an increased military presence consistent with the island being part of the Danish realm, while also taking the allies' concerns into account. That was important for all of NATO.

I also reminded Frederiksen that this was not the first time a neighbour had attempted to take Greenland from Denmark. In the summer of 1931, a group of Norwegian hunters occupied Eastern Greenland, and the occupation was ratified by the Norwegian government. Denmark brought a case before the Permanent Court of International Justice in The Hague, where Norway lost on all counts. The court concluded that Greenland was Danish.

The discourse around Greenland disappeared from the news cycle fairly quickly, but we were anxious in the lead-up to the summit in 2019. The United States had a president who might turn everything upside down. To tell the truth, as the summit approached we were unsure whether holding it was a good idea. But on the other hand, it would be an admission of failure and dangerous to NATO's future if we neglected to hold summits due to the risk of exposing discord and disagreements. The summits were what drove political cooperation forward. The alliance needed them.

In mid-November, I was in Washington to meet with President Trump as part of preparations for London.

Photographers came in to take the official photographs, but Trump quickly sent them out because he noticed some cans of Coca-Cola he didn't want included in the images. After they were cleared away, he called the photographers back in again. 'Everybody smile!' Trump said.

When the photographers had finished, we naturally enough turned to the topic of France. Trump slaughtered Macron for the brain-dead claim. 'A disrespectful and offensive statement. You can't go around talking about NATO like that,' he said. According to Trump, NATO actually only had one problem, and that was France.

'What do you think of Macron? He isn't doing so well in NATO, is he?' Trump asked. I didn't respond to the question directly, but explained that Macron's actions had no support among the other Europeans, and that it was important we stand united. I felt the urge to stick up for Macron. Or rather, to emphasise how important it was to keep France within the alliance. So I said a little about the country's relationship with NATO over the years.

This kind of dialogue had now almost become a standard part of our interactions – Trump asked me questions about major and minor issues, while I tried to steer the conversation towards an understanding that what NATO did was important for and of use to the United States.

I was keen to present Trump with the organisation's new defence spending figures. Europe and Canada had increased their defence budgets, and since Trump became president, these increases had gained momentum. Towards 2024, the figures would increase even further. Nine countries had now achieved the 2 per cent goal.

But none of this seemed to make any great impression on Trump. He asked why more countries hadn't reached the 2 per cent target. 'It's an insult. Couldn't most of them pay two per cent in a day if they really wanted to? Germany could. They're outsmarting us on trade,' he said.

As usual, Trump linked trade to security policy. He brought up many of the same topics as before, but he seemed more relaxed. There was less confrontation in the air.

The Nord Stream 2 gas pipeline also came up again. 'Germany are making themselves Russia's hostage,' Trump said. But he also went on to make a lengthy argument about how the United States could sell gas to Europe, explaining that he had just opened the world's largest facility for liquid natural gas in Louisiana.

'The biggest facility I've ever seen. My people say we can transport this gas cheaply,' he said.

After our delegations entered, Trump directed Mike Pompeo and myself to two chairs in front of his desk, while he sat behind it. On the desk, beside the two telephones, I noticed a small wooden box with a red button on it – if I didn't know better, I might have thought it was the infamous nuclear button. A little way into the meeting, Trump smiled coyly, leaned forward and pushed the button. A few seconds later a staff member came in with some cans of Diet Coke for us – it turned out to be Trump's Coca-Cola button.

A few weeks later, I met with Trump again, at a breakfast meeting in Winfield House, the residence of the US ambassador in London, just before the summit was about to kick off. Our staffs had agreed that we would only do a brief photo shoot that morning, but it didn't work out that way. Instead, the event ended in an hour-long press conference, in which Trump and I each sat straight-backed on our chairs in front of all the journalists. I got the impression he had decided to do things that way there and then, on a whim.

This time, however, Trump had nothing but praise for the alliance and me. It was completely different to the performance in Brussels the previous year, when he had lashed out at Germany before the cameras. I was able to finish my sentences as I explained the work to strengthen NATO, and the progress we had made on sharing the burden more fairly. No interruptions, no irritation.

'Shall we have breakfast now?' Trump asked, surprised, when the press conference was over. We were far behind the planned schedule, and he had completely forgotten the whole breakfast. Still, he was good-humoured when he realised there was more on the agenda.

'Out there at the press conference, I would have liked to say we don't protect the countries who refuse to pay, but I didn't say it,' Trump said, once we had sat down at the breakfast table and the media had left. 'You know, two per cent is so little. Should have been four.'

So he hadn't changed his views on the necessity of the allies paying more. But his tone was lighter, and the fear that he might withdraw the US from NATO was to all intents and purposes gone. Now the concern was that he would use the summit to announce a scheme of graded security guarantees – a kind of first- and second-class membership of the alliance. Only the countries who paid their way, who spent at least 2 per cent of GDP on defence, could expect a full security guarantee; the others would have to settle for less binding promises of American support. These concerns really began to gather momentum when we learned that Trump had arranged a separate meeting towards the end of the summit, to which only the leaders of nations who fulfilled the 2 per cent requirement and myself were invited. But that meeting, too, concluded without any new, dramatic announcements. Instead, a tweet emerged, in which Trump spoke highly of NATO.

The summit itself started with a magnificent reception at Buckingham Palace. At an audience with Queen Elizabeth II, I had the pleasure of becoming a little better acquainted with her. She told me about her friendship with Lord Ismay, Winston Churchill's chief of staff and closest military adviser during the war. Lord Ismay became NATO's first secretary general in 1952, and over the years Queen Elizabeth had met each and every one of us. I was now the thirteenth secretary general with whom the Queen had discussed the alliance's future.

Throughout the reception, she exhibited an impressive level of stamina – the ninety-three-year-old showed no signs of tiring. I introduced her to the longest-serving minister of foreign affairs, Luxembourg's Jean Asselborn. 'I've been minister of foreign affairs for fifteen years,' Asselborn said proudly. 'Yes, that is rather a long time. But not quite as long as I have been Queen,' she replied with a smile.

After the reception, there was a dinner in Downing Street hosted by the UK prime minister Boris Johnson. His roguish style was on full display, with his dishevelled hair and crumpled suit, while he quoted Roman warlords and Greek philosophers – possibly a little imprecisely, but it made his contributions colourful and entertaining. Johnson was a contentious figure among many of the allies, because he had pushed for the United Kingdom to leave the EU. But he was also a passionate supporter of NATO and the fundamental idea that Europe and America had to stand united. No matter what one might think of his political views, it was hard not to be charmed by his irrepressible energy and constant stream of audacious and pithy statements and self-deprecating remarks.

After the dinner, Johnson and I ended up standing alone for a while, upstairs in the prime minister's residence. We admired its Christmas tree, perfectly shaped and beautifully decorated with lights and sparkling baubles.

'What a fantastic Christmas tree,' I exclaimed.

Johnson shot me a look.

'Of course. But nowhere near as fine as the tree in Trafalgar Square.'

He was referring to the tradition in which Oslo sends a Christmas tree to London each year, to thank the British for their assistance during the war. His smile left me in no doubt that he shared the prevailing view among London's residents that Oslo had thanked the British by sending them a somewhat straggly tree this year, too.

The London summit went better than expected. The three most critical heads of state showed their most cooperative sides. President Erdoğan supported NATO's new defence plans, a resolution he had previously blocked due to the alliance's lack of support for the safety zone in Syria. President Macron took his brain-dead criticism no further. And President Trump expressed his clear support for NATO.

The summit's declaration was brief, and contained only nine paragraphs. But on one point, it represented an important breakthrough. For the first time, the alliance communicated a shared attitude towards China.

For several decades, the world had been witness to a formidable economic development in the Middle Kingdom. I'd had the opportunity to see this up close myself, when in the mid-1980s, as head of the Labour Party's Youth Organisation, I was invited on a tour of the country. I was impressed by what I saw. Not least, the country's leader, Deng Xiaoping, made an impression with his pragmatism and ability to reform Chinese society. Never before in human history had more people managed to escape poverty and want in such a short space of time, and to achieve a reasonable level of wealth and security. The infant mortality rate fell. Life expectancy increased.

When I returned home from China, I gave a newspaper interview in which I shared my experiences from the trip. It had clearly had a great effect on me, because I chose to claim that Deng Xiaoping was my political role model. A few years later, he ordered the attack on the demonstrators in Tiananmen Square in Beijing, and several thousand people were killed. My earlier newspaper interview was brought up, and I was forced to admit that my admiration for the Chinese leader hadn't exactly aged well.

But my enthusiasm for China's social and economic development was shared by many. The dominant attitude in the West was that China's inclusion in the world economy would bring about democratic reforms and the liberalisation of China itself.

We were wrong. As it turned out, one-party rule and control could be combined with an increasing free market economy and more private wealth. China has become an ever more authoritarian country. In the years leading up to the London summit, democracy in Hong Kong was crushed and several thousand protesters and journalists arrested. The idea of 'one nation – two political systems', which had been launched when Hong Kong was handed over to China, had turned out to be an illusion. More and more, ordinary Chinese citizens were being surveilled through the authorities' control of the Internet and social media, and the use of technology such as digital face recognition in public places. The suppression of the Uyghurs in the Xinjiang region turned more brutal.

In the West, people increasingly acknowledged that economic relations with China were not exclusively positive. They could have consequences for our security. Chinese control of critical infrastructure such as ports, airports and the 5G network could make us vulnerable. Exports of advanced, Western technology might come to be used against us, and unilateral dependence on the importing of rare minerals or other products from China constituted a risk. So although we all agreed that we should continue to trade with China, we must at the same time manage the potential impact of this trade on our security.

Beijing was undertaking a massive military build-up. China had become the world's second-largest military power with a rising number of intercontinental missiles and other advanced weapons systems. The Chinese were stockpiling a nuclear arsenal, and it was estimated that by around the year 2035, China would have around as many strategic nuclear warheads as the United States.

A far more China-critical line had gained a foothold within American foreign policy, and Beijing was progressively being seen as a security policy challenge. In 2015, the Obama administration had harshly criticised the way in which China was acting with carte blanche in the South China Sea, in violation of international law, and made it clear the United States opposed all further militarisation of the contentious islands. In 2017, with Donald Trump in the White House, this ever more critical line triggered a rupture in the United States' China policy. China was now referred to as a 'strategic competitor'. The following year, the US introduced high tariffs on a number of Chinese goods, including electronics and medical equipment. Chinese investments in the United States became subject to restrictions. One aim of these measures was to limit trade and other economic contact that might lead the United States to become dependent upon China, or give Beijing access to advanced technology.

At the time of the London summit, European countries had also become more concerned about these developments. In recent years, a more China-critical attitude had gained traction in Europe, too, but discussing that within the framework of NATO remained sensitive. There were many reasons for this. European NATO countries still defined their relationship to China in mainly economic terms. They saw immense gains in trading with China, and wanted to avoid NATO giving the impression that the alliance had acquired a new enemy. For the German automotive industry, the Chinese market was hugely important, and the Germans felt it was not necessarily in their national interest to latch onto Trump's hard anti-China line. France believed that many of the issues Trump was concerned with, such as energy security and 5G, were core tasks for the EU, and nothing to do with NATO. Poland and the other countries in Eastern Europe were not against placing greater focus on China per se, but they were worried it would draw NATO's attention away from their greatest concern – that is, the threat posed by Russia.

The considerations and interests were numerous and sprawling. Reconciling them was no small task.

In my address to the US Congress in April, I had given up on including anything about China because no joint negotiated standpoint existed. But in the months before the London summit, NATO's machine had worked slowly and methodically. The alliance's various committees trawled through many pages of documents about NATO's relationship with China. Assessments were made. Reports were written. Allied capitals were consulted. Previously, I had found myself exasperated at the slowness of such processes, irritated by all the details and nuances the various parties got hung up on. But in this case, it was necessary.

All this work ultimately culminated in the following sentence in the summit declaration: 'We recognise that China's growing influence and international policies present both opportunities and challenges that we need to address together as an Alliance.'

It was just a single sentence. But it expressed something utterly essential. Our relationship to the giant in the east was not just about trade and the economy. It was also about security.

27

Trump on the telephone

'HELLO, MR PRESIDENT, THIS IS JENS STOLTENBERG SPEAKING!'
Donald Trump had requested a call with me at short notice. I heard his voice on the other end: 'One of the greatest of all time, right? One of the greatest. The greatest.'

I wasn't totally sure whether it was him or me who was 'the greatest', but it didn't really matter. Trump's tone was light, despite the crisis that had arisen in the Middle East.

It was the eighth of January 2020. Five days earlier, the head of the Quds Force of the Iranian Revolutionary Guard Corps, Major-General Qasem Soleimani, had been killed in an American drone strike outside Baghdad. The Iranians were furious, and threatened retaliatory attacks. Soleimani was regarded as a national hero in Iran – it was impossible for the regime to allow the killing to pass without a response. All at once, the situation had become complex and dangerous. A military confrontation between Iran and the United States, with Iraq as the combat zone, was now a possibility, albeit one that nobody really wanted. The Iranians fired missiles at American military bases in Iraq. Eight soldiers were injured, but luckily no lives were lost. Had anyone been killed, Trump might have felt forced to respond militarily. He had already tweeted that fifty-two targets in Iran had been marked.

'You know,' Trump said, 'we hit them hard when we took out this terrorist, this general. He was the worst in the world. It's unbelievable what they had planned, they were going to attack one of our places, one of our embassies, another Benghazi catastrophe. It was supposed to happen this Saturday. So we took him out, may he rest in peace.'

The killing of Soleimani had made the American forces more vulnerable, and now Trump wanted the majority of the US operations in Iraq to be undertaken by NATO instead. Earlier that day, he had made a televised speech in which he made it clear he was going to ask NATO to become much more involved in the Middle East. And now he was following up on this with me.

'I hope what I said about NATO didn't give you a heart attack. But this is important. NATO has to step up,' he said. 'You know, we pay such a ridiculous amount for NATO. Ridiculous. But fine, it's about to become a little less ridiculous. NATO has to go into the Middle East instead of the United States. We're paying so much anyway, almost one hundred per cent. It will look smart, it will look genius,' Trump said.

As usual, Trump was concerned with burden-sharing, and felt that a larger role for NATO in the Middle East would reduce the strain on the US. This would also make it easier for Trump to say he had pulled the United States out of an endless war.

'Mr President, when we met for the first time in 2017, you urged me to do two things. To get the Europeans to pay more, and to get NATO to do more in the war on terror. And I completely agreed. So we're following up on these issues, and—'

Trump cut me off.

'NATO has to replace the United States, end of story. We're the ones who are paying, anyway. NATO represents the world in a different way than the United States. Less hostility, multilateralise the whole thing. Almost like the UN. Stroke of pure genius.'

'NATO can do more in the Middle East,' I said. 'I was intending on bringing this up with Secretary of State Pompeo later on. And I discussed the possibility of NATO doing more in my conversation with Security Advisor Robert O'Brien just before Christmas. So to follow up on the—'

Again, Trump interrupted me.

'I want to go one step further. We'll change NATO's name. NATO-ME, or something like that. NATO Middle East. A phenomenal idea. Just imagine your legacy. And mine.'

He brought up the mistakes his predecessors had made.

'The Middle East is a real problem, and that's because of Bush's stupidity. He stormed in there like an idiot. Even though Iraq didn't have anything to do with the World Trade Center.'

I promised to follow up, so that an expanded NATO role could be more concretely defined.

'I'll send my best people over to Washington right away. I'll send John Manza,' I said.

Manza was one of several NATO assistant secretary generals. He was a former Marine infantry officer, and had served in the war against Saddam Hussein in 1991, when Kuwait was liberated. I had met him for the first time in Afghanistan several years earlier, and had got to know him well when we travelled to Baghdad together the previous autumn. He was a fascinating guy who had grown up as one of eight siblings; the two oldest brothers had served in Vietnam. After twenty years in the Marine Corps, Manza took a PhD and began working for NATO. He was now the alliance's head of operations, an eager motorcycle enthusiast with a penchant for vintage cars, who felt most comfortable in jeans and leather jacket and never without his colourful braces. Manza also had a large sailing boat, in which he embarked on solo sailing trips for a few weeks each year.

'Send the right people over. I'll meet with them when they get here, okay?' Trump said.

'Excellent,' I replied.

'Thank you, my friend, I'll see you soon.'

Just after our telephone conversation, Trump held a press conference at which he hinted that NATO ought to be expanded, so that countries in the Middle East could join the alliance.

'[You have] NATO, right, and then you have M-E, Middle East,' he said excitedly, writing the letters in the air with his fingers. 'You call it NATO-ME. What a beautiful name. I'm good at names.'

Now that the West had decided to do more in the war on terror, there would, in my eyes, have to be very good reasons for *not* doing so through NATO, since it was a matter of our common security. We were now in a situation where my wish to increase NATO's involvement fitted perfectly with what the president of the United States was trying to achieve. The alliance agreed to strengthen the organisation's operation in Iraq.

Some months later, in June 2020, it was me who called Donald Trump, primarily to discuss the situation in Afghanistan. Trump had decided to withdraw American troops from the country. It was important that I discussed this directly with the president, and ensured that every move we made was coordinated within NATO. But it took a little while for our conversation to finally get around to Afghanistan.

'Hello, this is …'

'How are you, how are you doing?'

I was good, I replied, but before I could continue, Trump cut me off.

'China hit us so hard, those sons of bitches, they hit us with this plague.'

The coronavirus pandemic was now affecting the entire world. I said that I had seen from the latest figures that the number of Covid cases in the US was decreasing, and that the economy was also showing signs of improvement, with ever more people back at work.

'It only cost us $4 trillion and many human lives,' Trump said. 'It was terrible what they did to us, and they could have stopped it. Terrible thing, my friend. Terrible thing.'

I said a few words about how the NATO allies were helping each other during the pandemic, and about the military efforts to assist civilian society.

'Oh really? Well, to be honest, I haven't seen many NATO soldiers offering the United States any help. But fair enough. We've dealt with everything we had to deal with. But how's it going, by the way? Has everyone reached the two per cent target now? What about Germany?'

'Not everyone,' I replied. 'But I'm still pushing. Every time I speak with the NATO leaders here in Europe, I bring up—'

'Germany is paying less than one per cent. And Angela won't even come to the G7 summit because of Covid. She said: "Oh Covid, oh Covid!" But we don't have any Covid here in the White House, right? Where is Germany at now, Secretary General?'

I said that Germany would soon be above 1.5 per cent; that they were looking at more increases in the coming years, and that nine countries were now at above the 2 per cent target.

'Who else?' Trump asked. 'Who else is as bad as Germany? Are there any others?'

I said that Spain and Italy were still some way below the target, but that the countries in Eastern Europe and the United Kingdom were above it. A number of countries were now approaching the 2 per cent goal not because they had increased their defence spending, but because their gross domestic product had decreased due to the pandemic. I was therefore at least as concerned with the increase in absolute figures, I said.

Trump seemed content with this.

'Okay, so what else is going on?' he asked.

I was finally able to bring up Afghanistan, and made it clear that the allies welcomed the agreement the United States had entered into with the Taliban.

'But it's important that we all remain well-coordinated in the times ahead. I understand that the United States is planning further reductions of its troops, and I—'

'We are. We have to get the hell out.'

I told Trump we had to be certain the Taliban were sticking to their side of the deal, and that I was unsure whether they actually were. I emphasised in particular that the Taliban had to start negotiations with the government in Kabul, as they had pledged in the agreement with the US. I was anxious to see whether Trump would now plainly state that he had in fact moved away from this agreement, which made demands of the Taliban. But I was unable to finish before he began speaking again.

'But have you ever seen anything so stupid? Where we're spending so much money? Anything so stupid? Please. I've never been involved in anything like it in my life. The money we're spending. I don't even want to give you the numbers, because it's so embarrassing to even talk about it. So we're going to get out.'

Trump wanted me to get in touch with his security advisor, Robert O'Brien, so we could coordinate, and I confirmed that I had spoken with him several times. O'Brien had assured me that anything the United States did would be coordinated with the NATO allies. I told Trump that if the US did undertake further reductions in troop numbers, it might be necessary to close the NATO bases outside Kabul.

'Yeah, speak to O'Brien and General Kellogg. But it's time. It's time to get the hell out. We should have gotten out eighteen years ago.'

At the time, General Keith Kellogg was security advisor to vice president Mike Pence, and a colleague Trump obviously trusted.

'I'll be sure to keep in close contact with them, and we'll make sure that the Taliban keep their side of the agreement. We must do everything we can to prevent Afghanistan—'

'I totally agree. But we'd like to get out. We're pulling many troops out of Germany because they're so far behind on their NATO obligations. They're at one per cent, so we're taking soldiers out of Germany. We're at fifty thousand now.'

This was new. The US military presence in Europe had increased under Trump, but now it was set to decrease again. And cuts would be made in Germany in particular.

'And we're going down to twenty-five thousand as quickly as possible.'

Now Trump was really on a roll.

'They're criminals, with what they're paying. You know, the problem with Germany is that they can't be trusted. And she won't even come to the G7 summit. I can tell you now, if we ever needed them in a war, they wouldn't be there for us. You can be sure of that. She won't even come to a meeting.'

Trump stuck with this topic for quite some time.

'Angela is afraid of Covid. If she's afraid of Covid, then she'll definitely be afraid of bullets, right? They have this pipeline to Russia, they're paying the person we're supposed to protect them against. They can't be trusted. Would you say they're untrustworthy?'

'I would say they haven't yet reached the two per cent target, but that—'

'No, they haven't, and they never will. Because, you know, they think everyone else is stupid. And we can't allow them to think that way.'

We went back and forth for a little while on whether Trump would publicly confirm that the United States was withdrawing troops from Germany; I had seen some speculation in the press that US soldiers would be transferred to Poland. Trump sang Poland's praises – they were at 2 per cent. But his preference was to bring all the US soldiers home to the United States.

I once again repeated that I agreed the financial burden was unfairly distributed, and reminded Trump that NATO was now doing more in the Middle East, especially in Iraq. Which was also a way of ensuring fairer burden-sharing.

'Very good,' Trump said. He pointed out that the Middle East is much closer to Europe than it is to the United States, and said he thought the Europeans ought to be careful about allowing immigration from Arab countries. Since I knew how concerned Trump was with China, I tried to remind him of what we had managed to achieve at the summit six months previously. But again, I was unable to finish.

'The really big danger is China, more than anything else,' Trump said. 'That's a big risk.'

'Yes, China—'

'To me, that's your big risk.'

'China poses a significant challenge, and—'

'China's doing well. But, you know, we're keeping pace. I've built up a mighty defence, and I've spent $2.5 trillion. And, to be honest, NATO isn't responding to China at all. It's laughable. But Europe's big risk is China.'

'Yes, and that's what I emphasised in the speech I just gave about where NATO will be ten years from now. I said that NATO cannot remain neutral. NATO cannot forgo being part of the West's response to China's growth.'

But Trump didn't follow up on this. Instead, he suddenly returned to a topic I'd thought we were done with for this conversation.

'Yes, and, you know, they have to pay their bills. They can't think that we'll fight for Germany, and, well, Germany can't fight. They've lost their independence to Russia. They get sixty, seventy per cent of their energy from Russia. How ridiculous is that? They can't fight. Send them a white flag.'

Yet again, I tried to say that the Germans were increasing their defence budget, and that they had decided to buy some American fighter jets, which was good for the American defence industry. But I admitted that Germany had a long way to go.

Trump was unwavering. He claimed that the US was paying 100 per cent of NATO's expenses, and that the Germans were simply laughing.

'Yes, I agree that we must have fairer burden-sharing,' I said. 'But I also believe it's a great advantage for the United States to have many friends and allies in NATO. Especially with regard to China.'

'I don't know about that,' Trump replied. 'She won't even come over to a summit here in the United States. That would have shown that we stand together. That we're all getting over this Chinese virus. Everyone else wanted to come, except Angela. It would have been a great sign if we'd held the G7 summit at around the agreed time, with everyone present. But she didn't want to. So now we're cancelling the G7.'

'I understand. So there won't be a G7 in September, either? Has it been decided?'

'I don't know. Personally, I couldn't care less.'

'You know, NATO isn't a member of the G7. So it's hard for me to bring up the summit with the European allies.'

'No, no, I agree. I have no complaints about you. You're doing a great job. But everyone is using the United States. I've seen it for three and a half years now, and all I wanted was to put a stop to it. But you know, time passes, and you get … I'm determined to put a stop to it, I just think about all the money that's being spent … it's completely ridiculous. I actually think we might be dragged into a war, because someone gets into a war with Russia. And they won't do anything for us. You know this. But let's not talk about it. What else should we talk about?'

'No, I think we've covered the most important matters. And as I said, I'm glad you have Covid-19 more under control.'

'Yes, we're doing good. The latest employment figures are fantastic. The prognosis was that we'd lose nine million jobs, but it might end up being around five. Just think, we're losing all these jobs because of China. It's a shame for all of us. I was riding high. Then we see this plague come into our country. Where did it come from? From China. And the whole world was changed. We're bouncing back, but they screwed it up. Nobody else will be able to handle China. I'm the only one. And I'm not happy about it,' he said.

Trump was drawing the conversation to a close.

'Okay. Look after yourself, Jens. I'm with you one hundred per cent. I'm just asking for fairness, that's all.'

28

A power shift
in Washington

'JOE BIDEN'S GOING TO WIN.'

The US ambassador to NATO, Kay Bailey Hutchison, was firm in her belief when I met her at around midday on the day after the American presidential election. The vote was still being counted, and Trump was leading in several swing states. But Hutchison had stood for election a number of times, and been a member of the US Senate for twenty years. Over a long career such as that, you start to see patterns others might overlook. Hutchison was better positioned than most to predict what the outcomes of the remaining states would be. There were major differences between the congressional districts in which the vote had been counted and those that remained. Hutchison was certain the results would swing in Biden's favour as the count progressed.

On the third of November, the day of the US election, I had kept an eye on the TV throughout the evening, but nothing was clear when I went to bed. When I abruptly woke the next morning, however, things had begun to change. Trump was doing much better than expected. Of the Biden landslide, which many forecasts and several experts had predicted, there was no sign.

There were now few who dared to say anything for certain, and a number of experts believed Trump might actually win again. I began to mentally prepare myself for another term with Trump in the White House. A number of media appearances had been set up over the course of that morning, in which I was to congratulate the winner and offer my thoughts on the US election. We postponed everything. There was, as of yet, no one to congratulate.

Again, I had the curious feeling that there was something I had not understood, something I hadn't realised. Again, the predictions had underestimated support for Trump, and again I was reminded that the greater probability of a Biden victory did not preclude the opposite.

In a triumphant speech on the morning after the polling stations closed, Trump claimed he had won and called for the count to be stopped. He used words like 'fraud' and 'cheating'. While I was thinking that yet another term with Trump in the White House might prove challenging, I remembered a conversation I'd had with Angela Merkel a few months earlier. She had feared that Biden would fail to win over voters in the presidential debates, and that Trump would pull off a victory. 'But if he does, we'll just have to hang in there, Jens. We have to make the best of it,' she said.

I agreed. It would be possible to salvage NATO from four more years with Donald Trump.

Over the days that followed, Biden slowly closed in on Trump's lead, just as Hutchison had predicted. On the morning of Saturday the seventh of November, the situation was such that if Biden managed to secure the twenty electoral votes from Pennsylvania, it would all be over. Later that afternoon, I had just begun a session in the gym up in the residence's loft. The television that hung on the wall was on, and tuned to CNN. The anchors were discussing some new results in Nevada, and analysing results from some small, pro-Democratic districts outside Las Vegas, which Biden had won. They moved on to Pennsylvania, and a small county Biden had taken. Then, all at once, the call was made: CNN declared that Joe Biden would win the presidential election.

It happened so quickly I barely managed to take it in. But then the CNN anchors dug into the numbers from Pennsylvania again, and clarified how the marginal county would secure Biden a state victory. I abandoned my training session – instead, I watched the reporting on the election. Barack Obama's vice president had now become

president-elect Joe Biden, and Kamala Harris would become the
United States' first female vice president.

I had eventually figured out how to work with Donald Trump,
despite his unpredictability. One day he might threaten to leave
NATO; the next he might be a 'big, big, big fan' of the alliance. He
could harshly criticise Angela Merkel one moment, then declare 'I
love this woman' the next. But all the attention he had directed
towards NATO had led to the mobilisation of significant forces in
favour of the alliance among Republicans and Democrats in Congress.
Key individuals within Trump's administration were open and acces-
sible. Soon, Trump himself had become supportive of NATO's
involvement, such as in Iraq and in the war on terror.

At the Republican National Convention in August, Trump
described how he had pushed the Europeans to spend more on
defence. 'Our NATO partners, as an example, were far behind in their
defence payments. But at my strong urging, they agreed to up their
payments to $130 billion more a year. This will ultimately go to $400
billion,' he said. This was far more than had actually been agreed, but
Trump had continued to use the figure in his election campaign nonetheless. I didn't correct him. My job was to preserve NATO's unity.
The threshold for correcting one of the alliance's leaders therefore had
to be extremely high – especially when that leader was the president
of the United States.

Trump had pulled the United States out of the Iran nuclear deal; he
withdrew from the Paris climate agreement and introduced new
tariffs. None of this related to NATO directly, but splits and disagreements over such important issues affected the collaborative climate
within the alliance. My attempts to build bridges were mainly based
on reminding the European leaders that the number of American
soldiers in Europe had increased under Trump – and that this demonstrated that the United States stood by the security guarantee. This,
after all, was the most important thing.

But over the past six months, this argument, too, had been weakened. In the summer of 2020, Trump showed that Germany's
insufficient defence spending would have consequences. He

announced that approximately a third of the around thirty-five thou-sand American soldiers in the country would be withdrawn. How quickly this would happen, and whether the troops would be sent home to the United States or transferred to other NATO countries, was not confirmed. Mark Esper, who had been US secretary of defense since the summer of 2019, did a good job of limiting the impacts of Trump's decision when he had to implement it. But the task of defend-ing Trump in Europe was growing ever harder. I could no longer simply claim that Trump's actions spoke louder than his words.

With Biden, we would have a much more predictable president. But I was under no illusions that all our problems would simply vanish. Like Trump, Biden would demand the Europeans do more for their own defence.

Biden and I had worked together previously, including when he was Obama's vice president, and I remembered him as a steadfast and amiable man. He had been elected to the Senate all the way back in 1973; he belonged to a generation that had been shaped by the hostil-ities of the Cold War. Biden had held central positions in Washington over many years, and he had intimate knowledge of foreign policy from his time as chair of the Senate Foreign Relations Committee.

The transfer of power would not take place until the twentieth of January. At any given time, the United States has only one president. And for two more months, his name would be Donald Trump.

The autumn of 2020 was a kind of professional state of emergency. In effect, I stopped all overseas travel due to the coronavirus restric-tions. There were also extremely few visits and meetings between other NATO leaders during this period. Many of these visits are about cultivating and maintaining the solidarity and political connections within the alliance, and I began to fear that these bonds might be weakened because we hardly met. I would usually have met with the president of the United States several times, for example, but in 2020 there were no meetings between us at all.

Trump refused to accept the election result, and filed lawsuits in Arizona, Michigan, Georgia and Pennsylvania in an attempt to get the result overturned. This gave rise to uncertainty at NATO headquarters and among allied capitals. My hope was that the authority of America's institutions would ensure that the transfer of power proceeded smoothly and as it should, in spite of Trump's protests.

Just three weeks after the election, on the twenty-third of November, I had my first telephone conversation with Joe Biden. He was up to date on all matters relating to NATO, and his tone was relaxed and friendly.

It wasn't much more than a congratulatory call, but we spent twenty minutes going over the status of some of the most important issues: Afghanistan, Iraq, fairer burden-sharing.

'When it comes to Afghanistan, I'm aware that some difficult decisions will need to be made very soon. I'm going to look into this in detail,' Biden said.

When it came to defence spending, he expected the Europeans to meet their obligations. It was now more important than ever that the Europeans strive to achieve the 2 per cent target – were they to ease off the pressure, and end up lagging far behind again, Trump would be proved right. It would show that it was his threats that had made them pay up. The Europeans had to prove him wrong, Biden said.

I knew that Biden and his team were concerned that everything must proceed properly. We would enter into no cooperation before Biden had been inaugurated. With a sitting president who refused to concede, Biden and his people were acutely aware that *they* must make no formal blunders. I was therefore careful not to refer to our conversation in any way that might make it appear that the president-elect had provided signals about what he may do once in office.

December passed. My family and I celebrated Christmas and New Year, in Oslo this time. We had decided to sell Karin and Thorvald's apartment in Mogens Thorsens gate, but it was hard to let go of my childhood home with all its history; all those teenage parties and the conversations around the kitchen table. It had been the centre of my life for many years, and there were so many happy memories linked to it. Now the apartment had to be cleared out, and the process was starting to drag on. As director general of the Norwegian Institute of

Public Health, Camilla was in the middle of managing the pandemic. Her work situation was extremely challenging, but we hoped to make some progress around New Year, just as soon as we had a little free time together. There would be far less of this than we had hoped.

In the United States, preparations for the transfer of power were underway throughout the entire Christmas and New Year period. Trump continued to claim he hadn't lost the election. For weeks, he had referred to the election as 'stolen'. 'We can't let this happen,' he said. 'Stop the steal!'

Late in the previous autumn, Trump had also fired Secretary of Defense Mark Esper. It was hard to see why he had seen fit to replace the secretary of defense in the period between the election and the inauguration. It was an unusual step, in any case, and it gave rise to even more uncertainty.

On Wednesday the sixth of January, Ingrid and I had planned to have dinner together at home in Oslo. I enjoy cooking, when I have the time and occasion to do so. On that day, I put some fish in the oven and turned on Ingrid's iPad so that I could follow the debate in Congress, where the electoral college votes would be counted and the election result finally certified.

The first thing I heard was an address by Republican Senator Ted Cruz, who argued that an electoral commission ought to be established to eradicate all doubt regarding the result of the election. Apparently this had happened once before, in the mid-1800s. No one had anything to lose by doing this, Cruz believed. If the election had indeed proceeded as it should, then the commission would confirm this.

Cruz was contradicted by various Democrats, who pointed out that the states *had* investigated, and concluded that nothing had occurred which could overturn the result. The job had already been done – establishing such a commission would only serve to sow mistrust in a system that functioned well, they said.

A little later, I noticed the speaker of the house interrupt a representative who was in the middle of addressing the chamber. If it was time to take a break, it seemed strange that it would be necessary to interrupt someone this way. Then the sound suddenly vanished. I checked whether there was something wrong with the iPad.

Then people began to leave the chamber; I wondered whether the Capitol Building's fire alarm had sounded. We moved from the kitchen to the TV room, and began to flick through various channels. Like millions of other viewers, we watched the dramatic scenes unfolding in Washington as the Capitol was stormed. There was the ringing of shattering glass; people breaking down doors and shoving their way past desperate security guards, who were powerless to stop them. The violent protesters forced their way into the building that is the very manifestation of American democracy.

Donald Trump won the election in 2016. This gave him a democratic mandate to lead the world's most powerful nation and NATO's largest and most important member state. This was always my starting point, the basis of all my interactions with him. NATO provides the institutional framework for the United States' presence in Europe. Without the United States, there is no NATO. I therefore regarded it as my job, my responsibility, to make cooperation within the alliance function as effectively as possible.

Trump and I disagreed on important questions, and we were far from one another on the political spectrum. There were some tough periods and challenging meetings. Within the alliance, too, there were great contrasts in a number of areas. It's fine to disagree on defence spending, pipelines transporting gas from Russia, or tariffs. But to refuse to accept the result of a democratic election is something else entirely.

Trump's first presidential term ended in fire and smoke. Looking back, I've often thought that perhaps he couldn't have left the White House in any other way. That there was a kind of logic in him not simply bidding everyone a polite and conventional farewell.

All the same, things went well for NATO during Trump's first term as president. His initial standpoint was that the alliance had lost its relevance, but this changed as our cooperation gained momentum. The United States increased its military presence in Europe, the

Americans began to supply weapons to Ukraine, the member nations increased their defence budgets, we stepped up our efforts in the war on terror, and we managed to agree on a first joint stance towards China. Paradoxically enough, the alliance had been strengthened.

On the day of the Capitol attack, I maintained ongoing contact with my staff. The question was whether I ought to make a statement on the drama playing out on the screens before us. NATO's secretary general doesn't usually express opinions on events within member states.

But the storming of the Capitol was an attack on the very rules of the game – on democracy itself. It ran counter to the values upon which NATO was founded. At 21.30, I tweeted the following: 'Shocking scenes in Washington, DC. The outcome of this democratic election must be respected.'

A few hours later, the protesters luckily withdrew, and that same night the election result was finally certified. On the twentieth of January 2021, Joseph Biden Jr. was inaugurated as the forty-sixth president of the United States of America.

29

When the job comes first

FOLLOWING EXTENSIVE LOCKDOWNS AND MANY RESTRICTIONS, IN early 2021 Europe was finally vaccinating its population against Covid-19. This was a prerequisite for getting working life to function somewhat normally again. And that also applied to those of us in NATO.

The Belgian government had reassured us that everyone working at NATO headquarters would have the opportunity to take the vaccine. But time passed. We soon came to realise that the reassurance we had been given was no simple matter for the Belgians. They feared, understandably enough, that there might be a reaction if NATO was prioritised ahead of the country's own population.

Then Poland decided to offer NATO vaccines. Warsaw had long been asking NATO to stand up for the country, with more soldiers, heavier weapons and more frequent patrols. Now they saw an opportunity to give back to the alliance. The Poles would send four thousand doses of the AstraZeneca vaccine to NATO in Brussels, to show that Poland was a good friend and ally.

The problem was that several large European countries like Germany and Italy had just put the AstraZeneca vaccine on hold as a result of some rare but extremely serious side-effects. Norway and Denmark had already stopped administering this vaccine while they undertook more thorough investigations of episodes of blood clots and bleeding, which in several cases had proved fatal.

In March, various countries in Europe began administering the AstraZeneca vaccine again. The uncertainty around the vaccine had not been eliminated entirely, but that it had at least been partially readmitted into the vaccination programme made it easier for us to accept it. We asked all NATO employees to make use of the Polish offer and take the vaccine.

The only question was whether this should also include me.

Like many other NATO employees, I was registered in the health systems of both Belgium and Norway, and was in the ordinary vaccine queue in both countries. It just so happened that in the Belgian system, it was now my turn to be vaccinated. On the same day that we undertook a large-scale immunisation of the employees at NATO headquarters, I could visit a Belgian doctor's surgery and receive the vaccine there. The vaccine currently being offered in Belgium was the one manufactured by Pfizer.

The Belgians hadn't bumped me up the queue because I was head of NATO – since I was in the fifty-five to sixty-four age group and receiving treatment for ankylosing spondylitis, being offered the vaccine at this point was in no way a form of special treatment. Then came a message from my Norwegian GP, stating that I could also be vaccinated back home in Norway. No special treatment – it was simply my turn in the queue. I would receive the Pfizer vaccine there, too.

I spoke with Camilla several times on the phone. Norway had not yet resumed use of the AstraZeneca vaccine; there, it was still on pause. And Camilla was crystal clear: 'You mustn't take the AstraZeneca vaccine, Jens.'

The fact that other countries had resumed use of the vaccine made no impression on her. 'They have poorer data and much weaker registration than we do here in Norway. Although there's been most attention on younger women, we have no reason to believe the vaccine is any less of a risk for men over sixty,' she said.

Ingrid was back in Norway already, and of course I spoke with her, too. She agreed with Camilla. I should stay well away from the AstraZeneca vaccine.

For the private person Jens Stoltenberg, this would have been easy. All I would have had to do was turn up at the Belgian doctor's surgery, roll up my shirtsleeve and receive the Pfizer jab. But I had just encouraged all of NATO to take the AstraZeneca, in spite of the uncertainty, which of course everyone was well aware of. Could I therefore, as head of the organisation, choose Pfizer?

My colleagues told me that of course I had to decide for myself, but they were fairly sure it would cause resentment. How harsh the reactions would be was difficult to say. Some even thought it not inconceivable that I might have to step down.

Any special treatment of NATO's secretary general had to be avoided – that was the message from every last member of my staff. And I agreed. But then I tried to think through what the requirement of zero special treatment actually involved. Had I been an ordinary NATO employee, it would have been fine for me to reject the Polish vaccine on offer and take the Belgian one instead. A number of NATO employees had been vaccinated already, in their home countries or in Belgium. In other words: the principle that I should be treated like everyone else should mean that I could choose to take the Pfizer vaccine. If the conclusion was that I must take the AstraZeneca like most other NATO employees, then *that* would actually constitute special treatment.

But would it be possible to communicate such an intricate and apparently self-contradictory message? That equal treatment meant that I could take a different vaccine than almost everyone else?

My preference was for the vaccine from Pfizer. My big sister, director general of the Norwegian Institute of Public Health, who had stopped the administration of the AstraZeneca vaccine in Norway, was firm in her conviction. I trust Camilla absolutely when it comes to such things. My wife also urged me to listen to what she and Camilla said. The side-effects of the vaccine were extremely rare, but potentially life-threatening. I took immunosuppressant medications against ankylosing spondylitis. Whether I would be more vulnerable to the potential side-effects than those not taking such medicines, no one could say. But it didn't increase my desire to take the AstraZeneca vaccine. On the other hand, however, most countries in Europe now believed the AstraZeneca vaccine was safe.

I ended up taking the AstraZeneca.

Camilla was worried; Ingrid exasperated and irritated. In my last telephone conversation about it, I unfortunately hadn't worked up the courage to tell her what I had decided to do. Or, at the very least, I hadn't expressed it clearly enough. In any event, Ingrid learned through the media, and not directly from me, that I had not done as she and Camilla had asked. It wasn't good, to put it mildly.

'It's just so typical of you, Jens! You always put your job first, ahead of everything else. Your reputation, your standing in NATO, is more important than your health, than your life – *our* life.'

She was right that the decision wasn't just about me. If I became ill, then of course her life would be affected, too.

I tried to explain the hopeless signal it would have given had I refused to take a vaccine I had encouraged everyone else to take. 'I might have ended up having to leave NATO,' I said.

'Great! And then you could have simply come home. You're there on overtime anyway,' Ingrid replied.

The mood between us was poor for a few days, there's no reason to deny it. Dilemmas that had impacted our relationship for all the years we had been together grew more visible and exposed, perhaps more so than ever before. My job in NATO, versus my life and health. My position in the public eye, versus my private life and family. Heavy weights on either side of the scale. No compromises, no halfway solutions or grey zones in which I could take refuge.

It was either/or. And I chose my job, yet again.

30

China on the agenda

I FOLLOWED PRESIDENT JOE BIDEN WITH MY GAZE AS HE SLOWLY walked over to the 9/11 and Article 5 Memorial, the monument to the victims of the terrorist attack on the World Trade Center that stands outside NATO headquarters in Brussels. There, before a twisted steel beam from one of the destroyed towers, he stood alone with his own thoughts for a brief time before I went over to join him.

'I was on the train from Delaware to Washington that morning,' he said. 'My wife called and told me something terrible had happened in Washington and New York. But it was impossible to imagine just how bad it was.'

Biden was on his way to an ordinary workday in Congress when the hijacked planes crashed into the World Trade Center and the Pentagon. When he arrived in Washington, the Pentagon was on fire and parts of the building had been destroyed. He lost several friends in the attacks.

Biden and I stood side by side before the monument on that mild June evening.

'NATO came to our aid back then, after 9/11. The United States needs NATO. I really mean that,' he said.

Then he began to tell me about his son Beau, who had died of a brain tumour in 2015 at just forty-six years of age. For the second time, Biden had been struck by personal tragedy. He lost his first wife, Neilia, and their one-year-old daughter, Naomi, in a car accident in

1972. His sons Beau and Hunter, three and two years old, were also in the car and were injured.

'You know, I'm the president of the United States. It's a great honour to have been elected to this office. But every time I think about Beau, I tell myself he was the one who should have been president, not me. He was a much better person than I'll ever be.'

Many lines converged as we stood there before the remains of New York's fallen Twin Towers. The terrorist attack on the eleventh of September was the cause of the war in Afghanistan, where Americans and Europeans had been fighting side by side for almost twenty years. We spoke about the many manifestations of terrorism, and I told Biden about the 22 July attacks in Oslo and on Utøya, and the people the Labour Party and I had lost there. As the sun was about to set, I accompanied Biden to his car, where the security guards were waiting. There, we said our goodbyes.

It was Monday the fourteenth of June 2021, and we had just concluded another NATO summit.

The run-up to the summit had been hectic. As usual, it was important to have as many agreed positions as possible before the heads of government met. The summit in London in 2019 had been the starting shot for a political process we had named NATO 2030. My office was using this opportunity to prepare several concrete proposals for how the alliance could be strengthened. These were not only about familiar matters, such as increased defence investment and more troops, but also about formulating new policy linked to issues such as China, resilience and climate change. And last but not least, we had a chance to suggest a major boost to NATO's common budget. With increased tensions in Europe, greater security challenges and new member states, it was necessary to strengthen the alliance in order to build military facilities, organise exercises and run the organisation more effectively. The need was obvious, but it's never easy to obtain more money for international organisations like NATO. Doing so of course requires the member states to transfer money from budgets within their own control, to budgets controlled by NATO in Brussels.

The reform package was therefore received with a certain hesitancy and scepticism among the member countries, and most lukewarm of all was France. For Paris, the proposed significant strengthening of NATO was an example of me expanding my role far beyond its remit.

Early in the spring of 2021, a meeting was held in Paris between diplomats from several central NATO nations and a high-ranking official from the French Ministry of Foreign Affairs. In written minutes from the meeting, I read that the French diplomat expressed deep frustration at my leadership of NATO. The way he saw it, the alarming developments had begun when a former prime minister had been chosen as NATO secretary general, but now the situation was 'completely out of control'. I had apparently used the United States' ostensible absence from the alliance over the past four years under President Trump to give myself 'a more prominent role'. NATO was not 'my organisation', as I seemed to believe – my role was to serve the member nations.

France had 'a serious problem' with me, said the diplomat who believed I had taken too much control over the 2030 process. In revising its strategic concept, the alliance shouldn't have to simply say yes or no to my 'sexy slogans'.

I had expanded my role in an improper way, and was most concerned with my own legacy. This would come back to bite me, the diplomat said. It was vital the member states took back control.

I had been aware of France's dissatisfaction, but the intensity of the criticism and condemnation of me personally was rather concerning. France is an important country in NATO. It wasn't good for the alliance that key figures within the French Ministry of Foreign Affairs were so highly critical of me, and clearly also trying to get others to endorse this criticism. Throughout the winter and spring of 2021, they did their level best to clip my wings.

To garner support for the reforms and curb the French resistance, one thing was important above all else: to get the United States on our side.

The Biden administration wished to strengthen the alliance, that much was clear. Our strategy was therefore to convince the Americans that NATO 2030 could be an effective tool in achieving this. Our pitch in the winter of 2021 was also about making the reform package the United States' project, and at a meeting of NATO ministers of foreign affairs in March, we appeared to have achieved precisely this. Secretary of State Antony Blinken was extremely supportive. He made it clear that the United States stood behind the proposal to increase the organisation's common financing.

At the end of May, I travelled to Paris to meet with President Emmanuel Macron – one of the first journeys I made after the long break due to the coronavirus. The entrance to the Palais de l'Élysée is squeezed between other buildings, but the palace is revealed in all its splendour once you have made your way inside and see the magnificent building and beautiful park at the rear.

Macron stood ready to receive me on the steps, elegant and well-dressed as always. He smiled warmly, and firmly gripped my shoulders. Macron is a leader who greets people in a physical way that is both natural and genuine. We chatted as we made our way up to the meeting room. Macron is analytically inclined, and thinks long-term. Domestically, he stands for a policy of reform with which I sympathise, and we have spoken a lot about pension reforms, upon which we largely agree. He speaks good English, and our conversations were therefore more personal, more direct, than if we'd had to use interpreters.

The backdrop for my meeting with Macron on that day in May were the reports that Paris had grown tired of the secretary general with great ambitions for the alliance. I had ended up right in the firing line for French scepticism about NATO.

But my meeting with Macron was pleasant and constructive. He was far more positive about NATO than his previous statements might suggest, and more flexible than the officials and political team around him. He didn't repeat anything reminiscent of his brain-dead claims of 2019. Nor did the harsh criticism of me personally that had come from the high-ranking official in the French Ministry of Foreign Affairs earlier that spring come through in anything he said.

'It's clear that the Biden administration wants to develop the US's relationship with NATO. That can strengthen the alliance and open up a new chapter in the transatlantic relationship,' he said.

French positions on foreign policy often ran counter to mine. France wanted to limit what NATO did, while giving the EU a greater role in the continent's defence policy. But the contrasts were surmountable. We shared the same values and stood together.

Perhaps Macron, in his meetings with me, appeared more obliging than he really was. Maybe he allowed his diplomats and officials to express his criticism and push the French agenda, to give himself some leeway to appear more understanding and reconciliatory. It wasn't clear to me whether the president actually knew how French officials were almost constantly trying to block various NATO projects, large and small.

I had decided in advance not to start a discussion about increasing the common budget within NATO, which I knew France was against. I reasoned that Macron would bring it up himself.

I went through the other 2030 proposals, one by one. Macron's reaction was openly expectant. He didn't say a word about money. In the end, I handed a note to Stian, who was sitting next to me, asking whether I ought to bring up the budget. 'You could ask if he has any concerns regarding NATO 2030' said the note I received in return.

'Turkey,' Macron replied. He was worried about the challenge Turkey represented to the fundamental values upon which NATO is built. Relations between presidents Erdoğan and Macron were difficult. In Turkey, religion was becoming an ever more important political factor. By criticising Erdoğan, Macron could position himself as the advocate of the modern, secular state. Erdoğan, for his part, could use confrontations with Macron to position himself as the leader of the Islamic world, someone who would stand up against criticism and violations of Islam. It was challenging, having two presidents of major NATO countries who had become each other's ideal enemies.

Towards the end of the meeting, when we had run over time and were packing up our papers, came the words I had been expecting.

Macron said no mention had been made of any increase of NATO's common budget.

We discussed this for a while, Macron arguing against and I in favour. The tone was good, but the president stood his ground. For France, this was about extremely small sums, so the opposition was political. We would need help from the Americans if we were to have any hope of securing the budget increases.

On Monday the seventh of June, I had the last and most important of the preparatory meetings ahead of the summit. For the first time following the pandemic, I was back in Washington – this time to meet with President Biden.

The staging of the meeting was good. The guestbook had been set out, the chief of protocol read out the names of all the participants, and we had a clear agenda. I was worried I had chosen slightly too pale a suit, but my fears evaporated the moment I walked into the Oval Office. Biden appeared wearing a royal blue suit and flowered tie, and his socks were decorated with tiny dogs. He immediately struck an informal tone. The warmth he radiated reminded me a little of Thorvald; perhaps that also had something to do with Biden's casual style and shock of white hair.

Biden instilled trust and respect. And the domestic policies he was about to implement in the United States had impressed me, with major efforts relating to infrastructure and the climate crisis.

I steered the conversation towards NATO 2030 and the strengthening of the alliance's common budget. I explained that Germany and the United Kingdom were on board, as was Spain. 'I recently had a productive meeting with President Macron, but he's still against the increases. He made it clear he would rather spend the money on the EU's own defence, rather than on NATO. So we're not quite in full agreement, and I'll need your support,' I said.

'Well, you have it. What would you like me to say?' Biden asked.

'Be as clear as you can. Go through each point of the 2030 proposals in detail,' I replied.

Biden made it clear that he supported increasing the common budget and strengthening NATO early in our conversation.

With the United States behind us, I felt sure we would garner support for the reform package at the summit, but I was still concerned that Macron would oppose it. If he did, the disagreement between the United States and France would become the main focus at the summit, yet again giving the impression of an alliance in conflict.

Biden spoke at length about China, and what he referred to as a competition between democracies and authoritarian regimes. After winning the presidential election, he had spoken with President Xi Jinping twice on the telephone, and Biden confirmed how the United States' attention was now turned on the giant in the east. The priorities of US foreign policy could be summarised as the three Cs: China, Cyber and Climate.

I gave an account of the developments in Afghanistan, and said that the work to reduce our military presence was going as planned. With regard to NATO's engagement in future conflicts, I repeated Obama's old motto: prevention is better than intervention.

'Bingo,' Biden replied.

As the meeting approached its conclusion, Biden stood and showed me around the Oval Office. On the day on which a new president is sworn in, the staff of the White House have a few hours to install the items the incoming president has requested. Now Biden took me by the arm, pointing at the things he had asked to bring with him, and explaining why. In addition to busts of prominent leading figures like Benjamin Franklin and Robert Kennedy, he had chosen a bust of labour leader and civil rights activist Cesar Chavez, a pioneer in the fight for the rights and interests of American agricultural workers.

'Chavez has meant more to me than you know,' he said.

The brief guided tour stopped at the president's desk.

'I have something for you, my friend,' Biden said, pulling out a drawer. Then he handed me a pair of Ray-Ban aviator sunglasses, of the type he himself had worn for years, and which had become a kind of trademark of his. I thanked him, thinking that this was a gift I was actually going to enjoy.

Biden's broad experience within foreign affairs and security policy was impressive, and he was a passionate supporter of international cooperation. He had been involved in such work since the 1960s, and was able to reference details from American political history and international events like few others. It gave him a unique authority. But at the same time, my impression of Biden in this first meeting with him as president was somewhat mixed. He could stray from the point and get lost in trifles.

In his inaugural address, the president had assured American citizens that he would rebuild the United States' alliances, and that the country would engage with the world once more. There was no doubt that Biden and his team were in favour of NATO. Nevertheless, it is always a little uncertain how much energy, power and attention an American administration will be willing to give the alliance. But after our meeting, I was reassured.

In the brief time that remained before the summit, the tug of war over the decisions that would be taken continued. This happened through the countries' NATO delegations in Brussels, and it was therefore possible for me and my office to maintain control of the process. But on the last weekend before the summit, the leaders of the G7 nations met in Cornwall. In a separate meeting with Biden, Macron gave up his resistance to increasing the common budget. Biden himself commented on what had happened between them when, a little later, he met with Vladimir Putin in Geneva. On his way up the steps to board the plane back to Washington, a journalist wondered whether it wasn't a little naive to have met with Putin. Surely it wasn't possible to believe he was ever going to change?

'Sure, it's Vladimir Putin,' Biden replied. 'But, look, it was also – I don't want to compare him to Putin, but it was – the French President said he will never go for more money for NATO. Guess what? He's agreed.'

And with that, the NATO 2030 package fell into place. It involved a step change in response to a broader threat picture, with important clarifications on climate change, cyber threats, infrastructure, and not least, China. In addition, the package laid the foundations for a trebling of the common budget, and hundreds of new appointments in the coming years. The cooperation within NATO had to build upon an understanding of the term security in its broadest sense; one that covered much more than defence and credible military deterrence. It was about security in a wider sense, and our ability to protect and defend everything from gas pipelines and powerplants to mobile networks and IT systems.

We were expanding and strengthening the institution itself. This would make NATO more robust and less vulnerable to political shifts following many years of downsizing and cuts.

For me, the entire process around NATO 2030 was reminiscent of the processes I knew well from Norwegian politics, through which we prepared political programmes for the party and the government. The difference was that this time, the decisions were made on behalf of many countries. I saw how leading such a process can grant one great influence over the end result. My closest colleagues and I hatched the ideas; we then filtered them through the various capitals before the final resolutions were adopted at the summit, and these were surprisingly similar to the original proposals we had drafted. It paid to conduct political craftsmanship from the secretary general's office.

The summit defined climate change as one of the greatest security challenges of our time. Global warming intensified crises and conflicts; more extreme weather had an impact on how military operations could be conducted. If the world is to achieve its climate goals, the emissions from military activity also have to be cut. In the NATO 2030 programme, it was for the first time decided that the alliance would work on issues relating to climate change, including by reporting emissions and contributing to the development of technology that can provide effective as well as climate-friendly defence in the future.

The London summit had briefly stated that China represented a challenge the alliance could not ignore.

Xi Jinping's foreign policy had given rise to uncertainty and unease, particularly due to his threats against Taiwan. That Taiwan was not formally part of China represented a humiliation Xi was keen to do away with, and he had sharpened his language around the use of military force to reunify Taiwan with the People's Republic of China.

Now, two years later, the statement on China included in the 2019 summit declaration had been vastly expanded. Security and human rights were given much greater weight. In several paragraphs, NATO made it clear that China's assertive and provocative behaviour was a challenge to our security.

We must cooperate more closely with partner countries such as Australia, Japan, New Zealand and South Korea to defend the norms and institutions that had characterised the international community since the Second World War. NATO is a regional alliance, but the challenges we face are global, so it was imperative we continue to strengthen our global partnerships to deal with these challenges effectively.

The Americans were very pleased – they got the summit they had wanted. Joe Biden united the West around the United States in managing the mighty rival in the East. For the most part, Biden and Trump were aligned in their policy on China; the differences lay in how they each related to their allies. Biden wanted to bring them on side, and regarded NATO as an important platform for achieving this.

In terms of how the United States was viewed, we noticed a certain scepticism still lingered among the allies. Biden received a warm welcome, but doubts remained as to how long America's friendlier tone towards Europe would last. Furthermore, there were vastly differing opinions among the Europeans as to how this should be handled. Some countries – Italy, Belgium and Luxembourg among them, and with France at the helm – believed the doubt Trump had sown was an argument for making Europe less dependent on the United States and NATO. 'European strategic autonomy' was a kind of insurance against Trump or another future president with similar attitudes. On the opposite side were countries such as the United Kingdom, the Netherlands and Denmark. They believed the idea of a Europe solely responsible for its own security to be a dangerous one, which increased the risk of the United States turning away from Europe at some point in the future.

Germany appeared to be somewhere in the middle. We had to avoid France and Germany taking the same line in their view of transatlantic relations and cooperation – if this happened, we might end up with a constellation that included the United States and the United Kingdom on one side in important matters, against France and Germany on the other. And with this, we would risk much becoming deadlocked.

Everyone was relieved at Biden's faith in cooperation with Europe, and the fact that his attitudes clearly reflected recognisable American security policy.

'This is a new day. We are back in the game,' he reassured the allies during one of the informal gatherings at the summit.

'But for how long?' asked President Macron.

31

Exit Afghanistan

ONE DAY IN MID-APRIL 2021, I CALLED US SECRETARY OF STATE
Antony Blinken. He wanted to talk about the way forward in
Afghanistan. We had already touched on the subject in previous telephone conversations, but now Blinken wished to inform me of what
the Americans had concluded following their recent comprehensive
review.

Blinken was an experienced foreign affairs politician, and he had
worked closely with Joe Biden over a number of years, but he was still
new in his role as secretary of state. As a nine-year-old, Blinken moved
from his home city of New York to Paris, to live with his mother and
her new husband, Samuel Pisar. As a boy, Pisar had gone to school in
Poland along with nine hundred other Jewish children. He was the
only one of these children to survive the Holocaust. Blinken often
talked about the impression his stepfather's experiences had made on
him.

During the election campaign, Biden had promised to bring home
the US soldiers that remained in Afghanistan. He had been against the
war for a long time, but still, I felt anxious about how his decision
would play out. Both Obama and Trump had wanted to put an end to
the United States' war in Afghanistan, but neither of them had
managed to do it. Now Biden had been left with the responsibility – he
was the one who had to deal with the true weight of the war's dilemmas.

When I got Blinken on the line, he first confirmed that the Americans had completed their review. The president had made his decision. And he wanted out.

Just over a year earlier, around New Year 2020, Donald Trump had made a deal with the Taliban which stipulated that all foreign soldiers would leave Afghanistan by the first of May 2021. In return, the Taliban would stop their attacks on international forces before the withdrawal and sever all ties with Al-Qaeda and other terrorist organisations.

The United States had negotiated this deal without the other NATO allies really having much of a say. We received regular briefings from secretary of state Mike Pompeo and chief US negotiator Zalmay Khalilzad, but we were not permitted to view the texts being negotiated. Once the deal was in place, it became clear that it not only committed US troops to leave Afghanistan, but all other nations' forces to leave the country, too. That is, the United States had negotiated all of NATO's presence in Afghanistan, without the NATO allies being included in the negotiations. This caused some irritation and concern among the other allies. Even the Afghan government had been excluded from the proceedings.

The allies' concerns were linked to whether the conditions the Taliban were being asked to fulfil were strict enough. The deal made it clear, for example, that the Taliban and the government in Kabul must start negotiations regarding a new constitution, but there was no requirement that an agreement had to be reached before the United States and NATO withdrew their forces. The Taliban fighters were required to become part of the regular Afghan army, but it was not compulsory that this happen before we pulled out.

It was, however, reassuring that the withdrawal would take place in stages, contingent upon the Taliban keeping their side of the deal. The purpose of this was to prevent the Taliban regaining control of the country.

Some months after the deal had been made, in May 2020, I hosted a meeting on Afghanistan at home in the residence in Brussels.

Around the table sat the head of the NATO and US forces in Afghanistan General Scott Miller, SACEUR Tod Wolters, US NATO ambassador Kay Bailey Hutchison, head of NATO operations John Manza, and Stian and myself.

We were informed that Trump's patience had run out. He wanted a complete withdrawal from Afghanistan. No matter the cost and as fast as possible.

This was strictly confidential, those of us around the table were told. Only a few key individuals in Washington knew that the plan was to pull out unconditionally. 'The number of people who know about this has just doubled, now that we've told you,' the Americans said.

I wanted to be absolutely certain I had understood correctly.

'What about the requirement that the Taliban must fulfil several conditions – that they must stop their violent attacks, enter into negotiations and break with Al-Qaeda?' I asked.

'No, that no longer applies,' Miller answered.

This was a fundamental change in the premise for the withdrawal, and the Europeans had not been informed. The Americans were forging ahead, even though the pervading tone among the allies was in favour of remaining in the country. But the United States was still clearly pulling the greatest weight in Afghanistan. None of the NATO allies was exactly chomping at the bit to take over from them. Taking responsibility for the biggest military missions gave the US power, and the Americans knew how to use it. Of course their decision influenced NATO's situation, and put limits on what I was able to do.

The negotiations between the Taliban and the Kabul government began in Doha, the capital of Qatar, but quickly deadlocked. The Taliban exhibited no willingness to make compromises that would restrict their power.

At the start of October, one month before the presidential election, Trump tweeted: 'We should have the small remaining number of our BRAVE Men and Women serving in Afghanistan home by Christmas!'

Again, this came as a surprise to everyone. Completing the withdrawal before Christmas was far earlier than even Trump himself had prepared for. Such an expedited American withdrawal would put other nations' soldiers in an extremely difficult position, and extinguish any last hope of a negotiated solution. Besides, winding up the military presence in the country would be a much more complex process than Trump's tweet suggested.

All signs indicated that we would soon have another American president, and that we would be able to sit down with the new administration and discuss the various withdrawal alternatives. As I viewed the situation in the autumn of 2020, my most important task was to ensure an orderly process within NATO, and to prevent rushed decisions. Trump's first presidential term therefore also ended without him managing to complete a full withdrawal from Afghanistan.

Personally, I had long held strong doubts about what was the right thing to do, and there was also disagreement among my closest colleagues. Stian believed we had to stay – that it was about NATO and the West's credibility. The military presence was modest; NATO forces suffered few losses. The operation was at a level at which it could be continued, and there was a real risk the government would collapse and the Taliban return if we withdrew.

Deputy director of my private office, the German Lorenz Meyer-Minnemann, believed the opposite. When Stian had become head of my private office, he had requested that Lorenz join him as his right-hand man. Lorenz had worked in NATO for a long time, and knew the organisation extremely well. He was a well-read and broad-minded man of the somewhat unassuming type; someone who could quote the classics without it seeming like an affectation.

Lorenz believed that the choice we faced in Afghanistan was a typical example of the sunk cost fallacy – a phenomenon that describes the difficulty of accepting that an investment has been unsuccessful. Instead of acknowledging the loss, you invest even more in an attempt to save the project. According to Lorenz, we were simply refusing to accept that we had already been in Afghanistan too long. We needed to cut the cord and put an end to it.

The conflicting advice reflected our uncertainty around this challenging issue. It was in situations such as these that I felt the full weight of the responsibility inherent in my role as the alliance's leader. I reached a point where I needed to decide for myself what I thought was right.

I had met Afghanistan's ambassador to the United States, Roya Rahmani, a couple of years earlier. She was born in 1978, six months before the Soviet Union invaded her homeland. When Rahmani was a girl, her family fled to Pakistan, where she lived in refugee camps with her mother and siblings and went to a madrassa school. 'Not every student who went to that school ended up becoming a terrorist, but quite a lot of them did,' she said. She later moved to the United States, got a good education and ended up working as a diplomat and ambassador in Washington.

Rahmani feared what would happen if the Taliban came to power again.

'Secretary General, don't be naive. The Taliban haven't changed, I don't trust them for as much as a second. They will shove women back into burqas,' she said.

Up until the winter of 2020/2021, my conclusion had been that the cost of leaving Afghanistan was greater than the cost of staying. I had said this to Obama, I had said it to Trump, and this assessment was behind the reassurances I had given all the Afghans I had met on my many trips to the country. But slowly, and despite the dangers Rahmani had pointed out, I began to place greater emphasis on the uncertainty and the downsides of staying.

My belief in what we could achieve militarily had suffered a blow in recent years. We had not made the progress that Jim Mattis had been so confident of making when he, with my full support, convinced Trump to send in more troops. On the contrary – the Taliban had grown stronger. They now controlled around half of Afghanistan. The Taliban had suffered losses, but these were small compared to the number of people who continued to support the organisation. Taliban fighters constantly crossed the border to Pakistan, to rest and reorganise. They had a safe haven there.

Even with our support, the government army would never manage to inflict a military defeat upon the Taliban. And there was always the risk that our own or the US military operations could go horribly wrong, such as when an American plane mistakenly attacked a hospital in Kunduz in the autumn of 2015, and forty-two civilians were killed. To me, this tragedy was a prime example of what *can* happen while wars are raging. People make mistakes. Technology fails, with terrible consequences.

There was, at least, a deal on the table between the United States and the Taliban. It wasn't perfect, but it provided an opening for a controlled withdrawal.

The agreement would ensure that the Taliban didn't attack the international forces. But should we decide to stay in the country after the withdrawal deadline, we would have to be prepared for them to start attacking us again. This would make it necessary to send in more troops, and we would again see NATO soldiers injured or killed.

It was entirely possible to argue that this was a price we should be willing to pay out of consideration for the alliance's credibility, the war on terror and the rights of Afghan women. But I doubted whether the willingness to pay this price truly existed among the NATO nations. After almost twenty years, we had not managed to build a democratic Afghanistan that could stand on its own two feet – so what was the likelihood that we would manage it at some point in the next twenty? Afghanistan had become an example of what an ever-increasing number of Americans were referring to as 'endless wars'.

I felt a weighty responsibility for all the soldiers we had deployed to Afghanistan. I had felt this as Norway's prime minister, and I felt it now. But the pain of acknowledging that many lives had been lost could not be an argument for risking even more. I didn't suddenly change my mind and take a new position, but I began to weigh the arguments differently. The uncertainty involved in staying in Afghanistan had become too great, the price too high. My conclusion therefore changed, and I began to argue for it in meetings with NATO leaders and in my conversations with the decision-makers in Washington. A withdrawal from Afghanistan was also in line with the restructuring of the organisation I had been working towards since 2014 – to bring NATO back to its core task of defending Europe.

*   *   *

After my phone conversation with Antony Blinken on that day in April 2021, it was clear that no further assessments of the situation on the ground would be made that might make the Americans put the brakes on. The United States was about to pack up and leave.

'We've assessed two different alternatives, either that the withdrawal happens in accordance with a predetermined schedule, or that it must be based on certain conditions being fulfilled. The president has decided on the first alternative,' Blinken said. Like Trump, Biden neglected to set demands of the Taliban in order for the US forces to be withdrawn. The only difference was that while Trump had agreed to be out of the country by the first of May 2021, Biden decided that all American soldiers would be withdrawn by the eleventh of September. Twenty years after the terrorist attacks on New York and Washington, the United States' longest war would be over.

The decision was not unexpected. Still, it was affecting to hear Blinken say it straight out: *full withdrawal.* The Taliban, not the US and NATO, would represent the strongest military might in Afghanistan. The game had been turned on its head. Our strongest bargaining chip had been that we would continue, or perhaps even increase our presence in the country, unless the Taliban agreed to the Ghani government's demands to hold democratic elections, ensure freedom of the press and guarantee women's rights. Now this chip had been taken off the table.

The Americans were aware that the NATO allies would have problems with the decision, but hoped they would stand behind it all the same. Blinken emphasised that the United States would continue its diplomatic work in Afghanistan. Both financial support for the security forces and humanitarian efforts would continue.

For my part, it was important to coordinate the various positions and close ranks within NATO. The first person I spoke with was German minister of foreign affairs Heiko Maas, and his British counterpart Dominic Raab – both representatives of countries that opposed an unconditional withdrawal. They were not happy about what was about to take place. 'But the writing is on the wall for what will happen when the Americans withdraw. We'll just have to make the best of it,' Raab said.

Italian prime minister Mario Draghi seemed resigned when I spoke with him. 'Maybe we should just call it what it is, a defeat,' he said drily. Angela Merkel was also disappointed when I spoke with her.

'I don't like it. The only people smiling today are Vladimir Putin and Xi Jinping. They're the only ones happy that we're pulling out,' she said. The Europeans were even more critical than I had expected.

Nevertheless, the only realistic outcome was for NATO to reach the same decision as the United States. There was no way the Europeans could continue a war that had been triggered by an attack on the United States *after* the Americans had left. European leaders could not ignore the gravity of the politics surrounding this – getting their national assemblies to approve a new mandate to send soldiers to Afghanistan after the United States had withdrawn was utterly unthinkable. And they knew it.

'The conclusion is a given, so the decision should also be made pretty quickly, without hesitation. If it's postponed, it will only lead to greater frustration,' I said.

On Wednesday the fourteenth of April, President Biden announced his decision. He made a televised speech from the Treaty Room in the White House, the same room in which President George W. Bush had declared war on Afghanistan in October 2001.

'I'm now the fourth American president to preside over war in Afghanistan – two Democrats and two Republicans. I will not pass this responsibility on to a fifth president,' Biden said.

He left no room for doubt. A military presence in Afghanistan was no longer in the interest of US security.

That same afternoon, I chaired an extraordinary meeting of all the NATO ministers of foreign affairs and defence. It ended up being a long discussion. NATO allies would end their military engagement in Afghanistan. The withdrawal would start on the first of May, and would be concluded in the course of a few months.

Over the weeks that followed, I often heard European leaders say that the United States had acted obstinately, without listening to them.

When I met with him in Paris later in the spring, President Macron made a point of this, drawing a parallel with President Trump's decision to pull the American soldiers out of northern Syria in the autumn of 2019. According to Macron, French special forces operating in the same area had been hung out to dry. 'We can't trust the Americans,' he said.

But several NATO countries had withdrawn their soldiers from Afghanistan without consulting the other allies – including France. It's simply that when the United States makes this kind of decision, it has entirely different consequences. Indeed, there were now many European soldiers in Afghanistan, but these troops were to a great extent dependent upon American support. It was American drones and satellites that gathered most of the intelligence, and American bombers who came to the European soldiers' aid whenever the situation became critical. The Americans provided much of the transport capability and logistics we all used. No other country was intent on taking over the United States' role – and nor did they have the means to. The United States' size and military might means that whatever the Americans decide has consequences for everyone else. NATO could continue without the United States in principle, but in reality, Biden had decided on behalf of the entire alliance.

Besides, the Biden administration *had* consulted the allies in advance, at both ministerial and ambassadorial level. The fact that many disagreed with the conclusion was another matter.

It wasn't just Macron who was critical of the process. Other leaders in Europe were also frustrated at what they perceived to be a lack of involvement in the decision to leave Afghanistan. Much of the frustration was probably due to the fact that they had felt misled when Trump had negotiated the deal with the Taliban the year before. The bitterness this had caused in Europe was now rubbing off on Biden and his government. Clearly the mistrust could not easily be brushed aside.

After the meeting of NATO ministers on the fourteenth of April, it was important for me to speak with Afghanistan's president, Ashraf Ghani. He had to hear NATO's decision directly from me, and not second-hand. I got him on the line an hour after the meeting had concluded.

'This isn't the end, but the start of a new chapter. We're withdrawing our troops, but we will continue to support the Afghan security forces, train the soldiers and stand behind you in the peace negotiations with the Taliban. But I am of course aware that we have made a difficult decision, with significant risk,' I said.

Ghani was prepared – he had already received a call from President Biden. He was courteous as ever, and he thanked me for NATO's support, but of course I could hear the disappointment in his voice. 'There's no doubt that we are heading into a challenging period,' he said.

A little further on in the conversation, he allowed his vice president, Amrullah Saleh, to take over. The tone changed substantially.

'We've been abandoned,' Saleh said. 'The violence will increase. Jihad has defeated NATO.'

Saleh raised his voice.

'The world's most powerful military alliance has been beaten by a fanatical terrorist organisation,' he said.

President Ghani allowed his vice president to say what he did not wish to say himself. The Afghan government believed we had failed them.

32

Collapse in Kabul

'HOW DO YOU FEEL ABOUT IT?' I ASKED.

'I don't feel good, I don't have a good feeling.'

I considered the man before me. General Scott Miller was calm and level-headed, as I had found him to be at our previous meetings, but he made no attempt to hide that things looked bleak.

'It's not going to go well,' he said.

The Taliban were advancing on all fronts. They were taking over smaller towns and border stations; taking control of ever more of the road network. 'I've seen some analyses that show the Afghan forces can hang on for a couple of years. But I have no faith in that. I'm there, I know what's happening,' Miller said.

Miller had been head of the NATO and US forces in Afghanistan since 2018. He had just arrived in Brussels, having come straight from Kabul. As he entered my office he held out his hand; I was about to attempt the strange elbow greeting that had become commonplace during the pandemic, but changed my mind when I realised Miller would clearly prefer a handshake. It was a bit of a clumsy start, before we sat down.

The picture Miller painted on that day in early July 2021 was in keeping with the briefings I had received from our own people. After the United States and NATO had decided to end our operation, the Taliban had refocused and intensified their military efforts. The Taliban's offshoot in Afghanistan, the Islamic State – Khorasan

Province, had also become a serious threat. Miller was worried that the fragile machinery of power in Kabul was beginning to show cracks. President Ghani and the head of the High Council for National Reconciliation, Abdullah Abdullah, were bitter rivals, and in reality sat at the top of two parallel systems of government.

Ghani was increasingly isolating himself. The government forces were struggling, and soldiers were fleeing across the border to Tajikistan. Village leaders convinced local commanding officers to give up and lay down their weapons without a fight. The Taliban sought out pilots who were home on leave, and murdered them. It was a cynical but effective tactic. Without pilots, the government forces would lose their last advantage – control of the country's airspace.

Miller didn't believe the Taliban would attack Kabul. They would advance as far as the city limits, but prefer to take the city as part of a political solution. Fighting inside the city they would incur losses, and it would lead to significant destruction. This was in line with what we knew Taliban leader Hibatullah Akhundzada desired – he wanted a negotiated surrender of Kabul. NATO had a good overview of Akhundzada's assessments and priorities.

Miller had warned against the phasing out of our military presence. But now that the decision had been made, he didn't want the process to drag out. He wanted the withdrawal to happen quickly, because this would be safest. For the same reason, he wanted as few American civilians as possible to remain behind. An evacuation could then be undertaken swiftly, should one become necessary. The main problem was all the Afghans who worked for the Kabul government or the international forces – the moment they understood that the Americans were on their way out, they would have little desire to stay. They too would try to leave the country, and then things would rapidly begin to unravel. If we started to evacuate people, the fear of a collapse might become a self-fulfilling prophecy.

Miller had grave concerns about the situation for the Afghans who had worked for the international forces. 'I occasionally hear that they have no right to be helped to leave. In my mind they do, if the Taliban are going to kill them. And they will be killed,' he said.

On those days in July, I did a lot of work on how our presence in Afghanistan ought to continue after the troops had been withdrawn. The NATO resolution meant that our civilian presence would remain. Many contracts needed to be arranged and budgets established. The various NATO countries were withdrawing their soldiers, but at the same time making plans for the continued operation of their embassies and extensive relief work. The Afghan authorities and government forces would receive massive financial assistance, and NATO would continue to train Afghan soldiers outside Afghanistan. All this required a large number of NATO civilian staff to remain in the country.

The Americans were in a hurry, and wanted their troops out as soon as the fourth of July, Independence Day, more than two months before the date on which President Biden had originally planned to complete the withdrawal. The huge military operation that the withdrawal represented was not effectively coordinated within NATO, and therefore nor was it clarified for all the other allies. Soldiers from many other countries were also in Afghanistan. They were confused about when they would leave, how it would happen, and in what order things would take place.

Nor did the Americans sufficiently consider the fact that there would continue to be a significant civilian presence in Afghanistan.

Throughout the summer, the Taliban advanced and gained ground. But for the time being, Afghan government forces were managing to hold on to most of the larger provincial capitals, and Kabul was not under threat.

At the end of July, I spoke again with President Ghani on the telephone. He made no attempt to hide how difficult the situation was, and described in detail the attacks to which the government army was being subjected. Ghani felt bitterly towards the Americans. He begged for air support.

'I understand that you're withdrawing all the ground troops, but surely you can still send in planes from the bases in Qatar or elsewhere to help us hold off the Taliban,' he said.

I'd had several conversations with Ghani in recent months. Every time we had spoken, he had made it clear that the aim was to drive back the Taliban and win the war. But this time, he didn't do so.

'We're undertaking a strategic consolidation. We're regrouping our forces, withdrawing from some areas in order to be able to hold others. We're going to deadlock the military positions on the ground. And then we will have to negotiate with the Taliban. That's our goal now,' he said.

As July turned into August, the Taliban changed their ground strategy. Until then they had focused on taking smaller towns and obtaining control of rural districts, but now they went after the larger provincial capitals. In the south, Kandahar fell. The Taliban also made major gains in the north, where they traditionally hadn't been so strong. The battles were not especially hard won. Local leaders changed sides to ally themselves with the victors.

August is the month in which many people in Europe and NATO take holidays, and I eventually travelled to Norway. Whenever necessary, I went down to the Norwegian Armed Forces' operation room at Akershus, where I could have conversations with our people in Kabul, at headquarters in Brussels, and in the various NATO capitals. The military withdrawal was as good as completed, but the United States and NATO still had some soldiers in the country to provide protection to the alliance's embassies, among other tasks.

On Thursday the twelfth of August, I was at my family's cabin in Svartskog outside Oslo. I was out taking our newly acquired Buster motorboat for a spin when Lorenz called me from headquarters. I got myself ashore and up onto the terrace, where I sat gazing out across the peaceful Bunnefjord while Lorenz updated me on the situation. The Americans had been in touch. In around an hour, a press conference would be held in Washington at which it would be announced that all Americans would be leaving Afghanistan, including those who had stayed behind after Miller's swift and efficient withdrawal of the troops. Only a handful of diplomats would remain.

The United States was giving up its presence in Afghanistan altogether – including the US civilian presence. This meant they no longer believed Americans to be safe in the country. Which meant that nobody else was safe there, either. This would be evident to everyone.

This is a Saigon moment, I thought. In the final days of the Vietnam War, panic-stricken people had clung to the helicopters that took off from the roof of the American embassy in South Vietnam's capital, Saigon. Now everyone would rush for the exit in Kabul, too.

One of my employees connected the encrypted line. Secretary of State Blinken had requested a conversation.

'I'm so glad you called,' I said when I heard Blinken's voice.

'That's good to hear, because what I'm about to tell you isn't very pleasant,' he replied.

President Biden had decided to send several thousand soldiers to Kabul, with one sole purpose: to help American staff leave the country as quickly as possible. The paradox was therefore that, for a time, more people had to go into Afghanistan to get people out.

'The US embassy is going to be moved from the centre of Kabul and out to the airport,' Blinken said.

Just an hour earlier, the White House hadn't wanted to confirm this. It was serious news, since NATO's Kabul headquarters was right next door to the US embassy, which was like a small military base. Its extensive security systems also protected NATO's headquarters.

'This will have consequences for us. We're going to have to consider closing down the headquarters and moving all our operations out to the airport,' I said.

Most of the intelligence briefings I had received concluded that the Taliban would win in the end. But as late as May, even the most pessimistic assessments maintained that the Kabul government would hold until at least the end of the year. Now it appeared the collapse might happen over the course of just a few days. President Ghani would be visiting Brussels at the end of the month, but I was unsure whether he would have a country to return to.

I had to go back to Brussels. Early the following day, I was down at the cabin's pier, eyeing the motorboat with more than a little concern. I wasn't satisfied with the mooring; the rope out to the buoy was too long. A neighbour came chugging past, and told me it didn't look good – passing boats might get the rope caught in their propellers. But the cars and my bodyguards were waiting up beside the cabin. I simply had to go.

A short time later, the police escort and I turned into the military section of Oslo Airport Gardermoen, where a NATO plane was waiting. In front of the turquoise-coloured building a Norwegian flag fluttered. As Norway's prime minister, I had stood here and received the coffins of our fallen soldiers on their return from Afghanistan. Those were some of the hardest days I experienced as head of Norway's government, and I continue to send Christmas greetings to the families who lost their loved ones. Now the entire operation might be in its final hours.

That same day, Friday the thirteenth of August, I chaired an extraordinary meeting of the North Atlantic Council. The mood among the ambassadors was grave. We received a full review of the situation on the ground. The Taliban had now taken all the cities along the motorway that forms a ring around central Afghanistan, the country's main artery. Abdul Rashid Dostum and other warlords who had previously stood up to the Taliban had been defeated or changed sides.

The NATO employees who returned straight from Kabul gave a frank assessment of President Ghani. Many of them had long been critical of him, but now they were more exasperated than ever. 'He's self-centred, surrounding himself with yes-men, and out of touch with developments on the ground. Promotions within the army smack of nepotism,' we were told. NATO's staff found it incredibly painful to see how badly everything was going.

On Sunday, I received an update from NATO's head of operations, John Manza. The capital of the Balkh Province, Mazar-i-Sharif, had fallen the previous day. It was the last major city in the north to do so. In Kabul, police officers took off their uniforms. Manza had announced that all our key personnel would be moved to the airport, as would all contractors and local employees. The operation was just getting underway.

Huge Chinook helicopters shuttled Americans from the embassy complex in the city centre out to the airport.

It wasn't exactly Saigon 1975, but nor was it that far off.

Ghani had fled the country. Armed Taliban commanders took over the presidential offices.

A little later, I was told about the young dentist Fida Mohammad, and his story. On the morning of Monday the sixteenth of August, instead of going to work, he had made his way to the airport in an attempt to leave the country. Hundreds of people had stormed the runway. A huge American C-17 transport aircraft landed and taxied towards the terminal building, but when the pilot noticed the distressed crowd, he feared the plane would be overrun. He decided to take off again without unloading. As the aircraft was moving down the runway, Fida Mohammad had climbed into its wheel-well. Once they were airborne, he was faced with the choice of being crushed by the plane's wheels swinging into the well, or jumping out. He chose the latter. His body was found on a roof not far from the airport.

When the C-17 landed in Qatar later that day, the crew found several people's remains in the wheel-well. It is still not known how many died that day. The chaos at the airport illustrated just how desperate many Afghans became when the Taliban took control.

Over the past few months, we had made hectic preparations for our continued presence in Afghanistan. 'We're ending our military mission, but not our support,' I had repeated over and over. We had been planning how this support would be organised since as far back as April.

All these plans were now swept aside. Everything collapsed over the course of a few hours.

In Brussels, all focus turned to managing the crisis hour by hour. We had to get people out – not only our own citizens, but also the Afghans who had worked for us. They were in mortal danger now that the Taliban had taken over, but I was unsure whether we would manage to evacuate them.

Including our colleagues and their family members, there were several thousand Afghans we needed to help leave Afghanistan. Many of those who worked for us were already at the airport, but for their families in Kabul the situation was more complex. They had to be identified, in a country with no official ID numbers, and where it was easy to purchase fake papers. We risked transporting many people who had never worked for NATO. But we would fly those who had worked for us and their families out of the country, and they would also be given asylum. All the NATO nations made it clear they were willing to receive Afghan citizens. But getting them to the airport amid the chaos was an almost insurmountable task.

The Americans brought in an additional thousand soldiers, paratroopers from the 82nd Airborne Division, who would protect the airport and assist with the evacuation. Plenty of planes came in, but each nation thought mainly of its own citizens. Over the first few days, there was a lack of contact and coordination – many planes were only a quarter or half full upon taking off again. And almost no Afghans were on board.

The Taliban had agreed that the evacuation could continue until the thirty-first of August, but not a day longer – we would be taking an enormous risk if the operation continued beyond that date. Strikes might be launched from the hills around the airport; both the Taliban and the Islamic State – Khorasan Province had the capacity to undertake such attacks. I had seen as much myself, when the grenades began to rain down on the airport a short time after Jim Mattis and I had landed there in September 2017. Even military aircraft are vulnerable upon take-off, when they have the least manoeuvrability.

This would be a race against the clock.

We were drowning in letters and emails from desperate people begging for help to leave. Many of these pleas were addressed to me personally.

'Greetings from hell,' one letter began. 'I'm a medical student. As a young woman, I can no longer continue my education, they won't let us return to the university. I cannot bear their atrocities, I cannot stand the thought of going twenty years back in time. We can't live here anymore. I don't know if I'll be dead tomorrow, or if I'll be alive. I'm begging for help for me and my family. Hoping for a quick and positive reply.'

Another read as follows:

'Dear Sir. I am in Kabul. Before the government fell, I was a captain. I have the necessary papers to prove this. As you know, the situation is becoming harder with every day that passes for people like me (ethnic Hazara and Shia Muslim). Taliban soldiers are pursuing me and my family, and we have been forced to leave our home. We move from place to place every night. Our lives are in danger, I want to leave this country, together with my family. Hope you save us, please, please, please.'

Every one of the letters made a deep impression on me. We responded to all of them, but most importantly, they were forwarded to the 24/7 crisis team to see if we could help.

A profound gravity descended on me during these days in August. Not only were we receiving pleas for help, but NATO and I were also facing significant criticism; there were many who were particularly disappointed that we had left Afghanistan's women to the Taliban. The criticism affected me, but compared with the drama playing out in Kabul and the things to which many Afghans were being subjected, the condemnation directed at me was nothing.

Eventually, the evacuation from the airport was better organised. The Turks took charge, and did an excellent job. NATO also took clearer responsibility for the evacuation's coordination. The organisation's highest-ranking civilian representative in Kabul was sixty-four-year-old Stefano Pontecorvo, a robust and self-important Italian who was not overly concerned with diplomatic etiquette. He referred to himself as arrogant, and seemed satisfied being so. Now Pontecorvo grabbed the reins and began to hold at least two coordination meetings daily out at the airport, in which all the countries participated. We obtained an overview of all the various aircrafts' movements, and how many people were registered and ready to be evacuated at any given time. This put an end to the departures of half-full planes.

The biggest problem was still getting people out of Kabul. To be admitted to the airport, the Afghans had to be able to present documentation that they had worked for NATO or Western countries, or that they were relatives of our people. But it was mortally dangerous to carry these documents on one's person while leaving the city centre, where the Taliban had now established many checkpoints.

Incredibly, Pontecorvo managed to organise bus convoys, which picked people up at agreed secret meeting places in Kabul and drove them out to the airport. In some cases the buses were detained at the Taliban's checkpoints for several days – we received reports of people who had spent almost sixty hours on a bus, without being allowed to take so much as a step outside it. A few people gave up and left the buses; the bus drivers then sold the vacant seats to others. The sanitary conditions were horrendous, but we managed to get the buses through.

'I had a problem when it came to my cook's turn,' Pontecorvo later told me. 'The rule was that nobody could take more than one wife with them, but the cook said he had two. I figured it was worth a try. Both of them came along.'

Every time a plane took off, it was a huge relief. Many political decisions can seem rather remote and abstract, but now everything was so tangible – our decisions had direct consequences for many people. Get the planes in, fill them up, fly them out again, first to Qatar and then on to transit camps in Europe. This was the only thing that mattered.

On the day that Kabul fell, I spoke with UK prime minister Boris Johnson. 'Our dear American friends triggered all this with the decision to leave Afghanistan,' he said. 'The situation is not particularly beautiful, as we speak.' Johnson was worried about the consequences the collapse would have for solidarity within NATO.

It was a concern I shared. On Thursday the nineteenth of August I had a long conversation with Secretary of State Blinken. We would be holding a new, virtual meeting of NATO ministers of foreign affairs the next day, and I believed we already needed to take a wider view, rather than simply focusing on the evacuation and the situation at the airport. We must seek to avoid internal splits within the alliance.

'We have to ask some difficult questions about NATO's involvement,' I said. We needed to identify some lessons from what had happened, and we had to take the initiative to begin this process ourselves. Otherwise, somebody else would do it for us.

Blinken agreed.

Even Conservative British and German politicians were now speaking up in favour of becoming less dependent on the United States, and asking questions about the alliance. Former UK prime minister Theresa May, addressing the House of Commons, described the withdrawal from Afghanistan as the worst humiliation for NATO and the West in several decades. The tone in the European press and among leading European politicians was increasingly critical of NATO and the United States. A picture was drawn of a brutal defeat. In an editorial, the *Guardian* claimed that Angela Merkel, who wanted closer transatlantic ties, was wrong; Emmanuel Macron, who wanted European strategic autonomy, was right.

'We held a summit in June that strengthened the transatlantic ties, and now this. What do you think?' I asked Blinken.

'We read European newspapers here in the United States, too, Jens. But yes, I agree. We must demonstrate that we stand united.'

I feared that the meeting of NATO ministers of foreign affairs the following day would be used to apportion blame, but luckily, that didn't happen. It wasn't the time for accusations and criticism. Everyone understood the seriousness of the situation, and everyone had agreed to end the military operation, albeit with varying levels of enthusiasm. We knew we had to present a united front to the new rulers in Kabul. If the signals from Western countries and heavyweight institutions such as the EU and NATO differed, they would also be significantly weakened.

It was right that we demanded the Taliban respect human rights and combat terrorism. But the reality was that we could no longer enforce these demands. Without military backing, there was little we could do.

On Thursday the twenty-fourth of August I participated at a G7 summit. President Biden made a statement, in which he defended the decision to withdraw the US troops from Afghanistan. But he also admitted we wouldn't manage to evacuate everyone we wanted to by the thirty-first of August deadline. He was keen to use all possible means of exerting pressure on the Taliban after the evacuation was concluded, in order to force them to permit those who wanted to leave the country to do so. The Taliban were financially vulnerable. Biden wanted to freeze their accounts, withhold funds.

'We have to view this in perspective. The United States has spent over $300 million per day in Afghanistan for twenty years. $300 million per day!'

The president went on:

'We trained and equipped three hundred thousand Afghan government soldiers,' he said, with the emphasis on the three hundred thousand.

'Did you all know that everything would collapse in eleven days?' Biden lifted his gaze, looking at us and allowing the question to hang in the air for a moment before he continued. 'I didn't. If you knew, then you didn't tell me.'

'No matter what happens in Afghanistan, we must stand united,' I said in my address. In the times ahead, we had to be prepared to combat terrorist groups in Afghanistan from bases in other countries – 'over the horizon', as we say in NATO. The alliance was now assessing how we could contribute.

I highlighted the fact that the evacuation taking place at the airport in Kabul was something on which we were united. The Americans dominated – they had the most soldiers, and they had the most and the largest aircraft. But the impression given in the media was that the operation was purely an American one, and this was not correct. Over 21,000 people had been evacuated from Afghanistan in the last twenty-four hours. Almost half of them, around 40 per cent, left the country on non-American planes. So this was a joint effort.

Angela Merkel was in unusually low spirits. Elections were due to be held in Germany a few weeks later, and she had borne the brunt of the political fallout from Germany's first major military engagement since the Second World War. After sixteen years as chancellor, she was on her way out of politics, but her party was paying for what had happened. According to Merkel, all hell had broken loose.

'We must stand together, but I must say that I'm bitter. We must be under no illusions as to the impression Afghanistan gives of us across the world. In Germany, the reactions are strong. *Hölle ist los!*'

Two days later, the thing we had most feared occurred.

A suicide bomber attacked the dense crowd outside the airport fence. The death toll increased hour by hour, eventually stopping at 182, a figure that included thirteen American soldiers. Islamic State – Khorasan Province claimed responsibility.

Not long before, our intelligence division had reported the risk of a terrorist attack to be extremely high. There were several terrorists in the area outside the airport; they didn't meet in person, and they constantly changed their phones to make it as hard as possible for us to surveil them. Their orders had been to approach the fence, where the crush was greatest. One of them managed to make their way through to Western personnel before detonating their bomb. Had we had more resources in place in Kabul, our intelligence division believed, the attack could have been prevented.

Under chaotic conditions, the United States and the NATO allies managed to transport over 120,000 people out of Afghanistan during the days of the evacuation. One of them was Aryana Sayeed, the musical artist I had met when I visited Kabul in 2017. She was one of the tens of thousands of Afghans who had stood in the throng outside the airport before being let through and flown to Qatar. A little later, she travelled to the United States.

The NATO team in Kabul, with Stefano Pontecorvo at the helm, managed to evacuate our Afghan personnel and their families, a total of 1,899 people. But several thousand Afghans who had worked for us in earlier phases of the twenty-year-long operation remained in the country. How we would manage to help them was unclear.

President Biden called the evacuation an extraordinary success. It *was* an incredible logistical and technical achievement, with extraordinary efforts from all involved. Still, it was somewhat bold to denote the evacuation a success. One of the main arguments for ending our military presence in Afghanistan was that the agreement with the Taliban would enable an orderly, well-organised withdrawal. The chaos at the airport and the despairing masses of people outside the gates demonstrated to the entire world that the withdrawal had been anything but orderly.

Nobody had predicted the rapid collapse. Many people have exaggerated ideas about the kind of information intelligence agencies are actually able to provide. Intelligence can give insightful analyses of the current situation, but the problem is that both society and conflicts are in a constant state of flux. In Afghanistan, we received valuable assessments of the capacities of the Taliban and of the government forces, but our intelligence didn't pick up on the political developments and lack of leadership, or the fact that many were changing sides.

Later that autumn, we completed an evaluation of our involvement in Afghanistan. The report's main conclusion was that NATO and the entire international community's presence had suffered from what is known as 'mission creep'. Ever more ambitious targets had gradually been set. When the American soldiers and other NATO allies went into Afghanistan late in the autumn of 2001, the aim had been to defeat Al-Qaeda and prevent the country becoming a hotbed of international terrorism. In the main, this goal was achieved – Al-Qaeda were for the most part neutralised, and over the years in which NATO was in Afghanistan, no terrorist attacks were planned or attempted on us by the group. Osama bin Laden was killed in 2011, and with that, it was possible to declare the job done. Instead, however, the international community, along with the UN, EU, NATO and many others, had almost imperceptibly set themselves a much more challenging goal.

What had begun as a targeted, military counter-terrorism operation soon became an extensive nation-building project. We would build a country with equal rights for women and men, with a free press and effective state institutions. We attempted to create a democratic and united Afghanistan, something that had never before existed in many hundreds of years of Afghan history. The nation is a clan society, characterised by ethnic, social and cultural contrasts, and a country strongly opposed to all outside attempts to transform it into a centralised state.

Another conclusion was that we became victims of our own, overoptimistic narrative that things were constantly improving in

Afghanistan. The NATO countries paid a high price for being there, in the form of lost human lives, money and resources. Without progress, this price would seem insufferably high. Conditions in the country therefore simply *had to* get better. We placed too much emphasis on the bright spots, and neglected all the problems and signs of weakness that should have enabled us to realise that the Taliban were stronger than the Afghan government forces – even with us standing behind them.

We were in Afghanistan too long, and we wanted too much.

Millions of Afghans believed in us and supported our joint efforts to build a country free of religious fanaticism. I was among the many who long believed, and at the very least hoped, that democracy and freedom would triumph over oppression and brutality. But eventually, we had to acknowledge that we had been wrong. Nor was the international community, led by the UN, EU and NATO, able to establish a strong Afghan government that could take on the responsibility for the country when we withdrew. What should have been a strong and stable state structure simply collapsed like a house of cards.

The operation in Afghanistan is a good example of how military might alone has clear limitations. Once the evacuation was complete, President Biden claimed that not only was the United States' longest war now over – the decision to withdraw had also been about 'ending an era of major military operations to remake other countries'.

In the event of any future military operations beyond NATO's borders, the objective will have to be clearly defined. And above all else, we will have to be realistic about what it is possible to achieve.

The decision to leave Afghanistan will forever be marked by those chaotic first days of the evacuation and the terrorist attack outside the airport.

Had the Americans not been in such a hurry to leave, perhaps the withdrawal might have been more orderly. But it's impossible to know for sure. Above all, the situation was a reminder that withdrawing troops is difficult. It's important to get people out, but the more who leave an area, the more vulnerable are those left behind. Taking longer over the withdrawal could just as easily have *increased* the risk of lives being lost. Nevertheless, the seriousness of what happened during the withdrawal could not be permitted to overshadow the much bigger question of whether it was right to end our military presence in the region. Tactical and operational defeats do not alter the fact of a decision being the strategically correct one to have made. It was painful to leave, but there is nothing to indicate that we would have achieved any more by staying in Afghanistan for another twenty years.

Late in the evening on the thirtieth of August 2021, US Central Command released a photograph of the head of the 82nd Airborne Division, Major-General Chris Donahue. The image, shot in greenish night vision, was viewed around the world, and showed Donahue in his combat uniform, carrying a rifle in his right hand. Some planes and the terminal building could be glimpsed in the background; Donahue was making his way towards a cargo plane. The accompanying text read: 'The last American soldier leaves Afghanistan'.

The United States and NATO had lost the war.

The defeat was a fact.

There was now a kind of peace in the country, but the people of the young, future-oriented Afghanistan would have to manage on their own. And when it was all over, I couldn't help but think about the two students I had met in Kabul in 2017.

I had promised them that we would stay. It was a promise I didn't keep.

PART 6
WAR

August 2021–April 2023

33

Capability and intent

SATELLITE IMAGES AND LARGE MAPS LAY SPREAD ACROSS THE table before me. On the maps, a number of armed battalions were marked in red pen. The various symbols showed which kinds of military units were present at each location – these included infantry, armoured vehicles, air defence, and engineering and medical battalions. Their number was increasing day by day.

In the spring of 2021, Russia deployed large numbers of troops close to the border with Ukraine. Tens of thousands of soldiers, along with large quantities of heavy weapons, ammunition and supplies, were brought to the border regions. Landing craft were made ready in the Black Sea; fighter planes were deployed to the Crimean Peninsula. Satellite images clearly documented what the Russians were doing. The question was why.

In military intelligence, a distinction is made between capability and intent. Military capability can be measured by counting the number of soldiers, weapons, vehicles and everything else that determines the combat effectiveness of military units. It's usually easier to obtain knowledge about this than it is about intent, because to know the intent, you have to understand the thinking behind the military build-up.

Russia undoubtedly had the capability to launch a massive attack against Ukraine along a broad front. The question was whether this was in fact the intent – whether the purpose of the military build-up was to invade. Or whether the whole thing was simply an unusually large military exercise, as Moscow claimed.

In the 1990s, NATO and Russia entered into agreements regarding the notification and mutual inspection of larger military exercises. The purpose of these agreements was to build trust and reduce the risk of this kind of activity being used to conceal preparations for military aggression. The Russian authorities had provided no notice of their recent actions, and nor had they invited NATO allies to observe what they insisted was an exercise. This increased our unease, and I criticised Russia for not adhering to the agreements regarding transparency around military activity.

Relations with Russia had long been growing colder. As far back as 2005, Putin gave a speech in which he referred to the Soviet Union's dissolution as the greatest geopolitical catastrophe of the twentieth century, and a tragedy for the Russian people. Two years later, face to face with many Western leaders at the Munich Security Conference in 2007, he took issue with NATO and what he referred to as the United States' attempt to dominate the world. The speech was a disappointment to those of us who had hoped and believed that Russia would find its place within a new European security order characterised by trust and cooperation. In parallel with this, Putin also tightened his grip on the home front, smothering independent media, manipulating elections and ensuring that political opponents were either imprisoned or died under suspicious circumstances.

Viewed within a longer historical perspective, Russia is a weakened superpower. The country is a mere shadow of the former Soviet Union. But even a weakened superpower can be dangerous. The prevailing unease about the developments in Russia was heightened by the fact that in the spring of 2021, Vladimir Putin was increasingly isolated. He spoke with ever fewer people, and surrounded himself almost exclusively with members of his security apparatus – people with the same background and mentality as he has. The pandemic only served to increase this isolation.

It seemed Putin was no longer the person I had met in the early 2000s, and with whom I had begun a collaborative relationship. He had become more suspicious, more willing to take risks and more hung up on his own notions of recovering Russia's former greatness. Putin had become more dangerous.

Meeting with Russian political leaders as head of NATO was different from doing so as Norway's prime minister. NATO was the very symbol of what Moscow perceived as aggressive and threatening during the Cold War – a tool of American imperialism. And, after the Soviet Union was dissolved, a military instrument for suppressing Russia within Europe and maintaining a US-led world order. Viewed from Moscow, NATO was worse than the sum of its member nations.

The Russian regime's mistrust and suspicion increased; the propaganda machine against NATO churned on, and the troll farms worked around the clock to sow discord and division in Western countries. I was overcome with disappointment and a certain resignation; others might say I became more level-headed and realistic. The difference between interacting with Russia from NATO headquarters in Brussels, compared with doing so from the governmental offices in Oslo, was greater and deeper than I had envisaged. Nevertheless, I continued to work for maintaining a dialogue with Moscow – I believed it wrong to demonise the Russians. I recognised Russian art and culture in interviews; I thanked the Russians for their efforts during the Second World War. I tried to reassure them and make them less paranoid.

Throughout history, one source of Russian aggression has been the country's sense of insecurity. 'Those of us in the West must appreciate that the Russian mentality and way of thinking is different from ours,' Thorvald often said to me in our many conversations about Russia. The country wasn't going anywhere. We therefore had to develop a cooperation on a people-to-people level and keep the door open – even if keeping such an open line had always to go hand in hand with credible military deterrence.

These conversations gave me important reminders. The world can rarely be drawn in black and white. But what was nevertheless clear to me when Moscow was undertaking its military build-up around

Ukraine in the spring of 2021, was the nature of the Moscow regime to which *I* had to relate. This was a regime that had become increasingly more oppressive at home and more aggressive abroad.

We were not at war with Russia. But we were not in normal peacetime, either.

Any notion of normal neighbourly relations with the country seemed remote. The issue now was about managing the relationship, to ensure misunderstandings and a lack of contact and communication did not lead to dangerous situations, or in the worst case, trigger acts of war. The lack of openness and trust increased the risk that dramatic incidents might occur.

At the UN General Assembly in New York in September 2021, I would meet with Russian minister of foreign affairs Sergey Lavrov. The Russian military build-up around Ukraine in the spring provided a unique backdrop to the meeting. Not all the allies were equally concerned about what the Russians were up to; some believed the United States and NATO were exaggerating, and in fact only serving to increase security tensions. In the summer, the Russian military build-up suddenly stopped, and many of the soldiers returned to their permanent garrisons. Moscow – and some NATO nations – believed the withdrawal proved we had been overreacting and that we should therefore tone down our criticism of Russia.

As usual, the meeting with Lavrov was held at Russia's mission in the UN building, not far from the assembly hall. It was a sterile room without a view, rather cramped and with a wide table in the middle. Small Russian and NATO flags formed a kind of midline down the tabletop; a large Russian flag stood against one wall. Lavrov and I took our seats opposite one another, each with our close colleagues beside us, as we had so many times before in this very room.

Russian media were present at the start, and Lavrov said some friendly words to them. I was less obliging in my introductory comments than I had been at previous meetings. The situation was more serious, and there was always the risk that what I said might be misused by the Russian media. After a few minutes, the journalists were sent out. And the moment they were gone, Lavrov's tone changed.

On issue after issue he rattled off his deep dissatisfaction with NATO: the bombing of Serbia in 1999, the various waves of NATO enlargement and our ostensible lack of response to the Russian proposal of buffer zones that would limit military activity along the border between Russia and NATO. He accused us of supporting 'neo-Nazis' in Ukraine, and complained that we hadn't said a word when the Russians in Crimea were allegedly threatened by the authorities in Kyiv.

I brought up our concerns about Russia amassing so many forces in the border regions. Lavrov gave an irritated reply.

'This is normal military activity,' he said. 'You are exaggerating, you are hysterical. You shouldn't be poking your nose into what happens on Russian territory.'

I argued in favour of new meetings of the NATO-Russia Council, in order to discuss, among other matters, the proposed buffer zones. I knew that member nations such as Poland and the Baltic states were strongly opposed to the establishment of such zones, as they believed it would make it harder to defend their territories. But at the same time, I knew that NATO and Russia had previously managed to agree on geographical military limitations. If it was balanced and recast, it might help to ease the tensions.

But Lavrov wasn't interested. He knew that Ukraine would be top of the agenda should the council convene, and he was sick and tired of listening to us point out Russian breaches of international law there. 'Waste of time,' he said.

Lavrov shook his head.

'Why am I even sitting here? You have no opinions of your own, Stoltenberg. You say only what your bosses permit you to say.'

All my previous meetings with Lavrov had included an element of dialogue, an opening, something we might be able to build upon, even if his manner was rough and occasionally unpleasant. This time, there was absolutely nothing constructive. No matter what topic we switched to, I could hardly complete a sentence before he butted in.

'You're constantly interrupting me,' I said, before continuing. 'The Russian military build-up—'

'I'm not interrupting.'

My colleagues laughed, exasperated.

Lavrov's spokeswoman, Maria Zakharova, sat a little further down the table from him, fiddling with her phone. Whenever I spoke, she groaned and rolled her eyes. I concentrated on conveying my arguments without allowing myself to be affected by the atmosphere in the room. But the truth was that the meeting was actually rather tragic. At a time when NATO and Russia should be speaking with one another and seeking diplomatic solutions, it was impossible to have a dignified conversation with Russia's minister of foreign affairs. A little later, Lavrov gave an interview to the Russian news channel RT, in which he urged me to resign since I was unfit to do my job.

At the end of September, we expelled eight Russians who were accredited as diplomats to NATO, but who in reality were active intelligence agents. They rarely stayed in Brussels, and instead travelled freely around the Schengen Area on diplomatic passports. Not long before, we had discovered just how extensive the activities of Russian undercover and intelligence agents in Europe actually were. The two agents who attempted to kill Sergei Skripal and his daughter in Salisbury in the United Kingdom some years earlier belonged to an elite group of fifteen agents from the Russian military intelligence agency the GRU, who were stationed in the Haute-Savoie province of the French Alps. It was like something straight out of a spy film, with the agents moving between villages and houses in the Alps and undertaking missions all across Europe.

The advice from NATO's intelligence division was clear: Russia's mission to NATO was being used as a base for surveillance, and expulsions were necessary. After the assassination attempt on Skripal, we had cut the number of Russian diplomats in the NATO mission from thirty to twenty. Now the ceiling was lowered to ten. When I took office as secretary general, Russia's NATO mission was one of the largest of any nation within the alliance, with over eighty people.

I was ready for Lavrov to perceive the expulsions as a kind of response to our miserable meeting in New York, and that there would be reprisals. In mid-October, the Russians decided to close the NATO liaison office in Moscow, which had been established in the 1990s when there was great faith that better relations between Russia and NATO were achievable. A few days later, we were notified that Moscow was also suspending all activity within its mission to NATO. The remaining ten Russians would be returning home.

The Russians claimed we had been given advance notice of the closure of our Moscow office. This wasn't true – we learned of it via the media. But it didn't really matter either way. The doors slammed shut. For some years we had succeeded in maintaining a *kind* of dialogue with Moscow, but now even this appeared to be over.

Later in October, our intelligence services began to report that Russia was again amassing significant military forces close to the border with Ukraine. This was strongly reminiscent of the military build-up in April. Back then, forty-eight battalion tactical groups had been deployed, each of which consisted of around one thousand men and was equipped with all the tanks, artillery and air defence necessary for them to enter into combat. As October moved into November, we observed that the numbers of troops were increasing, and that more were on the way. Much of the heavy equipment had never been withdrawn, but remained in the border regions throughout the summer.

If they continued with the build-up, by January the Russians would have amassed a military presence that was three times as large as the build-up back in April, although they still lacked certain elements they would need before an attack could be launched, such as paratroopers and command units. We presumed these would be some of the final units to be brought in.

Within NATO, we continued our discussions about what Russia wished to achieve, and what were the most likely scenarios. Perhaps Moscow was waiting for a pretext to enter Ukraine. Maybe they would use discord and riots to argue that the region's stability was threatened, and then move in to re-establish law and order; Russian agents and infiltrators might provoke the unrest necessary to execute such a plan. Amassing large numbers of troops close to Ukraine also served a purpose in itself, even if the soldiers stayed put. If the government in Kyiv were to consider advancing on the separatists in the East, their desire to do so would be significantly reduced as long as 100,000 Russian soldiers were standing right across the border.

The possibilities were numerous. The Russians might turn the heat up and down, as they had long been doing. They might make threats, launch cyber-attacks, link the new military build-up to political coercion. They could test whether Western unity would hold when subjected to pressure. It was the kind of game they had played before.

What was growing ever clearer, was that Vladimir Putin refused to accept that Ukraine was becoming an increasingly West-facing country. In July, he had published a long article on the Kremlin's website, in which he explained the relationship between Ukraine and Russia, as he saw it, in great detail. He reeled off a history with roots going all the way back to the early Middle Ages; a cultural, religious and linguistic unity that had lasted for centuries. The Russians and the Ukrainians are one people, Putin wrote. He claimed that the current government in Kyiv did not serve Ukraine's true national interests but was subject to foreign powers, allowing itself to be used as an instrument in the West's fight against Moscow – 'the anti-Russian project', as he called it. 'I am confident that true sovereignty of Ukraine is possible only in partnership with Russia,' he concluded.

Throughout the autumn of 2021, ever more of the regular intelligence briefings I received were devoted to Ukraine. The briefings were normally given by a CIA staffer, or by people from NATO's own intelligence division. One day in mid-October, one of NATO's intelligence officers requested a confidential conversation. He came into my office, and after ensuring all phones were out of the room as usual, we sat down at the meeting table. The intelligence officer showed me a map of the Russian forces.

'As you know, Secretary General,' he said, 'we've maintained a precise overview of the Russian military build-up, but we've so far been unable to say anything certain about the intention behind it.'

He took a brief pause, lifted his eyes from his notes, and looked at me, his expression serious.

'Today, however, we know what the intention is. It's to invade Ukraine.'

34

Ultimatum

US DEPUTY SECRETARY OF STATE WENDY SHERMAN ALLOWED HER
gaze to wander around the large, round table in the meeting room at
NATO headquarters before it stopped on the two Russians. It was the
twelfth of January 2022, and we were in the middle of a long and difficult meeting of the NATO-Russia Council.

The atmosphere was strained and tense.

'Russian ministers, Russia is a large country, a colossal landmass,
and the country is a permanent member of the UN Security Council.
The country has the largest conventional military forces in Europe,
and is one of the world's two biggest nuclear powers.'

Sherman took a brief pause before she continued.

'I'm surprised that Russia can feel threatened by Ukraine.'

Sherman was one of the heavyweights of the United States' Foreign
Service; among other consequential processes, she had been involved
in negotiating the Iran nuclear deal. She said that she herself had
Russian roots; her grandmother was born in Pereiaslav, which at the
time was in the western part of the Russian Empire. Sherman's father
was an American who had served in the Marine Corps during the
Second World War, and who had fought in the Pacific.

'But in that war, as horrifying as it was, we and Russia fought
together for Europe's freedom and security,' she said.

'And I'm saying that as an American Jew,' she added.

As Sherman spoke, the Russian ministers leaned towards each

other and began to talk among themselves. Sherman stopped speaking, allowing silence to fall over the room.

'Gentlemen, may I have your attention?'

After a few moments the Russians noticed that the mood in the room had shifted, and they looked up. Sherman continued.

'A conflict will cost Russia dearly. It is a path I hope Russia will not choose to take,' she said. 'NATO's secretary general has offered another, better path. The Polish chairmanship of the Organization for Security and Co-operation in Europe, the OSCE, has offered another, better path. The French Presidency of the Council of the European Union has offered another, better path. And so has the President of the United States.'

One of the two Russians at the meeting was my old acquaintance, former NATO ambassador Alexander Grushko, who was now Russia's deputy minister of foreign affairs. But this time there was no place for small talk about our shared childhoods in Skillebekk, or reminiscing about 1960s Oslo. Deputy minister of defence Alexander Fomin was also participating.

'Today, we are again discussing Euro-Atlantic security. You have heard suggestions that diplomacy is the only practicable path. We are prepared to enter into concrete negotiations, quickly, but not on the basis of fear and threats. We hope you will agree,' Sherman concluded.

The council had convened because in December, Vladimir Putin had submitted proposals addressed to the United States and to NATO regarding a new security treaty. The treaty had three main elements. The first was that *no* new countries would be permitted to join the alliance. The second was that no country that had become a member of NATO after the dissolution of the Soviet Union would be permitted to have military forces or equipment from other NATO nations on its territory. The third element was that NATO would not deploy new offensive weapons in Russia's immediate vicinity, and that existing, long-range weapons would be withdrawn.

This wasn't just about Ukraine. In reality, Russia was demanding that the United States and NATO enter into a legally binding treaty that would change the security order that had ensured peace in Europe for many decades. The proposal was formulated as an ultimatum, and the Russians were now speaking this way, too.

The demand that NATO's doors be closed to new member nations broke with the principle that every country shall be able to choose its own security arrangements, a principle Russia had also supported several times. The second demand, that we must withdraw all our forces from the countries in the East, would mean that we would no longer be able to defend our newer members in the same way as the older ones – we would end up with two tiers of NATO member nations. The first two demands were therefore impossible to agree to.

But the third demand was different. It was always possible to negotiate on the deployment of forces and weapons systems. There was much the Russians could achieve here, as long as they were willing to enter into balanced and verifiable agreements. But a unilateral withdrawal was out of the question.

Although the divide between us was great, we believed it right and necessary to speak with the Russians. We offered a process that included several meetings and various working groups, which could look into the challenges in more detail – as long as the diplomatic track remained active, the risk of a military confrontation would be reduced. But the Russians never responded to our invitation. At the same time, they maintained a high public profile and communicated in capital letters, and all this indicated that they didn't actually desire a political solution. Moscow submitted the proposed treaty with demands they knew we would be unable to fulfil. In the next round, they would be able to say they had attempted diplomacy, but the West's rejection of their proposal legitimised a military response as a last resort to safeguard the country's security interests.

At the meeting, Grushko and Fomin maintained that the military activity close to the Ukrainian border was due to ordinary military exercises that were nothing to do with other countries. They also made strong accusations against NATO.

'The situation is unacceptable. NATO is refusing to consider Russian interests and is threatening Russia,' they said.

Fomin went through the treaty, which the Russians had made public in December, point by point.

'If NATO refuses to agree to these demands, then our assessment of NATO as an aggressive alliance will be confirmed, and things may move in the direction of a military confrontation,' he said.

It was difficult to interpret this as anything other than a threat. If NATO refused to accept Moscow's terms, there would be war.

Grushko and Fomin handed out maps, on which different colour codes marked the countries that were and were not members of NATO. The Norwegian archipelago of Svalbard was *not* a member of NATO, according to the map. Nor was Northern Ireland, Corsica or Sardinia. And nor was Denmark. It's possible that the purpose of these erroneous maps was to unsettle us, but it was more likely just an example of Russian sloppiness.

'I'll ensure correct maps are sent to you, so there are no misunderstandings in Moscow about what is and is not NATO territory,' I said.

The NATO ambassadors laughed, but both Grushko and Fomin remained straight-faced.

That we had managed to convene the NATO-Russia Council at such a critical time was a bright spot. But the outcome was disheartening. The Russians maintained a threatening tone, and we came no closer to a solution.

The underlying, unanswered question was what Vladimir Putin was going to do.

Almost three months had passed since our intelligence division had made it crystal clear that Russia was planning to invade Ukraine. The military build-up continued as our intelligence had envisaged. More soldiers and more equipment and *matériel* were deployed close to Ukraine's borders. By mid-December, fifty-two battalion tactical groups were in position – more than in the spring. At the same time, Putin's rhetoric was growing ever more extreme; he claimed a genocide was being committed against the Russian-speaking population in the Donbas. Such statements were intended to give the Russians a pretext to respond militarily.

Not since the Cold War had Europe seen a greater concentration of military forces than those now deployed around the Ukrainian border. But even if Putin had made plans to invade, that didn't mean he had given the final order that would make them a reality. Nor did we know the potential scale of any attack. The aim might be to tear the entire Donbas region out of Ukraine, once and for all. Or to obtain control over the Sea of Azov coast, and thereby create a land bridge to Crimea. Or to take Kyiv, topple the government, and install a pro-Russian regime.

The thought that the Russians might actually launch a large-scale invasion of a neighbouring country was surreal. It was something that belonged to another time. Nobody could predict the consequences such an attack might have, or whether a war in Ukraine might escalate beyond the country's borders.

Over these weeks in winter, I continuously discussed the situation with political leaders in a number of countries. A common thread that ran through all these conversations was the need to act as one. Now that Russia was waging a war of nerves and coercive diplomacy against the West, we had to stand united. I also had helpful conversations with the president of the European Commission Ursula von der Leyen. Late in the autumn, we had travelled to Lithuania and Latvia together. It was important that NATO and the EU show their strength and their solidarity with the countries in the eastern part of the alliance.

For weeks the allies had sat together, formulating an agreed stance. Documents were circulated and sentences polished to finalise our response to Russia's demands and coordinate our positions. The United States and Europe were closely coordinated, *through* NATO. Nevertheless, French president Emmanuel Macron prioritised his own political agenda and emphasised that Europe must maintain a separate dialogue with Russia to resolve the crisis.

'In the coming weeks, we need to bring to being a European proposal to build a new security and stability order. We need to build it between Europeans, then share it with our allies in the NATO framework. And then, we need to propose it to Russia for negotiation,' Macron said in a speech at the European Parliament in mid-January.

Within NATO, twenty-eight of the member nations and 600 million of the region's inhabitants are European. By comparison, the EU has 450 million inhabitants. Viewed this way, there is 'more Europe' in NATO than there is in the EU. But when Macron spoke of 'European sovereignty', he was referring to the EU, not Europe as a whole.

Part of the picture was that for many weeks, French and German intelligence had differed from that gathered by the Americans. While they didn't disagree on the military capability the Russians had built up at the border, they differed in their analyses of the intent behind it. This led to the German and French intelligence agencies painting a far less dramatic picture of the Russian military build-up. 'Seasonal variations' was a recurring phrase in the reports, and the French believed the warnings of an imminent invasion to be exaggerated.

This significant downplaying of the gravity of the situation from French and German quarters was something we had experienced before. Shortly after Russian forces were deployed in Crimea in late February/early March 2014, a meeting of the North Atlantic Council was convened. The meeting opened with a comprehensive intelligence review. There were several thousand Russian soldiers in Crimea; maps were shared, and we were informed of where they were. Intelligence agents almost always make certain reservations about the information and analyses they provide, but this time, the council was presented with an unusually detailed report, free of any such caveats. There was no doubt that Russia had invaded Crimea.

Nevertheless, the German ambassador called for caution when drawing conclusions. He suggested that the observed activity could be in line with the agreement the Russians had with Ukraine on the maintaining of a marine base in Crimea. NATO had to be reserved in its approach; be careful not to criticise. Avoid any escalation of the situation. Keep all channels open.

He was supported by his French counterpart, who in spite of the unusually clear intelligence report believed that at that particular point in time, there were no signs that Russian soldiers had been engaged in Crimea. NATO had to remain passive, and refrain from increasing the organisation's readiness. Instead, the alliance should emphasise the rights of minorities in Ukraine and the old cultural ties between Ukraine and Russia.

The French and German interpretation of events in January 2022 was therefore in line with their assessments of the crisis eight years earlier. Both occasions illustrated the deep disagreement among NATO nations in their views of Russia.

As the Russian military build-up around the Ukrainian border increased, so did the nervousness among the eastern allies. To reassure them, and ensure that Putin wouldn't so much as think about attacking a NATO country, we increased our military presence along NATO's entire eastern border. Greater readiness, more soldiers, more patrols using aircraft and ships. NATO enhanced its presence from the Baltic to the Black Sea.

In mid-February, I travelled to Romania, which in the north of the country has an almost four-hundred-mile-long border with Ukraine. I visited a military base close to the Black Sea coast, where German and Italian fighter planes had been deployed, in addition to an increasing number of American soldiers. I emphasised there should be not a shred of doubt about NATO's ability and willingness to defend *all* member states.

'There will never be first-class and second-class members of NATO. There are only NATO allies,' I said.

In a conversation with Romanian president Klaus Iohannis, I asked him whether he felt too many *Americans* had been deployed, as had been insinuated by the authorities in Slovakia and Hungary. Iohannis looked at me, perplexed.

'We've been waiting for the Americans since 1945. We're happy they've finally arrived,' he said.

Throughout these days in February, the situation became more threatening with practically every hour that passed. Russia had deployed ninety-eight battalion tactical groups to the borders; sixteen more were on the way. This meant that around 75 per cent of Russia's standing forces were now positioned close to Ukraine. A large-scale military exercise involving Russian and Belarusian forces was taking place in Belarus, which made the front longer and reduced the advance warning we would receive of any moves made.

General Tod Wolters, a former pilot with the US Air Force, was now NATO's supreme allied commander, or SACEUR. He gave a briefing at a meeting of the North Atlantic Council on the eleventh of February, in which he said that an attack might occur within ninety-six hours. Wolters expected the attack to begin with a cyber-attack, and strikes using precision weapons and cruise missiles on military command and communication centres. A primary objective would be to isolate President Zelenskyy, to prevent him from communicating with his people.

Not long before this, President Biden had taken the initiative to schedule regular meetings between a small group of international leaders, which made it easier for us to stay coordinated. The composition of attendees varied slightly from meeting to meeting, but the United States, United Kingdom, Canada, Germany, France and Italy were always present, in addition to the two EU presidents and NATO's secretary general.

On the evening of the eleventh of February, Biden chaired one of these meetings. He shared the latest, up-to-the-minute intelligence: all the necessary Russian troops, equipment and weapons were now in position. We would no longer receive any advance warning of an attack, and Biden believed one might be made on the sixteenth of February. 'They'll try to take Kyiv in two days. They're still looking for a pretext to legitimise an attack,' Biden said.

During the meeting, Ursula von der Leyen brought up the question of sanctions. There was broad agreement that the West must launch a package of sanctions that would hit the Russian economy hard and also impact upon individuals within Putin's inner circle. Boris Johnson suggested we also impose sanctions on hydrocarbons, but the proposed punitive measures linked to oil and gas received no support from the other European leaders. On the contrary – Italian prime minister Mario Draghi asked to take the floor one more time in order to say: 'No, no, practically all Italy's energy is based on gas, and we're dependent on imports from Russia. We must have and we shall have effective sanctions, but we must also be able to live with them ourselves.'

I explained how those of us in NATO perceived the developments. We were now facing the greatest concentration of military forces since the end of the Cold War. No one could know anything for certain until an attack was actually underway, but we had to view the situation with the utmost seriousness, and prepare for the worst.

The military assistance to Ukraine was stepped up. NATO would not deploy its own forces to participate in the fighting, but we made the Ukrainians better able to defend themselves. Air-defence Stinger missiles, Javelin anti-tank missiles and much more military equipment and ammunition was flown in, from the United States and the United Kingdom. In 2022, Ukraine's armed forces were in an entirely different state than they had been in 2014 – they were better equipped, better trained and better organised. An invasion would cost many Russian soldiers their lives. This was something we wanted Putin to take into account in his calculations.

On Friday the eighteenth of February, I attended the Munich Security Conference. The Russians claimed they had completed a military exercise in Crimea, and that the forces had been withdrawn across the Kerch Bridge, which connects the Crimean Peninsula with Russia. This was obviously another attempt to cause confusion, and lend credibility to the idea that in claiming a Russian attack was imminent, NATO and the United States were warmongering. But there was no sign of any true reduction of the Russian troops.

Many were surprised that President Zelenskyy attended the conference in Munich. He questioned whether an attack was in fact likely, as he had done several times in recent weeks. All the warnings of an invasion had led to capital flight from Ukraine, and the further deterioration of the country's economy, he said.

I emphasised how much was at stake. Relations between Russia and NATO. European and transatlantic security. Ultimately, how we want relations between states to be organised.

'Moscow is attempting to roll back history. And recreate its spheres of influence. It wants to limit NATO's right to collective defence …

Moscow also wants to deny sovereign countries the right to choose their own path. And their own security arrangements,' I said at the conference.

I'd had a sliver of hope that we might ward off a Russian attack – a plan to invade is not the same as a decision. We worked intensely, along three different tracks. We tried diplomacy, with offers of trust-building measures and disarmament negotiations. Then we made it clear that an attack would be met with heavy economic sanctions targeted at the Putin regime. Alongside this, we stepped up military aid to Ukraine and deployed more troops in our Eastern member nations, on land, at sea and in the air. The signal to Putin was unmistakable: we would defend every inch of the territory of all NATO countries. And if the Russians attacked Ukraine, they would pay a high economic and military price.

But this hope was dwindling. There were no signs that Putin was going to turn back. He was charging indefatigably towards war.

On the evening of the eighteenth of February, a videoconference was scheduled between the leaders of the largest countries, and I participated from my hotel room in Munich. Again, President Biden shared the most up-to-date intelligence. The attack date the Americans had pinpointed, the sixteenth of February, was already behind us, but now Biden said it was only a matter of days. The United States' intelligence had been impressively precise, but I was somewhat sceptical of the Americans' tendency to operate with specific attack dates. Whenever these turned out to be incorrect, it lent credibility to those who argued we were exaggerating the threat of an invasion.

On Monday the twenty-first of February, Russian media reported that two armed Ukrainian vehicles had crossed over to the Russian side of the border in the Donbas, in order to extract two saboteurs whose mission had been to blow up infrastructure within the Russian territory. At the same time, new statements were issued regarding the discovery of mass graves and genocide against the Russian-speaking minority in the Donbas. Both these claims were pure fabrications. They were good examples of the stories the Russians would try to plant to provide a pretext for an attack, a so-called false flag operation.

NATO had long been warning that such operations might be launched.

That same evening, I discussed the situation with my colleagues at home at the residence, and we went through the latest reports on the military build-up. One hundred and twenty battalion tactical groups, fighter planes, helicopters, special forces, many landing craft, para-troopers – everything that is needed to undertake a large-scale offensive operation.

The latest intelligence was that significant volumes of blood had been brought to the field hospitals, and that field crematoria had been erected.

We went upstairs to the living room to listen to President Putin hold a scheduled speech. It lasted for fifty-seven minutes, and it was frightening. It was the Bolsheviks who had created the modern Ukraine after the Russian Revolution in 1917, Putin claimed, but the country had never been a separate nation. Ukraine was an integrated part of Russia, and of Russian culture and history. The regime in Kyiv was controlled by the United States. According to the Russian presi-dent, all the bloodshed that was about to occur was the full responsibility of the Kyiv regime.

'I've made [the] long since overdue decision,' Putin said, looking straight into the camera, 'immediately to recognise the independence and sovereignty of the Donetsk People's Republic and the Luhansk People's Republic.'

Only one thing remained in the drama Putin was staging: to claim that the people of these two 'republics' had requested Russia's help to defend themselves against Ukraine.

On Tuesday the twenty-second of February, I learned that Russian soldiers had left their camps and driven out into the terrain to take up attack positions along the border with Ukraine. Putin received the Federal Assembly's approval to use military force beyond Russia's borders. The ultimatum to Ukraine was bluntly put: Crimea must be recognised as Russian territory; Ukraine must commit to never becom-ing a member of NATO; and the Ukrainians must return all Western weapons and undertake the full demilitarisation of the country.

On Wednesday the twenty-third of February, I was supposed to participate in a meeting about NATO's partnerships in The Hague, but was forced to tell Dutch prime minister Mark Rutte I would have to cancel due to the situation in Ukraine.

Each update I received throughout the day communicated only minor changes. But the situation was growing darker with every hour that passed.

Russian planes had been loaded with bombs and missiles; naval vessels were in position in the Black Sea. Over the course of the past three days, 80 per cent of the Russian forces had moved into combat positions.

The Russians evacuated their embassy in Kyiv. The flag was lowered.

A little before 18.00 I was in the car on my way home when NATO headquarters notified me that the assistant secretary general for intelligence and security David Cattler wanted to get hold of me. I took the call as soon as I got home.

Any hope of peace had crumbled away over the past few days and weeks, but still it was as if time stood still for a few beats when Cattler gave me the definitive confirmation.

There would be war in Europe.

35

Vladimir Putin's war

IN A BIOGRAPHY OF HIM PUBLISHED IN 2000, VLADIMIR PUTIN reveals a little about what has influenced him as both a person and a politician, and one incident is highlighted in particular. Late in the autumn of 1989, a few weeks after the fall of the Berlin Wall, a furious crowd gathered outside the KGB's Dresden headquarters, where Putin was serving. He and his colleagues felt threatened, and called the Soviet military camp close by to obtain protection. The camp's reply was that the soldiers could do nothing without orders from Moscow, and no such orders had been given.

Putin explains just how much of a shock Moscow's silence was to him. The centre of power was paralysed. This was a landmark moment, and probably instructive for much of Putin's conduct since. Never again would Russia be so weak, so paralysed, so incapable of standing up for its interests and defending its sphere of influence. Putin became a leader who regarded military might as the most important guarantee for securing Russia's position in the world. A leader who has been inspired by the rulers who expanded Russia's territory, and who now, yet again, wished to use military force to achieve his goals.

On the day David Cattler called to inform me that the order to attack had been given, we reviewed our plans and procedures: who should notify whom, what should happen during those first hours, who was responsible for what. Cattler had made it clear that the attack would begin between 22.00 and midnight.

As the evening progressed, I stayed up late to read the updates as they came in, while also keeping an eye on the TV news broadcasts. When the Gulf War broke out in January 1991, CNN showed live coverage of the first cruise missiles streaking towards Baghdad, and the subsequent explosions lighting up the dark city. Now the channel had reporters in place in Kyiv.

When no attack had started by a little after midnight, I decided to go to bed. It was impossible to know how much sleep I'd be able to get over the coming days.

I woke to the sound of my telephone ringing; a glance at its screen told me it was 04.25 on Thursday the twenty-fourth of February 2022. Stian was on the line. 'It's started,' he said.

The previous evening, we had agreed to gather at NATO headquarters as soon as any attack was underway. But I was now informed that US secretary of state Antony Blinken and US secretary of defense Lloyd Austin wished to speak with me. I decided that I might as well take the call at home, and then head out to the offices.

I dressed, drank the first of many cups of coffee, walked the few metres across the landing to my home office, and began to go through my emails. A little later, I turned on the television and watched another speech by Vladimir Putin.

A special military operation was underway in Ukraine, he said. This was necessary to protect the populations of Luhansk and Donetsk. The purpose of the operation was to 'demilitarise and denazify Ukraine'. Only precision weapons would be used, and only military installations would be targeted. The civilian population had nothing to fear. He urged all Ukrainian soldiers to go home.

I watched Putin closely. He was sitting in the same room, with the same flags behind him, in the same position at the same desk as when he had announced the recognition of Luhansk and Donetsk three days earlier. He was wearing the same suit, the same tie. The same intonation and delivery. The two speeches must have been recorded at the same time, in a single session.

Putin believed NATO was responsible for causing the Russian attack, because we supported Zelenskyy's government. 'No matter who tries to stand in our way or all the more so create threats for our country and our people,' Putin said, 'they must know that Russia will respond immediately, and the consequences will be such as you have never seen in your entire history.' It was hard to interpret this as anything other than a threat to use nuclear weapons.

Not long afterwards, I got Blinken and Austin on the secure line. We reviewed the situation, and I informed them of the actions NATO would take over the coming hours. Austin had been thoroughly briefed on the attack so far. Cruise missiles had struck Kyiv and Kharkiv. Ukraine's air defence was under heavy attack. Ground forces were moving in from several sides. This was not a limited attack to secure control of the Donbas or the stretch of coastline along the Sea of Azov, it was a full-scale invasion to take all of Ukraine. Kyiv was the target.

'This is big,' Austin said. But the Ukrainians had managed to put up an effective resistance.

In recent days and weeks, NATO and the United States had warned the Ukrainians and shared intelligence with them, so they had detailed knowledge of the Russian forces. The Americans had also advised the Ukrainians to move much of their air defences; many of the cruise missiles therefore struck positions no longer occupied by batteries. 'They only hit dust,' Austin said.

But he was worried about President Zelenskyy. 'We fear for his life. The Russians are definitely going to try to take down the government,' Austin said. It later became known that the United States had offered to help Zelenskyy leave Kyiv for a safe location. 'I need ammunition, not a ride,' Zelenskyy had replied.

After the conversation ended I made my way out to NATO head-quarters. In the car, I was informed that Zelenskyy wished to speak with me, and I looked forward to hearing from him. But once I arrived at headquarters I learned he had been forced to take refuge in a bunker, and that we were no longer able to make contact with him.

The atmosphere at NATO headquarters that morning was sombre but composed. On the surface everything was calm, there were no signs of nervousness or chaos, and everyone knew what they had to do. But we all understood that from now on, we would live in a more dangerous Europe. That one world existed before the twenty-fourth of February 2022, and another existed after.

We were well prepared, as we had been planning how we would respond to a possible invasion for many weeks. When Crimea was annexed and the Russians entered the Donbas in 2014, NATO did too little too late. The alliance had had no plans for how to respond. Now, in 2022, on the other hand, our response was immediate – precise and comprehensive intelligence had made this possible. An emergency meeting of the North Atlantic Council approved the activation of NATO's defence plans. NATO's SACEUR, General Tod Wolters, was granted comprehensive powers to command the deployed NATO troops and mobilise new ones. Within hours, additional reinforcements were on their way east. Two hundred aircraft, fifty naval vessels and forty thousand soldiers stood ready close to Ukraine's border. We were now seeing the benefits of the restructuring process we had been working on since 2014, to strengthen NATO's defence capabilities within Europe.

'For our generation, the world has mainly always seemed to be moving in the right direction. But that's no longer the case,' I wrote in a text to Norwegian minister of foreign affairs Anniken Huitfeldt. The ninth of November 1989, the day on which the Berlin Wall fell, was another fateful day in Europe's history. I was thirty years old, and Ingrid had given birth to our first child just a few months earlier; it was as if both Ingrid and I in our personal lives and the whole world stood on the threshold of something promising and new; that each day would be better than the last. The events that were currently unfolding were just as significant, only they were moving in the opposite direction. The fall of the Berlin Wall was the start of a period of stability that had lasted for over thirty years. Now that period of stability was over.

Setbacks and atrocities were nothing new. We had witnessed the Balkan wars in the 1990s, and the 9/11 terrorist attacks on the United States, but a war between two sovereign nations was something else entirely. Europe's largest country and one of the world's two biggest nuclear powers had begun a ruthless war of aggression against a neighbouring nation. Relations with Moscow had reached a low point which only a year earlier I would never have believed possible.

On Friday the twenty-fifth of February, an extraordinary virtual NATO summit was held. The NATO leaders concluded that the invasion represented the most serious threat to Euro-Atlantic security in decades, and that Russia bore full responsibility. 'President Putin's decision to attack Ukraine is a terrible strategic mistake, for which Russia will pay a severe price, both economically and politically, for years to come,' stated the summit declaration. I emphasised that we could not rule out Putin challenging the sovereignty and territorial integrity of NATO nations in the future. Looking ahead, further reinforcement of our own defence would be necessary to deter Russia from making an even greater mistake than to invade Ukraine – namely, to attack NATO. We must avoid any situation in which we had either to respond to a Russian attack with a massive counter attack or to witness a NATO country being attacked without being able to respond militarily for fear it would lead to a devastating large-scale war. The latter would undermine the solidarity principle and in reality be the end for NATO.

A few days later, early in the morning on Monday the twenty-eighth of February, I spoke with President Zelenskyy for the first time since the invasion had begun. He was under intolerable pressure. Russian troops were just miles away. Barricades had been constructed on the outskirts of Kyiv.

'My dear friend, I hope you're doing okay,' I said when I finally got Zelenskyy on the line.

'We think this is going to be a difficult day. The invading forces are ramping up their attacks, and we expect there to be more air strikes,' Zelenskyy began. He seemed calm and collected, but he spoke with greater intensity than he had in our previous conversations.

The Ukrainians' biggest problems were defending themselves against tanks and air attacks. 'Rocket batteries have been deployed in Belarus, and we are being attacked from there. I need to close Ukrainian airspace,' he said.

I knew this was the real reason Ukraine's president had wished to speak with me. He wanted NATO to introduce a no-fly zone.

His request was easy to understand. The Ukrainians were being attacked from the air by planes, helicopters and missiles around the clock. NATO and the United States had previously introduced no-fly zones, including over Bosnia and northern Iraq. We could do so here, too, but the first step would have to be to take out the Russian air defence that could shoot down our planes. In addition, we would have to shoot down any Russian planes or helicopters that violated the order. A no-fly zone above Ukraine would involve a direct military conflict between NATO and Russia.

I praised the Ukrainian people, the armed forces and Zelenskyy personally for their courage, endurance and resistance. 'You have garnered enormous respect for the way you are leading the resistance,' I said.

I reminded Zelenskyy of the support NATO countries had given Ukraine, support that was now being stepped up. 'But we have also been clear, and I understand that this is upsetting for you, that NATO countries cannot be party to this conflict,' I said.

But Zelenskyy forged on.

'If I hear correctly, you're saying that NATO cannot be party to the conflict. Can I ask why not?'

I repeated that we were providing support. Weapons. Equipment. Money. I promised to do everything I could to provide even more, as fast as possible.

'I understand. Only, we're being bombed. Civilians are dying, just yesterday sixteen children were killed. Are there legal restrictions that are preventing you from closing the airspace, or …?'

'I have a double message for you, Volodymyr. First: we're supporting you, with weapons and equipment, and second—'

Zelenskyy cut me off.

'I'm grateful for the military support. But my question is about whether it is possible to close the airspace above Ukraine, whether there are any legal restrictions that prevent you from doing this?'

He didn't intend to give up. I used the brief pauses between Zelenskyy's words and those of the interpreter to think through how I was going to answer the next question.

'The allies have been clear that they do not wish to be party to the conflict, not with troops on the ground or with planes in the air. I truly understand the desperate situation you are in. But closing Ukrainian airspace would mean us becoming directly involved in a conflict with Russia. That is the real problem, not the legal aspects.'

'I understand you talking about the risk of escalation. But listen, we're at war. It's strange to be talking about escalation. We are being attacked. Self-defence is not escalation.'

'I realise how difficult this is. The allies admire your bravery, and that of the Ukrainians. We are introducing strict sanctions, Russia and Belarus are paying a high price. But at the same time, I have to be honest with you. Yes, all-out war is raging in Ukraine, but the allies are also keen to ensure that this does not spin completely out of control. That is the dilemma right now.'

Zelenskyy was becoming resigned.

'I understand. But I ask you to please convey my message to the members of NATO.'

I assured him I would do so, and that I would also urge everyone to continue to provide Ukraine with support.

'Please don't hesitate to contact me again,' I concluded.

The conversation was painful. I needed a few minutes to myself after we had hung up. We would be there for the Ukrainians, but we were not willing to die for them. That was the hard reality, and I couldn't give Zelenskyy false hope.

In another video conference with President Joe Biden and several other high-ranking leaders later that same day, I presented Zelenskyy's plea for a no-fly zone. Prime Minister Boris Johnson was clear: 'It's not possible for us to shoot down Russian planes.' President Emmanuel Macron pointed out the risk of us becoming useful idiots for President Putin: 'If we overdo our support for Ukraine, then we will confirm Russia's image of NATO.'

Chancellor Olaf Scholz explained Germany's attitude. The German line had been to support Ukraine with military *matériel*, but not weapons. Now, however, Scholz would send advanced weapons to Ukraine. He had allocated an additional €100 billion to increase Germany's defence budget and ensure they were now meeting the target of spending 2 per cent of GDP on defence. He wanted to buy F-35s, the world's most advanced fighter jet. It suddenly appeared that Germany might surpass the United Kingdom to become the NATO nation in Europe with the largest defence budget.

This was a radical break with the reserve that had characterised German defence policy for many decades. Scholz had announced the plans in a speech to the Bundestag the previous day and been met with a standing ovation. After Putin's attack on Ukraine, the world was no longer the same, he said. *Eine Zeitenwende* was the expression Scholz used – 'a turning point'. That the German chancellor from the social democratic SPD, in coalition with the old 'anti-nuclear movement' party the Greens, had spearheaded such a dramatic rearmament and revision of German defence and security policy, also said a lot about the changing times to which we were all now witnesses.

I congratulated Scholz. Polish president Andrzej Duda did the same. Boris Johnson called the speech historic. Poland and the United Kingdom praised the German rearmament.

During the video conference, the heads of state and government were unanimous. Two tasks were important above all else. We would support Ukraine. But we must also prevent a large-scale war breaking out in Europe, between Russia and NATO. And unfortunately, these two tasks were not equal.

President Biden summarised the discussion: 'We'll support Ukraine, but we're not going to risk World War III.'

36

Nuclear sabre-rattling

THE RUSSIANS QUICKLY ENCOUNTERED PROBLEMS. NOT LONG after the soldiers crossed the border, a long military convoy got completely stuck a few miles outside Kyiv. These forces had been supposed to take the city, or to surround it from the west, but thanks to poor planning, old equipment and a lack of fuel, combined with an unexpectedly strong resistance, they had become bogged down.

The convoy included armoured vehicles, tanks and artillery, and was over forty miles long. When Ukrainian forces attacked, the wrecked vehicles at the front of the column formed an effective block-ade, forcing the Russians to abandon their plan to quickly take control of Kyiv.

In other sectors, however, things were going better for the Russians. A few days after the invasion they had taken the city of Melitopol in the south-east, and they were in the process of establishing a corridor between Donetsk and Crimea. After a little over a week, Kherson was captured. But all across the country, Ukrainian resistance was strong.

A few weeks after the invasion began, the Russians tested the SS-X-30 SATAN II missile – a weapon with a range of 11,000 miles, capable of transporting nuclear warheads and designed to evade anti-ballistic missile systems. A satisfied Putin appeared on television as his military leaders informed him of the test's success.

'This truly unique weapon will strengthen the combat potential of our armed forces, reliably ensure Russia's security from external threats and make those who, in the heat of frenzied aggressive rhetoric, try to threaten our country, think twice,' he said.

The missile test and television appearance were no accident. Yet again, Putin was playing on people's fears. The purpose of this nuclear sabre-rattling was to scare us away from supporting Ukraine.

Sergey Lavrov followed Putin's lead. He gave interviews in which he said that NATO was in reality at war with Russia, due to the alliance's weapons deliveries to Ukraine. The risk of nuclear war was real, he said, and should not be underestimated.

Such statements from Russia's leaders could not be ignored. They were based on the Kremlin's notion that NATO was threatening Russia by moving ever closer to the country's borders; during the years in which the government in Kyiv had turned westwards, it was ostensibly NATO who had been pulling the strings.

Such ideas also have their supporters in the West. The invasion of Ukraine was condemned broadly and unanimously, but nevertheless many held the United States and NATO responsible. The alliance had shown a lack of respect for Russia's legitimate security interests, and failed to understand how threatening NATO's enlargements had seemed to Moscow. We had therefore forced the Russians into a situation in which they had no choice, where they ultimately had no other option than to invade Ukraine to prevent this country, too, becoming a member of NATO.

There are no agreements or formal barriers that prevent NATO from expanding eastwards. Any such provisions would also be in contravention of the Helsinki Accords from 1975, which established the framework for the cooperation between East and West, and stipulate that all countries have the right to choose their own security policy alignments. The then Soviet Union signed up to this declaration. Neither the agreement from 1990 regarding the reunification of Germany, nor the cooperation agreement between NATO and Russia from 1997, contained provisions that prevented countries in eastern and central Europe from becoming members of NATO. Quite the opposite, in fact. In the agreement between Russia and NATO, Moscow indirectly accepted that NATO could expand eastwards.

But the fact that such steps are permitted is not the same as it being wise or right to take them.

According to the Washington Treaty, NATO's member nations may invite other European countries into the alliance if this can contribute to the security of the North Atlantic region. But it is not always obvious that this is the case. A new member nation will make NATO larger and stronger, but it may also make Russia feel more threatened, and thereby serve to weaken our security. It isn't only so-called Russian-friendly forces that have pointed this out – important foreign policy thinkers, such as Henry Kissinger and diplomat and Russia expert George Kennan, had long warned against NATO's enlargements eastwards. They believed such enlargements failed to sufficiently consider Russia's legitimate interests.

With every new NATO enlargement, the alliance has therefore discussed what is right, and how Russia might react has been part of the assessment. But at the same time, it would be deeply problematic to neglect to admit a new member state simply because Moscow opposed it. Ascribing Russia's interests decisive weight would mean that other countries' interests must yield.

This would be to accept a world in which global superpowers can control other countries – a world many of us hoped and believed we had left behind. A world that would undermine the rights of peoples and nations to control their own future.

The NATO enlargements since the end of the Cold War have not occurred because NATO has pushed eastwards – they have occurred because the countries in the East have pushed to become members of NATO. Through democratic processes, and with overwhelming majority support among their populations, countries such as the Baltic states, Poland, the Czech Republic and many others have worked determinedly to join the alliance. For them, NATO was the only guarantee of being able to keep their newly won freedom.

Still, the West has made mistakes. The United States' attack on Iraq in 2003 never should have happened, and many NATO nations, with Germany and France at the forefront, were opposed to the invasion. It is also possible to take a critical view of some of the events that happened during the dramatic and chaotic period directly after the dissolution of the Soviet Union in 1991. Even from Western quarters, I've heard that Ukraine's borders were arbitrarily drawn, and that the country ended up being too large. This was something Stalin had done directly after the war. The Soviet Union was, after all, a centrally controlled state, with the Communist Party in power, and it therefore didn't really matter where the borders between the republics ran. They should have been changed when the Soviet Union collapsed, but nobody ever dared to attempt it, it was said.

But missteps and contentious decisions made many years ago cannot be used to justify aggression today. Many have pointed out the unreasonable burdens the victorious powers placed on Germany after the First World War, and how Hitler, on his march towards power, was able to exploit Germans' discontent. But this doesn't mean that Britain and France were therefore responsible for the outbreak of the Second World War.

Following the end of the Cold War, the West, led by the United States, attempted to connect Russia to the democratic world through trade, cooperation and financial assistance. The idea was that we would face the security challenges of our age together – terrorism, ethnic and religious conflicts, and the risk of the spread of nuclear, biological and chemical weapons. That relations with Moscow might again become turbulent was always a possibility. But any drift towards conflict would be much more dependent on Russia's own choices and how the country defined its own role and status than it would be on any action taken by the West and NATO.

I am convinced that President Putin never considered Ukraine a military threat, and that he was not especially concerned about the people of Luhansk and Donetsk. A democratic and ever more West-facing Ukraine, on the other hand, was a *political* threat to the regime Putin spearheaded.

Throughout autumn and winter, we had received intelligence reports of an imminent invasion, which unfortunately had turned out to be correct. But the intelligence analyses we received about the course of the war, about what would happen after the Russians attacked, for the most part luckily turned out to be wrong.

It wasn't just Putin who believed the war would be brief – those of us in NATO did, too. There was a widespread perception that Kyiv would fall in a matter of days, and the rest of Ukraine after a few weeks. At the very least, the Russian forces would quickly take control of all of the Donbas and the areas east of the Dnieper River.

But when NATO leaders met at an extraordinary summit in Brussels on the twenty-fourth of March, it was already clear the Russians would win no easy victory. Hard battles were raging on several fronts, including north of Kyiv. Many were killed during Russian artillery and missile attacks on shopping centres, power stations and other civilian targets. Over one hundred thousand people had been evacuated from their homes.

But the Ukrainians stood their ground and fought back determinedly. We began to realise that the war might become protracted.

In these first weeks of the war, President Zelenskyy proved himself to be an effective spokesperson for Ukraine's cause. In his green, field-uniform-inspired attire, he spoke from Kyiv on large screens to almost every single European national assembly about the country's need for help, and about what was at stake for all of Europe. When addressing the NATO summit, however, his tone was tougher. Zelenskyy was disappointed in the alliance for providing what he felt was weak support due to a fear of getting involved.

'I thought it was supposed to be Russia that was afraid of NATO, not NATO that was afraid of Russia,' he said.

Zelenskyy again asked us to shut down the airspace above Ukraine, even though he knew we wouldn't do it. He followed this up with an appeal for weapons.

'Let us have one per cent of your planes, one per cent of your tanks, one per cent of your artillery. One per cent of all of it – and we win.'

I had never before heard Zelenskyy take such an admonishing tone. He was stepping up to lead his country's fight for freedom.

'And never, ever again tell me that our soldiers are not up to NATO standards,' he said.

Everything else I had been involved in within NATO – all the decisions I had made and dilemmas I'd been forced to handle – suddenly seemed small compared to what we now faced.

A large-scale war had come closer to us than ever before in my lifetime, with perhaps the sole exception of the Cuban Missile Crisis, when I was three years old. Back then, the world was on the edge of a precipice, but the clarification came quickly and the crisis was over within a fairly short space of time. It was hard to think of anything that compared. I knew only that never before in my life had I been jointly responsible for decisions with such potentially serious consequences.

I did what I've always done when the work seems overwhelming and I feel weighted down by responsibility: I made sure to get enough sleep, ate healthily and exercised whenever the opportunity arose. I went for bike rides, logged off for a while, and spoke about ordinary, everyday things with the people around me.

We spent a lot of time working on how to achieve the right balance in our support for Ukraine. It was difficult to know whether we were going too far with our arms support or doing too little. And where was the line for Putin?

The ongoing hostilities were a risk factor in themselves. An order to attack that is misunderstood. An off-course missile. Or a calculated provocation from Putin's side to drag us in, if, for political reasons, he saw it as being in his interest to expand the war. And how many attacks involving weapons of mass destruction could we sit back and watch before we simply had to retaliate? Our intelligence reports could not rule out that Putin might use such weapons.

It was important to me that Putin understood we were serious when we said we would not become part of the war, so that he knew to avoid forcing us into a situation where we had no other choice than to intervene. But we had no guarantees something like this wouldn't happen. Until now, the war had remained within Ukraine's borders, and it was easy to assume things would continue that way. Yet as long as the war was ongoing, the risk of escalation would endure.

At the same time, we could not allow ourselves to succumb to fear. NATO must decide for itself how we wished to support Ukraine.

Nor could we allow ourselves to be pressured into closing the door to new member nations. The invasion had triggered a security policy earthquake in two countries that were very close to me. Finland and Sweden now wished to join NATO.

37

Shuttle diplomacy

I'VE ALWAYS FOLLOWED POLITICAL DEVELOPMENTS IN FINLAND and Sweden extremely closely; I have many friends in both countries, and especially in Sweden. As prime minister of Norway I worked well with Swedish prime minister Göran Persson, and then with his successor, Fredrik Reinfeldt. The Norwegian Labour Party and the Swedish Social Democrats have always maintained a close cooperation. Swedish minister for foreign affairs Anna Lindh and I had met regularly since the 1980s. When she was stabbed and killed at a shopping centre in Stockholm in 2003, I lost not only a colleague, but also a dear friend.

I continued to stay in regular contact with the political leaders in both countries after I took office at NATO, and I noticed the way the increased security tensions in Europe after 2014 influenced their attitudes. The threat picture was perceived as being more serious. They sought closer contact with NATO, both politically and militarily. 'We want to be first among the countries who aren't members,' Finnish prime minister Alexander Stubb told me when I visited Helsinki in the spring of 2015. He had been Finland's minister for foreign affairs some years earlier, and had visited Norway often, so I knew him well. This time, Stubb made no attempt to hide that he supported Finland joining NATO, but also admitted that it was a political impossibility.

Late in October 2021, I had a long conversation with Finnish president Sauli Niinistö during another visit to Helsinki. The seventy-two-year-old Niinistö was a veteran of Finnish politics, and had been the country's president since 2012. Like other Finnish leaders, he had intimate knowledge of Russia, and was regularly in touch with President Putin. I asked what it was like to manage Finland's 832-mile border with the colossal neighbour in the East, which was longer than all the other NATO nations' borders with Russia put together.

'It's challenging. But it's better than the alternative, having no border,' Niinistö replied laconically.

He now offered to act as a bridge-builder between Russia and NATO – an offer I gratefully accepted, while also adding that a lack of bridge-builders was not the problem. The problem was that Russia lacked the will to find a way forward together with NATO.

Niinistö's uncle had fought in the Winter War of 1939–1940, when the Finnish had surprised everyone and garnered great respect by inflicting bloody losses on the Soviet Army by which they were vastly outnumbered. This willingness to fight was crucial in Finland managing to preserve its independence. 'My uncle was among those intent upon fighting again,' Niinistö said.

In all my encounters with the Swedish and Finnish leaders, I emphasised that Sweden and Finland were close partners for NATO. We shared the same values and faced the same challenges. It was hugely important that our military forces undertook more exercises together and became more coordinated. But at the same time, I always emphasised that NATO fully respected Sweden and Finland's non-alignment, and that any decision on NATO membership was up to the countries themselves. I didn't wish to say anything that might be interpreted as an attempt to pressure the two countries into joining the alliance.

When I visited Helsinki in the autumn of 2021, it was still out of the question for Finland to apply for NATO membership. What changed the situation at a single stroke, however, was the demand Vladimir Putin made in December, that no new countries be permitted to join the alliance. This threat diplomacy had a tremendous effect within Finland. Part of Finland's security policy was 'the NATO option' – the fact that NATO membership existed as an alternative, and that the country *could* apply to join the alliance. Putin, however, wanted to remove this option. When Russia began trying to close the door to NATO for good, it became important for Finland to step inside.

The assessment in Helsinki was that the most important thing to Putin were his demands to establish a new security order in Europe. Niinistö believed this was just as important to Putin as taking Ukraine – and these demands affected Finland and Sweden directly.

So a process in the direction of membership was already underway before Russia's full-scale invasion of Ukraine on the twenty-fourth of February, but afterwards everything suddenly started to speed up. Over the following weeks, I spoke regularly with the Finnish and Swedish leaders, in meetings and on the telephone, and we frequently exchanged text messages. There were some questions to which they were especially keen to obtain answers before they made any formal application to join the alliance. Were they welcome? If yes – could the process be completed quickly? Or would they need to be prepared to spend years in the waiting room, as other countries had done? In that case, they wouldn't apply. And last, but not least: what kind of security assurances could they expect during the period when they believed they would be especially vulnerable, from making their application until they became full members of NATO covered by the alliance's security guarantee? They had, after all, heard Putin say many times that any enlargement of NATO would be regarded as an act of aggression against Russia, and he had also threatened countermeasures.

Niinistö was anxious about what such countermeasures might entail. In Georgia in 2008 and Ukraine in 2014, the Russians had begun military operations in order to ward off NATO membership. Sweden's minister for foreign affairs Ann Linde brought up the possibility that President Putin might try to exploit the situation if Sweden applied to join NATO, implying that he might try to scare the Swedes, for example by launching a hybrid attack.

I was careful not to promise more than I was able to deliver regarding NATO support in the interim. But the moment they applied, and we responded by inviting them to join, the political decision would in reality have been made. For the alliance then *not* to stand up for them would weaken NATO's credibility.

Finland quickly forged ahead with the application process, with Sweden following more slowly behind. Part of the reason for this lay in the two countries' different historical experiences, especially in terms of what happened in the years immediately after the Second World War, when the Nordic countries went their separate ways.

In April 1948, Finland was pressured into signing a 'friendship agreement' with the Soviet Union, which limited the country's room for manoeuvre within foreign and security policy. This caused deep concern and fear in Norway, and that same year this unease led to the Norwegian authorities asking the British and the Americans about how they would respond in the event of a Soviet attack, and what kind of assistance Norway might receive. These enquiries contributed to the alliance-building project already embraced by the British, and which would eventually lead to the creation of NATO.

In the winter of 1948–49, lengthy negotiations took place between Norway, Sweden and Denmark regarding a Nordic defence union, and how this might fit within a broader, Western cooperation. The three countries didn't manage to come to an agreement. Sweden maintained a strictly neutral line, believing West-leaning ties would provoke the Soviet Union and increase the risk of the Nordic region being dragged into a major conflict. Norway and Denmark's experiences from 1940 pulled the two countries in a different direction – remaining neutral hadn't prevented Nazi Germany's attack on the ninth of April. The Norwegian and Danish authorities therefore believed it crucial not to stand alone. The Soviet Union must know that they could not attack them without triggering a large-scale war. As it turned out, these differing fundamental attitudes were impossible to reconcile, and the Nordic countries therefore went their separate ways. Norway and Denmark joined NATO, while Sweden remained non-aligned.

For Finland, neutrality has always been a virtue of necessity. It was something demanded of them during the Cold War out of consideration for the Soviet Union. But Finland had no ideological relationship to its non-alignment; the country's neutrality had no value in and of itself.

For Sweden, on the other hand, the country's neutrality and military non-alignment was extremely ideological – the Swedes revered it. That their country was non-aligned was deeply rooted in their national identity and in their history. To apply for NATO membership was therefore a much greater leap for the Swedes than it was for the Finns.

This was understandable. I'm not entirely sure what I would have thought myself, had I been a Swedish politician. The last time Sweden was at war was in the summer of 1814 – against Norway. The country has managed to stay out of military conflicts for over two hundred years. No one could deny that Sweden's neutrality had been highly successful. They were proud of it.

It is also possible to argue that this balance within the Nordic region, with Denmark, Iceland and Norway as NATO members, and Sweden and Finland as neutral states, has contributed to the lack of tensions in the north for many decades. There was also the deep-rooted scepticism the Swedish Social Democrats had of the United States and NATO, an alliance 'that has started wars of aggression and includes the use of nuclear weapons in its doctrine,' as NATO critics within the party often said. And the fact that joining NATO meant becoming an ally of a country like Turkey certainly didn't make matters easier. The changes in attitude in Sweden, especially among the Social Democrats, almost say more about just how much of a political earthquake Putin's invasion was than anything else.

After the twenty-fourth of February, Finnish opinion swung massively in favour of NATO membership. Finnish prime minister Sanna Marin was among the many who changed their minds following Putin's invasion. 'The current situation is challenging, but it might be even worse a decade from now,' she said in one of our conversations after the war broke out. That a large majority were in favour of applying to join the alliance was crucial in Finland, where there is a tradition of broad compromises on important political questions.

'It's no longer a question of if we're going to apply. It's a question of when,' Marin told me.

In Sweden, the rapid developments taking place in Finland put the government under pressure. This became palpable following an interview I gave to the *Dagens Nyheter* newspaper in mid-March, in which I said that we would manage to admit Finland and Sweden to the alliance quickly, and that security assurances in the interim would be worked out. This could be interpreted as me pushing the two countries towards membership. Swedish prime minister Magdalena Andersson and minister for foreign affairs Ann Linde were disappointed – my going significantly further than the Swedish government in my statements caused problems for them.

I was annoyed at myself – they were my friends. I first met Ann Linde towards the end of the 1970s, when she was active in the Swedish student union and I was on the board of Norway's counterpart. Since then, we had worked closely together in various political roles. I hadn't known Magdalena Andersson as long, but I had great respect for the job she was doing as party leader and prime minister. She combined an economist's cool analysis with human warmth. Now my statements had made things difficult for them. It was the Swedes who were in the thick of it, and they should have been able to decide for themselves whether they needed any extra help from me. It wasn't long since Magdalena Andersson and other leading Social Democrats had been critical of NATO, stating that Swedish membership of the alliance could have a destabilising effect. Nevertheless, NATO membership had suddenly become extremely relevant. They had been catapulted into the debate, and I shouldn't have said anything that might seem like me trying to lecture them.

'They're just moving so darned fast in Finland, much faster than we expected,' an exasperated Andersson told me. This put Sweden in a squeeze.

Early in April, the Swedes realised that the Finns had made up their minds. Immediately afterwards, Ann Linde made it clear to me that this would be of major significance for Sweden's decision.

Up until the invasion in February, the opinion polls in Sweden had shown that the population was fairly evenly split in their views on NATO membership. Sometimes the majority was in favour of membership of the alliance; at other times it was against it. But follow-ing Putin's attack, opinion swung markedly in favour of joining the alliance. There was a clear majority for NATO membership, including among social democratic voters.

The Social Democrats had initiated a major internal process, and the party leadership was concerned that this had to be real, and not perceived as being only for show. Only when this process had been completed did Prime Minister Andersson and the rest of the govern-ment offer their final decision. Sweden's defence plans rested on the premise that Finland was neutral. If Finland joined the alliance, the country's long border with Russia would become a NATO border. This changed everything. Sweden could not remain an island outside NATO. It was said that Finland decided to apply to join the alliance because of Ukraine, and that Sweden decided to apply because of Finland.

The Swedes felt that the Finns could have coordinated more effec-tively with them earlier in the spring, and that they then could have avoided the time pressure they were now under. But as the situation stood, both Magdalena Andersson and Ann Linde supported the two countries applying simultaneously. The Swedes expedited their sched-ule, in order to apply to join NATO alongside Finland in mid-May.

Both the Finnish and Swedish leaders exhibited impressive political drive over the course of that spring. The world changed. Well-established positions were overturned. Historic decisions were made.

One by one the questions were clarified, both within NATO and within Sweden and Finland. The two countries would be welcomed into the alliance, and the process would be concluded quickly.

Sauli Niinistö called President Recep Erdoğan, because there was a certain fear it might prove difficult to obtain the Turks' approval. But Niinistö was reassured that Turkey would view the applications favourably. I brought up the matter with minister of foreign affairs Mevlüt Çavuşoğlu, and he made it clear that Turkey would not oppose the enlargements. Several meetings of the North Atlantic Council, with the Turkish ambassador present, confirmed the same. We believed we had everything in place.

* * *

On Friday the thirteenth of May I wasn't in the office, because I had contracted Covid. I was at home, asleep in bed, when I was woken by a call from my communications adviser, Sissel Kruse Larsen. She told me that Erdoğan, without warning, had issued a statement that Turkey was not prepared to support Finnish and Swedish membership of the alliance. I pulled myself together and called Çavuşoğlu, with whom I had enjoyed a good working relationship for several years. He had just attended a meeting with Erdoğan in Istanbul, at which the matter of Finland and Sweden joining the alliance had been discussed.

'You know, Jens, we support keeping NATO's door open. We are in favour of enlargements, we have supported both Ukraine and Georgia in their wish to join the alliance,' he said. 'But unfortunately, Sweden openly supports the Kurdish PKK and YPG,' he continued. 'Their ministers for foreign affairs and defence meet representatives from these terrorist organisations regularly, and you know how the Turkish people feel about this. We must have clear assurances from both Finland and Sweden that they support neither of these organisations.'

The Turks had long been fed up with individuals they considered Kurdish terrorists being granted far too much liberty by many NATO nations – and Sweden was practically regarded as a safe haven for them. Turkey had problems with Finland, too, but there the contact between officials and the Kurdish organisations was neither so open nor so provocative. Erdoğan had told me many times that Turkey considered these organisations terrorist movements, and that there was no point distinguishing between them.

'This is serious,' I told Çavuşoğlu. 'This will cause concern, not just in Stockholm and Helsinki, but in other NATO capitals too.' If countries like Sweden and Finland couldn't be accepted into the alliance, then there wasn't much to be said for NATO's open-door policy.

Çavuşoğlu could see that the demands might give rise to unease. 'But we also have our concerns, with which you must sympathise,' he replied. He said that Turkey would also demand that restrictions on the export of weapons be lifted.

The following day, the fourteenth of May, NATO held an informal meeting of the ministers of foreign affairs in Berlin. I should have been there, of course, but I was forced to stay home and instead participated by video link.

Çavuşoğlu didn't sugarcoat the message. 'I have to be open and honest with you. Our people are against Swedish and Finnish membership right now, and that also applies to supporters of the opposition parties. My president's statements reflect the Turks' views on this issue,' he said.

Ankara first needed to see that Sweden and Finland were taking clear and concrete steps to meet Turkey halfway. Çavuşoğlu delivered some harsh criticism of Sweden, and of minister for foreign affairs Ann Linde, who he felt had been less accommodating than her Finnish counterpart, Pekka Haavisto. Both were participating at the meeting as specially invited guests.

'This has nothing to do with your so-called feminist foreign policy, Ann. We have followed your statements extremely closely, and you use threatening language,' Çavuşoğlu said. He consistently referred to the PKK and the Syrian-Kurdish YPG as a single unit, and claimed that Sweden was sending them weapons.

All at once, what we'd had good reason to believe could happen immediately was looking much more difficult. Without a solution before the summit in Madrid in the summer, the timeframe for Sweden and Finland becoming NATO members might be extended indefinitely.

The main problem was Sweden. Many people of Kurdish origin lived in the country, and people sympathised with the plight of the Kurds. Government representatives had contact with Kurds of various backgrounds; one of the first things Ann Linde had done when she became minister for foreign affairs in the autumn of 2019, was to condemn the entry of Turkish troops into Syria and to impose arms embargoes. Kurdish MP Amineh Kakabaveh was a former member of the Swedish Left Party, and had previously been a soldier in the Peshmerga, the armed branch of the regional Kurdish authorities in Iraq. Her voice had been decisive in Magdalena Andersson's government being able to form a majority. In return for her support, Andersson had had to promise that the Social Democrats would cooperate more closely with the YPG, and in parliament Kakabaveh was a visible spokeswoman for Kurdish interests. All of this was a source of endless irritation for the Turks.

The move by Turkey in mid-May triggered an intense six-week period of shuttle diplomacy, to try to save the Finnish and Swedish applications. Previous application processes had dragged on for years, and the Finns and Swedes were keen to avoid this happening to theirs.

'This will put us in the situation we're so keen to avoid. We've made ourselves vulnerable by applying, but don't have the protection that membership provides,' Magdalena Andersson told me.

Over the course of these weeks, I had a total of four long telephone conversations with President Erdoğan. He stood firmly by Turkey's demands. 'Sweden and Finland are ignoring questions that are of great importance for Turkish security. This makes it impossible for us to support them becoming members of NATO,' he said.

'Both countries are prepared to take several steps to address Turkey's concerns,' I replied. 'If this process drags on, it will only benefit those who wish Turkey and NATO ill, and those who would seek to sideline us and prioritise other security policy organisations.'

The matter was now squarely on Erdoğan's desk, and each and every step had to be approved by him personally. To start with, he wouldn't even accept that we needed a process, but on this crucial point he eventually conceded. Several challenging meetings were held between the Turks, the Swedes and the Finns. According to Ann Linde, the Turks were making objectionable demands that would limit freedom of expression in Sweden; she also believed that Turkey was making erroneous claims. Sweden had long since designated the PKK a terrorist organisation, and it was wrong to say that Sweden supported the organisation. And there were no Swedish arms being supplied to the YPG; consequently, there were no arms deliveries to stop.

After first attempting to negotiate on their own but getting nowhere, Erdoğan, Niinistö and Andersson eventually agreed that my office should take over in leading the process. We drafted an agreement between Turkey, Sweden and Finland, and the parties agreed that this draft would form the basis for negotiations going forward.

The Turks reacted to the fact that Sveriges Radio had sent a TV crew to northern Syria and interviewed Salih Muslim, whom the Turks believed represented the PKK, but whom the Americans and British deemed a member of the YPG. Muslim had criticised Erdoğan with some harsh words, and apparently believed Sweden would never turn its back on the PKK. To the Turks, it was incomprehensible that the Swedish government was unable to use the state radio broadcaster for its own ends, and couldn't simply notify Sveriges Radio that such interviews had to be stopped.

Trust between the parties was at an all-time low.

By mid-June, both the Finns and the Swedes were starting to lose hope; they had little faith in any solution being reached before the summit. We received no indication that a secret arrangement between Russia and Turkey might be behind the Turks' blocking of the applications, with Putin pulling the strings, as some media outlets speculated. But it was clear the Turks were in no rush to admit the two countries regardless.

Despite the poor relations, negotiations continued and our shuttle diplomacy proved effective. We made progress in the work to agree a deal. As we approached the summit, I believed a solution to be within reach. Finland and Sweden had given a lot. They condemned the PKK. They pledged to do more to combat terrorism. They would cooperate with Ankara to ensure terrorists were deported. They would place no special limitations on arms exports to Turkey. They would share intelligence and information. And in return, Turkey would invite Finland and Sweden to join NATO.

Erdoğan's security policy adviser, İbrahim Kalın, was optimistic: 'I think we have a deal.'

I, too, felt optimistic. But I knew from experience that nothing was certain until President Erdoğan had given his final approval.

38

A breakthrough in Madrid

MADRID IS A BEAUTIFUL CITY, WITH ITS MANY MAGNIFICENT palaces, towering church spires and inviting squares. Not quite as beautiful, however, is the Recinto Ferial Ifema Madrid, or IFEMA Madrid – the enormous exhibition hall situated outside the Spanish capital, not far from the airport. Both the hall and the surrounding area seem like a desert of concrete and cement; under the burning summer sun, the heat can become unbearable.

This is where the NATO heads of state and government gathered for a summit on the twenty-eighth to thirtieth of June, 2022. Security considerations mean that NATO summits are often held at such facilities – had the meeting been held in the centre of the city, it would have been necessary to shut Madrid down for three days. A few weeks earlier, Ingrid and I had spent a relaxing weekend with Spanish prime minister Pedro Sánchez and his wife Begoña Gómez at the popular holiday destination of Quintos de Mora. Sánchez had become a major political leader in Europe, and I was now looking forward to opening the summit together with him.

Inside, the exhibition hall was decorated with flags and various emblems in NATO colours. The colossal space had been divided into large and small meeting rooms using movable partitions, with a separate room allocated to me and my office. It looked great in the photographs, but the solution was somewhat makeshift. The meeting rooms had no ceilings, so much of the sound flowed between them.

The hall had been rigged for the summit in just twenty-four hours, and it would be de-rigged just as quickly. As usual, the NATO summit was being held among a landscape of stage sets.

Russia's war of aggression against Ukraine had now been raging for over five months. In mid-April, the Ukrainians had managed to sink the flagship of the Russian Black Sea fleet, the missile cruiser *Moskva*. After a prolonged siege, the Ukrainians had been forced to surrender the Azovstal Iron and Steel Works, one of the world's largest steelworks and site of the last organised resistance in Mariupol. At around the same time as NATO leaders were gathering in Madrid, Ukrainians retook Snake Island off the coast of Odesa, where at the very start of the war a small group of Ukrainian forces had refused to surrender to the Russians that greatly outnumbered them.

Intense fighting was ongoing, and now NATO issued yet another response: we agreed on the greatest reinforcement of our collective defence since the end of the Cold War, including with more stocks of equipment, ammunition and fuel in the eastern part of the alliance. This increased the strength of our deterrence.

I had a legitimate hope of resolving the complex issue of Finland and Sweden's NATO membership when presidents Recep Erdoğan and Sauli Niinistö and prime minister Magdalena Andersson and I sat down in one of the meeting rooms at around 15.00 on the twenty-eighth of June, the day on which NATO leaders gathered in Madrid.

Erdoğan and I sat next to each other on the same side of the table, with Andersson and Niinistö directly opposite. NATO on the one side, applicants Finland and Sweden on the other. Our advisers sat right behind us.

'Agreement is within reach,' I began. 'But it's important that we agree *now*, at this meeting. We are not leaving this room until we've achieved this.'

I was convinced we needed to make the most of this opportunity, now that we had the three leaders sitting around the same table. Besides, there were practical limitations that meant we had to come to an agreement. The following day, I would be chairing the sessions of the summit itself, and therefore stuck in the large conference room from morning to early evening. We could probably have arranged some meetings between the advisers, but Erdoğan would only attend if I also took part, and he had to be present for us to be able to make decisions.

The text that lay before us on the table condemned the Kurdistan Workers' Party, the PKK. But the YPG, the Syrian-Kurdish militia, was not mentioned by name. Nor was FETÖ, the organisation the Turks believed to be behind the attempted coup in 2016.

'We have a strong text concerning the war on terror, which it should be possible for everyone to endorse. What's important is that we do what we can to fight terrorism, not what we call the various organisations,' I said.

I gave Erdoğan the floor.

'You know very well it isn't sufficient to condemn the PKK,' he said. He demanded that the YPG also be named in the text, and alleged that Turkey was not being taken seriously. 'The Nordic countries are a playground for terrorists,' he complained.

His tone was tough and uncompromising.

Then Andersson and Niinistö spoke. They reiterated their familiar standpoints, and their positions were firm.

I've taken part in so many meetings at which no progress is made; where the discussion goes around in circles because political leaders fear how things will end up if they even hint at giving so much as an inch. I now decided to be clearer, more direct. To do this is always a risk. Either it will help to shift people's positions, because it impresses the seriousness of the situation upon everyone in the room, or the parties simply grow irritated at being lectured and dig their heels in even more.

I turned to Erdoğan and gripped his shoulder.

'Finland and Sweden have given a lot,' I said. 'And they have pledged to stand with Turkey in the war on terror.'

I searched Erdoğan's face for any sign that what I'd said had made an impression, but found none.

'They won't hesitate to deport people when this is in accordance with the law and following a decision by the immigration authorities,' I went on. 'Sweden is tightening up its counter-terrorism legislation.

And remember this: if we *don't* come to an agreement here, that will be a huge victory for the PKK and others like them. They'll be jumping for joy if NATO closes its doors to Sweden and Finland. You mustn't allow them that victory.'

Nothing in Erdoğan's body language indicated that he agreed with me, but nor was there anything to suggest he disagreed with what I said. He simply looked at me as he waited for me to finish speaking.

'The YPG must be included in the document, and they must be referred to as terrorists,' he replied, calmly and firmly. This was the single detail he was concerned with.

At one point I noticed Stian pass a note to Erdoğan's adviser, İbrahim Kalın, who had played a central role in the negotiations. I later learned that it said: 'Is there any point continuing?' Kalın read the note and nodded, slowly.

An hour passed. Then two. Niinistö grew frustrated. 'You said ages ago that this could all be worked out. What do you actually want?' he said. Erdoğan gave a sharp reply.

Things were not looking good. Anger and irritation would only make it even harder to come to an agreement.

Magdalena Andersson and Ann Linde started gathering up their papers, as if preparing to leave. I whispered to them in Norwegian: 'Wait, don't go!'

The room was rather small; people sat shoulder to shoulder along the walls. The air was thick and stuffy. We agreed to continue, but we needed to take a break before the air and the atmosphere in the room got even worse. Everyone else made their way outside, while I remained sitting alone with Erdoğan. I was focused on just one thing: ensuring he didn't disappear, that he didn't leave the meeting because he was upset or hungry or tired.

'Would you like anything? Coffee? Cake? A sandwich?' I asked.

'I'm not that cheap,' Erdoğan replied with a crooked smile.

Some sad-looking canapés were brought in, but Erdoğan wolfed them down as he and I continued the conversation one-on-one. I reminded him of everything Turkey had achieved in the negotiations. If we let Finland and Sweden in, it would show President Putin that

NATO's door remained open, and that he couldn't threaten sovereign, democratic states into staying outside the alliance.

Turkey's president listened as I spoke, but said that none of this changed his categorical requirement that the YPG be named in the text. This was what our people were now working on outside the meeting room, so we were both aware we were actually free to talk about other things. Our conversation moved on to how long we had known each other, and we touched on Norway, and the Norwegian oil fund and the fiscal rule. We had talked about this at previous meetings, too; Erdoğan appreciated how Norway only ever spends the fund's real returns.

'You promised to come to Istanbul with your wife, but you never did,' Erdoğan said suddenly.

This was true. A few years earlier, I had accepted an invitation from Erdoğan to visit Istanbul. I had made many official visits to Turkey, but his point was that I had *also* agreed to come to Istanbul with Ingrid – private dinners with Erdoğan and his wife, and visiting the city's landmarks together, would be an entirely different thing from sitting in meetings in Ankara. But my schedule had been packed, I didn't prioritise making Istanbul part of the plan, and then the pandemic had arrived and put a stop to all international travel.

Erdoğan had reminded me of the Istanbul invitation when I met with him for the first time after the pandemic, in Antalya some months earlier. Before Madrid, I'd had the sense that he might bring up the invitation again. I know him – he wants Turkey to be valued – and I had therefore spoken with Ingrid before leaving for Spain. 'If he asks about the trip to Istanbul, can I say that we'll go?' I had asked. Ingrid had agreed.

So when Erdoğan brought up the Istanbul visit yet again, I replied without hesitation. 'Actually, Ingrid and I spoke about that very recently – we'd love to come!'

It's hard to say how much of a difference this made, if any. But that Erdoğan and I got on the same wavelength, and that together we began to look forward to visiting Istanbul, Erdoğan's hometown and a city of which he is immensely proud – well, it certainly didn't hurt.

We sat there for over an hour before the meeting resumed. There had been some hectic activity out in the corridors and in some of the other meeting rooms. Our staffs came in with an adjusted draft text, which referenced the YPG in a section about Turkey's national security more generally, not in the paragraph about terrorism: 'As prospective NATO allies, Finland and Sweden extend their full support to Türkiye against threats to its national security. To that effect, Finland and Sweden will not provide support to the YPG/PYD, and the organization described as FETÖ in Türkiye.'

The wording and placement of the sentence meant that the YPG were not labelled terrorists in and of themselves; the political point for Sweden and Finland was that they didn't want to be forced into accepting Erdoğan's definitions of who is and isn't a terrorist. Both Niinistö and Andersson called home to secure political backing, and they were given the green light. Finland and Sweden believed the new text was acceptable.

I thought we were done, but no. Turkish minister of foreign affairs Mevlüt Çavuşoğlu demanded the inclusion of a passage that had been discussed earlier in the meeting, about how Sweden and Finland must first commit to taking several concrete steps before Turkey ratified the agreement. But following the insertion of the sentence in which Sweden and Finland promised not to provide support to the YPG, this passage was no longer relevant. Çavuşoğlu wanted to have his cake and eat it, too.

I felt the impatience surge within me.

'Mevlüt, you need to shut up!' I said, and gave him a hard look. Silence fell over the room. You can only speak that way to friends, I thought.

I read the complete text aloud, slowly, three times, to Erdoğan and all the others in the room. Sweden and Finland would do more to combat terrorism, and remove the restrictions on arms exports. In return, Erdoğan would support inviting the two countries to become members of NATO.

Then I went around the table. Niinistö said yes. Andersson said yes. Erdoğan looked first at me, then glanced at Niinistö and Andersson before returning his gaze to mine. 'Okay,' he said. The entire room burst into applause.

Goodwill now shone from the face that just hours earlier had been so difficult to read. We had come to an agreement.

It was vital that we wrap things up before anyone had second thoughts; I quickly shook Erdoğan's hand to make it clear we had a deal. We needed to get the new text typed up and translated, and new printouts made. It was important that the parties sign here and now.

Meanwhile, the summit gala dinner at the Royal Palace had begun and was now in full swing. In his welcome speech, King Felipe had joked it was a good sign that he couldn't see me among the guests, and this was indeed true – it meant that we were still sitting around the table with the Turks, Swedes and Finns, working to find a solution.

It was a little after eight in the evening when I sent Pedro Sánchez a text: 'We finally reached an agreement on Finland and Sweden. Apologies for not making it to the dinner tonight. Looking forward to seeing you tomorrow. Best, Jens.'

A little while later, Sánchez's reply dinged in: 'Congrats my dear friend!! Fantastic!!! Another achievement of the Madrid summit!'

The signing ceremony ended up being a somewhat curious affair. Since everything happened so quickly, no preparations had been made. Journalists came running when the news of a breakthrough started to trickle out – there was no announcement of what was about to take place. The delegations came in, the ministers of foreign affairs sat down, signed the documents, stood up again, shook each other's hands, and walked out. Not a word was spoken. As I was leaving, I called out to those present that I would return in half an hour to brief them on what they had just witnessed.

We had a deal. The decision was made – we had a consensus on inviting Finland and Sweden to join the alliance. All that remained was for the national assemblies of all the NATO nations to approve the two new members. This was usually just a formality.

39

The journey to Kyiv

THE TRAIN WAS DARK, THE WINDOWS COVERED WITH BLACKOUT blinds so not a chink of light could escape. The brakes screeched, and the carriages stopped with a jolt. I lifted the blind a few centimetres and peeked out. There were the two boundary markers, one painted in the colours of the Polish flag, the other in those of the flag of Ukraine. We were at the border.

I peered from under the curtain as the train began to move again, listening to the regular, clacking rhythm of the wheels bumping over the joints in the track. The sound reminded me of other long journeys I had made through Europe by rail, and of how the rail networks bound the continent together, both in good times and in bad. In the darkness outside I glimpsed lakes and marshland, some patchwork fields and miles upon miles of forest unfolding across the flat landscape; the occasional solid, slightly worn brick building from back when these areas belonged to the Habsburg monarchy, which dissolved following the First World War. At daybreak we passed villages; carts jangling along a dirt road and people just starting to go about their days. Several graveyards came into view. Before they disappeared from sight, I just had time to notice that the fences around them had been expanded to provide space for many new graves, which were covered with large quantities of fresh flowers.

It was dawn on the morning of the twentieth of April, 2023. The train rushed through Ukraine. I was on my way to Kyiv to meet with President Volodymyr Zelenskyy.

A few hours earlier we had landed at the Rzeszów military base in the far east of Poland, which had now become Europe's best-protected airport. Large volumes of weapons and military equipment were flown into this base, before being transported on into Ukraine. From Rzeszów it was just under half an hour's drive to the border city of Przemyśl, where the train stood waiting for us.

Tens of thousands of fleeing women and children had arrived here in the first days of the war, making the opposite journey of the one I was about to take. The Poles had swarmed in to help them, bringing food, clothing, nappies and toys. I walked quickly across the platform, glancing up at the makeshift roof. No aerial photographs would reveal who boarded or disembarked the train.

The train had an aura of pomp and grandeur, with chandeliers hanging from the ceiling, luxurious seats, dark wood trim and tables spread with white tablecloths. I had an entire carriage to myself, with both a meeting room and sleeping quarters with a large bathroom. The interior reminded me of the train in Agatha Christie's novel *Murder on the Orient Express*. Ukraine is a great rail nation, rightly proud of how well the service has always run, including during the war. This was important for military transport needs and for the machinery of civilian life. Overinvestments in staff and *matériel* in the period in which Ukraine was part of the Soviet Union meant that the Ukrainian railways were exceptionally robust. That the trains managed to stick to the timetables gave people a sense of normality amid the trials of war.

My small delegation and I got ourselves set up in one of the salons. For security reasons, only extremely few people at NATO headquarters knew that I was on my way to Kyiv. A normal daily agenda had been booked for me in Brussels, which was then cancelled just before I left.

I had long wanted to return to Ukraine, but making such a visit was contentious within the alliance. Some of the allies were concerned

that my presence in Kyiv would shore up President Putin's claims that
NATO's aggressive enlargements eastwards were the real cause of the
war, and strengthen his narrative about how this was actually a conflict
between Russia and the West.

But after Joe Biden had visited Kyiv in February, such considerations no longer weighed so heavily. If the president of the United
States was able to travel to Kyiv, then NATO's secretary general must
also be able to do so. Besides – was I supposed to refrain from travelling to Ukraine, a free and independent country, and a partner nation
for NATO, due to Putin's view on my making such a visit? We could
not give Russia the power to determine what the NATO secretary
general was and was not allowed to do, nor whom President Zelenskyy
was permitted to meet. In part, this right of self-determination was
actually what the war in Ukraine was about.

We believed the trip was important. Of course going to Kyiv was a
political act. NATO was clearly signalling its support of the Ukrainians'
legitimate resistance.

As the train rushed eastwards, Stian, Dylan White from the NATO
press office and I polished our message to the Ukrainian leaders and
the wording I would use during the subsequent press conference.
While in Kyiv, how I expressed Ukraine's relationship to NATO would
be especially important.

After a couple of hours' discussion, and steaming black tea served
by the Ukrainian train stewards, we turned to our separate tasks. I
withdrew to my spacious compartment, with the blackout blinds carefully drawn. My bodyguards were on board, and I knew that sniffer
dogs were searching every station we would pass along the way.
Special forces soldiers had been deployed close to our route, and
before I left Brussels SACEUR General Chris Cavoli had told me that
his people would have 'constant eyes on us'. Cavoli had taken over the
role a few months earlier, moving from his position as head of the US
ground forces in Europe and Africa. He was a man who inspired
confidence, educated at Yale in addition to his military training, and I
found it reassuring that the Americans were able to track our movements in Ukraine. Should the locomotive be rendered inoperative,

others stood ready along the entire route, and could be connected to the train within half an hour. I could therefore sleep soundly to the rhythmic ticking of the wheels along the track, but it was nevertheless a night without much sleep.

Early in the morning, we arrived in Bucha. At the start of April 2022 the images of the dead bodies that lay in the streets here, many with their hands bound behind their backs, had shocked the entire world. The massacres were a turning point. Attempts at negotiations became more contentious. The NATO nations' attitudes to the Putin regime hardened. Military aid to Ukraine was significantly increased.

I was now told the whole story. How the Russians had been driven back, the first time they tried to take the city. How mercilessly they advanced when they returned for a second attack. How the soldiers, many of them intoxicated, shot at anything that moved and went into houses to steal equipment and belongings – they even snatched coffee makers to take with them. Most of these soldiers came from poor Russian provinces, far from the large cities like Moscow and St Petersburg.

I was driven to a white church with bullet holes in the walls. Right beside it was where 116 bodies had been found, many of them obviously executed. A memorial had been erected there, and I laid a wreath in memory of the dead. A total of 462 people were killed in Bucha, and sixty-two were detained and taken to Russia. The Russians had prepared lists of leading figures within the local community, and systematically targeted them. Most of the victims were politicians, head teachers, newspaper editors and union representatives.

Bucha's mayor, Anatoliy Fedoruk, was among those who showed me around. 'The Russians came to my house, too, but I saved myself by making them believe I was somebody else,' he told me.

A little later that morning, our motorcade arrived in Kyiv. Cars and buses drove down the streets, the shops were open and people strolled along the pavements and through the parks, but it nevertheless struck me how much quieter it was, how many fewer people there were than on my previous visits. Cafés and restaurants closed early. People stayed home a lot, perhaps to remain closer to air raid shelters.

Everywhere, statues and monuments were covered with sandbags. The city's pulse beat more slowly.

We stopped at the Wall of Remembrance of the Fallen for Ukraine, the monument to all those killed in the war with Russia since 2014. When I first visited the site in 2015, I was told that the names and photographs of all the fallen would be displayed here. This was already no longer possible. The number of victims had grown far too great for the space.

I approached the wall and laid a wreath, then stood for a while with my head bowed in respect for the dead. The call of a solitary trumpet cut through the air. Behind the memorial wall, the golden domes of St Michael's Monastery towered against the sky.

When I visited Kyiv on that day in April 2023, almost fourteen months had passed since Putin began his full-scale invasion. The previous autumn had been characterised by dramatic changes in the front lines. The Ukrainians had managed to recapture significant territory, first in the north, all the way from Kyiv to Belarus, and then in Kharkiv in the east followed by Kherson in the south. Over the course of a few months, they managed to liberate half the territory the Russians had taken control of following the invasion. Large numbers of Russian troops were at risk of being surrounded. Putin responded to these military defeats by mobilising reserve forces, which according to the Russians would send 300,000 new soldiers to the front.

The Ukrainian advances were of course good news. But at the same time, this increased the risk of President Putin feeling forced to resort to dramatic measures, such as the use of chemical or nuclear weapons. In other words, Ukraine's counteroffensives might trigger what was referred to as a 'catastrophic victory'.

Our surveillance of what was happening on the Russian side of the front was escalated. The Russians had been using missiles that could carry both conventional and nuclear warheads since the very start of the war, which made it difficult to anticipate whether a nuclear attack might be imminent.

One bright spot was that the Chinese had made it clear the Russians mustn't even think about using nuclear weapons; US secretary of defense Lloyd Austin also warned the Russians in no uncertain terms. It was critical that Moscow understand that any use of nuclear weapons would have serious consequences.

Putin's assurances that he would defend the annexed provinces of Luhansk, Donetsk, Zaporizhzhia and Kherson by all available means deepened our concerns. In Putin's view, he could claim that NATO's support of Ukraine was tantamount to support for an attack on Russian territory. According to their own doctrines, the Russians could use nuclear weapons if the existence of the Russian state was threatened. And it was of course up to Putin himself to define what constituted such a threat.

In the intelligence briefings we received, the possibility of the Russians using tactical nuclear weapons in Ukraine changed from 'extremely unlikely' to 'unlikely'. But in this context, 'unlikely' means a probability of between 10 and 25 per cent. So a nuclear attack was far from an impossibility.

Several times that autumn, I was reminded that a nuclear war can never be won and must never be fought. I hoped our deterrence would be effective enough to prevent Putin from taking this suicidal step, but we couldn't rule out the possibility completely. The fact that the threat of nuclear war had been assessed as very real, was deeply unnerving. For the first time in my life, I went to bed in the evenings knowing that I might be woken by a telephone call to inform me that a nuclear attack was underway.

After the front lines stabilised again late in the autumn of 2022, the risk of nuclear war was thought to have lessened, but it certainly wasn't over. President Putin had repeatedly threatened to use nuclear weapons.

Drawing historical parallels is always risky, because doing so erases all differences and nuance. But I couldn't help thinking about the First World War, and the weeks before the war's outbreak in which the global superpowers had moved towards catastrophe. Putin's invasion had initiated an apparently unbreakable chain of reactions and counterreactions.

A desire for more weapons and equipment dominated all our conversations with Kyiv, and the Ukrainians' need seemed insatiable. They needed more artillery, more ammunition, and not least more air defence. Luckily, the United States, Germany and other allies provided Ukraine with some Patriot batteries. This is one of the world's leading air defence systems, which can shoot down incoming missiles from great distances away. The problem was that the NATO allies had only a limited number of them, and they were extremely expensive. A battery with radar, command unit and launchers costs around $1 billion, with each of the advanced missiles belonging to the system costing $4 million. In comparison, an Iranian Shahed drone, of which the Russians had plenty, costs less than $50,000. So it was clear that Patriot rockets had to be reserved for countering the more advanced Russian weapons, and not wasted on cheap drones. The waves of attacks on Ukrainian cities were not only intended to destroy important targets, but also to force Ukraine to use up its reserves of air defence ammunition. The country would then be defenceless in the event of aerial attacks, and this would turn the game around on the ground, making it much easier for Russian forces to advance.

There was soon a desperate lack of artillery ammunition, and the stockpiles in many NATO countries were also depleted to perilously low levels. Secretary of defense Lloyd Austin had become a key player in pushing for more military support to Ukraine, and led this work. For several months, he had been asking President Biden for permission to provide Ukraine with cluster munitions, which the Russians had long since begun using. These effective weapons scatter a large number of small grenades across a large area, and can stop advancing soldiers. But often, not all the grenades explode – instead, they can remain on the ground, causing casualties and fatalities months and even years after wars are over. Biden had said no. But eventually the dilemma was such that the Ukrainians could either be given cluster munitions, which the United States had a good deal of, or no ammunition at all. Biden finally changed his mind and said yes, and Austin informed me of the decision.

'We're aware that cluster munitions are contentious. Many of the alliance's member nations have signed the UN Convention prohibiting them,' Austin explained.

He didn't need to tell me this. In 2008, agreement had been reached regarding a convention to prohibit cluster munitions, and Norway had taken a leading role in this work. The convention was signed in Oslo, and the very first person to sign it was then Norwegian prime minister Jens Stoltenberg. And now here I was, sitting in a meeting with the US secretary of defense, feeling relieved that the United States had decided to provide cluster munitions to Ukraine.

In the autumn of 2022, the Russians dug themselves in, building fortifications and minefields behind the front line. If the Ukrainians were to be successful in getting back on the offensive, to push the Russians back and recapture more territory, they would also need weapons that could break through fortified positions – primarily, tanks. What the Ukrainians wanted most was the German Leopard 2, perhaps the best tank in the world, of which Germany and other European countries had many.

I had several conversations with Chancellor Olaf Scholz about supplying the Leopard tanks. Scholz held back, citing a fear of escalation. He pointed out that Germany was already among the countries sending the most equipment to Ukraine, and he was right. But nor did he try to hide how difficult it was to be responsible for German tanks rolling eastwards over the Ukrainian plains again. It brought back painful memories from the Eastern Front during the Second World War.

If Putin really wanted to escalate the war, I pointed out to Scholz, he had no shortage of pretexts. The Russians had been driven out of Kharkiv and Kherson, the missile cruiser *Moskva* had been sunk and the Kerch Bridge to Crimea bombed, and we had supplied the Himar multiple-launch rocket system and other long-range weapons to Ukraine. Many so-called red lines had *already* been crossed without the Russians making good on their threats.

Nonetheless, Scholz made it clear he was open to the possibility of supplying the Leopard tanks to Ukraine, as long as we did so via an orderly process. It was crucial that other allies also send tanks to Ukraine, so that Germany would not be doing so alone. If it were to happen in cooperation with the Americans, then the situation would be entirely different.

After a round of silent diplomacy, and conversations between Biden and Scholz, the Germans managed to arrange an agreement regarding tank deliveries to Ukraine from several countries. On the twenty-fifth of January, I spoke with President Zelenskyy on the telephone. He had turned forty-five that same day, and I was able to convey my congratulations and the news that the Germans had released the Leopard tanks for delivery to Ukraine. The United States and the United Kingdom would be sending tanks, too.

After the ceremony at the memorial wall on that spring day in 2023, we were driven to the Mariyinsky Palace, where the Ukrainian president's offices are situated. There were numerous blockades, and we were directed to an annexe where everyone in the group had to go through a security check, similar to that at an airport. I walked through the annexe and out into a large, open courtyard. On the steps on the opposite side waited President Zelenskyy.

I have always liked Zelenskyy, ever since I first met him in 2019. He is a warm and open man, anything but pompous; he's easy to talk to and has a good sense of humour. A modern and competent leader, who wishes to fight corruption and the abuse of power and to connect Ukraine to the Western world. But that he would become the towering, nationally uniting figure the world has come to recognise since the invasion on the twenty-fourth of February 2022, I never would have imagined. I was looking forward to meeting with him again.

Zelenskyy welcomed me with a smile, there on the steps in front of the extravagantly decorated and ornate palace, as usual in his green military attire. I had debated what I ought to wear. Zelenskyy wore clothing that showed he identified with his countrymen at the front – he was leading a country at war. I was there to visit memorials, lay wreaths and express support for Ukraine's fight on behalf of NATO. A suit and tie was my way of showing respect.

Zelenskyy is adept at noticing the people around him. We had met at the COP26 climate conference in Glasgow in 2021, where he and I had a spontaneous conversation about Russia's military build-up and the threats it posed. In the packed and chaotic conference centre, there was hardly a vacant chair to be had. Dylan White managed to conjure up two stools and a tiny table, little more than a plank, and there Zelenskyy and I sat, talking while Dylan kneeled beside us, taking notes. 'No, no, that won't do,' Zelenskyy said, interrupting the conversation. Unlike me, he wasn't willing to accept Dylan having to sit on the floor while he scribbled down his notes as if his life depended on it. Only when we found another stool would Zelenskyy continue.

Both Zelenskyy and Dylan remembered this episode, and they chuckled heartily at the memory of it as they greeted one another again.

NATO membership was one of the main topics of the conversations that took place in the Mariyinsky Palace that day. The Ukrainians found it utterly absurd that certain NATO allies feared that Ukraine joining NATO would 'provoke' Russia. When Russia annexed Crimea in 2014, Ukraine was a non-aligned country. In February 2022, when Putin began his invasion, there was still no formal process underway that would move the country in the direction of NATO membership. During the conversations in Kyiv, both President Zelenskyy and minister of foreign affairs Dmytro Kuleba made it clear how meaningless they felt it was to talk about provoking Russia.

'This argument has always been wrong. But today, following Russia's aggression towards a Ukraine *outside* NATO, I have only one response to those who talk about the fear of provoking Russia: Are you serious?' Kuleba said.

It wasn't hard to understand their thinking. Since Putin was attacking their country, they naturally found concerns about 'provocation' completely irrelevant.

Still, Zelenskyy understood enough to know that NATO membership would be unattainable while the war was ongoing, and he therefore now formulated his request differently.

'At the summit in Vilnius this summer, you must give us a political invitation,' he said.

By 'political invitation', he meant an official declaration that on the day the war was over, Kyiv would receive a formal invitation to join the alliance, as Finland and Sweden had done in 2022. The road to full membership for Ukraine would then be a short one.

'You have to lower your expectations,' I replied. 'You understand the situation and know how contentious Ukrainian membership of NATO is within the alliance.'

All the same, at the subsequent press conference I emphasised that I had come to Kyiv with a single message: NATO stands with Ukraine.

'Let me be clear,' I said. 'Ukraine's rightful place is in the Euro-Atlantic family. Ukraine's rightful place is in NATO.'

We were aware that this would attract attention – and probably cause some irritation – in capitals such as Paris, Berlin and Washington. But at the same time, it was a fact that all NATO's member nations had concluded that Ukraine shall become a member of the alliance. This had happened as recently as at the summit in Madrid the previous year. There is little difference between declaring that Ukraine shall become a member of NATO and saying that Ukraine's rightful place is in NATO. The political content is almost identical, and of course NATO's secretary general has to be able to communicate the matters the alliance has supported by consensus.

But it isn't always *what* you say that is important. It is *where, when* and *how* you say it.

I was in Kyiv. I was standing beside President Zelenskyy, with the NATO and Ukrainian flags flying behind us. The war was raging. For over a year, Zelenskyy had led a heroic resistance against the Russian forces. And I had emphatically stated that Ukraine's rightful place was in NATO.

On this day in Kyiv, Zelenskyy was as I remembered him. His beard made him look older, and there was a new tautness to his features, but he had the same energy, the same vitality and the same good humour. Over lunch, talk turned to the old, historic bonds between Ukraine and the Nordic region, and to King Harald III of Norway who married

Princess Elisiv of Kiev, daughter of Yaroslav the Wise, Grand Prince of Kiev. They had at least four children together.

'So maybe we're related,' Zelenskyy said with a laugh. He was living under inhuman pressure, but it was impossible to tell this from simply being in his company. It was good to spend time with him, but bittersweet, too. His country was at war, and my time in NATO was drawing to a close. I didn't know how many more meetings between us there would be.

PART 7
PARTNERSHIP

January 2023–March 2024

40

One more year

'I NEED FIVE MINUTES ALONE WITH YOU,' SAID US PRESIDENT JOE Biden. It was the twenty-second of February 2023, and we were at a meeting with NATO's eastern member nations in Warsaw, Poland, where our main topic of discussion was the alliance's partnership with Ukraine.

When the usual family photograph with the heads of state and government had been taken and we were alone, Biden brought up NATO's seventy-fifth anniversary and the summit in Washington, which was eighteen months away. I said it would be a great occasion on which to mark the significance of the alliance. Biden agreed.

'But we need a secretary general,' he said.

Yes, of course, I thought. And by then, a new secretary general would long since have been found. So I reminded Biden that my term would soon be coming to an end, and that there were several good candidates who might take over from me.

Biden didn't respond. Instead, he looked at me in a somewhat expectant way.

By now, my term as secretary general had been extended yet again, to the first of October 2023. This had happened shortly after the war in Ukraine broke out, and I'd therefore had to decline the role of governor of Norges Bank, the central bank of Norway. I had felt this was an excellent job to have lined up, not least because the head of Norway's central bank is also chair of the country's oil fund. I'd been looking forward to moving home and starting work at Norges Bank alongside colleagues I had known since my student days.

But we were living through a fateful time. Supporting Ukraine while also helping to prevent a large-scale war had become my life's work, to which nothing else could compare. With war raging in Europe, the allies wanted to avoid the uncertainty that would be involved in the process of selecting a new secretary general. I was asked to stay on for another year, and said yes.

So when I met with Biden in Warsaw in February 2023, I was already on overtime of my overtime. But Biden made it clear he wanted me to stay on for yet another year.

'But, Mr President, your people haven't said anything about this,' I said.

This was true. On the contrary – US ambassador to NATO Julie Smith had informed us that the Americans would not be requesting another extension of my term.

'I don't know what they say,' Biden said.

He looked me straight in the eye.

'What I *do* know, is what *I* am saying to you. I'm the President of the United States of America, and I'm saying that you have to stay on.'

This made quite an impression on me, even if I was a little confused.

'That you're asking me,' I said, 'of course carries great weight. But I'll need to discuss it with my wife.'

While it was true I would need to discuss the matter with Ingrid, mentioning her also gave me a reason not to answer there and then. It was an excuse I had used before, and which gave me time to think.

'I understand,' Biden said, adding that I must give his regards to Ingrid and offer his apologies, but this was how it had to be.

We had to find out what Biden actually meant, and my staff checked in with the Americans. The message we received in reply was that Biden's statements mustn't be perceived as a formal request from the United States that I continue in the role of secretary general. Both Biden's security policy advisor Jake Sullivan, and ambassador Smith, were clear: this was Biden's way of telling me how pleased he was with me. They had seen the same thing when he was vice president – when he wanted to praise a person for a job well done, he was prone to saying things like: 'Of course you have to stay on, stay here in the White House!' This way of giving compliments could lead to misunderstandings and confusion. They apologised that the president hadn't been a little more careful.

The impression I'd got from my conversation with Biden in Warsaw was different, but we could do nothing other than draw the only possible conclusion: there was nothing more to think about. My brief conversation with the president didn't actually change anything; in the autumn I would travel home to Norway, as I had long been preparing to do. And in many ways, this would also be for the best. For Ingrid and me, and our relationship, it was undoubtedly best. Our agreement was that I wouldn't stay in Brussels for so much as a day beyond the first of October 2023. After multiple extensions of my term in NATO, this date had become something more than a date. It had become a symbol of whether I was in fact capable of keeping the promises I made to my wife.

Throughout late winter and early spring, the media began to speculate about my possible successors. Estonian prime minister Kaja Kallas was often mentioned. The media wrote about Mette Frederiksen, but she made it clear she had no plans other than to be prime minister of Denmark. Dutch prime minister Mark Rutte would have been a strong candidate, but he clearly stated that at this point in time, he wasn't interested. British secretary of state for defence Ben Wallace was the only person who openly said he wanted the job, but he didn't have a background as prime minister. A head of NATO who had not previously held the office of prime minister could easily be perceived as a downgrading of the role's significance, which would be unfortunate, considering the current security policy situation. President of the European Commission Ursula von der Leyen carried more than enough political weight, but then the decision would have to be postponed for a year, and it would become part of the wider negotiations surrounding the most important positions within the EU – a situation the United States, the United Kingdom and Canada were keen to avoid.

Because the media also continued to speculate about me, we checked in with the Americans once more, just to be on the safe side. Again, the response was unambiguous, and came in the form of a message from US ambassador to NATO Smith in March. It was not the United States' position that my term should be extended further.

My Norwegian colleagues started cancelling their children's school and nursery places in Brussels. Notice was given on rental contracts. Plane tickets were booked. Like me, several of them were also looking forward to going home after many years in Belgium. They began to speak with prospective employers about new roles. Everything pointed towards being back in Norway from the autumn.

On Monday the fifth of June, Mette Frederiksen visited President Biden at the White House. When I spoke with her afterwards, she said something that surprised me. Biden had told her he thought I should stay on in NATO.

The following week, on the thirteenth of June, it was my turn to meet with Biden. This was supposed to be an ordinary work meeting of the kind I always had with the US president in advance of a NATO summit, to go through the matters for discussion. Only a month remained until all the heads of state and government would gather in the Lithuanian capital of Vilnius.

After a few minutes in the Oval Office, Biden asked everyone else to leave the room. Then he started talking about my role in NATO, and how he felt that I always managed to find unifying solutions. And how these were critical times, with war in Europe.

He turned to me as we sat there in the wingback chairs on either side of the fireplace. 'Continuity is important,' he said. 'So that's why I'm asking you again to stay on.'

I thanked him, and said that it had been a privilege to serve in NATO. 'But there are many other good candidates. And I've now made other plans. I'm going back to Norway, as I've also promised my wife, and—'

Biden interrupted me.

'This isn't about you and your wife.'

He leaned forward slightly in his chair.

'This is about the alliance.'

Moreover, he had already made it clear in Warsaw in February that he thought I should continue as secretary general. 'So I assume you've had the opportunity to speak with your wife since then?' he said, almost reproachfully. As if nothing had happened in the interim. As if the Americans hadn't sent out other signals.

I didn't give in immediately – I had, after all, been prepared to reject the offer. We had several exchanges back and forth, but their content was largely the same. Biden didn't say a negative word about the other candidates, but he emphasised the need for stability in critical times. I pointed out that I'd already served as head of NATO for an extended period, and that the initial, most precarious phase of the war in Ukraine was now behind us. I could step down, and there were others who could take over.

Biden eventually realised that I wasn't going to say yes there and then. 'I'm going to make some calls, and then I'll get back to you,' he concluded. I tried again to dismiss the idea of another extension, but my protests weren't especially convincing.

I had a tough job, with weighty responsibilities and hardly a moment's peace, but the truth was that I enjoyed it. It was deeply meaningful to be involved in the processes and decisions that constituted the West's responses to the crises we faced. Over the years, I had accrued extensive experience and a high level of knowledge of the matters on which we worked. My network and connections with the other political leaders were close and effective, and NATO's organisation was no longer obscure and confusingly complex. I was ready to leave NATO, but the thought that in a few months my time with the organisation would come to an end also made me sad.

After this, things moved quickly. It became clear that countries like Germany, the United Kingdom and France also supported another extension of my term. Ingrid understood that I had been prepared to come home, and that I had made the necessary plans and practical arrangements to do so. And that it wasn't easy – and in fact nigh on impossible – to refuse to continue in my post with the situation as it was.

I'm sure Biden didn't think I was irreplaceable – no one is. And I'm sure he laid it on a bit thick to convince me to stay on a little longer. Biden was a pragmatist, and I believe he wanted me to continue in the role of secretary general because it was the solution that caused the least possible uncertainty at a time when we were still building up our support for Ukraine and the US was heading into an election year.

On Thursday the fourth of July the North Atlantic Council adopted the formal resolution to extend my term until the first of October 2024. For my employees who had terminated contracts and un-enrolled their children from schools and nurseries, there was nothing to do but reverse the decisions and make the necessary preparations for yet another year. This time, my feelings were more mixed than on the other occasions my term had been extended. But when the extension became a fact, I said that I felt honoured. And truly, I was.

41

Ukraine's future is in NATO

AT THE VERY END OF MAY 2023, THE NATO MINISTERS OF FOREIGN affairs met in Oslo. I was happy to have the opportunity to wish them welcome to my hometown.

Oslo is large enough to offer a proper city experience, but small enough that the surrounding nature feels extremely close. The forests of Marka in the north, the fjord to the south, and all the enveloping green hillsides – few capitals are more attractively situated. I always long for Oslo when I'm not there, and the city is at its most beautiful on a spring day with the sun shining down from a high sky. Just as it did on this day in May.

King Harald hosted the reception at the Royal Palace, a gesture much appreciated by the guests. We also held a ceremony at the 22 July Memorial in the city's government quarter. Norwegian prime minister Jonas Gahr Støre gave a moving speech, and all the ministers laid flowers. It was a poignant service that set the mood for our discussions to come by emphasising the values that were at stake: freedom, the rule of law and democracy.

The meeting the next morning was held in Oslo City Hall, an oft-frequented haunt of mine when I was leader of the Labour Party's Oslo branch, and when Thorvald was the city's deputy mayor in the mid-1980s. And, as I told Antony Blinken as we took our seats in the elegant meeting room where paintings by Edvard Munch adorned the walls: 'In 1987, Ingrid and I got married in this room.'

'Well then, no wonder you love the City Hall so much,' he replied, smiling.

It was an informal meeting of the ministers of foreign affairs that we had gathered for on that day. No advance conclusions had been prepared, and no resolutions were to be adopted. This time, there would be nothing but an open and free discussion around the meeting's sole subject: Ukraine's relationship to NATO.

On the battlefield, the situation was demanding. Just a few days before we met in Oslo, Russian forces had taken control of Bakhmut in Donetsk Oblast, after nine months of intense fighting around the city. The Ukrainians' long-threatened spring offensive, which we had believed would start in April, was still yet to begin.

The ministers of foreign affairs were alone in the room, without colleagues present, and we sat in a circle, with no table before us. 'Have we been invited to a therapy session?' one of the ministers playfully asked at the opening of the meeting. Such a set-up was unconventional, and it seemed to enable us to *see* one another more clearly, in sharper focus than usual.

Those of us in NATO had spent a long time working to find a solution to the question of Ukrainian membership that the entire alliance could stand behind. Poland and the Baltic states represented the outer fringes, believing it was best to make Ukraine a member of the alliance as quickly as possible. At the opposite end of the scale were Germany and the United States, who, while they didn't rule out Ukrainian membership in the long-term, feared that all forms of NATO involvement increased the risk of escalation and all-out war between NATO and Russia.

The divide between the allies was therefore great, but this provided scope for my office and I to steer the process. Our starting point was that Russia's war of aggression had revealed the political core of the conflict. The real reason for the war was not about who should control the Donbas. And nor was it about Crimea. It was about Ukraine's place in Europe. The in-between position Ukraine had occupied since 2008, when the country was promised NATO membership but without being given any timeframe for when this might be granted, was

untenable in the long-term. Either Ukraine would be dragged mercilessly into Russia's sphere of influence, or the country would have to
be incorporated among Europe's democratic nations. The question of
NATO membership had to be put back on the table.

I reminded the circle of ministers of the sheer range of the member
nations' positions, from those who wanted Ukraine to join the alliance, and for us to agree on an invitation as quickly as possible, to
those who believed that even repeating the membership promise from
2008 would be going too far. In doing so, I was able to establish the
two extremes. Everyone understood that neither of these positions
could be the conclusion of the meeting. Instead, I put forth our
proposal as a unifying solution that sat somewhere in the middle.

'It's too early to issue a formal invitation, but at the same time we
must bring Ukraine closer to membership,' I said.

We had prepared a proposal in advance that consisted of three
elements: comprehensive practical and financial support, which would
ensure Ukraine's military forces became ever more coordinated with
NATO's; the establishment of a NATO-Ukraine Council for closer
institutional cooperation; and the removal of the requirement for a
so-called Membership Action Plan, or MAP – a prerequisite comprehensive reform programme for nations applying to join the alliance.

I considered the ministers of foreign affairs, all sitting there free of
any documents or scripts. We had a genuine, open debate. The
Icelandic minister of foreign affairs, thirty-five-year-old Thórdis
Gylfadóttir, analysed the security situation in Europe following
Russia's attack and maintained that it had become impossible to keep
Ukraine outside the alliance. Iceland has no armed forces of its own
and is a small country within NATO, but on that day in Oslo City
Hall, all the arguments were balanced against each other and granted
independent weight and significance, regardless of who made them.
Many addressed the session to express opinions along the same lines
as Gylfadóttir's. Ukraine was a democratic country that wished to
become a member of NATO. This was a wish that deserved our
support, and the country must be linked to our most important partner institutions.

I was pleased to see that the ministers we had worried might shoot down our three-point proposal were either open to it, or even viewed it positively. The proposal received broad support, and the Oslo meeting became a crucial breakthrough in achieving a collective stance on the question of Ukraine's NATO membership.

In the weeks leading up to the summit in Vilnius in July, we continued to work at a high tempo. Over the spring, we had noticed how the desire to bring Ukraine closer to NATO was garnering ever greater support among many of the allies. I also noted that former US secretary of state Henry Kissinger had done a U-turn in a speech to the World Economic Forum in Davos. When I met with him in 2015, he had been against Ukrainian membership of the alliance. But now, after Russia's invasion, he believed the idea of Ukrainian neutrality no longer made any sense.

In our presentation to the allies, we emphasised that the proposal represented the best possible outcome. Without unanimous support for this package, we risked open disagreement and confrontation at the summit itself, as had happened in Bucharest in 2008. The message hit home, especially among the Americans – they wanted no discord or negotiations at the summit. When I met with President Biden in Washington in June, he told me that the Americans had been working on various alternatives for how they ought to respond to Ukraine's wish to join the alliance. He now made it clear that the United States supported the Oslo proposal.

Nevertheless, right up until the opening of the Vilnius summit on the eleventh of July, and even after the meeting had begun, the wording of the summit declaration continued to be honed and polished. The decision regarding Ukraine's membership of NATO would have to be made as the result of a political assessment at some *later* point in time – in the summer of 2023, it would be impossible to reach a consensus on anything else.

Our proposed wording for the summit declaration was therefore: 'We will be in a position to extend an invitation to Ukraine to join the Alliance when conditions are met.'

For some allies, however, this reservation wasn't strong enough. The final text therefore read: 'We will be in a position to extend an invitation to Ukraine to join the Alliance when Allies agree and conditions are met.'

The qualification that all allies must agree added nothing in terms of the statement's content – no decisions are ever made in NATO without a consensus being reached. So the two versions of the text actually said exactly the same thing. But by explicitly stating that all the allies had to agree, it was emphasised that each and every member nation would have the right to say no on the day Ukrainian NATO membership was brought onto the agenda.

Many years earlier, when I had gone around ruminating on whether or not I wanted to be put forward as a candidate for the role of NATO secretary general, it was precisely the thought of having to deal with such verbal hair-splitting that had most put me off. But almost a decade at the very top of the NATO system had done something to me. To coax forth a consensus by twisting and turning symbolic, linguistic turns of phrase had become part of my political skill set. I had become one of those people who actually believes the world can be changed by moving a comma.

We had cleared the three points of our proposal with the Ukrainians in advance; it was important that they were reasonably satisfied. Had President Zelenskyy said the proposal wasn't good enough, some of the other allies almost certainly would have insisted it was the best we could offer. But luckily, we had also managed to secure support for our proposal in Kyiv.

What happened on the first day of the summit therefore caught us off guard. On his way to Vilnius, Zelenskyy tweeted some strong criticism of NATO. He called it 'absurd' that the alliance had no schedule for when Ukraine should be invited to join the alliance, or when the country could become a full member. According to Zelenskyy, the vague wording about conditions meant a window of opportunity was being left open for bargaining with Russia about Ukraine's NATO membership, and this would therefore motivate Russia 'to continue its terror'.

We became aware of Zelenskyy's tweet just as the discussions on the summit declaration were drawing to a close. Several allies spoke up to say that we must do more, go further, to meet Zelenskyy halfway. The Americans grew irritated, and for a time were prepared to cancel everything relating to support for Ukraine. President Biden, sitting next to me at the large meeting table, leaned over, smiled, and said: 'As we say in America, he's a pain in the ass.'

I knew the summit declaration was important for Zelenskyy. 'It will be read in the Ukrainian trenches. Our soldiers need weapons and ammunition, but they also need hope. A promise that Ukraine will be invited to join NATO will make it easier for them to keep going,' he said to me.

'The summit declaration from this meeting is a great step forward for you. You must receive it as a victory,' I said. Zelenskyy nodded.

On the summit's final day, Zelenskyy and I held a joint press conference.

'Today we meet as equals. I look forward to the day we meet as allies,' I said, casting a glance at Zelenskyy.

He looked up from his papers, and seemed pleased – I presumed he had been hoping that I would say something like this, but his reaction was important to me all the same. And he too confirmed that he believed we had laid the foundations for a closer partnership between Ukraine and NATO in the times ahead.

The mood was good as the summit drew to a close, but the Americans seemed a little aloof. They were probably left with the sense that Zelenskyy and other Ukrainian leaders had pushed too hard on the question of NATO membership. But on the other hand, it was a fact that 85 per cent of Ukrainians were in favour of joining the alliance. This gave Zelenskyy a democratic duty – political marching orders – to do all he could to achieve Ukrainian membership of NATO as quickly as possible.

Gathering NATO leaders in Vilnius was a major event for the host country of Lithuania. The enthusiasm for the alliance reminded me of the welcome I had experienced during my visit to Ukraine – we couldn't even move from the hotel reception and out to the waiting vehicles without being met by cheers and rounds of applause from the crowds who gathered everywhere we went. But it wasn't me who had suddenly achieved rockstar status, no matter how much I might have liked to think so. I represented NATO, and they were thanking the alliance for their freedom.

At the summit, a banquet was held at which Ingrid and I sat together with Zelenskyy and his wife Olena, and our host, President Gitanas Nausėda, and his wife Diana. We talked about everything from our children and our plans for the upcoming holiday to the war in Europe and the way forward for Ukraine.

In 1988, when he was twenty-four years old, Nausėda had joined the Communist Party of the Soviet Union. Little did he know what was to come. The following year the Berlin Wall fell, and three years later the Soviet Union dissolved. And now, in 2023, he was hosting a magnificent dinner for the leaders of NATO. Nausėda was evidently moved and happy. He did his utmost to ensure that the leaders of countries that during the Cold War had been his enemies would have a pleasant evening.

To belong to the family of Western democracies, protected by NATO's solidarity principle and the United States, has enormous significance in a country where many still remember what it was like to be part of the Soviet Union.

42

Finland and Sweden cross the finish line

EARLY IN NOVEMBER 2022, INGRID AND I VISITED ISTANBUL, AS I had agreed with President Recep Erdoğan during the break at the summit in Madrid a few months earlier.

Erdoğan did everything possible to make us feel welcome. The hour-long boat trip Ingrid and I were to take, together with Erdoğan and his wife Emine, turned into a long and eventful evening out on the Bosporus Strait. Our guide told us about all the historic places we sailed past, helped along by more than a few anecdotes from Istanbul's former mayor – Erdoğan himself. The bridges, usually lit in the red of the Turkish flag, were now illuminated in NATO blue. The mood was good, and the conversation flowed easily.

It was no sacrifice for me to keep the promise I had made to Erdoğan, but it was still difficult for Erdoğan to keep the promise he had made to me and to the rest of NATO. After he had agreed to invite Finland and Sweden to join the alliance, little had happened.

'They haven't done enough to combat terrorism. It's the steps they take that will determine how the ratification process proceeds,' he said in one of our conversations.

It was of immense importance that we finalise the process of admitting Finland and Sweden into NATO. After all, the decision had been made. We had to show that NATO's door remained open to countries who fulfilled the organisation's conditions, and who wanted to join the alliance. The matter also meant a lot to me personally, because these were countries with which I had an especially close relationship.

It was still clear that Erdoğan's dissatisfaction was directed much more at Sweden than it was at Finland. At New Year 2023, the Finns received clear signals that the Turks were prepared to give them the green light first – even before the presidential and parliamentary elections that would be held in Turkey in May. But dividing the applications this way would put the unity of the Nordic countries to the test. Finland and Sweden had applied simultaneously and negotiated the accession protocol simultaneously, and the intention had always been that they would become members of NATO simultaneously. The Swedes might feel betrayed if Finland became a member without them.

I had said, both in private meetings and in public, that Finland and Sweden would join the alliance at the same time. But sometimes, U-turns are necessary. To me, it wasn't critical that the countries join the alliance simultaneously. The most important thing was the end result – that both countries became full members of NATO.

It was President Erdoğan who held the key. Relations between Turkey and Sweden had worsened significantly after a right-wing extremist burned a copy of the Quran outside the Turkish embassy in Stockholm on the twenty-first of January. Erdoğan made it clear that a country which tolerates such blasphemy could not expect Turkey to support its application to join NATO. All meetings in the negotiations between Turkey, Finland and Sweden were suspended.

The way we saw it, it would help Sweden if we managed to make Finland a full member before that summer's NATO summit. This would eliminate the risk of Erdoğan saying yes to Finland joining the alliance at the summit, while leaving Sweden hanging indefinitely. Those of us in NATO could almost certainly have prevented the two applications being handled separately, had we advised Turkey and Finland against such a solution. But we didn't – in fact, we did the opposite. We began to pave the way for a separation.

During a meeting of the NATO ministers of foreign affairs in Brussels in February, I suggested for the first time that the process didn't need to be completely coordinated.

'My position is that both [Finland and Sweden] can be ratified now. But the main issue is not whether they are ratified together. The main issue is that Finland and Sweden are ratified as soon as possible,' I told the press.

This signal was supported by the Americans. Just a few days earlier, I had been in Washington and discussed the NATO enlargement with US secretary of state Antony Blinken. He hurried into the meeting apologising, because he was a few minutes late. His two children, aged three and four, had been difficult that morning, and they hadn't made it out of the door in time. It was the easiest thing in the world to forgive him for. I remembered what it was like having young children in the house, and trying to get them dropped off at nursery before meetings I really couldn't be late for. It's good that politicians are also able to live an ordinary family life.

When Blinken had composed himself, he expressed his scepticism at the idea of splitting the ratification process, as had security policy advisor Jake Sullivan when I met with him. But both quickly concluded that NATO shouldn't stand in the way of such a process. The Turks confirmed to us what they had already told the Finns: Turkey was prepared to ratify Finland's Accession Protocol.

In February, I met with Finnish president Sauli Niinistö and the new Swedish prime minister, leader of the Moderate Party Ulf Kristersson. A conservative coalition government under Kristersson's leadership now held the responsibility for bringing the Swedish NATO application safely into harbour.

The atmosphere at the meeting was tense. 'It's a bad idea for Finland to go first,' Kristersson said. He feared it might be a long time before Sweden was permitted to join the alliance; that new demands would be made of them, and then the agreement from the Madrid summit would in effect be dead.

Niinistö made it clear that Finland still wished to proceed in parallel with Sweden, and that they would not be taking the initiative to separate the two application processes. But at the same time, the Finns made decisions that meant they *could* move ahead, and expedited the Finnish parliament's ratification of Finland's NATO membership.

Then it was up to Turkey. This, of course, was the purpose of the Finns hurrying things along, since they knew that Erdoğan was prepared to let them into the alliance.

'I'm against us not becoming members at the same time. And if you hadn't expedited the ratification in parliament, then Turkey wouldn't be in the position of being able to say yes to Finland alone,' Kristersson said.

'I have to correct you, Ulf,' Niinistö said. 'It isn't Finland who is *going* first. It is Finland who *has to go* first.'

'This is bad, really bad,' Kristersson said. He could see what was about to happen, but there was little he could do to stop it. He felt that Sweden had gone to great lengths to meet Turkey's demands, and now the Finns were in effect simply saying thanks for the company.

According to Kristersson and other Swedish politicians, the close military cooperation between Sweden and Finland would be complicated by the separating of their NATO application processes. They argued that a postponement was dangerous for the security of all NATO nations, in a situation with war in Europe. Apparently, if the alliance couldn't live up to the expectations it had created around the ratification of both countries occurring simultaneously, then NATO couldn't be trusted.

I cautioned against such notions, in both my conversations with the party leaders and in interviews with the Swedish media. I could understand the Swedes' irritation. But they had a tendency to depict the problem as being bigger than it was, and thereby also risked it *becoming* bigger.

'The way you talk about these questions is important,' I said.

Regardless, the Swedes wouldn't be left standing out in the cold – they were halfway inside already. The country's status had changed completely after NATO had invited Sweden to join the alliance at the summit in Madrid. They had been integrated into almost everything that happened within the alliance; they participated in meetings, and there was now a significant NATO military presence in Sweden. They had received security reassurances, including from the United States.

That NATO would fail to react to threats or attacks made against Sweden had become unthinkable.

'And if Finland becomes a full member before you, Sweden's security won't be weakened. It will be *strengthened*,' I said. All you had to do was look at a map – and see a Sweden surrounded by NATO nations.

'You can relax,' I said.

While it was slow going for Sweden, the process for Finland proceeded as we had hoped. Late in the evening on Thursday the thirtieth of March 2023, the Turkish national assembly unanimously voted to accept Finland's membership of NATO. Not even a week later, on the fourth of April, the Finnish flag was raised outside NATO headquarters for the first time. The wind took hold of it, and the flag unfolded perfectly.

Finland had left its post-war neutrality behind.

Ever since Finnish and Swedish membership of the alliance had been brought onto the agenda in the spring of 2022, the Americans had left it to those of us in Brussels to manage the process. The assessment was that if the United States put something into the pot to encourage the Turks to give the two countries the green light, then Ankara would make new demands, and the Biden administration wished to avoid such a bilateral game. In February 2023, however, it became clear that the Americans were open to something the Turks were extremely interested in: the purchasing of fighter jets. Specifically, Turkey's purchasing of forty new F-16s, technology to upgrade existing planes, 900 air-to-air missiles and 800 bombs, at a total value of $20 billion. The Biden administration was in dialogue with Congress to get the sale approved, and the response from Congress was that political demands needed to be made. If the Turks wanted the acquisition to go ahead, they would have to stop threatening neighbouring nations, improve the human rights situation within Turkey, and allow Sweden to join NATO.

So the United States Congress created a link between the sale of the F-16s and Swedish NATO membership. In the run-up to the Vilnius summit in the summer of 2023, the US worked actively to convince the Turks that no F-16s would be sold to them unless they ratified Sweden's NATO application. But did this mean Turkey would receive the fighter jets if they said yes to the Swedes? Would the approval of Sweden be enough? For a long time the Americans were not entirely clear on this point, and only in June did the clarification arrive: the F-16 sale would go through if Sweden received a yes.

On Monday the tenth of July, I sat down with Erdoğan and Kristersson in a small meeting room at the conference centre in Vilnius where the NATO summit was due to begin the following day. 'We now have an historic opportunity,' I said. 'We have to make an honest attempt to come to an agreement.' Both leaders confirmed that they were intent upon finding a solution.

Again, we reviewed everything the Swedes had done to meet the Turks halfway. I believed Turkey no longer had any reason to block Sweden's membership of the alliance.

The atmosphere reminded me of the meeting in Madrid the previous year. During a break, I ended up sitting alone with Erdoğan in the small meeting room. I said that it was always pleasant to meet with him, but it shouldn't really have been necessary for the two of us to come together again to enable Sweden to join NATO. All the problems had actually been resolved with the deal that had been agreed at the summit the year before.

'But the Swedes haven't stuck to the agreement,' Erdoğan replied, referring among other things to the burning of the Quran in Stockholm. It wasn't easy for Erdoğan to understand that it was impossible for the Swedish authorities to put a stop to demonstrations at which the holy Quran was set alight. I pointed out that in a country like Sweden, such a prohibition was not an alternative. But while I tried to explain the Swedish attitude, I also acknowledged that there was a difficult balance to be struck between freedom of speech and respect for religion.

Our colleagues hurried in and out with various papers as Erdoğan and I sat there in the cramped room, our knees almost touching. The draft statement was adjusted several times; phrases were inserted before being taken out again. After several hours of back and forth, we were nearing a solution. Just the final pieces of the puzzle were left.

In the end, only the timing of the ratification remained to be settled. A point in the agreement text stated that the Turks would now send the Accession Protocol to the national assembly to be processed quickly. Erdoğan wanted the words 'now' and 'quickly' to be removed.

'That won't weaken the text. But at the press conference, it will be important that I'm able to say the ratification will happen as soon as possible,' I said.

'That's fine,' Erdoğan said. 'But it's the national assembly, not me, that will approve the ratification,' he reminded me. 'So I can't promise anything in writing on their behalf.'

That shouldn't be a problem, I thought. Erdoğan's party led the coalition that held the majority in the Turkish parliament. But I was aware he would be dependent on his nationalistic coalition partner also supporting the agreement.

We agreed, and shook hands. I quickly informed Kristersson of what we had achieved. Any timeframe for the ratification was removed, in exchange for me being able to publicly use the expression 'as soon as possible'. Erdoğan also used this wording at his press conference.

A NATO photographer was sent into the room, and Erdoğan, Kristersson and I lined up in front of the Turkish and Swedish flags, with the NATO flag between them. After a round of handshakes, the agreement was sealed.

I had been sure the Turks would proceed quickly, but weeks passed in which nothing happened. On the first of October, the Turkish national assembly reconvened following the summer recess, but the ratification paperwork still hadn't been submitted. Measured against Erdoğan's promise to ratify Sweden's application as soon as possible, we were already on overtime. It required a significant degree of goodwill to think that the Turks were moving as quickly as they could.

I was due to travel to Stockholm at the end of October to participate in a NATO conference with the defence industry, and I knew that

I would be bombarded with questions about how the ratification process was going from members of government and the media. If I arrived in Sweden empty-handed, it would be difficult to avoid giving the impression that Sweden's NATO membership was lost somewhere in the ether.

I therefore wanted to speak with Erdoğan before I left. A telephone conversation was scheduled for Saturday the twenty-first of October.

Two weeks earlier, Hamas had committed a bloody terrorist attack on Israel. Almost 1,200 people were killed, the vast majority of them civilians, and 250 hostages had been taken to Gaza. The Israelis responded by launching a merciless war on Hamas. Tens of thousands of Palestinian civilians were killed in Israeli bombings and missile strikes on Gaza.

Understandably enough, Erdoğan was deeply concerned about the war in Gaza, and his top priority was achieving a ceasefire. I praised Turkey's efforts to provide humanitarian assistance, and in helping to protect the civilian Palestinian population. Then our conversation turned to Sweden. I told Erdoğan I would soon be visiting Stockholm, and reminded him of the promise he had made in Vilnius. 'I know that the Turkish national assembly has reconvened, and I hope that the ratification paperwork can be submitted before I arrive in Sweden,' I said.

Erdoğan repeated his old arguments yet again. The PKK were marching through the streets of Stockholm while the police simply stood by and watched. No terrorists were being deported. The Quran had been desecrated. The Swedes were not doing enough. Erdoğan himself had prepared the ratification papers, but unfortunately the Turks still needed to see that the Swedes were stepping up their efforts to combat terrorism.

Disappointment settled over me as he spoke. I hadn't expected Erdoğan to be so opposed. I began to doubt how I should try to steer the rest of the conversation.

Stian sat beside me, listening to what was said. I pushed the sheet of paper with talking points on it towards him and pointed to the word 'disappointed'. He nodded.

'Thank you for the update. But, my good friend, I have to be honest with you and say that I'm disappointed,' I said.

It was an expression I had rarely used in conversations with Erdoğan. If I pushed too hard, there was a risk of everything becoming deadlocked. And then the whole process would in effect be over.

'I really had hoped to see some progress,' I said. I listed all the contents of the agreements from Madrid and Vilnius, point by point; everything Sweden had done to meet Turkey's demands. New counter-terrorism legislation, closer cooperation on intelligence, allies lifting their arms sanctions on Turkey, tightened-up NATO action plans to combat acts of terror. And American promises on the sale of F-16 fighter jets.

In closing, I said that I understood it was painful to see the Quran being burned. But the protection of holy texts was not part of the deals we had agreed upon in Madrid and Vilnius. And it therefore couldn't be used as an argument for blocking Sweden from joining NATO.

'Now all we've achieved is at stake because the ratification paperwork hasn't been submitted to parliament. I'll be in Sweden on Tuesday and Wednesday. If the papers haven't been submitted by then, that will put me in a difficult situation, and it won't be easy to defend Turkey. It—'

Erdoğan interrupted the interpreter, who was still in the middle of translating.

'Old friend ...' he began. Stian and I looked at each other. This could go either way.

'... I would never do anything that puts you in a difficult situation.' It was still unclear what he actually meant by this.

'We'll do everything we can to get the papers sent over,' he said.

I wasn't sure that I'd heard correctly, but simply had to seize the opportunity.

'Thank you. The two of us have worked together for a long time and achieved a lot. But it's urgent that the papers are submitted *before* I get to Sweden. Then—'

Erdoğan interrupted me again.

'We'll send the paperwork next week.'

'This really is excellent news. I'll arrive in Sweden on Tuesday, so I hope—'

'You don't need to worry, I'll do what's necessary.'

'And that means the ratification papers will be submitted before I land?'

'Yes. We'll send the papers over before that,' Erdoğan said.

For the first time, we had been given a concrete timeframe, and Erdoğan did as he had promised. The paperwork was submitted to parliament. However at the final juncture, it wasn't just relations with Sweden that everything rested upon, but also the purchase of the F-16 fighter jets from the United States.

After some back and forth, Ankara and Washington agreed on procedures that ensured the Turks were reassured that the sale would go ahead.

Late in the evening on the twenty-third of January 2024, the Turkish national assembly said yes to Sweden joining NATO, with 287 votes for and 55 against. Finally, the Swedish flag would also be raised outside NATO headquarters in Brussels. Or so we thought.

Because Hungarian prime minister Viktor Orbán then entered the mix. On the day that Turkey ratified Sweden's Accession Protocol, Orbán tweeted that he had invited Swedish prime minister Ulf Kristersson to Budapest so they could 'negotiate' Sweden's NATO application. Orbán had repeatedly offered assurances that the Hungarians would not be the last to ratify Sweden's membership of the alliance, but now here they were. The Swedish government publicly rejected that there was anything to be negotiated with Hungary, but the move gave rise to unease in Stockholm.

Over the next twenty-four hours, I spoke with both Orbán and Kristersson on the telephone. Orbán reassured me that he personally supported the ratification, and that it would all be worked out when parliament reconvened in February. I could reassure Kristersson.

'Relax. When you've waited two hundred years to become a member of a military alliance, you can wait another month,' I said.

And at the end of February, Hungary's national assembly approved Sweden's membership of NATO.

On the eleventh of March, Victoria, Crown Princess of Sweden, and Prime Minister Kristersson, led a large Swedish delegation on a visit to NATO headquarters in Brussels. Not even the pouring rain could put a damper on the atmosphere – it was a historic day for NATO, for the Nordic region and for Sweden. For the first time since the age of the Kalmar Union in the 1400s, the entire Nordic region was bound by a collective defence cooperation. I ended my speech outside in front of the flagbearers by switching to Norwegian: 'So to all Swedes, I say – *velkommen til NATO*. Welcome to NATO!'

The Swedish guests were visibly moved. I, too, felt happy and proud as I stood there and watched the Swedish flag being slowly raised to the sound of Sweden's national anthem. Welcoming Finland and Sweden into the alliance was one of the last major goals I had set myself as head of NATO.

Less than two years after Finland and Sweden had applied to join the alliance, both were full members of NATO. It took longer than I had imagined and hoped that it would, but it was nevertheless still one of the fastest processes in NATO's history.

NATO became stronger. Vladimir Putin wanted less NATO close to Russia's borders, but ended up with more. It was a strategic defeat for Moscow.

PART 8
DEPARTURE

March 2024–October 2024

43

Endgame

ON THE FOURTH OF APRIL 1949, US PRESIDENT HARRY TRUMAN gave an address at the venerable Andrew W. Mellon Auditorium in Washington, DC. The auditorium is situated in the heart of the American capital, in a neoclassical building featuring columns and pediment sculptures; huge chandeliers hang from the ceilings of the vast space. Truman was chairing the meeting, and in a semicircle around him sat the ministers of foreign affairs from twelve different nations. Against the wall behind him, each of the countries' flags were lined up, one after the other.

His speech was short, the message clear.

'Men with courage and vision can still determine their own destiny. They can choose slavery or freedom, war or peace,' Truman said.

Europe and North America had to stand united to preserve peace. Truman's generation had lived through two devastating world wars, and they wanted to do everything in their power to avoid a third.

But it was not a given that the United States and Europe would stand together. Ever since the American War of Independence almost two hundred years earlier, the prevailing view within the US had been that the country was best served by avoiding permanent alliances with foreign nations. Towards the end of his time in office, the country's first president, George Washington, warned of foreign states – both friendly and hostile – who might try to influence the United States government and the American people. The United States should take advantage of its isolated location, remain neutral, and concentrate on itself and its own interests. Washington cautioned against entering into alliances, believing it was especially important that the United States stay out of hostilities in Europe.

It wasn't until the First World War, when the United States eventually entered the conflict, that this view was ultimately relinquished. When there was finally peace in 1918, after the four-year-long bloodbath at Ypres and on other European battlefields, the American soldiers were quickly brought home. The plan was for the same to happen after Nazi Germany was defeated in 1945 and the Second World War was over, the Americans having come to Europe's aid yet again. Vast oceans on either side and safe borders to the north and south gave the United States the security the country needed. Many Americans believed that it was not in their interest to have to protect Europe from itself and from the Soviet Union.

But forward-looking leaders on both sides of the Atlantic had learned from previous mistakes. The battles fought together against Nazi Germany had strengthened the bonds between the United States and the country's European allies. A few years after the end of the Second World War, the fronts between East and West in Europe hardened, and a new, Cold War began. The United States and Western Europe came together again in the defence of freedom and democracy.

Now these leaders had gathered in the Mellon Auditorium. When Truman finished his address, the document that would become known as the Washington Treaty was placed on a table before the rostrum. One by one, the secretaries of state and ministers of foreign affairs from the United States, Canada and ten Western European nations signed the document.

NATO was founded. A transatlantic alliance that could stand against the threats posed by the Soviet Union. The American soldiers remained in Europe. One for all, all for one.

Seventy-five years later, on the ninth of July 2024, I addressed the same auditorium. At the start of the summit, the United States had invited the NATO leaders to a grand celebration of NATO's seventy-fifth anniversary. Behind me, the number of flags had increased from twelve to thirty-two.

I was keen to emphasise that we must never take NATO for granted. Throughout its entire history, at every crossroads, the alliance has survived by adapting and making difficult choices. To simply agree that an attack on one ally would be regarded as an attack against all was a contentious decision that broke with previous attitudes and historical traditions in many of the member nations. This was also the case when NATO and the United States later entered into a dialogue with the Soviet Union in an attempt to build trust, and began disarmament negotiations. And again, after the fall of the Soviet Union – the decision to open the alliance's door to countries who had formerly been our adversaries.

Nor have military operations outside NATO's territory – the Balkans, Afghanistan and Libya – been easy choices. There was uncertainty and risk associated with each of them. And sometimes, we chose wrong. But without political leadership and the willingness to make difficult decisions, NATO would crumble. To remain passive, to shy away from demanding decisions, would also be to make a choice – perhaps the most ill-fated of all.

'Allies showed clarity and determination then,' I said. 'As we must continue to do now.'

It was both a festive and a deeply serious event. The gathering of heads of state and government was marked by the fact that the NATO anniversary was being celebrated at a dramatic time. For me personally, it was also a moment of great reflection. These were my last weeks as head of NATO.

Like other major crossroads in NATO's history, the alliance's support of Ukraine has not been an obvious choice; providing this support also comes with risks to us. 'There are no risk-free options in a war,' I continued. 'And remember: the biggest cost and the greatest risk will be if Russia wins in Ukraine.'

On the battlefield, things were not looking good. Ukraine's long-awaited counteroffensive in 2023 had been a disappointment. Hardly any territory had been liberated, and Ukraine had suffered significant losses. The Ukrainians and NATO's military leaders had various assessments as to why the counteroffensive hadn't succeeded. Ukrainian generals claimed that our support had been too little, too late. They were especially disappointed that they hadn't received planes to support the ground offensive.

NATO generals, on the other hand, said the problem was that the Ukrainians had waited too long to attack, giving the Russians time to establish strong lines of defence. Our people also argued that the attack had been too tentative, and not concentrated enough once it was finally launched. In 1940, France had more tanks than Germany, but the Germans assembled their forces and broke through the French front lines. In Ukraine, the forces were too thinly spread across the long front, and where the Ukrainians did attack, they quickly withdrew if they suffered losses.

'You have to be willing to risk the force in order to achieve the mission,' said our generals. This was probably true, but it was easy for us, sitting in our safe surroundings in Brussels, to ask the Ukrainians to sacrifice even more of their own.

Throughout the winter and spring of 2024, intense fighting continued with many killed on both sides, especially around the city of Avdiivka in Donetsk, which the Russians ultimately captured. They continued to forge ahead and to advance, and slowly took control of more territory, even though they failed to achieve any major breakthroughs.

In Ukraine, frustration was increasing. Western leaders travelled to Kyiv one after the other and promised more support, but what was delivered often didn't correspond to the promises that had been made. For every artillery shell the Ukrainians fired off, they were bombarded by up to ten from the Russians. Sometimes, the Ukrainians had nothing to defend themselves with. As NATO's supreme allied commander Chris Cavoli summarised a little drily: 'In a war, if one side shoots and the other doesn't, then it's usually the side doing the shooting that finally wins.'

And the Russians were shooting. Missiles and drones rained down over Ukrainian cities, power stations and other critical infrastructure.

The aim was to grind down the Ukrainians' determination to defend themselves, while at the same time depleting their air defences.

Ever more Ukrainian soldiers were killed because they didn't have enough artillery shells to hold back the Russian attackers. NATO allies tried to increase supplies, but hesitated because their own stockpiles were approaching perilously low levels. Many had decided to increase arms production, but it would take time for this to have an effect. Several countries said they couldn't give more to Ukraine without breaching NATO's guidelines around how much ammunition each country must hold in reserve. I made it clear before all NATO defence ministers that if they had to choose between NATO's minimum stockpile requirements and support for Ukraine, they should choose Ukraine. This was probably the first time a NATO secretary general had declared it acceptable not to meet the alliance's capability targets.

All the same, the work to secure weapons and ammunition for Ukraine reached a standstill. The United States' significant support package was stuck in Congress for almost six months because it had been dragged into a polarised American election campaign, but it wasn't just the US which was letting Ukraine down. The EU had promised to provide Ukraine with a million artillery shells from March 2023 to March 2024, but less than half had been delivered.

The Ukrainians' problems were heightened by the fact that not only were they receiving too little equipment and ammunition, but much of what they did receive couldn't be used because it was old and run-down. An even more frequent issue was that they received *matériel* lacking many of the parts necessary for it to be of use over time. This illustrated the difference between a weapon and a capability. A tank is a weapon, but for it to be used, much more than the tank itself is required: ammunition, fuel, spare parts, armoured recovery vehicles, mobile specialist workshops, manuals in Ukrainian and much more. Only when all the additional equipment is in place does the tank become a capability – and that was what the Ukrainians sorely needed.

It bothered me deeply that we weren't doing enough. At the time, I often asked myself whether *I* could have done more, whether I could have taken greater initiative to help Ukraine in their plight. More than ever during the war, I felt a sense of inadequacy. Ukraine was in the midst of a life and death battle for its existence as a sovereign nation, and we hadn't managed to give them the help they needed. Had we provided more support earlier on, many Ukrainian lives could have been saved. Ideally, we should have provided extensive military support following the illegal annexation of Crimea in 2014; in the best-case scenario, this might have prevented the invasion eight years later.

During another visit to Kyiv in April, I accepted on the alliance's behalf all the criticism for the fact that we had not delivered what we had promised. I openly admitted that the lack of help had had consequences on the battlefield. The Ukrainians were not solely responsible for the Russians' advance.

At NATO's Kyiv office, I also met Maryna Kozyr. On the very day she began working for us, she had lost her son, Oleksandr. He had been killed by a mine at the front in Bakhmut. At the time, Maryna had been unable to bear the thought of meeting with us, but now, a year later, she had a little more strength. When her son was killed, her husband was also at the front, but he had since returned home and resumed his job on the Ukrainian railway – legislation stipulated that if a family lost a member in combat, close relatives could be discharged. So the two of them were at least together in their grief.

'I'm proud of Oleksandr. He fell for his country,' Maryna said. It was difficult to find the right words. No parent should have to bury their child, the way tens of thousands of Ukrainian parents had in recent years. Clearer than in any of the reports I received, I could read in Maryna's face what war actually means in terms of pain and loss. And even more painful was the thought that so many lives had been lost because we hadn't managed to give the Ukrainians what they needed to protect themselves.

'You have reason to be proud of your son. We are all in his debt,' I said.

*   *   *

There are many areas in which you can get far with collective voluntary efforts, but war isn't one of them. Wars must be waged in an
organised, prescribed fashion. Life and death battles cannot be based
on voluntariness. We had to establish a system that gave the Ukrainians
greater endurance and predictability. It was absurd that something as
important as the support for Ukraine's defence was based on short-
term, voluntary contributions – and that a handful of countries were
pulling all the weight, while others were content to provide more
symbolic help. Things could not go on this way.

In the spring of 2024, we prepared a proposed package of measures
that would involve NATO as an organisation taking over the management of the support work – an important motive being to establish a
system that would be less vulnerable to shifting political winds on
both sides of the Atlantic.

The first measure was to establish a NATO mission for Ukraine,
with a detailed and binding plan for the kind of support that would be
provided, and to what extent. The second was to secure long-term
financing – at least €40 billion per year for at least five years. We hoped
to get this package approved at the summit in Washington.

After over two years of war, every aspect of Ukrainian society was
more run-down, and the political wear and tear was perceptible in
several respects. President Zelenskyy remained in a strong position,
but opinion polls showed that support for him wasn't as great as it had
been when Russia invaded. He had fired the popular commander-in-
chief of the country's armed forces, Valerii Zaluzhnyi, and replaced
various cabinet ministers, including the minister of defence; it was
also rumoured that his minister of foreign affairs Dmytro Kuleba and
several other members of government were about to go. Zelenskyy
had problems getting a new mobilisation law voted through, which
would cover younger age groups and ensure more soldiers were sent
to the front. Most of the soldiers in a war are usually in their early
twenties. In Ukraine, the average age at the front was over forty.

In my conversations with Western leaders that spring, I argued that
the Ukrainians had to be given the opportunity to use Western weapons against targets on Russian territory, in order to defend themselves

more effectively. President Putin, naturally enough, took a rather dim view of what I said. In a statement carried by TASS and other Russian media outlets, he mentioned that we had worked together when I was prime minister of Norway. 'Although I'm sure he wasn't suffering from dementia back then,' Putin said.

He had previously referred to our effective cooperation during my time as prime minister to highlight the contrast between the past and all the crazy things he believed I'd done since taking office in NATO. That I was suffering from dementia was a new twist. The comment was yet another discouraging sign of just how dismal relations between Russia and NATO had become.

Preparations for the Washington summit in July 2024 had not been the easiest. As always in NATO, it was crucial to obtain US support for what we were trying to achieve, but there was something passive and defeatist about our partners in Washington. They risked little, they failed to take the offensive, and they hid away their president.

This was regrettable but understandable. Over the past couple of years, in several of our meetings and conversations, I had experienced how Biden periodically struggled to keep the thread and mumbled, making it difficult to understand what he was saying. Our joint press appearances were kept as short as possible, and Biden relied on written notes, even when he was only supposed to make brief statements. This was in striking contrast to President Trump, who had allowed press conferences scheduled for a few minutes to last up to an hour.

That spring the Biden administration struggled. The polls ahead of the upcoming presidential election in November weren't good – Biden was trailing nationally and in the crucial swing states. Questions were raised about his ability to lead the country.

In interviews, I was asked about Biden's age and fumbling, and whether I was concerned that the commander-in-chief of the alliance's largest military forces by far might be weakened by old age. I replied that I personally had good and productive conversations with Biden. As head of NATO I couldn't weigh in on the discussion surrounding his candidature, but I sometimes felt a stab of guilt.

Biden had always been kind and generous towards me, and an important supporter of NATO. I now dodged these questions as best I could.

I had met with Biden in the White House a few weeks before the summit. The main topic for discussion at the meeting was our proposal for a strong Ukraine package, with obligations and long-term financial support. 'It will send a strong signal to Putin,' I said. 'The more long-term the support, the more likely it is that Putin will realise he cannot achieve his military aims. And the war might therefore come to an end more quickly.'

Biden sat without speaking for a while.

'This is difficult. The other guy will say that the United States is being weighed down by another endless war,' he said finally. As usual, Biden didn't mention Donald Trump by name.

The president was deeply sceptical of the proposed financial support for Ukraine over several years – not because he believed it was wrong or unimportant, but because such a commitment would serve as an extremely poor message in the context of his election campaign. Trump would use it against him. We saw an example of this soon afterwards. 'Zelenskyy is maybe the greatest salesman of any politician that's ever lived,' Trump said in a speech in Michigan. 'He just left with sixty billion dollars and announces that he needs another sixty billion. It never ends. It never ends.'

Trump had previously waded into the debate about how the war in Ukraine could be ended; he believed it could be done in twenty-four hours. How wasn't clear, but one of his advisers had submitted a plan in which international forces would secure the border between Russian- and Ukrainian-controlled areas, while Ukraine would receive significant military support. This plan ruled out Ukrainian membership of NATO.

Towards the end of the meeting, Biden rejected our proposal of long-term economic support for Ukraine. I repeated the arguments two or three times, and emphasised that the financial support we favoured would involve the Europeans taking responsibility for a greater share of the total financial burden. But Biden was firm, and for the first time I felt that he seemed almost irritated.

The compromise agreed at the summit ended up being that we would support Ukraine with €40 billion over the next year, in combination with a political goal of providing equivalent support the following year. This was less binding than the quantified support over five years that I had suggested, but a step in the right direction nonetheless. We also managed to set up a NATO mission, NATO Security Assistance and Training for Ukraine, through which the alliance would coordinate military support and training. A dedicated headquarters would be established, led by a three-star American general and with seven hundred military personnel responsible for the implementation. NATO would take over the running and protection of the Rzeszów logistics base in Poland, where the majority of the military support was brought before being sent across the border into Ukraine. Twice a year, NATO would prepare overviews of what each country had contributed; the alliance would take a central role in assessing the kind of support that was required, and in ensuring that the countries actually delivered what they had promised.

NATO became the hub of the support efforts for Ukraine.

Luckily, President Zelenskyy took the NATO resolutions regarding Ukraine as a victory, and made no public objections about how the country had once again not received an invitation to join the alliance. Ukraine was on an 'irreversible path' to NATO membership, the summit declaration stated. How much this really differed from previous summit declarations can be debated, but Zelenskyy emphasised it. That it was important to him was a point in itself.

Support for Ukraine would become more binding and more predictable. But at the same time, we had to be clear on the big picture. Financial and military support of the scope offered by NATO would better equip the Ukrainians to defend themselves against Russia's aggression. But it would not be sufficient to enable them to drive Russian forces out of Ukrainian territory. We were giving Ukraine enough support to avoid losses, but not enough to win the war.

The war in Ukraine had become a war of attrition.

In a war of attrition, it is the total resources the parties are able to mobilise that is ultimately decisive – the side with the most resources wins. Russia's population is four times greater than that of Ukraine; the country's gross domestic product is almost ten times larger. They have more soldiers, and are able to tolerate greater losses over a longer period of time.

China was keeping Russia's economy afloat with extensive deliveries of raw materials and advanced technology that made it possible for the Russian arms industry to manufacture bombs and missiles. North Korea sent large volumes of ammunition and other *matériel*, and eventually also soldiers. Iran supplied drones and other weapons to Russia. If you compared the total resources at Russia's disposal against those of Ukraine, there was little doubt as to who had most.

Moreover, a perception spread that Russia always wins its wars because the country is willing to make greater sacrifices and accept greater losses. Russian forces thwarted Napoleon's great army in 1812, and forced Hitler's soldiers to retreat during the Second World War. But history also contains many examples of Russia losing wars – and whenever this has happened, it has often led to internal political upheavals. Russia's defeat in the Crimean War in 1856 helped lay the foundations for reforms that abolished serfdom; the farmers were therefore no longer subject to the landowners, and could no longer be sold as slaves. The country's defeat in the Russo-Japanese War in 1905 led to the Tsar being forced to accept a separation of powers, and the introduction of elections to the national assembly. The loss of the First World War in 1917 triggered the Bolshevik Revolution. The Soviet withdrawal from Afghanistan in 1989 contributed to the changes that led to the dissolution of the Soviet Union a few years later.

Russia was receiving significant support from other countries, but on the other hand, NATO nations were also providing extensive support to Ukraine.

We supplied large volumes of weapons and ammunition, and gradually a consensus was also reached on providing modern tanks, long-range cruise missiles and F-16 fighter aircraft. Together with the Ukrainian forces' persistence, this inflicted major losses upon Russia. Thousands of weapons and military vehicles were destroyed. In the past few months, in excess of a thousand Russian soldiers had been killed or wounded every single day. Many Russian citizens of working age had fled the country to avoid being sent to the front, and the arms industry was occupying an ever-greater share of the workforce. It became harder to recruit soldiers, and to encourage more to enlist the military was forced to offer salaries at multiple times the usual level. It became more expensive to wage war.

The Russian economy was put on a war footing, which also had its price. Inflation was at over 10 per cent, the central bank interest rate at over 20, and there was an increasing lack of labour. Moscow was struggling financially.

The NATO nations' collective gross domestic product is ten times greater than that of Russia – we should therefore have had the economic standing to support Ukraine's defence. But in 2024, the NATO countries' support comprised less than 0.1 per cent of the alliance's total GDP. We could have given considerably more, had there been the political will to do so.

In the conversations I had with NATO leaders at the summit in Washington, it became evident why it was nevertheless difficult to increase our support: it wasn't easy to find the money in state budgets without adopting unpopular cuts in spending or increasing taxes. Increasing the deficit wasn't an option, because the national debt was already perilously high in many countries. Several NATO nations spent more paying the interest on their national debt than they did on their defence. Borrowing even more was not sustainable.

All the same, the support for Ukraine was a question of priorities, of political choices. In Denmark, prime minister Mette Frederiksen obtained majority support for removing a public holiday to finance increased support for Ukraine; Prime minister Kaja Kallas implemented tax increases in Estonia to do the same. Neither of these alternatives was especially popular, but they demonstrated brave political leadership. Where there's a will, there's a way.

For other allies, however, the distance between words and action was vast, and something became clear to me at the summit in Washington. There was an obvious difference between the way many leaders *talked about* this war and the nature of their policies. Some spoke as if it were an existential threat to their own country – and if that truly was the case, one had to ask why they weren't doing more to stop Putin. It was incomprehensible that a number of nations simply offered the bare minimum in support.

During the summit, several leaders pointed out how unreasonable it was that Kyiv should have to give up Ukrainian territory. 'We would never accept having to cede parts of our own country,' people said – and therefore nor could we demand this of the Ukrainians to achieve a ceasefire. They argued convincingly for a position that was correct in principle, but as they spoke, I couldn't help thinking to myself: 'Is that *actually* possible? Is this realistic?'

We couldn't change President Putin's way of thinking. His objective was to take control of Ukraine. But we could change how he calculated his next moves. If the price he had to pay for achieving his goal was sufficiently high, this might force him to accept a negotiated solution. And what happens around the negotiating table will always be inextricably linked to the balance of power on the ground.

The problem wasn't Ukraine. The problem was that Russia had started a war, and appeared to show no signs of ever giving up hope of controlling its neighbour. As long as Putin believed he could achieve more on the battlefield than at the negotiating table, the war would continue.

I therefore repeated my message that the way to secure peace was to provide Ukraine with more weapons. But at the same time, we in NATO had to obtain a clear understanding of what constituted a realistic goal for the Ukrainians. We needed a transparent and agreed notion of what 'victory' might actually mean.

I brought up these questions in the conversations I had with President Biden, Secretary of State Blinken and Secretary of Defense Austin in Washington. We had previously discussed how the war might be ended, and what a negotiated solution might look like. But it was always useful to receive an update on how the Americans viewed a possible endgame.

All three had the same message: 'Nothing about Ukraine, without Ukraine.' This meant that it was up to Ukraine to decide what might constitute an acceptable, negotiated end to the war. But at the same time, we knew that NATO's support was vital to the Ukrainians. When questioned directly, the American leaders acknowledged that it was not realistic for Ukraine to liberate all the land that had been occupied.

'The most important thing now is to prevent further Russian advances,' Biden said.

Any ceasefire agreement would therefore involve Ukraine having to accept Russian control of some Ukrainian territory – at least temporarily. But both Biden and Blinken emphasised that this was not the same as designating the areas in question as Russian. They reminded me of how the United States had never recognised the Baltic states as part of the Soviet Union, but always maintained that Estonia, Latvia and Lithuania were sovereign nations with claims to independence.

Over the past year, in various conversations with President Zelenskyy, I had personally used Finland as an example. During the Winter War of 1939–1940, Finland fought heroically and inflicted great losses upon Stalin's Red Army, but in the end was forced to capitulate. When Hitler's Germany attacked the Soviet Union in 1941, the Finns allied themselves with Germany in order to recapture the areas they had lost in the Winter War. To achieve peace following the end of the Second World War, Finland was forced to cede 10 per cent of its territory and the country's second-largest city, Vyborg, to the Soviet Union. But Finland survived as an independent state with a border with Russia that was respected. Finland exchanged land for security. This was a choice the Finns had been forced to make, and in much the same way, only the Ukrainians themselves could decide if this was a price worth paying.

On the first occasions I hinted at a 'Finnish solution' to the war in Ukraine, Zelenskyy had rejected the idea of ceding any territory outright. But that summer, he and his advisers had become less dismissive of a temporary cession, on the condition that the new borders and Ukraine's security would be guaranteed through Ukrainian NATO membership. Zelenskyy eventually also expressed this view publicly.

I told Zelenskyy that I wished to support him in the work to achieve such a solution, and that this would make it more realistic for Ukraine to become a member of NATO. We also had to remember what the Russian demands before the invasion had entailed. The Russians had demanded an entirely new security order in Europe, and required that NATO close its doors to all new members. Ukraine had to be 'demilitarised and de-nazified', the Russians had said. Their intention was to re-establish their old sphere of influence in Eastern Europe.

More important than anything else was that Ukraine survived as a democratic and sovereign state. The country must have safe borders and strong armed forces, in order to be able to defend itself and maintain credible deterrence against future attacks. And Ukraine must be welcomed into the Euro-Atlantic family – that is, become a member of both NATO and the EU.

This was what the war was about: Ukraine's right to choose its own path. If the war ended this way, it would be a defeat for Vladimir Putin, even if he continued to control Crimea and Donbas.

It would be a huge victory for Ukraine.

In Washington, I noticed just how much I had appreciated this final year as head of NATO. That I was able to take part in the organisation's seventy-fifth anniversary celebrations probably meant more to me than I had previously allowed myself to admit. It was a fine way to end my time with the alliance. I knew I was going to miss the work and all my exceptionally skilled colleagues in Brussels. Being at the centre of major events in international politics, and working with questions of critical importance for our time. Driving change and transformation within NATO, so the alliance would be best placed to face new challenges.

My ten years as secretary general of NATO would soon be over. It had been an eventful decade.

Twenty-three countries had now achieved the goal of spending 2 per cent of their GDP on defence. We had completed the first comprehensive revision of NATO's defence plans since the Cold War. Forces had been deployed in the east of the alliance. We had adopted a new strategic concept, an overall assessment of our security challenges which stated that China posed a risk to the interests, values and security of NATO nations. NATO had assisted in combating the terrorist state of IS in Iraq and Syria. The twenty-year-long war in Afghanistan was over. Finland and Sweden had become full members of the alliance. And even though we should have done more, we had supported Ukraine in a way hardly anyone had believed possible.

The leaders I met with in Washington had become close colleagues. We had been through a lot together, but now it was all coming to an irrevocable end.

I had thought as much the previous year, too, but I knew it to be true this time. Shortly before the summit, NATO had agreed on the appointment of Dutch prime minister Mark Rutte as my successor. Rutte and I had enjoyed a successful working relationship for many years, and he would make an excellent secretary general.

The political framework surrounding the summit was shaped by President Biden's age and health. He had hardly been seen in public before the summit, with the exception of a debate with Trump that gave rise to serious concerns that he was too old to serve another term. Now he made several public appearances; I was standing right behind him when he called his vice president 'Trump', and when, towards the end of the meeting, he introduced President Zelenskyy as 'President Putin'.

A sigh ran through the hall. Everyone present wished Biden well, and anyone can muddle up names – I've done it myself. But he kept making these mistakes. And while Biden had long had an unfortunate tendency to blunder on important occasions, what we were seeing now was something else entirely. More and more of his most ardent supporters were acknowledging his weakened state.

During the anniversary celebrations in the Mellon Auditorium, President Biden gave a speech in which he assured the government in Kyiv that they had NATO's full support, and made it clear that President Putin would never win the war. In closing, he began to talk about me. 'I asked you to put aside your own plans and stay in NATO longer. Forgive me,' he said, addressing Ingrid in the front row.

Biden asked me to come back up to the podium, and I stood a few feet from him as he finished his speech. Then he came over and tied a ribbon bearing a heavy medal around my neck.

It was the Presidential Medal of Freedom. I was usually given a hint in advance of receiving any honours or recognition, but this time it came as a complete surprise. I was deeply moved. Not only did the award feel like an expression of gratitude for my efforts as head of NATO, but it also seemed a recognition of my entire political career spanning forty years. It was impossible to view my time in NATO in isolation from all that had gone before. Had I not been leader of the Labour Party and Norway's prime minister, nor would I ever have become secretary general of NATO. And had Norway not been a good and loyal ally over the years, nor would I have been a relevant candidate for the position.

Norwegian minister of foreign affairs Espen Barth Eide is one of the people with whom I've worked closely ever since my years in the Labour Party's Youth Organisation. He was in attendance at the Mellon Auditorium that evening. As soon as the ceremony was over, my phone dinged with a text from him: 'I think it's probably a good thing we secured a majority for NATO at that national convention in 1987, all things considered.'

44

Farewell to NATO

BRUSSELS, SEPTEMBER 2024. ALL AROUND THE LARGE RESIDENCE in the Avenue Louise, half-full crates and boxes gaped at me. The removal company was in the process of packing up the house. We had to decide what we wished to take with us, and what would stay or be thrown away – our semi-detached home in Oslo wasn't big enough for us to take everything from Brussels. Books that meant a lot to us, gifts from all corners of the world. The photographs – there wouldn't be space for all of them on the walls back home. Ingrid and I agreed we would have to get rid of a lot, but that was easier said than done. We ended up keeping much more than we intended to.

A long chapter of our life was about to close.

The residence's home office was strewn with binders and documents. I had sorted a number of papers for safekeeping, but most ended up on the pile to be shredded. My gaze alighted on some small objects on one of the shelves: two fragile tin boxes that have been in my family for many years. My grandfather Emil had been given them by Russian fellow prisoners towards the end of the Second World War.

I carefully took the tins down from the shelf. In intricate detail, the Kremlin's walls were etched into the lids of both of them, with a star at the top of a slim donjon, and with two small fighter planes in the air above. Two dates, 21 – III – 1945 and 5. IV 1945, indicated that just weeks remained until the war would be over. *Kaptein Emil Stoltenberg* was written in elegant script along one edge, together with his prisoner number, *1489*.

My grandfather was one of the many Norwegian officers who were arrested on Hitler's orders in the summer of 1943. Towards the very end of the war, in April 1945, he was a prisoner of war in the camp at Luckenwalde south of Berlin, and he had told me about the fighting that had raged in the pine forests close by. Eventually, the German commanding officer decided to evacuate his men, and the Norwegian prisoners were forced to take over responsibility for the camp. An entire day passed. Then, on the twenty-second of April, Emil and the other prisoners saw a Russian armoured vehicle at the main gate. The prisoners were ordered to stay where they were. Soon, several Russian T-34 tanks rolled up, hardly stopping before they continued on at full speed in pursuit of the fleeing German soldiers. Later that same day, the infantry arrived.

The camp was liberated – by the Russians. This, too, is a tale of how the historic pendulum can swing the other way in a short space of time.

Luckenwalde was a camp that housed prisoners who had been held in various locations around German-occupied parts of Europe, and who were brought there as the Allies advanced. The Norwegian prisoners were officers who had fought in uniform, and who came from a 'Germanic' country. The Nazi regime therefore considered them legal combatants, and gave the Norwegians protection under the Geneva Convention's provisions regarding the treatment of prisoners of war. They were able to exchange letters with their relatives in Norway, and they received food parcels from the Red Cross. Things were far worse for those who had undertaken illegal activities; members of the resistance and saboteurs. Those who received the poorest treatment in Luckenwalde were the Russians and prisoners from other Slavic countries. They were given little food, many were executed, and others succumbed to starvation and disease. It was the emaciated Russian prisoners who from empty tins and with their own bare hands had created the beautiful little boxes to say thank you for the bread they had received from the Norwegian prisoners.

* * *

I was born in 1959, fourteen years after Nazi Germany was defeated. I was spared the trials and suffering of which my grandfather's tin boxes are a reminder. When I grew up hearing about the war, both my grandparents and Karin and Thorvald told such vivid stories that I sometimes felt I lived through the war myself. My maternal grandfather, Ørnulf Heiberg, had also made an important contribution. Ørnulf was an engineer, and with the help of his father-in-law, who was an archaeologist, he came up with a story about how they were undertaking archaeological investigations on Rørosvidda. In doing so, he managed to get himself a travel pass. And in the autumn of 1942, he took Susanne Krømer and her young son Peter with him to Røros, and helped them to cross the border into Sweden, just before over five hundred other Norwegian Jews were deported on the SS *Donau* and sent to the gas chambers in Auschwitz.

Like that of so many others, our family history contains deeply affecting narratives about the war. My respect for the women and men who don their uniforms and dedicate their lives to defending their country is rooted in the admiration I have for people like my grandparents. The stories of the things they did and experienced remind us of just how precious peace is.

The First World War was so brutal and destructive that many believed it 'the war to end all wars' – such a nightmare should never be experienced by anyone, ever again. Norwegian resistance hero Gunnar Sønsteby was born in 1918, the year the war ended, and he told me he'd believed he was born into a post-war age. This became an interwar period that lasted little more than twenty years. Those of us who have grown up after the Second World War have also lived in a post-war age. War has been unthinkable. We have lived in what is sometimes referred to as a time of deep peace.

Our task has been to break with the tragic pattern of Europe's history – all the post-war periods that became interwar periods. This is now harder than we would have imagined just a few years ago. Russia's war of aggression against Ukraine has reminded us that peace is not a given.

Precisely because of the horrors of war, it is important to do all we can to preserve peace. This means that we must always seek diplomatic solutions before resorting to military means. Compromises seldom lead to perfect solutions, but they prevent war, destruction and the loss of human life. I therefore agree with Thorvald, who maintained that the world needs more conflict-averse leaders.

A strong defence is necessary to deter potential attackers and prevent wars. And this costs a great deal.

But there is a price which cannot be measured in currency. In 1939, it was Hitler's invasion of Poland that triggered the British and French declarations of war against Germany, but after six years of war they nevertheless left allied Poland to Stalin's dictatorship. During the uprisings in Hungary in 1956 and in Czechoslovakia in 1968, many Western leaders gave passionate speeches supporting all those taking a stand for freedom. But we did nothing that actually made a difference. No weapons, no NATO soldiers. We didn't wish to risk a third world war for the freedom of a few million people on the other side of the Iron Curtain.

NATO's war in Afghanistan is now over. But the dream of a free and democratic Afghanistan has been crushed, and the Afghans must live with the consequences of those of us in NATO no longer being willing to fight for their cause.

In all these cases, the price of peace was high. But I believe the choices made were the correct ones.

It can, however, also be right to choose war. On the ninth of April 1940, Nazi Germany attacked Norway. A German envoy sought out the government with demands that it step down immediately, and a new, pro-German government led by Vidkun Quisling be appointed. Johan Nygaardsvold's government refused. And this meant war. Norwegian cities were bombed, civilians were killed, and soldiers fell in battle. But that the government chose to fight also meant that some painful losses were inflicted upon the country's attackers. Norway joined the Allied forces' fight against Hitler's Germany, which ultimately ended in an Allied victory in 1945.

When, on the morning of the twenty-fourth of February 2022, President Zelenskyy and his government were faced with the Russian demand not to resist, they could have chosen to surrender. And this would have prevented the bloodiest war in Europe since the Second World War. But Ukraine would have lost its freedom and independence. And it would have been a great loss for everyone who believes in a world governed by law and justice, and not the law of the jungle.

The choice between resistance or compliance, to fight or to capitulate, is one of the most difficult a political leader can face. Decisions often have to be made under immense time pressure and in the midst of extreme uncertainty, with no overview of what the consequences might be. On the scales, the price of peace is balanced against the pain of war.

I opened the double doors at the rear of the house and allowed the still-warm September air to flow into the rooms. Outside, the sun winked through the foliage of the lush garden. Ingrid and I had spent many pleasant evenings together out on the wide, tiled terrace; she was much better than me at inviting friends and colleagues over to join us. Now the outdoor furniture had been packed away under a grey tarpaulin.

Long historical threads become clear when standing at a crossroads in one's life. Now my time in NATO was at an end, and in a few months I would take over as chair of the Munich Security Conference. This would provide me with both continuity and a break. I would continue to work with foreign and security policy, but in a different role and from another perspective than I had for the past ten years.

The year 1945 has been called Year Zero – the year the Second World War ended and my grandfather and hundreds of thousands of others returned home from the POW camps. Many tens of millions had lost their lives, and Europe lay in ruins. But at the same time this was a year filled with optimism and belief in the future; the hope that a new age was dawning and a better world order would be built.

NATO is the trueborn child of the war in which my grandfathers fought. Organisations such as the UN, EU and NATO were founded to prevent the world from once again being plunged into a large-scale war. Through our ability and willingness to defend ourselves, peace would be safeguarded and preserved. A rules-based world order would be established, in which disagreements would be solved without the use of violence, and where cooperation and open borders would ensure growth and prosperity.

I have always had an unfailing belief that tomorrow will be better than yesterday – this optimism is in my political genes. It is a belief that is founded on all the progress humanity has made: across the world, life expectancy is higher, infant mortality lower, and ever more people have access to schooling and education. Since 1945, the number of people killed in armed conflicts has significantly reduced. Such global trends show that the conditions in which people live have on the whole improved over many decades. Of course, that the world has so far been moving in the right direction is no guarantee that it will continue to do so. But it does show that it is possible.

After the dissolution of the Soviet Union, democracy and freedom spread across Europe. We had great faith in globalisation, free trade and growth.

There was talk of the end of history, that our social order with democracy and the rule of law had proved so superior to all other systems that there was, in effect, no alternative. It could never be reversed or replaced by a fundamentally new world order. I was among the people who once thought that way.

All this now seemed very distant. And sometimes, despite my fundamental optimism, I can feel a gnawing sense of unease about the direction in which we are heading. We are no longer getting rid of weapons, but increasing stockpiles. The easing of tensions has been replaced with high tensions and a new war. Democratic countries are coming under pressure from authoritarian regimes on the outside, and disintegration from within.

I took office in NATO in 2014. Ten years later, the world had become a more dangerous place.

New wars, greater rivalry between superpowers, less predictability. It happened on my watch.

Room after room of the beautiful house was cleared. The dining room, with the long, oval table that friends and colleagues had gathered around. I had eaten breakfast and dinners here, and also had confidential conversations with heads of state and close colleagues. It was in my home office upstairs that I had spoken with Afghanistan's president, Ashraf Ghani, before the fall of Kabul. It was there, too, that I received the call that informed me the decision to invade Ukraine had been made, and where I was later told by Sanna Marin and Magdalena Andersson that Finland and Sweden would apply for membership of the alliance. Incidents that had shaped my years as secretary general. They were all different, but what they had in common was that when I first arrived at NATO, nobody had expected they would happen.

So it is with many of the great events that have shaped our time. We long believed the Berlin Wall and the Soviet Union would last forever, and were surprised when the wall fell so swiftly and the Soviet Union dissolved a short time later. The terrorist attack on the United States on 9/11 gave rise to a new security reality – nobody saw it coming before the planes crashed into the Twin Towers. Nor was the Arab Spring, with its change of regime in many countries, foreseen by experts or intelligence agencies.

Because it is so difficult to predict momentous events, I'm among those who like to be careful about anticipating what the defining events of our future might be. More than believing that we can predict what lies ahead of us, we have to be prepared for the unforeseen.

I do not know what the next crisis or war will be, nor the next great threat against Europe and North America. But NATO countries represent half of the world's economic might, and have over half the globe's military might. What I do know, is that our ability to face future threats is much greater when we stand together.

We have been there for one another for over seventy-five years, in good times and in bad. This hasn't happened by itself.

In my time as NATO secretary general, the relevance of the alliance has been challenged. The organisation was described as divided, obsolete and brain-dead. But in reality, when it really counted, NATO nations stood united. They made decisions that led to the strongest reinforcement of our collective defence since the Cold War.

The world has become more dangerous. But NATO has become stronger.

I held in my hands a pair of treasured possessions as I stood and considered my grandfather's tin boxes. On the inside of their lids a few words had been etched in Cyrillic. These were the home addresses of the prisoners who had created the tiny works of art; their apartment numbers were also included. For many years, my grandfather and I had spoken about visiting the men who made the boxes.

Now travelling to Russia had become unthinkable. But I'm sure that one day, it will be possible again.

I took my leave of the house in the Avenue Louise, where the rooms grew emptier as the removal boxes filled. Some of the rooms were stripped almost bare, and gave only a hollow echo when I entered them, but the sounds from the streets and the park outside remained the same, life taking its usual course.

The moving boxes were organised into stacks. Clothes, photographs, books, letters and memories – all properly sorted for the next leg of the journey. My grandfather's tin boxes I set in one of the very last crates, carefully wrapped in tissue paper.

I was ready to go home.

.

About this book

THIS IS THE STORY OF MY TEN YEARS AS SECRETARY GENERAL OF NATO, an open and honest account of what it was like to lead the world's mightiest military alliance.

After I had completed my term as Norway's prime minister in the autumn of 2013 and started work on the book *My Story*, about my years in Norwegian politics, I realised that I had taken very few notes. When I took office in NATO, I therefore decided to document things in more detail. Routine references are kept from meetings and conversations in NATO, but I wanted to complement these with more personal documentation.

This documentation took several forms.

My closest colleagues, and I personally, made written notes on my business trips, meetings and conversations.

In addition to this, I made my own voice recordings, like a kind of diary, featuring my reflections and personal thoughts on the ongoing work. I often also made such recordings together with close colleagues, and they contributed their assessments. We discussed the developments in major matters, like the withdrawal from Afghanistan, the war in Ukraine and the work to make Finland and Sweden members of NATO, but we also talked about and analysed important one-off events, such as all the summits and significant official visits. This has all been vital in enabling me to write this book several years after many of the incidents took place.

The audio material consists of several hundred hours of recordings, and the recorded conversations with my colleagues have enabled me to reproduce many conversations and incidents to the level of detail with which they are described in this book. Wherever possible, the accounts have been cross-checked with other documentation, such as interviews, press coverage and other publicly available information. Some details of a more historic nature have been taken from NATO's archives and from reference works.

Some linguistic adjustments have been made to make the book more reader-friendly. For example, the Kurdish militia the People's Defence Units is referred to using the acronym YPG, which are the initials of the organisation's name in Kurdish. When President Erdoğan and other Turkish leaders discuss this movement, they also include the organisation's political wing, and consistently use the acronym YPG/PYD.

On My Watch is a book for a broad, socially engaged readership, but I also hope that experts in foreign and security policy will benefit from and enjoy it.

This is my story, and therefore not an objective account of the period discussed. Nevertheless, I have attempted to give a nuanced and balanced view of the events in which I've been involved. Instead of simply describing the people I have met and worked with, I wanted to accurately recount events as they happened, along with what was said.

In the main, I describe events in which I participated personally, and the book has thereby become a first-hand account of important matters and events. As a result of this choice, many central questions in which I myself have had no direct role have been excluded. I neglect, for example, to discuss a number of parliamentary and presidential elections and important decisions made internally within the EU, because neither NATO nor I were part of the decision-making process.

The choice to write mostly about matters in which NATO has been directly involved also means that I have given a lot of attention to Ukraine, for example, but little to the Middle East, where the alliance has a limited role. To prevent the book becoming too long, I have out of necessity given little attention to topics that deserve more discussion. This applies, for example, to the Western Balkans, where NATO has played a central role for several decades, and which I visited a number of times as secretary general. The organisation's increasing cooperation with several countries in the Pacific region is only briefly touched upon, and there are other examples I could mention.

Just over a month after I completed my term as secretary general, Donald Trump was again elected president of the United States. In many ways, Trump's second term as president is different from his first. The president and his administration displayed greater self-confidence and determination than when he was elected the first time around; a number of executive orders and political initiatives demonstrated this.

Trump's return to the White House has made many uncertain about the future of the transatlantic cooperation, and triggered new discussions, including about many of the questions I write about in this book. The tone among the allies is sometimes sharp. The requirements regarding fairer burden-sharing within NATO have been tightened up. Trade and tariffs are not topics that affect the alliance directly, but disagreement on such important questions naturally has an impact there, too.

However, the administration's views on security policy and NATO cooperation are recognisable. China continues to be considered the United States' most important challenger and strategic competitor; the pivot towards the Indo-Pacific region is ongoing and intensifying. Demands that Europe and Canada spend more on their defence are far from new.

Trump's first term also presented challenges. During the 2018 summit, the alliance was on the verge of collapse. And towards the end of his term, Trump still stood by much of his criticism of the Europeans.

Throughout all four years, in both difficult and less difficult times, we met with the president and his administration often. We had discussions, listened to suggestions, and put our objections on the table in order to find a way forward. Our main message was always that a strong, well-functioning NATO is in the United States' interest.

I believe we succeeded. When Donald Trump's first term as president came to an end, NATO was stronger than it had been when he took office.

The road ahead may be bumpy. In some areas, the United States' policies are challenging, and the situation is characterised by significant unpredictability.

We must be prepared for the United States to reduce its military presence in Europe, and for the burden between NATO's member nations to be shared differently. But that doesn't mean the end of NATO. Regardless of what the United States says and does, it is both right and necessary for the Europeans to focus more on their own defence. The European pillar within NATO has to be strengthened. This will also increase the probability of Washington standing by its commitments to help defend Europe.

Relations with the United States are challenging, but they can be managed. How the relationship develops will depend not only on what happens in Washington, but also on us Europeans and our ability to act in concert and with composure. We have to demonstrate our willingness and ability to take our share of the responsibility for our collective security.

My fundamental belief stands firm. A strong and vital NATO is the best framework for Western defence and security cooperation.

My time as NATO secretary general has taught me that cooperation between friends can also give rise to problems. I have chosen to be as candid as I can, including about my own anxieties, because I believe that disagreements must be brought out into the light.

Dilemmas benefit from being discussed. Openness about conflicts is also necessary for us to learn from them.

But the way I see it, this isn't a story about disintegration or what divides us. This book says something about why it is so important that

North America and Europe stand together. *On My Watch* is a love letter to NATO, to international cooperation and to the wider global community. My hope is that with this book, I might contribute to strengthening the unity upon which we all depend so strongly.

Acknowledgements

I WOULD LIKE TO START BY THANKING EVERYONE I HAD THE
pleasure of working with in NATO. The alliance's international staff
consists of highly skilled individuals, who over the years I was there
demonstrated an unrivalled capacity to support me in my duties.
Practical support, excellent professional advice and all kinds of assistance meant that we achieved much together, and that my time in
Brussels became a fantastic period in my life.

A few people are mentioned in the book because they played a role
in the events I describe. Most are not mentioned by name, but everyone should know that I am deeply grateful for all their contributions.

A special thanks to everyone who in various periods has been part
of my Norwegian staff – Gjermund Eide, Vegard Ellefsen, Stein
Hernes, Stian Jenssen, Sissel Kruse Larsen, Torgeir Larsen, Trude
Måseide, Randi Ness, Anne-Marte Vestbakke and Mari Aaby West.
All have been outstanding and loyal colleagues who did their utmost
to help me succeed in my work.

This book would not exist without Per Anders Madsen. For over five
years he has collaborated with me on this project, interviewing me
and my colleagues, listening to audio recordings and composing draft
texts. Per's skilled pen, analytical prowess and broad knowledge of
foreign and security policy have been of immense value, and utterly
crucial to me being able to write about my years in NATO. Simen

Ekern was also involved in the early stages of the project, but this cooperation came to an end when he became Norwegian broadcaster NRK's correspondent in Brussels.

At Gyldendal, publisher Cathrine Sandnes was an excellent source of support when we began work on the book. Later, publisher Reidar Mide Solberg and editor Stine Aspebakken Linstad followed the project closely and were constructive readers and important advisers. It has been a close and trusting collaboration.

Many of my employees have also made valuable contributions to the work on this book. Sissel Kruse Larsen and Stian Jenssen in particular have offered immensely helpful assessments, and made many insightful suggestions regarding the text. Gjermund Eide was always a great help.

Many others, both experts and friends, have read the manuscript and offered good and useful feedback.

My sincere thanks to all of you.

The greatest thanks go to Ingrid. Without her, none of this would have been possible, and life would have been far from so good, in NATO or anywhere else.

Index

Trudeau, Justin 112, 147
Truman, Harry 18, 423, 424
Trump, Donald: 2016 presidential election 99–101: 2017 inaugural address 105: 2018 Fox News interview 208: 2018 meeting with Kim 164–5: 2019 State of the Union address 212–13, 215: 2020 presidential election 278–80, 281–2, 283–5: 2024 presidential election 431: Afghanistan War 129: concerns about China 267: conciliatory meeting with Obama 104: criticism of Europe 150, 152, 166–7, 210, 260, 280–1, *see also* defence budget of NATO states, Trump's criticisms: criticism of Merkel 106, 148, 150, 156, 273, 274–5, 276: criticism of Nord Stream 2 pipeline 150, 158, 159–60, 223, 263, 274–5, 276: European distrust of 143–4: First World War centenary event, Paris 209–10: G7 summit, Canada (2018) 146–7, 154: handshakes 111–12: isolationism 144, 260: Kavanaugh's Supreme Court nomination 153–4: nationalism 210: and NATO *see* defence budget of NATO states; NATO (North Atlantic Treaty Organization), and Trump: trade tariffs 147, 166–7, 267: Ukraine–Russia war 241, 431: US killing of Soleimani 269–70: US–Taliban deal 302, 303–4: wanting to buy Greenland 261: wanting withdrawal from Afghanistan 127, 272, 273–4, 303–4: withdrawal from IMF Treaty 199, 200, 202: withdrawal from Iran agreement 152: withdrawal from Syria 213, 251, 255, 309
Trump, Melania 164
Tsipras, Alexis 92
Turkey: 2016 coup attempt 245–6, 378: 2016 coup countermeasures 247–8: Aegean Sea refugee agreement with EU 70, 75: bordering countries 249: ceasefire deal with Syria 255: evacuation in Afghanistan 319: fight against YPG/PKK 243, 250–1, 251–2, 372–5, 378–9, 380, 381: humanitarian support for Palestinians 417: invasion of Syria 243, 249–50, 251, 253–4, 255: and Islam 294: Jens' 2012 visit 244: Jens and Ingrid's visit to Istanbul 410: low score on Democracy Index 247: and NATO *see* NATO (North Atlantic Treaty Organization), and Turkey: relations with Greece 67–8: Russian influence in 255: shooting down Russian plane 63–8: and Syrian safety zone 250–1, 253: US F-16s 414–15, 419
Turkmen 64
Tusk, Donald 73–6, 141

Ukraine: 1991 referendum 59: 2014 presidential election 56: Biden's 2023 visit 385: bonds with Norway 393–4: borders 361: Budapest Memorandum (1994) 53: corruption 240: East–West divide 60: fight for independence 57: history 56–7, 237: Jens' visits to 237–42, 383–8, 391–4, 428: joint civil

emergency exercise 55: NATO assistance to 55, 58, 62, 237–9: NATO membership; 2008 promise 57–8, 404–5; 2023 ministers of foreign affairs discussions 404–6; 2023 Oslo proposal 405–6; 2023 summit declaration 406–7; desire for 57–9, 62, 238–9, 241; increased support for 406; Kissinger's argument against 60; 'political invitation' request 392–3; removal of MAP requirement 405; Zelenskyy's criticism of 2023 summit declaration 407–8: NATO-Ukraine Council 405: Orange Revolution 56: as political threat to Putin 361: in-between position 404–5: proposed constitutional amendment 61: railways 384: separatists 21, 27–8, 60, 61–2, 241, 336: territorial integrity 59: Ukrainian Socialist Soviet Republic 57: war with Russia *see* Ukraine–Russia war: Yanukovych's removal and exile 21, 51
Ukraine–Russia war: 2022 invasion 350–1: 2022 Munich Security Conference 346–7: 2022 Western video conference 347: Biden's meetings 345–6: Bucha massacres 386: changing world 353–4, 357, 363, 442: considering peace options 435–6: countries supporting Russia 433: economic impacts on Russia 434: economic impacts on Ukraine 240: economic sanctions against Russia 345–6, 347: and Europe's dependence on Russian gas 345–6: Grushko's defence of Russian actions 40–1: importance of containing 357, 363: increasing NATO solidarity 342: Kissinger's views on 59–60: Lavrov's defence of Russian actions 51–3, 55: Malaysian passenger plane shot down 27–8: Minsk agreement 60–1: NATO 2014 North Atlantic Council meeting 343: NATO 2022 North Atlantic Council meeting 345: NATO extraordinary summits 354, 362: NATO military build-up on eastern border 81, 89–91, 344, 347: NATO-Russia Council 2022 meeting 338–41: NATO support for Ukraine; 2024 NATO measures 429, 432; disagreements 69–70, 343–4, 431; financing 429, 432; inadequacy of weapons/supplies 62, 427–8, 434–5; Jens' 2012 visit 237–40, 241; Jens' 2015 visit 55–6, 57, 58–9, 61–2; Jens' 2023 visit 383–8, 391–4; NATO-Ukraine Commission 240; NATO's readiness in 2022 353; Putin's threats 352, 358–9, 388; risks 363, 425; training Ukrainian soldiers 239, 258, 432; weapons and supplies 62, 239, 241, 346, 347, 357, 377, 433–4: NATO's diplomacy attempts 332–4, 338–41, 347: political reason for 404–5, 437: pushing Sweden and Finland to join NATO 366–7, 369, 370–1: Putin's anti-Kyiv rhetoric 336, 341, 348: Putin's invasion-day speech 351–2: Putin's security treaty proposal 339–41: Russia and others blaming NATO 359–60: Russia-supported conflict in the Donbas 21, 27–8, 40, 43, 51, 52,